# Complete Book of Australian Folk Lore

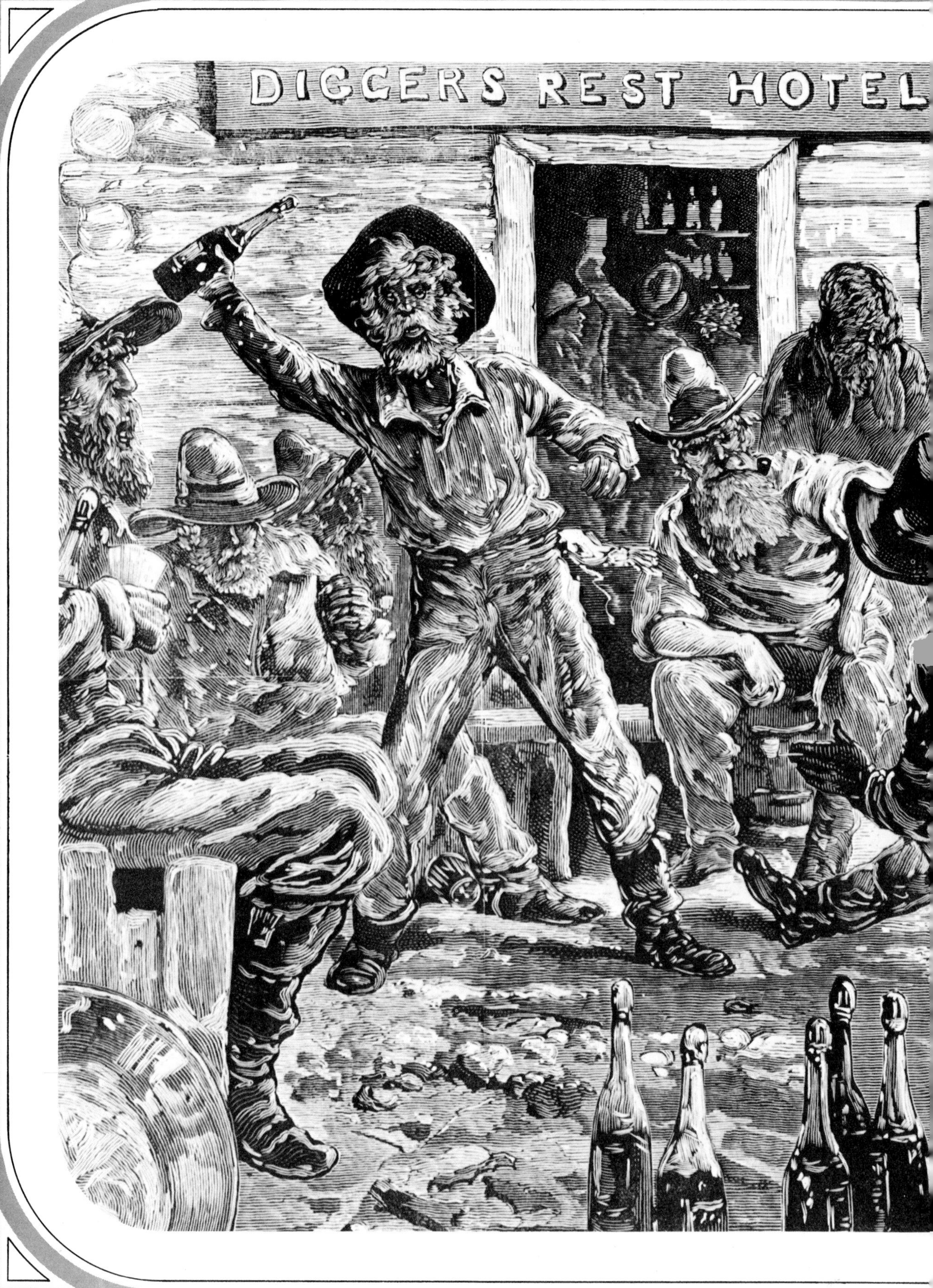
DIGGERS REST HOTEL

# Complete Book of
# Australian Folk Lore

## Compiled and annotated by Bill Scott

SUMMIT BOOKS
Published by Paul Hamlyn Pty Limited
Sydney·Auckland·London·New York

**Summit Books**
Published 1978 by Paul Hamlyn Pty Limited
176 South Creek Road, Dee Why West, NSW, Australia, 2099
First published 1976
by Ure Smith, Sydney
2nd impression (limp) 1978
This collection © copyright Ure Smith 1976
Produced in Australia by the Publisher
Designed by Snape and Gallaher Graphics, Sydney
Typeset by The Dominion Press, Victoria
Printed in Australia at Griffin Press Limited, Adelaide

**National Library of Australia Cataloguing-in-Publication Data**

Scott, William Neville, 1923– .
  Complete book of Australian folk lore

  Index.
  ISBN 0 7271 0312 1.

  1. Folk-lore — Australia — collections.
  I. Title.

398'.0994.

# Dedication

Dedicated to the memory of Vance Palmer and A. B. Paterson, and to all the field workers in Australian folk lore without whose patience and persistence these treasures might have been neglected.

# Acknowledgements

I would like to express my grateful appreciation to the following people for their permission to use material researched or created by them—Wendy Lowenstein, Ron Edwards, Russel Ward, Alan Scott, Ian Mudie, Graham Jenkin, Bill Wannan, Shirley Andrews, Mrs Margaret Whitworth, Bob Michell, and John Callaghan. For assistance with the research material and preparation of manuscript, I would like to thank John Collins and Anne O'Donovan.

Special thanks are due to Stan Arthur for his preparation of all the musical notation in the section on traditional songs, and his help with information on sources of collection of the songs.

For permission to use the following copyright material, my thanks to Mrs P. McLean for the quotes from *Time Means Tucker* by the late Duke Tritton, to Dal Stivens for his story "The Snoring Cod", to Jacaranda Press for the material quoted from *Roll the Summers Back* by the late Joseph Porter ("Spinifex"), to Angus & Robertson for the material quoted from *The Best of Lennie Lower* by Cyril Pearl, and also for "The Austra—laise" from *Selected Verse* by C. J. Dennis, to the estate of the late A. B. Paterson for "The Road to Hogan's Gap", to the Australian National University Press for the extract from *An Autobiography; Tales and Legends of the Canberra Pioneers* by Samuel Shumack, to

G. S. Casey for "The Hairy Men from Hannigan's Halt" by Gavin W. Casey, to *Singabout* for "Armatree Brown Jug Polka", "Four Sisters' Barn Dance" and "The Galopede", to the editor for "On the Queensland Railway Lines" from *The Queensland Centenary Song Book*.

For permission to reproduce the illustrative material, my thanks to the National Library of Australia for the Frontispiece and the plates on pages 25, 43, 47, 51, 55, 58, 68, 72, 77, 83, 92, 93, 99, 105, 116, 128, 130, 137, 139, 145, 149, 155, 157, 165, 184, 189, 191, 193, 199, 205, 209, 226, 235, 243, 246, 253, 255, 260, 265, 270, 282, 289, 293, 299, 302, 308, 312, 316, 320, 326, 332, 336, 339, 340, 344, 349, 352, 366, 372, 375, 377, 380, 392, 396, 406 and 409, and also for the plates on pages 16, 21, 30, 61, 87, 219, 296, 323, 330 and 360 from the Rex Nan Kivell Collection, and for the plate on page 277 from the Gundagai Collection; to the Art Gallery of New South Wales for the plates on pages 35, 276, 371, 373 and 391; to the Mitchell Library, Sydney for the plate on page 279; and to Dover Publications Inc. for the plates on pages 29, 40, 49, 64, 76, 159, 241, 263, 275 and 317.

Every effort has been made to trace ownership of copyright material used in this book; should some omission have been made, the editor and publishers apologize.

# Contents

# They'll tell you about me. . . .

## Ian Mudie

Me, I'm the man that dug the Murray for Sturt to sail down,
I am the one that rode beside the man from Snowy River,
and I'm Ned Kelly's surviving brother (or did I marry his sister?
I forget which), and it was my thumbnail that wrote that Clancy
had gone a-droving, and when wood was scarce I set the grass on fire
and ran with it three miles to boil my billy, only to find
I'd left the tea and sugar back with my tucker-bag,
and it was me, and only me, that shot through with the padre's daughter,
shot through with her on the original Bondi tram.
But it's a lie that I died hanging from a parrot's nest
with my arm in the hollow limb when my horse moved from under me;
I never die, I'm like the Leichhardt survivor I discovered
fifty years after the party had disappeared; I never die,
I'm Lasseter and Leichhardt both; I joined the wires of the O.T.
so that Todd could send the first message from Adelaide to Darwin;
I settled everywhere long before the explorers arrived;
my tracks criss-cross the Simpson Desert like city streets,
and I've hung my hat on Poeppel's Peg a thousand times.
It was me who boiled my billy under the coolabah,
told the bloke in the flash car to open his own flamin' gates,
put the goldfields pipeline through where the experts said nobody could,
wanted to know, "Who's robbing this coach, you or Ned Kelly?",
had the dog sit on my tucker-box outside of Gundagai,
yarned with Tom Collins while we fished for a cod someone'd caught years before,
and gave Henry Lawson the plots to make his stories from.
Me, I've found a hundred wrecked galleons on the Queensland coast,
dripping with doubloons, moidores and golden Inca swords,
and dug a dozen piles of guilders from a Westralian beach;
I was the one that invented the hollow woodheap,
and I built the Transcontinental, despite heat, dust, death, thirst and flies.
I led the ragged thirteen; I fought at Eureka and Gallipoli and Lae;
and I was a day too early (or was it too late?) to discover Coolgardie,
lost my original Broken Hill share in a game of cribbage,
had the old man kangaroo pinch my coat and wallet,
threw fifty heads in a row in the big game at Kal,
took a paddle-steamer seventy miles out of the Darling on a heavy dew,
then tamed a Gippsland bunyip, and sooled him on
to capture the Tantanoola Tiger and Fisher's Ghost
and become Billy Hughes's secretary for a couple of weeks.
Me, I outshore Jacky Howe, gave Buckley his chance,
and have had more lonely drinks than Jimmy Woods;
I jumped across Govett's Leap and wore an overcoat in Marble Bar,
seem to remember riding the white bull through the streets of Wagga,
sailed a cutter down the Kindur to the Inland Sea,
and never travelled till I went to Moonta.

Me, I was the first man ever to climb to the top of Ayers Rock,
pinched one of the Devil's Marbles for the kids to play with,
drained the mud from the Yarra, sold the Coathanger for a gold brick,
and asked for beer off the ice at Innamincka.

Me, yesterday I was rumour,
today I am legend,
tomorrow, history.
If you'd like to know more of me
inquire at the pub at Tennant Creek
or at any drover's camp
or shearing-shed,
or shout any bloke in any bar a drink,
or yarn to any bloke asleep on any beach;
they'll tell you about me,
they'll tell you more than I know myself.
After all, they were the ones that created me,
even though I'm bigger than any of them now
—in fact I'm all of them, rolled into one.
For anyone to kill me he'd have to kill
every single Australian,
every single one of them,
every single one.

# Introduction

During my boyhood in the bush near Brisbane in the early 1930s if my brother and I complained about anything my father silenced us with the comment, "You're too soft for this country!" Later, when I was working as a boilerman at a linseed oil factory near Brisbane, one of my workmates, a fellow called Ernie Harvey, who came from Miles in the southwest inland of Queensland told me about a boss drover he had worked for. This man had taken my father's attitude to extremes. If his men complained of the cold as they crouched round the campfire in the freezing dawn of a winter day on the plains, he would tear off his waistcoat, unbutton his shirt, and roar, "What's the matter with you blokes? I'm boiling!" In the dust of the tail of the mob, in the windless molten heat of summer, he would shout, "I'm freezing. Where's my overcoat!"

This attitude of most Australian men to difficulty, discomfort and danger was so much a part of my childhood that it never occurred to me to question it. I stared with some dismay at men of other races who could weep as unashamedly as children at joy or sorrow. I felt embarrassed for them. It didn't occur to me to question their attitude or my own, for I knew instinctively that I was "right". This sense of "rightness" I accepted completely, in this instance as in other factors that had gone into the shaping of my character as a young man. It was only borne upon me in the middle years of my life that there were alternative ways of reacting to outside circumstances, and that none of them is necessarily "right" as such. So I began to wonder at the attitudes of Australians that differ from those of folk from other countries. Further, I tried to discover why certain kinds of behaviour were acceptable here that would seem harsh and unfeeling to people from other lands.

When I came to the considerable reading of history that was needed for the compilation of this book it came to me that the solution of this problem lay in the way the traditional beliefs brought from older countries by the earlier settlers had been modified by the conditions of life here, particularly in the first eighty years of settlement. The harsh land and even harsher social conditions of our early settlement altered the prejudices and behaviour patterns of our forefathers in a manner that has survived to the present day.

The savagery of the treatment shown to convicts in Australia was worse than that shown any slaves on plantations elsewhere in the world. The slave was after all an investment, a chattel worth money, and some thought had to be given to protecting the investment he represented. He received some care and nourishment, much as was given to a draught animal. A convict labourer, on the other hand, who collapsed or died could be returned by his master to Government responsibility, and a replacement secured. The men who first scratched the surface of the land at Port Jackson, who built the stone barracks and churches at Port Arthur and Moreton Bay were less than slaves. Perhaps it is small wonder that the attitudes and traits that these men developed for survival should have remained to some degree extant until the days of my boyhood.

If you take men and work them to the edge of destruction in unspeakably bad conditions and with scanty rations, holding them in check only by the use of the lash and the gallows it becomes understandable that they will hate the uniformed symbols of authority that control their destiny. This hatred will continue after the worst of these abuses have been removed. Under these conditions it becomes understandable also that resentful men will do the absolute minimum of work they can get away with and that an enormous gulf of resentment and hostility will grow between the governed and the governors. This bitterness is not to be cured by a ticket of leave, or a pardon. The man who escapes the system will continue in his steadfast and abiding hatred, and his attitude will be passed on to his children by his example and experience. They will share his wariness and dislike of "screws" and "squatters", the authors of his previous misery.

The one source of spiritual comfort, the consolation of religion which had held the labouring classes of Great Britain in "their proper stations" was largely denied them. Chaplains were provided, but only too often these men were concerned with the lining of their own pockets at the general expense of the community rather than with their proper duties. The memory of Samuel Marsden, the "Flogging Parson", was still so bitter even in the 1930s as to cause Kenneth Slessor to write what is probably his most venomous poem, "The Vesper Song of the Reverend Samuel Marsden". Under conditions such as are described above, most men became rapidly devoid of hope, calloused to their own sufferings and almost indifferent to the suffering of others. Men at the penal settlements of Moreton Bay and Norfolk Island murdered each other by arrangement, for by this means the victim was released from his sufferings and the murderer could expect transport to Sydney for trial and his own release on the gallows. Men cast lots to see which would be the murderer and which the victim in perfect indifference as to which way fate would fall. Their only pride was in those of their fellows who defied the system, either through outlawry or stubborn defiance of the worst treatment that could be inflicted upon them.

These men were our first folk heroes, the wild colonial boys. Men in chains composed poems and songs about the bushrangers like Bold Jack Donahue, and his shout of defiance when called upon to surrender:

"Resign to you, you cowardly dogs, a thing I never would do.
I'll fight this night with all my might," cried bold Jack Donahue.
"I'd rather roam these hills and dales like wolf or kangaroo
Than work one day for the Government," cried bold Jack Donahue.

As with the later outlaws of the goldfields days, these men could not have remained at large for so long if it had not been for the active support of their many sympathizers. Those who remained defiant though in chains also had their admirers. Songs like "Jim Jones at Botany Bay" were popular. Bill Derrincourt, in his book *Old Convict Days*, describing the occasion when he was about to get one hundred lashes, remarks, "If a man, while receiving his hundred strokes, shouted out through pain, he was looked upon as a 'sandstone' or 'soft crawler'. Knowing this, I would have suffered cutting in pieces without a cry." There was the man, too, beaten at the Bathurst courthouse until the flesh hung in ribbons and the white bone showed, who on being released spat in the flogger's face and said, "You couldn't flog the wings off a butterfly." The spirit of these men lingers on,

however remotely, in the words of my father, "You're too soft for this country!" and in the words of the Wild Colonial Boy, "I'll fight but not surrender." The code was harsh, and the remnants of it linger still with some of us who breathed an echo of it in with our childhood. We remember the code, and find it difficult to surrender the thought that it is "the right thing to do".

These attitudes run through the folk culture of our country, even in the tall stories that were designed to entertain. The tales of incredible difficulties and dangers, of impossible achievements, served to reinforce men's good opinions of themselves and boasts of their hardihood allowed them to withstand the worst that their fellow men or their country might inflict upon them. Many of the ballads and songs describe the cleverness of bushmen and how they might

. . . astonish the newchums
With the way we can travel the land.

In the songs and poems one senses that they needed reassurance of their own worth and dignity.

The Australian today remains brave, aggressive, sensitive to ridicule, destructive and sentimental, blindly loyal to his fellows, resentful of outside authority when he disagrees with its dictates, and usually uncaring about world events unless they are sporting events and Australia is represented. Of this last indifference to overseas events, perhaps the conditioning began because of the remoteness of European civilization as it then was. This theme was explored by Geoffrey Blainey in his book, *The Tyranny of Distance*. Once in Australia, most settlers and convicts could not hope to see the lands of their birth again. Some achieved this of course, but for most, when hope of quick riches died, there was the saving attitude that they preferred their adopted country to their original homes. The major exception to this attitude was in the field of Imperialism, for most colonials seem to have been loyal to the dream of British Empire, to the extent of blindly following with armies whenever a war was entered upon by the parent nation, and usually physically assaulting those of their own population who advocated a more independent line of action.

Many of the attitudes listed above have tended to attenuate or change in urban Australians under the influence of better education and changed conditions of life, but enough of the unwritten law remains to regulate the conduct of the fight outside the dance hall, the game of two-up, and a general community standard of what is the "right thing to do". Naturally one would expect to find these persuasions reflected in the folk culture, and they are there of course. But there were also other influences at work in the broad scheme and these can be laid to the exposure of the native folk culture to that of two other lands, Ireland and the United States of America.

There are curious similarities and discrepancies between the folklore of the United States and Australia, the two frontier countries of the nineteenth century. American folklore, particularly the songs, sprang from a rich heritage of Anglo-Saxon, Celtic, African, Spanish, French and Central European cultures, brought there by the original settlers and those who followed after. The result of this transplantation into fresh soil has been a magnificent diversity of folk tales; ballads and blues, songs and stories from log huts, sod shanties, bunk houses, whaling ports, loggers' huts and mining camps. These form a varied and diverse miscellany of rich humour, great beauty and haunting persistence. Australia, on the other hand, with its harsher environment and the more limited social background of its settlers who were mainly Anglo-Saxon or Celtic, has shown a sparser development of song with regard to variety of music and subject. However, the ballad poem has flourished here to an extent unparalleled anywhere else in the English-speaking world. The folk culture of our country has produced a rich enough field in the boundaries set by the limitations of background, society, people and countryside. Peculiarly Australian attitudes as expressed exemplify an ironic humour that is largely lacking in the material from other lands.

It is not surprising that folk material from the two countries bordering the Pacific should share many things, particularly when one remembers the continual contact there has been between the people of both lands from the early days of settlement at Sydney Cove. There were American sealers harvesting the islands in Bass Strait and to the south of New Zealand along with their Currency and Vandiemonian cousins. The whalers of New Bedford and Martha's Vineyard, following the annual migration of the humpback whales from the Antarctic to the sheltered waters inside the Great Barrier Reef called at the infant settlement for stores and water. I have been in the cave on Booby Island, that bare knob of rock in the Torres Strait, where outward-bound whalers left their mail to be picked up by their compatriots and taken home to the States for posting. There were some bloody clashes between the crews of the two nations, fought with flensing spades and seal clubs, but I have no doubt that there were times when the men of both sides foregathered on the remote beaches and lonely islands to share the news and the colonial rum.

On two occasions in the last century there were major exchanges of citizens between the two countries. In 1849 one-tenth of the population of Sydney embarked for the Californian diggings, seeking gold, and in the next ten years there was a reverse flow after the discovery of the precious metal at Bathurst and Bendigo. If American music and tall stories are to be found, thinly disguised, in material still extant or available from printed sources it is small wonder; and Australians, on their part, made some impact on American folklore. The wholesale emigration of Sydneysiders to California added a word to American slang that is still extant there. As might be supposed from the background of these Australians, there were many violent and dishonest men among them. There was little organized law west of the Pecos River, so the presence of the "Sydney Ducks", as they were named, led to the formation of vigilante committees and "Kangaroo courts" among the diggers of other nations who were determined to stop their depredations. John Greenway, in one of his books, says that twelve of the first sixteen men arrested in San Francisco in 1849 were Australians. The culture and traditions that had made the Rocks district in Sydney infamous around the waterfronts of the world had much to do with the establishment of the equally infamous Barbary Coast beyond the Golden Gate. The slang word mentioned above, "Kangaroo court", that is, a place where a man is judged by a self-constituted body, is still used in America to describe a trial with no legal standing. The phrase echoes the origin of the defaulters they were instituted to deal with, the "Sydney Ducks". The court was usually presided over by what has been described as "Judge Lynch", in other words the justice dispensed was normally summary and final.

Something of the same type of activities and spirit among Australians abroad has been noted in London in the past twenty years, where Earls Court has become known as "Kangaroo Valley".

The first publicized goldfield in Australia was discovered by an Australian who had been re-

*Australian gold diggers, 186–? (artist unknown, oil painting)*

latively unsuccessful on the Californian diggings and who had returned to his native land. Gold had been found around Sydney on a number of occasions previously, but the information had been carefully suppressed by those in authority in the settlement where law was precariously maintained by "Judge Lash" instead of "Judge Lynch". They were fearful of the effect the knowledge of easy wealth would have upon the prisoners and their gaolers. When the Reverend W. B. Clarke showed Governor Gipps specimens of gold he had found near the Fish River while on an exploring expedition with Count Strzelecki, the Governor's response was to say hastily, "Put it away, Mr. Clarke, or we shall all have our throats cut!" One supposes that the news of Hargraves's discovery was only made public because the government of the day was concerned that the majority of the free population would otherwise leave for California. The population of New South Wales was about 200,000 when the major exodus took place in 1849, and those who went would almost all have been able-bodied men; so a counter attraction would have been needed to bring them back to Australia where their absence from the work force must have had serious effects on the economy of the young colony. When they did return they brought many Americans with them, thus reversing the flow of population and influencing the folk tradition.

So the contact between the two nations was reinforced and extended. There was less contact with Canadians. After Papineau's and Mackenzie's rebellions, the British Government sent rebels to Australia as transportees. In 1839, fifty-eight rebels, mostly *métis* of French-Indian ancestry arrived at Port Jackson to serve their sentences, and another eighty-three men were transported to Van Diemen's Land. These men appear to have mostly returned quietly to their homeland when they became "time-expired" men. Canadians came for the gold, of course. John Gilbert, one of Ben Hall's gang of bushrangers, had been brought to this country when a boy of twelve by his father who came to the diggings in New South Wales. This is the same John Gilbert about whom "Banjo" Paterson wrote his ballad, "How Gilbert Died".

The second major influence from overseas on our traditions and beliefs was curiously allied to the American. In 1798 large numbers of political prisoners were sent to this country after the rising of the Young United Irishmen against British rule. This was intended to place them far away so they could not raise any further mischief in their native land. These were the men who mutinied in an abortive revolution at Rose Hill (Parramatta) in 1804, but their march on the port of Sydney was halted by a small force of British regular troops before they could take any effective action. About this time, one writer estimated that one-third of the population of the colony was Irish by birth. The potato famine later in the nineteenth century had driven many Irishmen to emigration from their unfortunate country. Many went to New York, and from there went on to fill the police forces of their new nation and to have a major part in the building of the railroads across the continent, but many more came to Australia, first to the goldfields and later to settle on the land. The links of their common origin and their hatred of John Bull were so strong among the Irish emigrants that in 1876, when Fenian convicts were retrieved from Western Australia in the famous *Catalpa* incident, Irishmen in Liverpool, the United States and Australia were all involved, and it was an American whaler that was chosen to rescue the men. They were taken to America after their escape, where one of them, John Boyle O'Reilly (who had escaped previously in 1869) had been the chief mover in planning the rescue of his friends. O'Reilly was a war correspondent with one of the Fenian armies that invaded Canada from California and across the Great Lakes. O'Reilly later took the rank of General to himself, and led the retreat back down the west coast through Oregon.

Irish and American tunes remain the background to much of the Australian muster of folksong. We also appear to have brought some Irish traditional behaviour into our midst and kept it! An acquaintance of mine visited Ireland and attended a dance at a country hall, and he says that it was just like an old-time bush dance, with women at one end of the hall while the men either congregated round the keg or fought one another outside.

Although most of the tunes for Australian folk music both in dance and song come from the British Isles and America, the links abroad for the Bush Lie, the local tall story, are almost exclusively American. Although the two cultures share many things in some fields there is also a surprising lack of Australian equivalents for some features of traditional material that are common overseas. For instance, American folksong abounds in sacred songs, from the spirituals of the African people to the hymns of the primitive Fundamentalist sects and the Revivalists. I have never discovered a local religious song, nor have I ever heard one with a serious sacred theme. Once I thought I had found one. A shipmate aboard the Commonwealth Lighthouse Vessel *Cape Leeuwin*, Noel Sligar by name, sang a song for me in Cairns called "The Murrumbidgee Flood", part of which went as follows:

> We'll never know the reason these great disasters come,
> But we must all remember to say, "Thy Will be done!"

I produced this song in triumph to my brother Alan, who has done much more in the field of collecting songs than I have, and he told me that he had also collected words and music for this particular song. However, investigation had shown that it was almost a word for word copy of a similar earlier American song with the word "Murrumbidgee" substituted for "Mississippi". So our country still remains devoid of a collected sacred song, though hymn tunes have been used in some cases to words bearing little relationship to the original sentiments, mostly in the field of playground rhymes and bawdy ballads. Another kind of song that we lack in the homegrown variety in which America abounds is the lullaby and the song for children. There are some extant, of course, but none seem to be of local manufacture. Not that our children lack for songs of their own. Ian Turner has collected a great range of playground rhymes and ditties, and published them under the title, *Cinderella, Dressed in Yella*. This fascinating book is out of print at the moment of writing but I am reliably informed that a new revised and enlarged edition is being prepared and will be available soon. See the final section of this book for some examples of songs, rhymes and chants of the playground.

One of the remarkable features of Australian songs and stories is that they are rarely regional. They have a wide distribution, and one is liable to encounter them in all parts of the Commonwealth. There are a number of possible reasons for this wide spread of traditional material, but the most important was undoubtedly the itinerant worker in country districts from earliest times to the present. These men are growing fewer as mechanization catches up with the pastoral and farming industries. For instance, the major movement of men up and down the east coast for the sugar harvest is largely a thing of the past since the invention of a suitable and reasonably priced mechanical harvester. Cotton is now picked by a sort of giant vacuum cleaner, and a friend of mine in the tobacco industry tells me that mechanical harvesting is about to be introduced to that crop. The two industries still needing large numbers for hand labour, the wool and fruit growing interests, are also investigating methods of mechanical harvesting. In the case of the wool industry it is a chemical process rather than a mechanical one; and if successful, the sheep will simply have its wool pushed off with the bare hands instead of being shorn with machines. Australia without shearers? Impossible. But twenty years ago who would have thought that the canecutter would become so quickly redundant? The day of the traveller with the new songs and stories is almost past now, but sixty and a hundred years ago he spread them widely across the land.

It was the very life style of these men that led to the creation of much of this material in the first place. Unlike the successful goldseekers, who could afford to pay entertainers to come to them, these men were thrown back entirely upon their own resources for entertainment. Any diversion beside the camp fire had to come from the audience itself. I will speak more of this later, but for now would like to speak about another function these men performed that made them welcome and desirable to the society in which they lived. This was their role as news gatherers and news spreaders.

Settlers and fellow travellers welcomed the newcomer to hut or camp. The news carried by such a man could be of the greatest importance to them. Had rain fallen along the track? This was important to the drover with a travelling mob. It meant better feed for the mob and less worry about water for them. It was important to the horse teamster or bullocky, with eleven or twelve tons of wool "up", heading for a railhead or a wharf on the Murray River. For such a man it meant a careful assessment of the blacksoil plains with their attendant bogs and "gluepots", and these were so bad that after rain a bogged wagon often had to be off-loaded before it could be extricated from the wet soil. Those who know wet black soil will also know that even a powerful vehicle fitted with chains for steering and traction has to be halted often so that the sticky black mud can be chopped from under the mudguards to enable the wheels to turn. Even to walk on it when it is wet builds up a deposit on the soles of the boots so that one is forced to scrape them constantly to remain mobile. Small wonder then that the camped teamster, meeting a traveller from the direction he was headed, looked to him for news of the road ahead. In dry weather, the news of grass and water along the road was also of vital importance.

Travellers also carried the gossip of hundreds of square miles of country with them, for the country in those days was so sparsely populated that settlers living far apart from each other often knew of each other's joys and sorrows, triumphs and disappointments without ever having met. Within living memory the south of the Territory was still like this. In Mount Isa, at the mine barracks where I was living at the time, there was a Territorian living in the room next to me. He was a quiet middle-aged man, and he was a little worried one day when he was arbitrarily told that he was to share the room with a younger man. Luckily this young fellow was also from the Territory, and when the older man heard his name the following conversation took place:

"Any relation to old Bob?"

"Yeah, I'm his son."

"I met him once at Top Springs about thirty-seven or eight. You'd be the young fellow that went with that mob of stores from Banka to Lilydale, and then took them on to Fermoy when they'd spelled?"

"Yeah."

"I heard about you. You can move in, son."

So contact was made and reputation established though they had never met previously. This was one of the functions of the "bush telegraph", a man's history and reputation often preceded him and had much to do with his reception at a place where he had never been before. The same grapevine of information existed further south and east in earlier times. A careful study of the first chapter of *Such Is Life* by Joseph Furphy ("Tom Collins") shows how such information and gossip was passed along around the fire of a temporary camp.

Settled families also visited each other for the pleasure of human contact and conversation in the remoter areas, though their journeyings were not the odysseys of the Gulf drovers or the shearers making their annual round of their "run" of sheds;

but local gossip was also important. There was a strong district feeling and a rigid etiquette about such calls, even among the poorest families. These were the selectors, the stringybark cockatoos, the failed goldseekers turned settlers, battling it out on the thin edge of survival. Dame Mary Gilmore gives a clear account of their customs as well as their dreadful poverty in her book *Old Days, Old Ways*.

The bachelor wanderers, the rambling bush workers, cedar cutters, shearers, ringbarkers, rabbiters, doggers, shepherds, sheepwashers, fencers and canecutters, would live in the most primitive conditions for long periods of time and then have a glorious spree while "blueing their cheques". These men were not necessarily brutish or unintelligent, though certainly some of them were bad potatoes, like Sam Holt in the old song. When one considers the background, the wonder is that there were not many more villains among them. The community of convict suffering combined with the later experience of the exigencies of bush life demanding that men travel in pairs for survival led to the development of many of the customs that remain as traits of the Australian character. These traits give character to much of the material in this book and make it peculiarly ours. Sydney Baker, in his book *The Drum*, lists what he considers to be the distinctive qualities of the Australian character, and his listing has stood the test of time.

These itinerant workers who travelled by foot and horseback, and later by pushbike, were needed by the farmers and pastoralists as a seasonal work pool. Extra men were needed for crutching and shearing of the sheep, for the muster on the great cattle holdings and for the harvesting of the wheat, fruit and sugar crops. These large temporary groupings of men, during the time of the work or later as they cut out their cheques at a pub or shanty, were left completely without access to outside entertainment until Mr Edison invented his wax cylinder gramophone. As mentioned previously, they were thrown back upon their own resources for entertainment, and it was from this need that arose the ballads, the songs, the tall stories, and the bush jokes that continually well up from the inexhaustible spring of the people. I hope in this book to show something of the historical background, the kinds and varieties of people, the poems and songs they found entertaining, and also to demonstrate that some of it lives on today in the oral lore and literary wealth of our country.

I was born long enough ago to remember bullock teams snigging logs; and four and six horse teams pulling freight in the capital city of my State. I recall also the social evenings at homes, when all present were expected to contribute to the entertainment of the company. These musical evenings were a city as well as a country event but they lasted longer away from the radio and the talking pictures.

After taking a short look at some of the history of our country as seen through the eyes of contemporary individuals, having looked at its relationship with its fellow culture that developed in its sister continent in the northern hemisphere, it is worth looking a little more closely at what the two frontier cultures enjoyed in common. These were the ballad folksong and the tall story. In this country, both seem to have moved from the popular to the literary field, and both seem to be losing their struggle with their electronic counterparts that are so simply available. It is possible to get entertainment with no more effort than the flick of a switch or the press of a button. In most branches of folk culture the leaves are withered already. The few shoots left with a tinge of living green are beginning to yellow, though, except for enthusiasts, these have lingered longer in this land than in any other country except perhaps the Celtic nations. But the "Man From Snowy River" still rides in the hearts of the older generation, and it remains our best known and most quoted poem. I do not know if young people quote poetry at all; I suspect that if they do it is probably that of the cult heroes of their generation, Bob Dylan, Rod McKuen and their fellows.

The popular movement in Australia, the ballad, still holds on here though it receives little notice and less encouragement than other forms. There is a genuine need for expression among the people of Australia, and the poem still most likely to be found coming from the mass of the people is almost certain to be the familiar "sevener" of the bush ballad. Anyone who doubts this has only to refer to the enormous amount of verse sent over the years to the recently deceased Australian Broadcasting Commission programme, the "Hospital Hour". Any of the men who compered this session from the A.B.C. studios in Brisbane will witness to the spate of verse that arrived daily. None of it was truly great poetry, little of it was even readable poetry; but it pointed the enormous need of some of the folk of Australia for a voice that their "official"

poets no longer seemed to use for them. This country is almost certainly the last stronghold of the ancient popular form of the ballad. It shows in the entries for the Bronze Swagman poetry award at Winton each year, and I am sure it is equally well represented among the starters at the Henry Lawson Memorial Competition at Grenfell, in New South Wales, though I cannot speak from personal experience in the latter instance.

This book is an affirmation of the roots which our young society sank into the rarely welcoming, often hostile, soil of our adopted homeland. It represents a sampler only of the homespun songs and stories that sprang from that combination of circumstances mentioned previously. In case any reader feels that undue prominence has been given to the tall story in this book, I plead that it is a largely neglected field in our folk culture, the only one outside the ballad to achieve much literary expression. Australia is probably now the only country in the world where both these forms are widely used by practising writers. Also, the stories are in themselves so delightful when properly told that they deserve more attention than they have been given heretofore in the study and publicizing of our folk culture. They occupy that role that in older civilizations was taken by the myths and legends of gods and heroes. There have been some sporadic attempts at their assembly and dissemination, but the only book I know to be devoted solely to them in recent times has been *Crooked Mick of the Speewah,* by Bill Wannan. Because this book is available I have not included any of the Speewah stories, and have confined myself to literary stories, traditional paragraphs from the old "Aboriginalities" section of the *Bulletin,* and stories I have heard myself during my life.

Many Australian tall stories in our country spring from, or are allied to, similar stories current in the United States, but most folklore, where a common language is shared, spreads rapidly between countries. And what is really original? Probably the best known literary tall story from the States is "The Celebrated Jumping Frog of Calaveras County" by Samuel Clemens ("Mark Twain"); and an American researcher, B. A. Botkin, has shown that it is a development of a fake newspaper report that was printed twelve years before the Frog was first published. The scope and range of these stories is timeless, and fresh examples keep coming to my notice. The great tradition of the tall story marches into the future,

*Sydney Harbour showing the Heads (Conrad Martens, watercolour)*

keeping pace with the times and I am sure it will keep going as long as people enjoy laughter and mental provocation. The yarns about the country where it is so dry that you have to prime yourself before you can spit, where the Boss makes you wait until an inch of rain has fallen before you can have water in your tea, and where the trees follow the dogs around, keep turning up beside the similar stories that have been inspired by our more mechanized civilization. As will be seen by reference to the section, the Speewah might have been cut up for soldier settlement, Big Burrawang may have been irrigated and turned into citrus orchards, but the ghosts of Crooked Mick, Clancy, the Ragged Thirteen and the Wild Men of the Goldfields live on in the hearts of the people. This book tells a little of them and the men who made them and their legends.

Quite obviously, it was not possible to include all the available material in this collection. I made the arbitrary choice from that historical and traditional material which seemed to me to be most illuminating on the standards of conduct and entertainment at the various stages of our development as a nation. I leave it to the reader to decide for himself just how relevant our history and folklore have been in influencing our social behaviour which is unique in the world. Where a source book is available I have in most cases quoted author and title, so the interested reader can seek the material for himself for further information. While many of these books may be out of print, most are available from libraries.

There has been some academic and critical discussion as to the existence of an Australian ethos. I suggest that it has been there all the time but that it has been so obvious as to be either overlooked or dismissed as being of no consequence. Many writers, for example, have expressed reservations about mateship, the theme so beloved of Henry Lawson and others of the bush school of writers. I can only say they are talking about something outside their experience. I am sorry for them, for they are the poorer by their lack. While it is true that in the first instance mateship sprang from social necessity, the reality did exist and continues to exist. While nowadays the circumstances grow fewer when it is needful to have a man at your back in whom you can place implicit trust, there have been times in my not uneventful life when I have been glad that the man behind me was a mate. A man may have many friends and acquaintances, but a real mate is rarely found. I have known several, and for anyone to allege that mateship was a myth is to deny basic trust and unselfishness such as can exist between two men in difficult circumstances. Having had the experience myself, I pity the man who has not known it.

As a nation, we should treasure these songs, poems, tales and ballads which give character to us. The alternative is that the unique genius that informs the brain of Everyman will be lost in a morass of nonentity as bland and textureless as a cauldron of gruel. I do not mean that we should blindly subscribe to the sentiments expressed or the values expounded, but we should treasure the memories of the makers of these songs and poems and the tellers of tales that can make us laugh or cry. They have brought a savour to our lives that is peculiarly ours, and sometimes they speak for us when we do not have the words to say what is in our minds to say. Readers are sure to find something familiar in this book. It would be strange if they did not, because they are of the folk and, except for those individual authors whose work is included because it has become common folk property, these are poems, songs and stories of the folk. It is my hope that you will not only renew your acquaintance with old friends but that you will also find some new acquaintances who will become firm favourites.

# Section 1

# The History That Shaped a Tradition

Australian history is almost always picturesque; indeed, it is so curious and strange, that it is itself the chiefest novelty the country has to offer, and so it pushes the other novelties into second and third place. It does not read like history but like the most beautiful lies. And all of a fresh new sort, no mouldy old stale ones. It is full of surprises and adventures, and incongruities and contradictions and incredibilities; but they are all true, they all happened.

*From* Following the Equator, *Samuel Clemens ("Mark Twain")*

# Introduction to Section I

Unless some attention is paid to the background, the full meaning of much of the following material is lost. I have here tried to find historical fact as seen by direct observers of places and events; and in some cases have chosen to include differing and conflicting accounts of the same things so that the reader can gain some insight into the history of this country directly rather than from secondary writers. Much of it makes horrifying reading, but it clarifies attitudes that might otherwise remain obscure. It ceases in point of time at Federation.

Some of the byways of our history make fascinating reading, and much of it can never be fully explored now because there are no written records; not surprising in a land where few of the early settlers could write or read. The best and most comprehensive social history as seen by personal observers and commentators of early Australia remains Russel Ward's book, *Such Was Life*.

*Fleet in command of Governor Phillip and Captain Hunter (engraving from* Illustrated Sydney News, *18 March 1871)*

*Port Jackson, New South Wales (Skinner Prout, from* Australia, *ed. Edwin Carton Booth)*

Captain Arthur Phillip, R.N., the commander of the first fleet and the Governor of the new settlement, after making an examination of the surroundings of the Bay, decided that the place was unsuitable to his purpose. He therefore ordered the fleet to remain at anchor, while he himself set out in an open boat to explore the coast and to look for a home.

The undertaking was a bold one. The coast was wild and surf-beaten. Its dangers were many and unknown. Immense rollers broke upon the rugged shore, and seemed to leave no safe landing-place for any boat. The shores were peopled by unfriendly natives, who, standing in large numbers on the tops of the cliffs, hurled threats and defiance at the boats as they approached.

Suddenly, after sailing north for about twelve miles, there came a break in the coast-line about a mile in length from headland to headland. Seen from the open sea, this opening appeared of little size, but as the boats rounded the inner head the immense extent of the harbour was displayed. After exploring the different bays, that which showed the deepest soundings was selected. "The different coves of this harbour," says Captain Phillip himself, "were examined with all possible expedition, and the preference was given to one which had the finest spring of water, and in which ships can anchor so close to the shore that at a very small expense quays may be constructed at which the largest vessels may unload. In honour of Lord Sydney the Governor distinguished it by the name of Sydney Cove." Two days afterwards Captain Phillip returned to Botany Bay, and on the 25th of the same month, seven days after the arrival of the *Supply*, he left Botany and sailed to Port Jackson.

As at that time it happened to be blowing a strong gale, the rest of the fleet was left under convoy of the *Sirius*, with orders to proceed to Sydney as soon as the gale abated. Scarcely were the leading vessels out of sight when a strange sight appeared. "About daylight, just as they were preparing for a start," two strange sail showed themselves on the horizon. These gradually approached, and as they came nearer it was seen that they were the *Boussole* and *Astrolabe*, ships of the great French explorer La Pérouse.

On the 26th of the month, according to Captain Phillip, the transports and storeships under convoy of the *Sirius* finally evacuated Botany Bay, and as in a fair wind the journey only occupies a few hours they were soon all safely anchored in Sydney Cove.

Without any delay the disembarkation was commenced, and all persons able to work were set to clear the ground for the camp and to cut wood for the buildings. The clearing of the bush was then, as it has always been, a task of great difficulty. "The labour," says the Governor, "which attended this necessary operation was greater than can easily be imagined by those who were not spectators of it. The coast, as well as the neighbouring country in general, is covered with wood, and though in this spot the trees stood more apart, and were less encumbered with underwood than in many other places, yet their magnitude was such as to render not only the felling but the removal of them afterwards extremely difficult. By the habitual indolence of the convicts, and the want of proper overseers to keep them to their duty, their labour was rendered less efficient than it might have been. In the evening of the 26th the colours were displayed on shore, and the Governor, with several of his principal officers and others, assembled round the flagstaff, drank the King's health" (George III.), "and success to the settlement." The first house to be completed was that of the Governor, the materials and framework of which had been brought out ready-worked from England. Other houses and huts of various sizes soon appeared, and all seemed fairly in progress, when a dread enemy appeared in the midst of the camp.

On the voyage out there had been very little sickness, but now dysentery showed itself, and soon took hold of a large number. Of the sufferers many died. Scurvy also attacked the little colony, the members of which had for months been deprived of fresh food. Even after landing, fish or other fresh provisions or vegetables could rarely be procured. For the dysentery the red gum was found to be useful, while for the scurvy the chief thing that could be done was to grow vegetables and fruits with as little delay as possible. Very little, however, could yet be done in this direction, and, meanwhile, recourse was had to the various species of plants that were growing wild—celery, spinach, and parsley—all of which, fortunately, were found in abundance round the settlement.

At that time, according to the historians of the young colony, the public stock consisted of one bull, four cows, one bull calf, one stallion, three mares, and three colts. These were carefully preserved for breeding, and were shortly removed to the bay adjoining Sydney Cove, which bay was none other than Farm Cove. Here, where the

Botanical Gardens now extend their pleasant glades, a small farm was started, from which Farm Cove took its name. After strenuous efforts, matters began to improve a little, and by the end of February or beginning of March the settlement was in fair progress. The public storehouses had been well begun, and although the stumps of the trees had not been removed, the ground was cleared over a considerable extent, and Sydney town was no longer a mere hope, but had become an accomplished fact.

*From* Cassell's Picturesque Australasia, *Vol. I, ed. E. E. Morris*

Screw Pine

Saturday, 26th (January, 1788)
   The two Ship that Wee Seen of this Bay on
      Thursday 24th Jany. , Came
   in this Day Which proved to be French Ships on
      Discovereys

   At AM. the fleet. Got on thier Way. Came to an
      ankor at. $\frac{1}{2}$ p. 6 OClock
   in Port Jackson Close to the New town
   Which Was Crisned this Day & 4 Vollies
   of Small Arms. Fired.
Sunday, 27th
   I & Serj.! Clayfield Was Order.d on B.d   the
Charlotte Transp.! to Do Duty
   A Number of Male Convicts Went
   On Shore this Day to Work _ _

Monday 28th
   The Whole Detachment of Marines
   Wives & Children Desembarked
   & Encamped Immedetly, _ _
   The Male Convicts imploy'd in clear,g
   away the Ground.
Feb.y 5th
   a Seaman belonging to the Alex.r Was
   Drume,d out of Camp, for being Drunk
   and Afronting Some of the Officers

Thursday 7th
   The King's Commissions Was Read
   in Pressents of the Battallion &
   Convicts. there Was 3 Vollies fired
Coulers flying, &.c
   After the ~~Comm~~ King's Commission Was
   read the Laws ~~of~~ that this Country
   ~~W.~~ Is to be Governed by Was Read;
and then the Governer Made A Spech to the
   Convicts. Reletive to thier Behaviour
   & Every ~~thing~~ Crime that Was Committed
   before he freeley forgave _ _ _
   the Governer & All the Navey & Milatery
officers Dinned together in a(E Larbetery) [?]
   tent for that porpose _ _ _ _
   Same day the Governer Returned
   the Marines thanks for thier Manley
   & Soldierlike Appearance _ _ _ _ _ _

Sunday 24th
   Tho.s Harmsworth (Son to (Tho.s Harmsworth
a Marine). Died of A feaver _ _ _
   A few days after our Arrival here
   Major Ross had 7 sheep & one Hog
   Kild ~~kild~~ by Thunder and Lightning.

Wednesday 27th
   Tho.s Barrett, a Convict, Was tried for
   Breaking Open the Publick Stores, &
Exacuted the Same Evening at 6. OClock
Hen.y Lovel & Jos. Hall, Convicts
   was tried the Same day. for the Same
   Crime. & sentinced to Death; But
   Was Respited. for 24 Hours.(Afterwards
repreved)

Feb.y 29th
   Two Convicts by the Name of Dan.!
   Gordon & Freeman Was Cast for death
   & Reprived under the three Where
the Ware to be Execute.d the Latter
   Was forgave on Account. of his being
in futer Publick Exacutioner

*From* "Remarks on a Passage to Botany Bay", *James Scott, Sergeant of Marines*

Garden Island in a Fog

In this January, 1788, a great sight broke upon the view of the Botany Bay tribe. Ships they had perhaps seen before, but so many sailing in at once, and such large ones, was more than they had ever seen. . . .

For not only were ships anchoring in their bay in number beyond all precedent, but boats were descending, and seemed determined to possess the land, while the ships possessed the water. The first boat came nearer and nearer, and all the crew made such demonstrations of peace and good intentions, that they forgot their right to the land; forgot the legend about the small shot in their countryman's legs, and fraternized with the intruders. The leader of the company who stood before them in the full splendour of naval cocked-hat and gold braid, was no less a person than Captain Phillip, or Governor Phillip, who was charged by the Home Government to take away the land from the blacks, and give it to the men he had with him; who were principally sent out from England because they would not let other people's property alone. It was thought that they would thus reform.

The expedition was a very large one: it consisted of one thousand souls with suitable stores all packed up in three men-of-war, six convict ships, and three store ships. The colonists were selected in the most miscellaneous manner. Some, probably the majority, were political offenders, or sent out for offences of so slight a nature that society would have risked nothing by keeping them at home.

*From* A History of the Discovery and Exploration of Australia, *Rev. Julian E. Tenison-Woods*

The Kangaroo

New England was given to the Puritans by no earthly potentate, their title came direct from heaven. Increase Mather said: "The Lord God has given us for a rightful possession the land of the Heathen People amongst whom we dwell;" and where are the Heathen People now?

Australia was not given to us either by the Pope or by the Lord. We took this land, as we have taken many other lands, for our own benefit, without asking leave of either heaven or earth. A continent, with its adjacent islands, was practically vacant, inhabited only by that unearthly animal the kangaroo, and by black savages, who had not even invented the bow and arrow, never built a hut or cultivated a yard of land. Such people could show no valid claim to land or life, so we confiscated both. The British islands were infested with criminals from the earliest times. Our ancestors were all pirates, and we have inherited from them a lurking taint in our blood, which is continually impelling us to steal something or kill somebody. How to get rid of this taint was a problem which our statesmen found it difficult to solve. In times of war they mitigated the evil by filling the ranks of our armies from the gaols, and manning our navies by the help of the press-gang, but in times of peace the scum of society was always increasing.

At last a great idea arose in the mind of England. Little was known of New Holland, except that it was large enough to harbour all the criminals of Great Britain and the rest of the population if necessary. Why not transport all convicts, separate the chaff from the wheat, and purge out the old leaven? By expelling all the wicked, England would become the model of virtue to all nations.

So the system was established. Old ships were chartered and filled with the contents of the gaols. If the ships were not quite seaworthy it did not matter much. The voyage was sure to be a success; the passengers might never reach land, but in any case they would never return. On the vessels conveying male convicts, some soldiers and officers were embarked to keep order and put down mutiny. Order was kept with the lash, and mutiny was put down with the musket. On the ships conveying women there were no soldiers, but an extra half-crew was engaged. These men were called "Shilling-a-month" men, because they had agreed to work for one shilling a month for the privilege of being allowed to remain in Sydney. If the voyage lasted twelve months they would thus have the sum of twelve shillings with which to

*A fleet of transports under convoy (Carrington Bowles, 1781, mezzotint, hand coloured)*

commence making their fortunes in the Southern Hemisphere. But the "Shilling-a-month" man, as a matter of fact, was not worth one cent the day after he landed, and he had to begin life once more barefoot, like a new-born babe.

The seamen's food on board these transports was bad and scanty, consisting of live biscuit, salt horse, Yankee pork, and Scotch coffee. The Scotch coffee was made by steeping burnt biscuit in boiling water to make it strong. The convicts' breakfast consisted of oatmeal porridge, and the hungry seamen used to crowd round the galley every morning to steal some of it. It would be impossible for a nation ever to become virtuous and rich if its seamen and convicts were reared in luxury and encouraged in habits of extravagance.

When the transport cast anchor in the beautiful harbour of Port Jackson, the ship's blacksmith was called out of his bunk at midnight. It was his duty to rivet chains on the legs of the second-sentence men—the twice convicted. They had been told on the voyage that they would have an island all to themselves, where they would not be annoyed by the contemptuous looks and bitter jibes of better men. All night long the blacksmith plied his hammer and made the ship resound with the rattling chains and ringing manacles, as he fastened them well on the legs of the prisoners. At dawn of day, chained together in pairs, they were landed on Goat Island; that was the bright little isle—their promised land. Every morning they were taken over in boats to the town of Sydney, where they had to work as scavengers and road-makers until four o'clock in the afternoon. They turned out their toes, and shuffled their feet along the ground, dragging their chains after them. The police could always identify a man who had been a chain-gang prisoner during the rest of his life by the way he dragged his feet after him.

In their leisure hours these convicts were allowed to make cabbage-tree hats. They sold them for about a shilling each, and the shop-keepers resold them for a dollar. They were the best hats ever worn in the Sunny South, and were nearly indestructible; one hat would last a lifetime, but for that reason they were bad for trade, and became unfashionable.

The rest of the transported were assigned as servants to those willing to give them food and clothing without wages. The free men were thus enabled to grow rich by the labours of the bondmen—vice was punished and virtue rewarded.

Until all the passengers had been disposed of, sentinels were posted on the deck of the transport with orders to shoot anyone who attempted to escape. But when all the convicts were gone, Jack was sorely tempted to follow the shilling-a-month men. He quietly slipped ashore, hurried off to Botany Bay, and lived in retirement until his ship had left Port Jackson.

He then returned to Sydney, penniless and barefoot, and began to look for a berth. At the Rum Puncheon wharf he found a shilling-a-month man already installed as cook on a colonial schooner. He was invited to breakfast, and was astonished and delighted with the luxuries lavished on the colonial seaman. He had fresh beef, fresh bread, good biscuit, tea, coffee, and vegetables, and three pounds a month wages. There was a vacancy on the schooner for an able seaman, and Jack filled it. He then registered a solemn oath that he would "never go back to England no more," and kept it.

Some kind of Government was necessary, and, as the first inhabitants were criminals, the colony was ruled like a gaol, the Governor being head gaoler. His officers were mostly men who had been trained in the army and navy. They were all poor and needy, for no gentleman of wealth and position would ever have taken office in such a community. They came to make a living, and when free immigrants arrived and trade began to flourish, it was found that the one really valuable commodity was rum, and by rum the officers grew rich. In course of time the country was divided into districts, about thirty or thirty-five in number, over each of which an officer presided as police magistrate, with a clerk and staff of constables, one of whom was official flogger, always a convict, promoted to the billet for merit and good behaviour.

New Holland soon became an organized pandemonium, such as the world had never known since Sodom and Gomorrah disappeared in the Dead Sea, and the details of its history cannot be written. To mitigate its horrors the worst of the criminals were transported to Norfolk Island. The Governor there had not the power to inflict capital punishment, and the convicts began to murder one another in order to obtain a brief change of misery, and the pleasure of a sea voyage before they could be tried and hanged in Sydney. A branch pande-

*Goat Island (Skinner Prout, from* Australia, *ed. Edwin Carton Booth)*

monium was also established in Van Diemen's Land. The system was upheld by England for about fifty years.

*From* The Book of the Bush, *George Dunderdale*

The prisoners on Goat Island . . . amount to about 200, most of them are in irons; they are employed in erecting a powder-magazine, which is nearly completed, and is of sandstone. Internally, it is an arch, of 25 feet wide, and 100 feet long. The prisoners are lodged in twelve wooden "boxes", which are whitewashed inside and out, and are very clean. Each of these boxes is furnished with a few Bibles, Testaments, and Prayer Books.

*From* A Narrative of a Visit to the Australian Colonies, *James Backhouse*

# Lower Away
# for the Landing

Just fancy! It was way back in 1788 that Governor Phillip and I landed in Botany Bay. How time flies!

As we sailed into the bay we got a whiff from the boiling down works. "My goodness, this country smells!" said Phillip.

"I told you we were landing in the wrong place," I replied. "Why couldn't you land in some genteel place like Rose Bay?"

"Who's Governor of this colony?" he replied heatedly. "All right! All right!" I said. "Don't do your block in front of the convicts."

So we landed at Farm Cove. Thus is history made.

It was a pretty wild spot, and the natives were a bit suspicious. "Blime!" said one convict. "Tike me back to Dartmoor!" We put him in irons.

"I think we'll build a gaol first," said Phillip. The first sign of civilization was the gaol. Then we built the barracks.

After that I said to Phillip: "What about lunch?" "Good idea!" he said.

"Lunch ho!" I bawled, and there was a great clashing of leg-irons as the convicts collapsed in their tracks.

"I'm glad you thought to pack some sandwiches before we left England," I said. "There doesn't seem to be much to eat in this place."

"I think of everything," said Phillip, somewhat boastfully, I thought. "I've even brought a couple of rabbits and a potted prickly pear which I intend to plant shortly. They ought to do well in this country."

We were sitting down munching our sandwiches when Sir Joseph Banks came rushing up with a piece of lantana in one hand and a sprig of Bathurst burr in the other.

"Look what I've found!" he cried delightedly.

"How quaint!" said Phillip. "We must plant a lot of that, too. Come and have a sandwich, Joe."

We had just finished the last of our sandwiches when a soldier came up, saluted, and said, "Sir, one of the convicts has just bitten a piece out of his pick. Did it deliberately."

"Hang him," said Phillip.

"Yessir."

And that was that.

"You're a bit drastic, aren't you?" I asked, when the soldier had gone.

"We can get plenty more convicts, but we're a bit short of picks."

"I suppose you're right."

"Of course I'm right!" That's the sort of man he was. Bombastic.

"What's this track they're cutting here?" I asked him.

"That's George Street. I called it after the ship's parrot. Holy Moses!"

"Wasser matter?"

"It's all right. It must be the heat. I thought I saw a big brown thing standing upright on two legs with a long tail and it jumped fifteen feet and disappeared into the bush."

"You want to lay off that rum," I told him. We found out later that they were real. Kangaroos—not rum, after all.

All this time, Blaxland was away in the hills with Lawson and Wentworth. We were beginning to get a bit anxious about them. However, they came back after a while and said that they had discovered three railway stations. They had had the effrontery to name them after themselves. Phillip immediately named a street after himself. He was very annoyed. He even went so far as to name a whole bay after himself and called it Port Phillip in order to make it sound more important.

He was a man who was inclined to bicker about trifles. One day when he found me fraternising with the aborigines he was quite furious until I told him that I had learned a number of real good names for towns, such Wagga Wagga, Coonamble and Wantibadgery. That soothed him a bit.

After a few months, when we had the town pretty well fixed up and had imported a few bushrangers to liven things up a bit, darn me if Macarthur didn't arrive with some merino sheep he'd picked up somewhere.

"You fool!" said Phillip, bitterly. "They'll eat the grass and then how will my rabbits get on?"

"I never thought of that," said Macarthur, biting his nails.

"A fine team of colonists I've got," went on Phillip.

"You must admit," I said, "that we have made progress. When we first landed here there was nothing else to see but scenery. Now look at it. We've put up two new scaffolds, we've got a street, planted a whole lot of prickly pear . . ."

"Yes! Yes! I know all that, but nobody is ever

here when they're wanted. There's Bass and Flinders gone off in a boat somewhere, fishing, I suppose. They can get somebody else to be Governor. I'm fed up.''

It was a very nasty scene and has rightly been left out of most history books.

Still, when I look around today and see the result of our labours I say to myself, ''Well, we certainly gave the town a good start.''

I'm still able to give the town a bit of a start when I've got the money. The old pioneer spirit lives on.

*From* The Best of Lenny Lower, *ed. Cyril Pearl and W. E. Pidgeon*

*As settlement spread outward from Sydney Town to Parramatta, the Hawkesbury, and eventually to the Hunter River and the South Coast, convicts were assigned to landowners as servants. Depending on the landowner, the convict could find himself in a very wide range of circumstances so far as living and working conditions were concerned. Unfortunately, most masters were ruthless and reflected the official attitudes of the times.*

''But the fact is, flogging in this country is such a common thing that nobody thinks anything of it. I have seen young children practising on a tree, as children in England play at horses. I have now got a man under me who received 2600 lashes with the cat in about five years, and his worst crime was insolence to his overseer. The fact is, the man is a red-hot Tipperary man; and when his blood gets up, you could not make him hold his tongue if you were to threaten to hang him. Since I have had him he has never had a lash, just because I take no notice of what he says. The consequence is, there is nothing in the world that man would not do for me if he could. Some years ago, a little way up the country, a man actually died under the cat: of course it was all quietly hushed up.''

''But do you really think such things can be true?''

''Why, of course, when I see the very like of them under my own eyes. For instance, there is a lieutenant (a mere boy), who is now magistrate over a gang that are making a road not three miles from the farm where I stop. Whenever this lad means to send a man to the lock-up for the night, he makes

the lock-up keeper start three or four buckets over the floor, under pretence of keeping it free from vermin, but really for the purpose of tormenting the culprit by compelling him to walk about all night; and then he will have the poor wretch tied up to the triangles the first thing in the morning, before breakfast. This I know to be true, because I have it from the lock-up keeper himself. The fact is that officers, and especially young officers, when made magistrates, get irritated at the hardihood of a class of men whom they have made up their minds to despise; and the cat being a soldier's natural revenge, they fly to it directly. It is as common, you know, for one soldier to revenge himself upon another by getting him flogged, as it is for women, when they fight, to pull one another's hair.''

''One can hardly conceive such things possible.''

''Ah! you must not judge of this country by England. What I tell you now, I can tell you on the authority of my own eyes. I was sent for to Bathurst Court-house to identify a man supposed to have taken the bush from the farm I have charge of. I had to go past the triangles, where they had been flogging incessantly for hours. I saw a man walk across the yard with the blood that had run from his lacerated flesh squashing out his shoes at every step he took. A dog was licking the blood off the triangles, and the ants were carrying away great pieces of human flesh that the lash had scattered about the ground. The scourger's foot had worn a deep hole in the ground by the violence with which he whirled himself round on it to strike the quivering wealed back, out of which stuck the sinews, white, ragged, and swollen. The infliction was a hundred lashes, at about half-minute time, so as to extend the punishment through nearly an hour. The day was hot enough to overcome a man merely standing that length of time in the sun; and this was going on in the full blaze of it. However, they had a pair of scourgers, who gave one another spell and spell about; and they were bespattered with blood like a couple of butchers. I tell you this on the authority of my own eyes. It brought my heart into my mouth.''

''Well, I can only say that, for disgusting brutality, it exceeds anything I ever yet heard of as practised under the sanction of British law.''

''It is nevertheless true; and many much worse things than any I have yet enumerated are true. For instance, there are some magistrates who habitually flog to compel men to confess anything of which they suppose them guilty. I heard of a case

*Rounding up a straggler (Frank Mahoney, detail, oil on canvas)*

only the other day where a man had several 'fifties', on several consecutive days, to compel him to confess a robbery. No doubt in many such instances there is a sort of certainty of the man's guilt; but then again there have been very many cases where it turned out that the suspicion was totally unfounded. I know of several poor creatures who have been entirely crippled for life by these merciless floggings; and, which is worst of all, oftentimes for offences which no considerate and right-thinking person would dream of considering heinous and unpardonable. I will give one instance more of the summary jurisdiction of magistrates. The commandant at—, a police station near my hut, was walking out one summer-evening about twelve months ago with his lady: he was in plain clothes, all but his military foraging cap, an article of dress that many private gentlemen wear. Two men accosted him, and asked the way to a farm in the vicinity, to whose owner they had been assigned. Considering they did not address him quite respectfully enough, he gave them some sharp language, which they returned: hereupon, but still without telling them that he was a magistrate, he laid hands on one of them, who immediately tripped him up. On this his lady began to shout most lustily, which brought the soldiers of the party under his command out of their hut close by. The men were presently seized and confined. The next day the worshipful peace-breaker deposed against them himself, before himself, pronounced them guilty himself, and sentenced them himself to twelve months at an Settlers iron-gang."

*From* Settlers and Convicts; or Recollections of Sixteen Years' Labour in the Australian Backwoods, *Alexander Harris ("An Emigrant Mechanic")*

Laughing-Jackass and Snake.

It is not necessary, for the purposes of the present work, to detail the early difficulties, disappointments, privations, and perils, including the danger of famine, encountered by the colony during the first few years of its existence.

By an almost unaccountable oversight, on the part of the government at home, the infant colony was unfurnished with either agriculturists or mechanics sufficiently skilful or capable of instructing and training the promiscuous herd of felons transported from London and the towns of England, in those regular and productive efforts of labour, in the field and in the workshop, requisite even for the self-supply of the colony with the principal necessaries of life. So deplorable, indeed, was the deficiency in this respect, that there was but one individual in the colony who could either instruct the convicts in agriculture, or successfully manage them in other respects; and these qualities were the chance possession of a man whom Governor Phillip had hired in England as his body servant! Even of this valuable person, the colony was deprived by death so early as in 1791.

By another strange mistake of the home government, not only were no free settlers sent out with the convicts, but it was for a long time its policy not to permit free emigrants to proceed to and settle in the colony.

When the transported felons of England used to be poured into Virginia in North America, they were immediately dispersed amongst and absorbed into the numerous, industrious, and moral population of that country. They were a valuable supply of labourers, much wanted by the American planters. Their numbers, compared to those of the settled and orderly population, were insignificant. They were therefore easily constrained, by the numerical superiority of the people amongst whom they were cast, and by the united force of the law and of example, both to habits of industry and to moral observances in their conduct; and thus two of the objects of their transportation were accomplished by the very nature of the circumstances in which they were placed.

*From* The Felonry of New South Wales, *James Mudie*

Captain King assumed the government in September, 1800. Under his administration, it has been said, "the colony consisted chiefly of those who sold rum, and those who drank it."

The turbulent, immoral, and avaricious officers of the New South Wales corps carried things with so high a hand, that Governor King was frequently apprehensive of being put under arrest by them; and so flagrant did the misconduct of the government officers, both military and civil, become, that on the governor sending a gentleman to England with a written complaint against an officer of the corps, it was found, when the box which had contained the complaint and his excellency's dispatches, was opened in Downing-street, that its lock had been picked in the colony, rifled of its contents, and a harmless parcel of old newspapers put in their place.

This incident alone should have given the home government a pretty striking specimen and proof of the habits of the convict officers of the government who were suffered to be about the person of the governor, and to pollute the public offices and employments of the colony.

*From* The Felonry of New South Wales, *James Mudie*

About four miles from [Parramatta] is another settlement—Toongabby [sic]—where the greatest number of migrants are, and work very hard (there is also a good crop of corn standing, and promises well). Their hours for work are from five in the morning till eleven; they then leave off till two in the afternoon, and work from that time till sunset. They are allowed no breakfast hour, because they have seldom anything to eat. Their labour is felling trees, digging up the stumps, rooting up the shrubs and grass, turning up the ground with spades or hoes, and carrying the timber to convenient places. From the heat of the sun, the short allowance of provision, and the ill-treatment they receive from a set of merciless wretches (most of them of their own description) who are their superintendents, their lives are rendered truly miserable. At night they are placed in a hut, perhaps fourteen, sixteen, or eighteen together (with one woman, whose duty is to keep it clean and provide victuals for the men while at work), without the comfort of either beds or blankets, unless they take them from the ship they come out in, or are rich enough to purchase them when they come on shore. They have neither bowl, plate, spoon, or knife but what they make of the green wood in this country, only one small iron pot being allowed to dress their poor allowance of meat, rice, &c.; in short, all the necessary conveniences of life they are strangers to, and suffer everything they could dread in their sentence of transportation. Some time since it was not uncommon for seven or eight to die in one day, and very often while at work, they being kept in the field till the last moment, and frequently while being carried to the hospital. Many a one has died standing at the door of the storehouse waiting for his allowance of provision, merely for want of sustenance and necessary food.

*George Thompson, in a letter (1792)*

We left the Cape the 29th of April, and anchored in [Sydney] harbour the 26th of June. Would I could draw an eternal shade over the remembrance of this miserable part of our voyage—miserable, not so much in itself, as rendered so by the villainy, oppression, and shameful peculation of the masters of two of the transports. The bark I was on board of was, indeed, unfit, from her make and size, to be sent so great a distance; if it blew but the most trifling gale she was lost in the waters, of which she shipped so much; that, from the Cape, the unhappy wretches, the convicts, were considerably above their waists in water, and the men of my company, whose berths were not so far forward, were nearly up to the middles. In this situation they were obliged, for the safety of the ship, to be pen'd down; but when the gales abated no means were used to purify the air by fumigations, no vinegar was applied to rectify the nauseous steams issuing from their miserable dungeon. Humanity shudders to think that of nine hundred male convicts embarked in this fleet, three hundred and seventy are already

*Interior of a convict ship*

dead, and four hundred and fifty are landed sick and so emaciated and helpless that very few, if any of them, can be saved by care or medicine, so that the sooner it pleases God to remove them the better it will be for this colony, which is not in a situation to bear any burthen, as I imagine the medicine-chest to be nearly exhausted, and provisions are a scarce article.

The irons used upon these unhappy wretches were barbarous. The contractors had been in the Guinea trade, and had put on board the same shackles used by them in that trade, which are made with a short bolt, instead of chains that drop between the legs and fasten with a bandage about the waist, like those at the different gaols; these bolts were not more than three-quarters of a foot in length, so that they could not extend either leg from the other more than an inch or two at most; thus fettered, it was impossible for them to move but at the risk of both their legs being broken. Inactivity at sea is a sure bane, as it invites the scurvy equal to, if not more than, salt provisions; to this they were consigned, as well as a miserable pittance of provisions, altho' the allowance by Government is ample; even when attacked by disease their situations were not altered, neither had they any comforts administered.

The slave trade is merciful compared with what I have seen in this fleet; . . .

*Captain William Hill, Officer in the New South Wales Corps, writing of the Second Fleet (1790)*

Save for the natural setting around the finest harbour in the known world . . . everything was wretched—the filthy ships in the Cove, the rude lines of sodden barracks, the tents that held the sick sagging in the downpour along the waterfront; the night fires in the region of the Rocks, a sink of evil already and more like a gypsy encampment than part of a town . . . the stumps and fallen trees, and the boggy tracks wending their way round rock and precipice; the oozy Tank Stream spreading itself over the sand by the head of the Cove.

*Mrs John Macarthur, in a letter (1790)*

Snakes!

Early in the morning the gates of the convict prison were thrown open, and several hundred convicts were marched out in regimental file and distributed amongst the several public works in and about the town. As they passed along—the chains clanking at their heels—the patchwork dress of coarse grey and yellow cloth marked with the Government brand in which they paraded . . . and the whole appearance of the men, exhibited a truly painful picture. Nor was it much improved throughout the day, as one met bands of them in detachments of twenty yoked to waggons laden with gravel and stone, which they wheeled through the streets; in this and in other respects they performed all the functions of labour usually discharged by beasts of burden at home.

*From* Reminiscences of Thirty Years' Residence in New South Wales and Victoria, *R. Therry (referring to c. 1820)*

. . . I have a place at a farm-house, and I have got a good master, which I am a great deal more comfortable than I expected. I works the same as I were at home; I have plenty to eat and drink, thank God for it. I am allowed two ounces of tea, one pound of sugar, 12 pounds of meat, 10 pounds and a half of flour, two ounces of tobacco, the week; three pairs of shoes, two suits of clothes, four shirts a year; that is the allowance from Government. But we have as much to eat as we like, as some masters are a good deal better than others. All a man has got to mind is to keep a still tongue in his head, and do his master's duty, and then he is looked upon as if he were at home . . .

*Henry Tingley in a letter from Van Diemen's Land (about 1820)*

Flying Fish

Wednesday, Jan. 4. William McLoughlin was charged by his master with excessive insolence. On being desired to make a Welch rabbit, he exclaimed, "You're a d—— pretty fellow, an't you? I'll see you genteely d———d first," for which he was ordered to receive fifty lashes.

An assigned servant to Mr. Prout, who had been entrusted to bring six cwt. of potatoes to Sydney, but thought proper to appropriate half of them to his own use, was sent to six months in an iron gang.

James Pyne, for inhaling the sea breeze on the South-head road for the last nine weeks, instead of the smoke in his master's kitchen, was sentenced to receive 75 lashes—50 on that day, and 25 on the following Tuesday.

*Sydney Newspaper Reports (1832)*

A Bushman's Hut

In what manner were the convicts lodged? —Government had also provided bedding for every convict, and every man upon his arrival in the colony was supplied with it; this belonged to the Commissary's department, who always had his orders to do so from the Governor.

Had they their separate houses?—There were houses which were called Government-huts, which by the superintendent of convicts were appropriated to their purpose; and the others who were distributed to the different settlers in the colony. The settlers were under injunctions to give them lodgings as well as board.

How many were lodged in each of those Government-huts?—There might be five or six; I do not know exactly how many might sleep there, but that was in the discretion of the superintendent of the convicts, according to the size of the apartment.

Was any distinction made in favour of those who were married?—Yes; I made very great distinctions, and gave great encouragement and preferences to those who did marry.

Can you state some of these encouragements?—The principal superintendent had liberty to assist them in building a little hovel, which they might build for themselves; and, on all occasions, where he could oblige them by indulgences, he was to do it to the married persons in preference to the single, and particularly in preference to those who cohabited with women in a state of concubinage.

*From evidence given by Governor Bligh before the Select Committee on Transportation (1812)*

Mr Robert Arlack belonged to a class at that time very numerous in New South Wales, both among the very great and very little, who looked solely upon their assigned servants or government men as machines for getting money, and whom with this view worked them most unmercifully, extracting from each the full quota of work stipulated by the regulations; and if they broke down, returned them to Government obtaining fresh ones in their places. In fact, they considered convicts to be only a more expensive kind of labouring cattle, and on account of their not being able to live upon grass, a trifle less worthy than working bullocks. With such views they never thought of giving these unfortunate wretches a single ounce of any nourishment they could possibly avoid or a single article of raiment unless absolutely compelled . . .

*From* Ralph Rashleigh, *James Tucker*

The Flying Opossum of New South Wales

Happy and luxuriously lodged was the [wretch] who was master of a few pieces of sheepskin however acquired. The rest made beds of corn husks, thrown loose on their berths; these however, could be obtained only once a year. For a covering to sleep under they stitched together layers of the paper-like inner bark of the Australian tea-tree. These rugs, indeed, were exceedingly fragile, and when they became perfectly dry, would tear like tissue-paper. Some others wove a kind of matting of long grass. But all these expedients were wretchedly inefficient, and were it not that fuel were abundant, so that the prisoners could thus maintain large fires at night in the winter season, they must have suffered more severely than they did. As it was most of the elder men were periodically laid up with the rheumatism, and not a few lost the entire use of their limbs from paralysis.

*From* Ralph Rashleigh, *James Tucker*

Government House Sydney

The convict Superintendents, and their numerous followers, as well as most of the constables, and many of the settlers of the inferior class, have adopted a practice of compounding with convicts assigned them as servants, by which they derive a certain income from those convicts for allowing them respectively the free disposal of their own time. This compromise is usually productive of a revenue amounting weekly to a sum varying from five to twenty shillings per head, or even more, as the circumstances may allow; as, for instance, when the convict is a mechanic, who, by being apparently on his own hands, can easily earn more than double the sum he pays in consideration to his master, who, from a necessary connexion with the Superintendent, generally knows the surest way to have those of any trade he chooses assigned him.

*Thomas Reid, in a letter (1820)*

*more* than is requisite to keep them in health, as they have no work to do; but it is not more than is *politic* to allow them; because, if you stint them on the voyage, you must keep them under greater restraint, and their healths will suffer in consequence. . .

The ship is fitted up in the same way for the women as the men, excepting the addition of tables and shelves upon which to iron their clothes and stow away their tea-ware. Their rations are the same as those enjoyed by the men, with the addition of tea and sugar for the service of which there is a kettle supplied to each mess, and a tin-pot to each female, tea being usually made night and morning.

*From Two Years in New South Wales, P. Cunningham (referring to c.1820)*

Stockwhip.

Before leaving the Hulk, the convicts are thoroughly clothed in new suits, and ironed; and it is curious to observe with what nonchalance some of these fellows will turn the jingling of their chains into music whereto they dance and sing. Two rows of sleeping-berths, one above the other, extend on each side of the between-decks of the convict-ship, each berth being six feet square, and calculated to hold four convicts, every one thus possessing eighteen inches space to sleep in—and *ample* space too! . . .

Scuttle-holes, to open and shut for the admission of air, are cut out along the ship's sides;—a large stove and funnel placed between-decks, for warmth and ventilation; swing stoves and charcoal put on board, to carry about into the damp corners;—and in fact every thing that can be thought of provided to secure health and proper comfort to the convicts during their voyage. Each is allowed a pair of shoes, three shirts, two pairs of trousers, and other warm clothing on his embarkation, besides a bed, pillow, and blanket—while Bibles, Testaments, prayer-books, and psalters, are distributed among the messes.

The rations are both good and abundant . . .

The common diet of the convicts is certainly

"Domestic servants . . . assigned in Australia are well-fed, well-clothed . . . and are as well-treated in respectable families as similar servants" in England.

"As every kind of skilled labour is very scarce in New South Wales", a skilled convict "is worth three or four ordinary convicts". So he had to be well-treated.

"The condition of those employed as shepherds . . . and in agriculture . . . is inferior to that of a convict who is either a domestic servant or mechanic" (skilled worker); but "they are better fed than . . . agricultural workers" in England.

*From Findings of the Select Committee on Transportation (1838)*

In order to show the opinions entertained by some of the convicts, as regards the colony, I will give an extract from one of sundry letters which I have read, written by them to their friends in England, using the writer's own language and punctuation, but altering the spelling. He requests that his wife will come out, and bring their children with her, and then proceeds as follows:

"I am perfectly well satisfied with my situation thanks be to God that has placed me under those that does not despise a prisoner. No, my love, I am [not?] treated as a prisoner but as a free man, there is no one to say a wrong word to me. I have good usage plenty of good meat and clothes with easy work. I have 362 sheep to mind, either of our lads could do it with ease. The best of men was shepherds. Jacob served for his wife, yea and for a wife did he keep sheep and so will I, and my love we shall be more happy here than ever we should be at home if happiness is to be found on earth. Don't fail to come out I never thought this country what I have found it. I did expect to be in servile bondage and to be badly used but I am better off this day than half the people in England, and I would not go back to England if any one would pay my passage. England has the name of a free country and this is a bond country, but shame my friends and country-men where is your boasted freedom. Look round you, on every side there is distress, rags, want, and all are in one sorrowful state of want. Happiness and prosperity has long taken their flight from Albion's once happy isle."

He then alludes to the low price of provisions, and adds: "Except you live in a town you have no rent to pay, for each man builds his own house, no tithes, no poor-rates, and no taxes of any kind. And this is bondage is it?"

There are some other amusing remarks in this original composition, but the above will suffice to show that convicts lead not always the unhappy life they are supposed to do, unless through their own bad conduct. The writer of the above letter bears such an excellent character that his master has sent to England for his wife and family, with the intention of trying to be of some use to them. Those employed at the stock-stations have little to do save to ride about and look after the cattle, or sheep; indeed, much of their time is passed in hunting kangaroos, or emus, and a most independent kind of life they seem to lead, as indeed I have already shown.

*From* Excursions in New South Wales, Western Australia, and Van Dieman's Land, *Lieut. Breton*

The accused very seldom got the benefit of the doubt in the Penal days. The Government floggers at the Penal Stations were generally wretches who volunteered for this brutal work, so as to escape the penalties of the Iron-gang, of which they were often originally members. The author particularly remembers two such callous fellows, viz.: Billy O'Rourke (the Towrang flogger), and Black Francis—a negro—the Goulburn castigator, from 1838 to 1841. Billy O'Rourke was a small wizened-looking object, but muscular, and he revelled in his work. Before he began flogging, he would often say to the man chained up for punishment: "Heavy weather, byes (boys); heavy weather; but aisy now, sure it might be worse."

Black Francis used to lay the cat on with savage ferocity. He met with a sudden and tragic end—being found one morning "as dead as a door-nail", in the bush near the Run of Water, with three leaden slugs in his carcase. He used to make it his business to inform on some "ticket-o'-leave" men (after sometimes sharing their plunder), who were in the habit of robbing teams of spirits, that carriers were taking up-country. On several occasions he had "treed" and flogged his man for the offence referred to. But at last Nemesis overtook him, as stated, and Francis resigned the gentle art of flogging and everything else on this side of the Jordan.

Some of the convicts, as may be imagined, were made of the sternest human stuff, and men of that type never flinched under the lash. On two occasions I saw men—after undergoing, one a flogging of fifty, and the other, seventy-five lashes, bleeding as they were, deliberately spit, after the punishment, in the flogger's face. One of them told Black Francis "he couldn't flog hard enough to kill a butterfly". Old Tim Lane—the "Receiver" of Convicts—who took the particulars of men sent down from the country to the Head Depot in Sydney, etc., was a man of savage temper. One of the stories told of him was that he marked his daughter's face with a red-hot branding iron for an act of trivial disobenience.

*From* Old Pioneering Days in the Sunny South, *C. MacAlister (privately published, Goulburn, 1907)*

*The first cricket match between New South Wales and Victoria, played in the Sydney Domain, January 1857 (S. T. Gill, watercolour)*

Yet with much that was then pleasant in colonial society, it had its severe aspect. It must not be forgotten that my remarks apply to a convict settlement, in which the possession of wealth afforded but dubious evidence of a previous career of respectability. Many persons, originally transported for crime, had displayed the recuperative energy that is in man, by which though he sinks he but sinks to rise again, and resume the position that in early life he had forfeited. No doubt, the easy acquisition of property by convicts on their becoming free, and the circumstance of becoming heads of families, largely contributed to this happy consummation. It is obvious we cannot judge of motives; and whether principle or self-interest be the cause of reformation, society is the gainer when a bad man is transformed into a well-conducted citizen.

When, therefore, amendment in the mode of life was accomplished, charity and policy united in recommending the formation of the whole free community into an equal and united people. So thought not "society" in those days: not only were persons who had been transported excluded from the upper circle of the place, be their wealth or worth what it might, but the exclusion extended, at least partially, to their connexions. In the few instances, with regard to them, in which this too rigid rule of exclusion was relaxed, it was painful to witness the averted eye and the unwelcome shrug of the shoulders that the young and blameless relations of the strictly-excluded class had to encounter on appearing, as if they were intruders, at places of evening entertainment. The term *pure merino*, a designation given to sheep where there is no cross-blood in the flocks, was applied to mark a class who were not only free and unconvicted, but who could boast of having no collateral relationship or distant affinity with those in whose escutcheon there was a blot. These *pure merinos* formed the topmost round in the social ladder. The inequitableness of this rule of judgment may be seen by a simple illustration. Tried by such a test, a most estimable man, a late cabinet minister of England, and through a long and useful public life the representative of one of the finest counties in England, would have been deemed unfit for admission to a Sydney ball; and a late very learned and eminent bishop would have been a *tabooed* member of the "upper circle" in Sydney at this period, because they both happened to have near relations who by their misconduct brought disgrace, not on those excellent and eminent persons, but *on themselves*. The rule of disfavour did not end even here; for some against whom no social objection could be raised were designated a "convict-ridden set", because they did not adopt this doctrine of exclusion to an extent that appeared to them impolitic and indefensible. By a parity of reasoning, it might as well have been contended that the rule of social propriety that visits, perhaps wisely, "an erring sister's shame" with exclusion from respectable society, should be extended to every blameless female of her family and kindred. In truth, the objection was one affected, not really felt, by those who made it; and in urging it, they were alike unjust, uncharitable, and insincere.

*From* Reminiscences of Thirty Years' Residence in New South Wales and Victoria, *R. Therry (referring to c.1840)*

An Up-Country Coach

Money was plentiful then, and we used to have some tremendous sprees. Why didn't I save my money? There never was a chance to save. First of all, when we got our wages, the cheque wasn't a right cheque: it was an order written on flimsy or soft paper, on the nearest agent of the squatter, an' cashed by the nearest publican, who, of course, never handed over a cent. A man was compelled to stay there and knock his cheque down "like a man". Then if the order didn't happen to be drawn on a

merchant close by, it was all the same. If it was drawn on somebody in Sydney, how could a poor devil get away to Sydney—perhaps a four or five hundred mile tramp, without a farthing in his pocket? A man was obliged to go to the publican to advance him some money, and once you took a drink (for you couldn't go away without taking a nip) it was all up with you. The liquor was hocussed, and you got mad, and before you knew where you were your cheque was spent—at least so the landlord told you, and he bundled you out neck and crop. If he was at all a decent sort of fellow, he would give you a bottle of rum to help you to recover from your spree, and you returned to the station in a few days penniless. I've no heart to begin to save. I was well-to-do once— had a station of my own; but what with foot-rot and scab, and not looking after my own place, I soon went to the wall, and I've been getting lower and lower, till at last I became a shepherd. It *is* a lonely life.

*Quoted in* Old Colonials, *A. J. Boyd*

. . . I next desire to draw your Lordship's attention to the Social and Moral evils, which such state of things, if left unameliorated, must of necessity lead to. We see here a British Population spread over an immense territory, beyond the influence of civilization, and almost beyond the restraints of Law. Within this wide extent, a Minister of Religion is very rarely to be found. There is not a place of Worship or even a School. So utter indeed is the destitution of all means of instruction, that it may perhaps be considered fortunate that the population has hitherto been one almost exclusively male. But Women are beginning to follow into the Bush; and a race of Englishmen must speedily be springing up in a state approaching that of untutored barbarism.

The Occupiers of this vast wilderness, not having a property in any part of the soil they occupy, have no inducement to make permanent improvements on it—here and there a Building has been erected, which may deserve the name of Cottage; but the Squatters in general live in Huts made of the Bark of Trees; and a Garden, at least anything worthy of the name, is a mark of civilization rarely to be seen.

On the other hand,—there are, amongst the Squatters, and living the life which I have described, great numbers of young men every way entitled to be called gentlemen, young men of Education, and many of good family and connexions in Europe. The presence of young men of this description beyond the Boundaries has been highly advantageous; first, in lessening the rudeness of society in what is called the "Bush", and secondly, in affording the materials for a local Magistracy.

*Governor Sir George Gipps to Lord Stanley, on the practice of "Squatting" (3 April 1844)*

"You will find, I think, that high breeding and training are conditions of superiority in the human as well as in the equine and canine races; pedigree being, of course, the primary desideratum. *Non generant aquilæ columbas,* we say."

"Don't run away with the idear that nobody knows who Columbus was," retorted Bum. "He discovered America—or else my readin 's did me (adj.) little good."

"More power to yer (adj.) elbow, Bum," said Mosey approvingly. "But, gentleman or no gentleman, if a feller ain't propped up with cash, this country 'll (adj.) quick fetch him to his proper (adj.) level."

"Pardon me if I differ from you, Mosey," replied Willoughby blandly. "A few months ago, I travelled the Lachlan with a man fitted by birth and culture to be a leader of society; one whose rightful place would be at least in the front rank of your Australian aristocracy. How do you account for such a man being reduced to solicit the dem'd pannikin of flour?"

"Easy," retorted the sansculotte: "the duke had jist settled down to his proper (adj.) level— like the bloke you 'll see in the bottom of a new pannikin when you 're drinkin' out of it."

"Mosey," said Cooper impressively; "if I git up off o' this blanket, I 'll kick"—(I did n't catch the rest of the sentence). "Give us none o' your (adj.) Port Phillip ignorance here."

"You can git a drink o' good water in ole Vic.,

anyhow," sneered Mosey, with the usual flowers of speech.

"An' that 's about all you can git," muttered Cooper, faithfully following the same ornate style of diction.

*From* Such Is Life, *Joseph Furphy ("Tom Collins")*

In the colony of New South Wales, there are also *two castes:*—

First, a caste of free emigrant settlers, voluntarily seeking therein the advancement of their own views and interests,—by the exertion of their enterprise and capital promoting the interests of the colony at large,—and entitled, as free and untainted British subjects, to all the rights, privileges, and immunities which can be conferred upon them consistently with the accomplishment of the peculiar purposes for which this colony was founded and is maintained, and consistently with its well-being and its security as a dependency of Great Britain. As voluntary exiles to the country of their adoption, to which they have not been compulsorily *sent,* but to which they have freely *gone,* even *they* are bound to modify their expectations, and their rights are necessarily restrained and limited, by the considerations which have just been stated.

It is incumbent upon both the governors and the governed continually to remember and take into account the peculiarities of the social constitution of the colony. If there be any thing inherent in that constitution which necessarily involves a state of things repugnant to their preconceived notions of government, on the one hand, or of the rights of British subjects, on the other, they should remember that things which would be unconstitutional in England, are strictly, essentially, and inevitably constitutional in the colony. They ought not, therefore, either to undertake the government of such a colony, or to become subject to its regulations and laws, without first adapting their inclinations, principles, and maxims, to its constitutional and unalterable peculiarities. If those peculiarities give birth to political combinations that jar with their own pre-conceived opinions and habitual feelings, they must be told that it is a maxim of law, that he who seeks the nuisance is not entitled to require its abatement.

The second caste of the society of New South Wales consists of convicts who have been sent thither from England, by sentence of the law, for crimes committed,—sent thither, not as *colonists,*—not as retaining the attributes of British subjects,—not for the purpose of bettering their social condition,—but as *felons,*—as men whom the violated law has divested of their natural and legal rights,—sent thither, in short, as to a place of punishment,—where they are not only to remain divested of the protection of the ordinary laws of the realm, but where they are to be subjected to *new laws,* having for their object both their punishment and their reformation, but regarding their *punishment* as a means of deterring other persons in England from the commission of similar crimes, and therefore justifying the prolongation of the *punishment,* even in cases in which the reformation may already have been accomplished.

*From* The Felony of New South Wales, *James Mudie*

Our colonial-born brethren are best known here by the name of *Currency,* in contradistinction to *Sterling,* or those born in the mother country. The name was originally given by a facetious paymaster of the seventy-third regiment quartered here, the pound currency being at that time *inferior* to the pound sterling. Our Currency lads and lasses are a fine interesting race, and do honour to the country whence they originated. The name is a sufficient passport to esteem with all the well-informed and right-feeling portion of our population; but it is most laughable to see the capers some of our drunken old Sterling madonnas will occasionally cut over their Currency adversaries in a quarrel. It is then, "You saucy baggage, how dare you set up your *Currency* crest at me? I am *Sterling,* and that I'll let you know!"

To all acquainted with the open manly simplicity of character displayed by this part of our population, its members are the theme of universal praise; and, indeed, what more can be said in their favour, than that they are little tainted with the vices so prominent among their parents! Drunkenness is almost unknown with them, and honesty proverbial; the few of them that have been convicted having acted under the bad auspices of their parents or relatives. Nearly all the Currency criminals have, indeed, been furnished by three roguishly prolific families in the colony; and if the whole of the numbers of these have not hitherto been convicted, there are few who do not believe them deserving. This fact forms, indeed, the best test of the utility of marriage in ministering to criminal reform; for the pliable disposition of youth can, in general, be so readily bent towards good or evil, that parents have almost always the power of forming the infant mind in whatever way their own ruling inclinations may tend; and as so few of our Currency youths have been trained up in the paths of vice, we may naturally infer their parents have, at the least, made no attempts to mislead them. Hence the benefit of matrimony in a new colony does not less consist in peopling its dreary wilds with youthful and active native-born inhabitants, than in turning the inclinations of the old importations from thieving and immorality, towards honesty and virtue. The Currencies grow up tall and slender, like the Americans, and are generally remarkable for that Gothic peculiarity of fair hair and blue eyes which has been noticed by other writers. Their complexions, when young, are of a reddish sallow, and they are for the most part easily distinguishable,—even in more advanced years—from those born in England. Cherry cheeks are not accompaniments of our climate, any more than that of America, where a blooming complexion will speedily draw upon you the observation, "You are from the old country, I see!"

The young females generally lose their teeth early, like the Americans and West Indians, this calamity always commencing about the period of puberty: it may possibly be ascribed to the climatizing process, as we see nearly all plants and animals suffer considerable change in appearance on transplantation to a different latitude: we may therefore hope this defect will subside when a few generations have passed away. "The Currency lads" is now a popular standing toast, since it was given by Major Goulburn at the Agricultural dinner, while "The Currency lasses" gives name to one of our most favourite tunes.

The young men of low rank are fonder of binding themselves to trades, or going to sea, than passing into the employ of the settlers, as regular farm-servants. This no doubt arises partly from their unwillingness to mix with the convicts so universally employed on farms, partly from a sense of

*Boating at Berry's Bay, Port Jackson (engraving from* Australasian Sketcher, *26 October 1878)*

pride; for, owing to convicts being hitherto almost the sole agricultural labourers, they naturally look upon that vocation as degrading in the same manner as white men in slave colonies regard work of any kind, seeing that none *but* slaves *do* work. It is partly this same pride, as much as the hostile sentiments instilled into them by their parents, that makes them so utterly averse to fill the situation of petty constables, or to enlist as soldiers.

The young girls are of a mild-tempered, modest disposition, possessing much simplicity of character; and, like all children of nature, credulous, and easily led into error. The lower classes are anxious to get into respectable service, from a laudable wish to be independent, and escape from the tutelage of their often profligate parents; and like the "braw Scotch lasses", love to display their pretty curly locks, tucked up with tortoiseshell combs—and, slip-shod or bare-footed, trip it merrily along. They make generally very good servants, their

wages varying from ten pounds to fifteen pounds per annum. They do not commonly appear to class chastity as the *very first* of virtues, which circumstance arises partly from their never being tutored by their parents so to consider it, but more especially from never perceiving its violation to retard marriage. They are all fond of frolicking in the water, and those living near the sea can usually swim and dive like water-hens.

The Currency youths are warmly attached to their country, which they deem unsurpassable, and few ever visit England without hailing the day of their *return* as the most delightful in their lives; while almost every thing in the parent-land sinks in relative value with similar objects at home. Indeed, when comparing the exhilarating summer aspect of Sydney, with its cloudless sky, to the dingy gloom of a London street, no wonder a damp should be cast over the ethereal spirits of those habituated to the former; and who had possibly been led into extravagant anticipations regarding London, by the eulogiums of individuals reluctantly torn from its guilty joys. A young Australian, on being once asked his opinion of a splendid shop on Ludgate Hill, replied, in a disappointed tone, "It is not equal to *Big Cooper's*", (a store-shop in Sydney,) while Mrs Rickards' *Fashionable Repository* is believed to be unrivalled, even in Bond Street. Some of them also contrive to find out that the English cows give *less* milk and butter than the Australian, and that the choicest Newmarket racers possess *less* beauty and swiftness than *Junius, Modus, Currency Lass,* and others of Australian turf pedigree; nay, even a young girl, when asked how she would like to go to England, replied with great *naivete,* "I should be afraid to go, from the *number of thieves* there", doubtless conceiving England to be a downright hive of such, that threw off its annual swarms to people the wilds of this colony. Nay, the very miserable-looking trees that cast their annual coats of bark, and present to the eye of a raw European the appearance of being actually *dead,* I have heard praised as objects of incomparable beauty! and I myself, so powerful is habit, begin to look upon them pleasurably. Our ideas of beauty are, in truth, less referable to a *natural* than an *artificial* standard, varying in every country according to what the eye has been habituated to, and fashion prescribes.

The youths generally marry early, and do not seem to relish the system of concubinage so popular among their Sterling brethren here. In their amorous flirtations, I cannot find that they indulge in exchange of love-tokens, mementoes of roses, shreds of ribbons, broken sixpences, and the like tender reminiscences, fashionable among the melting striplings of humble birth in England; the only approach to these antique customs witnessed by me consisted of a hock of pickled pork and a pound of sixpenny sugar, conveyed by way of *sap* to undermine the virtue of one of our Newgate nuns; but whether in accordance to colonial custom, or to minister to the lady's refined *penchant* for such delicacies, I cannot take upon me to decide.

*From* Two Years in New South Wales, *P. Cunningham*

The Australian boy is a slim, darkeyed, olivecomplexioned young rascal, fond of Cavendish, cricket and chuckpenny, and systematically insolent to all servant girls, policemen and newchums. His hair is shiny with grease, as are the knees of his breeches and the elbows of his jacket. He wears a cabbagetree hat with a dissipated wisp of black ribbon dangling behind.

*From* Southern Lights and Shadows, *Frank Fowler*

Indeed, if you do not understand larrikinism you will never understand the Australian character. Clannishness and toughness are two of its characteristics. So are cruelty and wanton destructiveness, and all these qualities are latent in many of us.

*Sir George Stephen, in a lecture, in Melbourne (1871)*

There is a great deal of this mutual regard and trust engendered by two men working thus together in the otherwise solitary bush; habits of mutual helpfulness arise, and these elicit gratitude, and that leads on to regard. Men under these circumstances often stand by one another through thick and thin; in fact it is a universal feeling that a man ought to be able to trust his own mate in anything.

*From* Settlers and Convicts; or Recollections of Sixteen Years' Labour in the Australian Backwoods, *Alexander Harris ("An Emigrant Mechanic")*

With regard to this, the present Principal of the Brotherhood of the Good Shepherd writes of—

The Beauty of Home Life in the Bush.—The courage of the women and girls in resisting the tendency to let things slide, insisting on all the refinements and courtesies of the home in spite of isolation and trying weather; *every girl a lady and every boy a gentleman in the poorest "humpy".* One fruit of our social equality being not to degrade our "aristocracy," but to elevate our democracy; no fear of our getting down to a dead level. The care the girls take about their dress, although there is no one but their brothers to see that they are dressed nicely. The fine chivalrous spirit of the boys. (A house of bags and tin, but manners and dress fit for court.)

*From* The Church in Australia, *Rev. C. H. S. Matthews*

The Opossum of Van Diemen's Land

Gentlemen foreigners of all nations may be met with now in our Sydney streets, tempted by the fineness of our country and climate to take up their permanent abode among us. French, Spaniards, Italians, Germans (Americans I had almost added, but kindred feelings proclaim the impossibility of ever classing them as such), all add to the variety of language current among us; while even the subjects of His Celestial Majesty cannot resist the fascination of the name of Australia; and several ingenious and industrious individuals of that distant region now flourish as members of our community. Over a snug cottage at Parramatta, for example, may be seen the sign of "John Shan, (or some such spelt name,) carpenter, and dealer in groceries, teas, &c.," with his tidy English wife and groupe of Anglo-Chinese descendants around him. In the streets of Sydney, too, may often be seen groupes of natives from various of the numerous South Sea islands, with which we trade, in all their eccentricities of costume. A considerable portion of Otaheiteans and New Zealanders are employed as sailors in the vessels that frequent our port; and in the evening, as you stroll along the picturesque shores of our harbour, you may be often melted with the wild melody of an Otaheitean love-song from one ship, and have your blood frozen by the horrific whoop of the New Zealand war-dance from another.

*From* Two Years in New South Wales, *P. Cunningham*

What the doings of the larrikins are, every well-disposed person in a colonial city knows to his cost.

It is well known that boys in all ages have been given to what is called sky-larking. But this, although it might be called "larrikinism" in a mild form, was never productive of injury to the hoaxed ones. To my shame, I must confess that, as a youngster home from sea, or from school, I have assisted at jokes which quite threw "Captain Pindar's pig" into the shade. But the upshot of our worst pranks was at most a scolding, and "I'll tell your pa, you naughty boy."

But these larrikins are villanously mischievous in their pranks. Their ranks are recruited from the lowest scum of the towns. Born of parents vicious themselves, these unfortunate children are thrown upon the streets, and in time become a pest and scourge. In the old country they are pickpockets and assistants of burglars, from which professions they are gradually drafted off into the reformatory schools, and on board the training ships, whence they emerge in time as respectable and useful members of society. Pass down any street of a colonial city at night. Hordes of ruffian boys (many past the age when the word boy will apply) troop along the footpaths jostling the passers-by, insulting unprotected females, throwing stones, careless who is injured, howling and shouting defiance at any one who interrupts their game.

Watch them, when they have scented out a wedding. They collect all the kerosene-tins, pots and pans they can lay their hands on, and in the evening, if the luckless pair have not previously departed on a tour, their ears are assailed with a most atrocious din. Tins are battered under the windows, stones are thrown on the roof, and yells and cheers make night hideous.

If they are unheeded, they take stronger measures. Their ranks are reinforced, stones and sticks are rained in volleys on the house, and at last (as the scoundrels anticipated) the maddened benedict rushes out and distributes either money or liquor. This obtained, they depart howling their satisfaction.

I know of one instance, where a young lady's first introduction to her new home was seeing a case of brandy being opened on the verandah ready for the purchase of immunity from the attack of the larrikin.

It is of no use for a newly-married couple to go away for six weeks or so. Their return is known to the ringleaders of the orgies, who instantly summon their adherents, and relief has to be bought with liquor.

One irate father once fired on a band of the kerosene heroes, and severely wounded one or two. He was acquitted by law; and perhaps if all people who were assailed in like manner were to do the same, the results would be beneficial to the community at large.

Should the "largesse" thus rudely demanded be persistently refused, showers of stones and brick-bats demolish the windows. All possible damage that can be done in a short time is perpetrated, and before the police appear on the scene the actors have vanished.

But it is on New Year's Eve that the larrikins are seen in their worst form. Nothing is sacred to them on this anniversary. They parade the town in mobs. Men, boys, and hobbledehoys, of all ages and sizes, go from house to house with their kerosene band, and demand liquor, or money wherewith to purchase it. They—at least the elder portion of the prowling band—are half drunk, and inclined for any act of ruffianism. Outhouses are destroyed or carried off bodily. Lamps are extinguished. Signs are carried off and exchanged for others, causing ludicrous combination.

*From* Old Colonials, *A. J. Boyd*

Sydney is not without its public amusements. Of the Theatre I may fairly say that, as far as dramatic talent is concerned, it is conducted at the least as well as the generality of provincial houses in England. To be sure, we are compelled to be satisfied all the year round with the efforts of stationary performers; for it must be an eccentric Star indeed which would shoot so far out of its orbit as to reach New South Wales.

In decency of demeanour the audience of the Sydney Theatre Royal is a prodigy compared with that of similar establishments in the seaport towns of the old country. The "gods" are particularly well-behaved. The dress-boxes are always un-peopled, unless an impulse be given by a bespeak or by the benefit of a favourite. These appeals act as a sort of mental gad-fly on the society. The herd rushes together with one consent, and disports itself in crowded discomfort; and once more, for a month perhaps, the play-goer, whom a love of the drama only attracts, has the house all to himself.

In the pit of the Sydney Theatre one misses the numerous bald heads of an European *parterre*, for the people of New South Wales have not yet had time to grow old. On the other hand, the eyes of the stranger wander with surprise over the vast num-bers of new-born babies—three or four dozen little sucklings taking their natural refection, whilst their mothers seem absorbed in the interest of the piece; their great long-legged daddies meanwhile sprawl-ing over the benches in the simplest of costumes—a check shirt, for instance, wide open at the breast, moleskins, and a cabbage-tree hat. It was a pleasant thing to see these good folks thoroughly enjoying themselves in this manner on a Saturday night—a week's wages and the door-key in their pockets, and all the family cares deferred till Monday morning. Every one knows—at least every foreigner knows—how cold and undemonstrative is an English audience. Perhaps the warmth of the climate infuses a degree of fervour into a Sydney "house". It would be a lesson to the used-up man of the world, to witness the raptures with which some of the public favourites, and their efforts histrionic, musical, and saltatory, are received and rewarded. Oh! it is delicious to mark the gratified countenances, and to hear the thundering plaudits which are especially awarded to the latter branch of theatric art. Well may Madame . . . , the Sydney Columbine and Maitresse de Danse, most spheri-cal of Sylphides, bounce like an Indian-rubber ball; well may Signor . . . , Harlequin and Dancing-master, half kill his fatted calves in acknowledgment of so much flattering appro-bation!

There are to be found around the doors of the Sydney theatre a sort of "loafers", known as the Cabbage-tree mob—a class whom, in the spirit of the ancient tyrant, one might excusably wish had but one nose, in order to make it a bloody one! These are an unruly set of young fellows, native born generally, who, not being able, perhaps, to muster coin enough to enter the house, amuse themselves by molesting those who can afford that luxury. Dressed in a suit of fustian or colonial tweed, and the emblem of their order, the low-crowned cabbage-palm hat, the main object of their enmity seems to be the ordinary black headpiece worn by respectable persons, which is ruthlessly knocked over the eyes of the wearer as he passes or enters the theatre. The first time I attended this house, I gave my English servant, a stout and

*Opening of the new Theatre Royal, Sydney (engraving from* Illustrated Sydney News, *12 January 1876)*

somewhat irascible personage, a ticket for the pit. Unaware of the propensities of the Cabbagites, he was by them furiously assailed—for no better reason apparently than because, like "noble Percy", "he wore his *beaver* up", and, his hat being driven down over his eyes, in his blind rage he let fly an indiscriminate "one, two", the latter of which took effect upon a policeman! "Hinc!" a night in the watch-house, and the necessity of proving in the morning the "glaring case of assaulting a constable in the execution of his duty" was not intentional and "of malice aforethought".

Much has been spoken and written by influential persons in England about the hideous depravity of the Sydney populace. I do not think they deserve that character. Although the streets are ill-lighted, and the police inefficient in number and organization, Sydney appears to me to have on the whole a most orderly and well-conducted population. Public-house licences are so profitable a source of public revenue, that perhaps too many of these conveniences for crime are permitted to exist; yet drunkenness is kept quite as well out of sight as in English towns; and, although a pretty strong squad of disorderlies figures in the morning reports of the Police courts, the better behaved inhabitants are but little annoyed by their misdemeanours. All strangers notice with praise the extreme tranquillity of the streets at night. Whatever debaucheries may be going on "à huis clos"—and Sydney is no purer perhaps than other large seaport towns —they are not prominently offensive. If a noctambulist yourself, you may indeed encounter, towards the small hours, an occasional night-errant wandering in search of adventures; or having found some to his great personal damage; but he is an exception to the general rule of the social quietude of the Sydney thoroughfares. I do not believe, in short, that person or property, morals or decency are more liable to peril, innocence to outrage, inexperience to imposition, in Sydney, than in London or Paris. On the contrary, I am convinced, that from our own country, not only *might* come to New South Wales, but actually and frequently *do* come, individuals of every order of society—from the practised *debauché* of high life to the outcast of the London back-slums—capable of giving lessons in vice, in their several degrees, to the much abused Sydneyites, and who do absolutely astonish the colonials by their superior proficiency.

*From* Our Antipodes: or, Residence and Rambles in the Australasian Colonies, *G. C. Mundy*

Hail sons of Freedom, hail!
  Who dwell in Austral's isle;
Oerwhelm'd by stream corrupt, impure,
  The refuse and the vile.

Shall fathers weep and mourn
  To see a lovely son
Debas'd, demoralis'd, deform'd,
  By *Britain's filth and scum?*

Arise, then, Freeman—rise:—
  Secure your liberty;
Ne'er rest till Transportation dies;
  An Austral's isle be FREE.

*Anti-transportation poem, Anon. (1848)*

The original settlers were hardy folk—the pick of their respective homelands—and were mainly immigrants from England and Ireland who sought the freedom of a country unhampered by oppressive land and industrial laws. Many of them were obsessed by a sense of the injustice of the laws and of the conditions applicable to rural workers in their homeland, and were determined that in this new home these conditions should not become established. It was not remarkable, therefore, that they regarded with suspicion any attempts to assert "authority", and were quick to resent any interference with what they considered their liberty in a free land.

*From* The Inner History of the Kelly Gang, *J. J. Kenneally*

It might assist in meeting the difficulty now experienced in disposing of Irish convicts and at the same time afford the means of relieving Western Australia from its present difficulties if a very limited number of convicts were sent out to be employed there . . .

*Earl Grey, Secretary of State for the Colonies (1849)*

The West Australian convict system has many excellent points. It does not, as with the case under the old assignment arrangements of New South Wales and Tasmania, place the convict at the mercy of a master, who may be both brutal and vicious. Neither is his punishment, as was the case at Norfolk Island, simply cruel and vindictive. The men have a constant inducement to behave well, as they know that by doing so they better their condition. During the probationary stage, they are aware that each mark they earn brings them nearer to their ticket-of-leave, and when they obtain these a continuance of good behaviour has been required to entitle them to their conditional pardons. This requiring a man to find employment before he is liberated upon his ticket works well, forcing him for a time, at least, into habits of industry. During his detention on the roads he sees the settlers and learns what is to be done, and by the time he has served his ticket-of-leave out, and is wholly thrown upon his own resources, he ought to have acquired some little money and a full measure of colonial experience.

No one can say that the convicts work hard, and, as far as my experience goes, I found them remarkably comfortable both as regards shelter and diet. They are always as hospitable as they can be to a visitor. I put up several nights with road parties, and partook of meals with them which any man might heartily enjoy. The meal over, the men would produce their tame cockatoos or opossums, would enjoy a smoke or a stroll, would read books from the prison library, or spin yarns by the blazing fire. I found them all eager for information regarding the "t'other side", as they call the eastern colonies, and one and all stated their determination to get there. After an evening spent thus, we would turn in to comfortable beds and be up early next morning for a wash in the creek. If they do not return thanks for having their lives cast in pleasant places, the men are a most ungrateful set.

*Melbourne* Argus *(1864)*

Pething a Bullock

The history of Western Australia up to 1850 contains little of interest. Cut off from communication with the other Colonies, the few settlers laboured under the disadvantage of having no market for their agricultural produce, and no labour to develop the natural resources of the country. Shortly after this period, the settlers petitioned the Home Government to make Swan River a convict settlement; this was promptly acceded to, and several shiploads of convicts were sent to the Colony. In the nine years between 1850 and 1859, 5169 convicts were introduced, with 6364 other persons, many of them families of the prisoners. It was the neighbouring Colonies that first appealed to the Home Government to discontinue transportation to Western Australia, on the plea, that convicts made their way from that Colony to Adelaide and Melbourne. Transportation ceased altogether in 1868. It is said by that time Western Australia had absorbed nearly 10,000 of England's criminal population, and that, "undesirable as such a class of immigrants as this may be, it must be conceded that since their introduction the Colony has progressed year by year, exports have increased, the settlers have a market for their stock and produce, public works are progressing, and the statistics of crime show an immunity from transgression against property that could hardly have been anticipated". As the population of the Colony is now about thirty thousand, there is some truth in the statement that it is considerably tainted with convictism, though the dangerous elements of this disease seem to have been soon eradicated by residence in the Colony.

*From* Under the Southern Cross, *Henry Cornish*

*One convict in Western Australia has had the distinction of being the source of inspiration for at least two books. John Boyle O'Reilly, the Irishman who himself not only escaped but arranged the escape of six of his fellows (see "The Catalpa" in the folksong section for more detail), wrote a novel called* Moondyne, *and more recently, Randolph Stow wrote an excellent children's book called* Captain Midnite. *Both were to a degree inspired by the*

*numerous escapes from captivity of a West Australian convict, Joseph Johns, better known as "Moondyne Joe". He escaped from the closest surveillance on a number of occasions, once only being recaptured after two years through breaking into a gentleman's wine cellar and incapacitating himself before escaping. He developed something of a duel with G. E. Hampton, son of the Governor of West Australia at the time, who held the office of Comptroller General and as such was in charge of prisoners. After one of his more spectacular escapes, the following ditty was popular with all and sundry in Perth and Freemantle.*

> *"The Governor's son has got the pip,*
> *the Governor's got the measles.*
> *For Moondyne Joe has give 'em the slip,*
> *Pop goes the weasel!"*

*For a good account of Moondyne Joe and his activities, see* Tell 'em I Died Game, *Bill Wannan, published Lansdowne Press.*

*I have sometimes wondered whether the paucity of folk material from South Australia (save for the "Cousin Jack" miners' stories about the Burra) was because there were no convicts permitted into the Province, though convicts from other States certainly went there and became settlers.*

Now, Father, I think this Australia is the Promised Land, but there are faults in it, the water is bad, most of it tastes salt. Adelaide is a very drunken place. Trade is very good here; they get 7s. a day for plastering. The natives are black, some are almost naked. They get a very good living with begging about Adelaide. We have a beautiful cottage in a gentleman's garden. Wood and water, vegetables and a cottage to live in, and I have 20s. a week. I am under gardener. We call it Paradise, for we have all the richest fruits and vegetables that's grown; we have melons and every sort of pumpkins; we have the tree of knowledge, peaches, oranges, lemons, grape vines, the tobacco plant. Provisions are very cheap, flour 2d. a pound, mutton 2d. per pound, legs 3d. per pound, beef 3d. per pound, sugar 3d. per pound, best tea 2/6 per pound, tobacco 3/0 per four pounds. Drapery goods are as cheap as in London; furniture, pots, iron pans; using things are very dear. They think nothing of money here.

Ale is 10d. a pot, spirits are very dear, Cape wine is 1s. the bottle. The colony is in a very prosperous state. I often think of my poor Father and Mother and brothers and sisters dragged very near to death for half a bellyful of meat, while we have plenty of everything and to spare. We ofttimes talk about the poor white slaves of England, the woolcombers, that said they would not transport themselves to the land of full and plenty. I hope you will let the gentleman read this letter, that gave the money to me to help me to the Promised Land.

*From a letter in the* Bradford Observer *(7 December 1848)*

Churches abound in every Australian city, especially in Adelaide, where they are so numerous as to excite the ridicule of the less devout Victorians. I forget how many there are; but at any rate, they bear a very small proportion to the public-houses, against which I think they may fairly be pitted. Still, there are plenty of them; and no sinner will easily be able to find an excuse for not going to church in the non-representation of his particular sect.

*From* Town Life in Australia, *R. E. N. Twopenny*

In 1829 hadn't a white man in it. In 1836 the British Parliament erected it—still a solitude—into a Province, and gave it a Governor and other governmental machinery. Speculators took hold now, and inaugurated a vast land scheme, and invited immigration, encouraging it with lurid promises of sudden wealth. It was well worked in London; and Bishops, statesmen and all sorts of people made a rush for the Land Company's shares. Immigrants soon began to pour into the region of Adelaide, and select town lots and farms in the sand and the mangrove swamps by the sea. The crowds continued to come, prices of land rose high, then higher and still higher, everybody was prosperous and happy, the boom swelled into gigantic proportions. A village of sheetiron huts

*City of Adelaide (engraving from* The Three Colonies of Australia, *Samuel Sidney)*

and clapboard sheds sprang up in the sand, and in these wigwams fashion made display; richly dressed ladies played on costly pianos, London swells in evening dress and patent-leather boots were abundant, and this fine society drank champagne, and otherwise conducted itself in this capital of humble sheds as it had been accustomed to do in the aristocratic quarters of the metropolis of the world. The provincial government put up expensive buildings for its own use, and a palace with gardens for the use of its Governor. The Governor had a guard and maintained a court. Roads, wharves and hospitals were built. All this on credit, on paper, on wind, on inflated and fictitious values—on the boom's moonshine, in fact.

This went on handsomely during four or five years. Then all of a sudden came a smash. Bills for a huge amount drawn by the Governor upon the Treasury were dishonoured, the land company's credit went up in smoke, a panic followed, values fell with a rush, the frightened immigrants seized their grip-sacks and fled to other lands, leaving behind them a good imitation of a solitude, where lately had been a buzzing and populous hive of men.

Adelaide was indeed almost empty; its population had fallen to three thousand. During two years or more the death-trance continued. Prospect of revival there was none; hope of it ceased. Then, as suddenly as the paralysis had come, came the resurrection from it. Those astonishingly rich copper mines were discovered, and the corpse got up and danced.

*From* Following the Equator, *Samuel Clemens ("Mark Twain")*

55

In the distance across a vast expanse of rural scenery, the Hawkesbury River, like a silver-backed serpent dragged its lengthy coils through long vistas of drooping greenery that stooped to kiss the rippling surface of the water. Thickly wooded hills rose sharply to the sky-line on one side and sloped to the plain on the other, where cornfields, with their tall stems, whispering leaves and blond-tasselled tops, stood side by side, all summer through, with the fields of golden wheat.

The river, always lovely, brought not only their stores and contact from the outside world but a great deal of their entertainment as well. On regatta days it was overhung by an atmosphere of happy excitement. Booths were erected on the river bank and were freely patronized, while the town's sixteen hotels were full. Local talent, represented by Tommy Burns on his concertina and Blind Loftus on the fiddle, was in great demand by the publicans. These artists entertained the holiday-makers with such current song-hits as *Bold Jack Donohoe*, which told of a Liverpool-Penrith bushranger of that name, or perhaps with the sailor's hornpipe or an Irish jig. Four-handed reels were also danced, for music and dancing were then popular in the pub bars. Here, too, the drovers—the "Bosses of the Roads"—congregated to drink and play with cards and dice-box, often from dusk to sunup.

Children found amusement on the merry-go-round or at the wax-works, where they shivered before gruesomely visaged figures of murderers and bushrangers. They always hailed with delight the appearance of those quaint characters, "Peg-leg Hobbs" and "Billy-the-Bell," the bellringers of the district, who on festival and auction days cried the wares of the booth-keepers and auctioneers.

"Come on now, ladies and gintlemen. If y' want t' buy corn or chaaf or praties that'll milt in y' mouth, y'll find 'em all here in O'Connell's stalls," Billy-the-Bell would shout, the saliva from his toothless mouth spraying before his face.

"Shure, an' ye can buy punkins, an' swades, an' paches; an' cabitches wat is small and cabitches wat is large. The cabitches wat is small ain't cabitches at all, but they is brussels sprouts," Peg-leg Hobbs shouted lustily, every now and then giving a loud sniff and wrinkling his nose like a fox-terrier after a rat.

Any sport by which money could be won or lost found favour. For large wagers men would compete, rolling in empty casks, starting from high ground with the bottom of the hill as the winning post. They would run races carrying all sorts of objects, such as pumpkins on their heads or small boys on their backs. Some preferred to swing from horizontal bars; or jumping off bottles laid on their sides, to compete in broadjumping (the last proved a rather difficult feat, as the bottles had a somewhat alarming tendency to roll and it required great skill to jump two feet from such a starting point). Another exciting sport was to see who could stay on a cartwheel the longest time, the competitors getting into position among the spokes and hanging on with legs and arms while the cart was driven, slowly or fast for a given distance.

These and many other queer activities attracted stakes of as much as 100 pounds. The stake for cricket was 1 pound per bat, and the losers, besides forfeiting their stakes, provided a dinner for the winning team. No matter what the sport was, horse racing, cricket, boxing, walking, rowing or cockfighting (which at that time was legal) the stakes were high and money was spent freely and without regrets.

*From* Captain Thunderbolt, *Annie Rixon (referring to c. 1840)*

On the whole, the old hands have been of essential service to the country, and when kept in order by persons who understand what is their duty, and who make them perform it, they are useful servants. They are, however, a disagreeable set of men to deal with; rarely, if ever, identifying their master's interests with their own, but looking upon him as a person to be overreached and imposed on, and despising him when he permits them to do so. The person who excites their greatest respect is the man who is alive to their attempts, (or, as they express it themselves, *who drops down to their moves,)* and the highest encomium they can pass on such a one is, that *there are no flies about him.*

They are very fond of change, wandering about the country generally in pairs, and rarely remaining more than a year in one service. They are to be found more at the distant stations and in newly-settled country where wages are higher, and there is more difficulty to contend with, than in the more civilized parts where the emigrants have in a great measure superseded them. Still, through the whole country the great mass of shearers, splitters, and even bullock-drivers are old hands. They have a strong *esprit de corps,* which is kept up by their speaking a language so full of cant expressions as to become almost a separate dialect. Their best trait is their liberality towards each other; and indeed when money was more easily made than at present, this was carried to a pitch of reckless profusion. When a man was paid his wages, or had made a good sum of money by shearing, splitting, or other job-work, he used to go to Melbourne and treat all his friends, and frequently keep open house at a public-house for a week or a fortnight together. In this way, I have known some of them to have spent upwards of a hundred pounds in that short time; they were, of course, extensively plundered by the publicans. Now, however, that money is not so easily earned, they are something less lavish, but still a large proportion spend all their earnings of several months', or even a year's hard labour in a few weeks' dissipation; and it is a common thing to deposit a sum with the landlord upon the understanding that he is to furnish drink while it lasts. When the money is out, they start away in search of new scenes and fresh employment, carrying on their backs their heavy packs, containing cloths and blankets or kangaroo rug. Two generally travel together, who are called mates; they are partners, and divide all their earnings.

Though amongst this class of men the standard of morality is very low, yet they are not without their rude notions of honour, modified, however by a kind of public opinion amongst themselves, which exercises a considerable influence over their actions. They have a pride in fulfilling their engagements; and when they undertake a piece of job-work, they generally adhere faithfully to their contract, although it may turn out an unprofitable job. I have known several instances in which money has been lent to them to the amount of two or three pounds, and I have never known it not to be repaid; and in general, when a confidence is reposed in them for the performance of any particular service, they acquit themselves creditably, though, as this arises from that pride which urges a man to show himself worthy of being trusted, and as it is a feeling which, however creditable in itself, is inferior to that principle which prompts a man to do his duty irrespectively of all other considerations, it might not, perhaps, be safe to count on a prolonged exertion of this kind. A man guilty of crimes of a mean and unmanly nature is despised by them; and one who robs from his fellows, but especially from his mate, is regarded as infamous. On the other hand, drunkenness and debauchery of any kind are not regarded as crimes—indeed to omit an opportunity of getting drunk would be considered as a kind of breach of privilege; nor are they very scrupulous on the subject of honesty, if the person injured be not a poor man. Defrauding one not of their own class they seem to regard as a spoiling of the Egyptians. I have always considered the observation of the effects produced on these men by their peculiar position as a most interesting study; and although this effect may be modified by peculiarity of disposition, yet I think that I have correctly delineated the leading characteristics of the class. . . .

The emigrants, or new hands, contrast in some respects very favourably with the class which I have sketched. They are more easily managed, have fewer tricks, are less fond of change, often remaining for a long time in the same situation, seeming to become attached to their employers, and to take an interest in the property committed to their charge. They are less reckless about money, several of them having made considerable savings out of their wages. When they were new in the country, the old hands, vain of their own knowledge, looked down on their inexperience, while the emigrants in turn despised them for being convicts: so that it seldom answered to have them on the same station; but now the two classes amalgamate better, for the emigrants have had time to gain experience, and are able to hold their ground—indeed some of them are in every respect as useful, even in those departments, which were at first exclusively in possession of the old hands.

*From* The Present State and Prospects of the Port Phillip District of New South Wales, *C. Griffith*

*Sunday in the bush (engraving from* Town and Country Journal, *10 January 1874)*

His dress consists of a pair of very tight strapped moleskin trousers, a shirt of many colours, like Joseph's coat, a cabbage-tree hat well-coloured, and worn, as a rule, on the back of his head, giving a still bolder and more impudent expression to a face already insolent enough, and destitute of any expression beyond that which may be found in the bullock or sheep. All the animal propensities are highly developed, but of intellect there is nothing. The greasy hat is suspended to his head by a string, which is conveniently caught in his mouth or under his nose. In his mouth he wears a short black pipe. I say wears, because the pipe appears to be part and parcel of the Nut's physiognomy. It is never removed except to be filled or to be lighted. Finally, his heels are ornamented by a pair of huge, sharp spurs, which always bear tokens of having been ruthlessly applied to the bleeding sides of his horse. No Nut ever rides quietly. His pace is either a furious gallop or a jog-trot. The furious gallop is, however, the favourite pace. Now, having described our friend, I will consider him as he rides up to the public-house on a Sunday morning. Far away down the road, a cloud of dust heralds the approach of half a dozen of these roughs. As they approach they may be heard yelling at their horses, cursing each other, and generally making a most terrific uproar to notify their speedy arrival.

Pulling up their panting animals, they dismount, and hitch them up to the rail, studded with wooden pegs, which is provided for the use of travellers.

Entering the house, each Nut sprawls his arms over the bar, and one of them, with a volley of blasphemy, asks what the others are going to drink.

Now ensues a strange dialogue, only to be heard amongst such a strange crowd. It proceeds something in this fashion:—

"Now then, Harry, you old ——, what the —— is it going to be? Give it some —— name or other."

"No fear, Jack," says Harry, "this is my —— shout. Come on, boys, what's it to be?"

Then begins another Nut.

"Look here, Jack, 'tain't no —— use a-talkin'. I means to knock down my —— cheque, and d—— if I ain't goin' to shout. Here, you howlin' old ——, fetch out the poison!"

So the last Nut carries the day: the point of honour is conceded to him, and the landlord fills up a number of glasses with the only liquor affected by these noble spirits—rum.

As soon as the glasses are filled, a shake of the elbow, a round swing of the glass, or a "Here's luck" and "More fun," do duty for health-drinking, and a desultory conversation ensues. This conversation invariably turns first on the merits of their respective stations, herds, flocks and bosses, and next on reminiscences of old hands, and other Nuts, long since departed the district. Sprawled across the barcounter, with his arms tucked under him, one of the Nuts commences the highly intellectual conversation by a demand to know whether the others remember old Jim the Crawler. This elicits a chorus of "Ah! I mind that old sinner. He was a wunner to drink, that cove was. I've seen him take a dozen stiff nips before breakfast, and never a wink out of him. And there was Jim Steele—he was another; you mind Jim; he used to be boundary-riding for Griggs the Nipper—old Squeezem, as the chaps used to call him." Then chimes in another Nut: "Why, yer don't mean him as used ter tie up the niggers, and lambaste 'em with a stock-whip?"

*From* Old Colonials, *A. J. Boyd*

In 1851 the ground on which Ballarat now stands was virgin forest and park-like lands, untouched by the hand of man, barely even visited by him. It is true, it was part of a sheep-run, owned by some brothers named Yuille, but a solitary shepherd, or an occasional tribe of wandering black fellows, were the only human beings who visited the site of what is now a bustling town and an important mining centre.

The Presbyterian minister, Mr. Hastie, was then, and is still, settled at the older town of Buninyong, seven miles away. He gives the following description of the place:—"I often passed the spot on which Ballarat is built, and there could not be a prettier spot imaginable. It was the very picture of repose. There was, in general, plenty of grass and water, and often I have seen the cattle, in considerable numbers, lying in quiet enjoyment after being satisfied with the pasture. There was a beautiful clump of wattles where Lydiard Street now stands, and on one occasion, when Mrs. Hastie was with me, she remarked, 'What a nice place for a house, with the flat in front and the wattles behind.' Mr. Waldie had at that time a shepherd's hut, about where the Dead Horse Gully is, on the Creswick Road, and one day when I was calling on the hut-keeper, he said that the solitude was so painful that he could not endure it; for he saw no one from the time the shepherds went out in the morning till they returned at night. I was the only person he had ever seen there who was not connected with the station."

The greater part of Victoria was a wilderness in those days, but of danger there was little, save that every-day danger of the Australian bush, want of water. An occasional wandering tribe of aborigines, too, might prove troublesome, but that hazard was lessening daily. They had never been very numerous, and the squatters had from the first been waging continual war against the dark-skinned denizens of the bush, who, now reduced to half their original numbers, entertained a wholesome fear of the white man's firearms. Into the virgin forest, then, went these prospectors, among the hills and into the gullies, where the foot of civilised man had never yet trod. What if they did disturb the ferns and the trailing creepers, and turn the pretty silver creeks rushing down the rocky hill-sides into dirty, yellow-tinged streams, and the fern-clad gully into a desolate waste? No one ever saw the beauty they spoiled, no one very likely ever would have seen it, and these men, selfish as they no doubt were, have helped to build up a mighty colony.

It was along the banks of the creeks and water-worn gullies that these prospectors first sought gold. For of the two sorts of gold-mining, viz., alluvial and quartz, alluvial was the one first in vogue, being the easiest, and requiring little or no technical knowledge. The newest "chum" could trace the bed of a dry creek above ground. Equally easily recognised was the bed rock, though it might be a hundred feet below the surface; and the water-worn gravel and sand, which the diggers washed for gold, and consequently termed wash-dirt, was nothing, in point of fact, but the bed of an ancient creek, which in olden days had carried down the gold from its home in the quartz hills. Having found what they sought, their natural desire was to keep it to themselves. But this was well-nigh impossible. It began to be whispered in the nearest township that So-and-So's party had struck gold in paying quantities at such-and-such a place, and within a week thousands of men had "rushed" the creek, which a few days before the little party of prospectors had called their own.

A "rush" on the early gold-fields was like nothing else in the world. One day the lovely gully, the wild, dense bush-land, untouched by the hand of man, and in less than a week a place thronged with busy life. Rushes varied in size, sometimes consisting only of a few hundred men, while at others there were thousands in the field. The newcomers on their arrival hastened to "peg out" their "claims" in what appeared to them the most desirable spots, or took gratefully what the first comers had left for them. The ring of the axe was heard, the great forest trees fell before strong and sinewy arms that had learned to wield the axe in the forests of California. For miles around the land was denuded of timber, tent-poles, firewood, and timber for the new claim being an absolute necessity.

The climate of Victoria is mild compared with that of England, and the summer is very hot—hotter, perhaps, thirty years ago than it is now—but, south of the dividing range, at least, there are certainly three months of bitterly cold weather, when some shelter is necessary from the cutting wind and the driving rain. Consequently, as by magic, in less than a week a large canvas-and-bark town had sprung into existence. A somewhat ramshackle and tumble-down town it was, cer-

tainly, for each man was in haste to be rich, and gave little thought to his personal comfort mean-while. The great aim of all was to have the dwelling close to the claim. This, of course, was not possible where the ground was rich and the claims lay close together, and, accordingly, there sprang up a long, irregular line of huts and tents. Tents were most in favour, as being the simplest and easiest shelter to provide; but bark and slab huts were by no means uncommon. Uniformity there was none: each man built his house according to his own taste. Here was a frail bark hut, through the holes and crannies of which the cold wind must have whistled full often; there a neat white tent, the property of some new "chum" who had been fortunate enough to get it safe up country. In marked contrast would be the tent next door—a piece of tattered canvas, so old and ragged and brown that it is surprising it held together at all. Farther down the embryo street might be seen a neat hut built of slabs, with a weather-proof bark roof: the property of an old bushman, this. He and his mate understand how to make themselves comfortable, and the axe, which the new "chum" next door—residing in a tumble-down mia-mia, a mere shelter of boughs or bark, of which a black fellow would be ashamed—finds an unconquerable difficulty in using, is in his deft hands a powerful and useful tool.

Inside these huts and tents very little furniture was to be seen. The floor, of course, was the bare earth, and a standing bed-place or bunk was generally considered a necessity, but there was very little else. Some luxurious soul might make himself a rough wooden table, or rig up a few convenient shelves, but this was rare. Boxes and the flour-barrel, as a rule, did duty as seats, and the early digger's sole possessions were his mining imple-ments, his blankets, a tin billy, and a frying-pan. All else was considered superfluous, and looked upon as luxurious. The digger himself was usually attired in a blue or red shirt, mole-skin trousers tucked into high boots, and a slouch hat, while at his waist were pistols and knife, without which weapons of defence and offence no man was seen. In the middle of the camp was the inevitable grog shanty and general store, a place where anything was to be bought, from a needle to a sheet anchor, from the digger's tent to the chamois leather bag in which he carried his gold. The owner had found, in the sale of bad liquor at exorbitant prices, a surer road to wealth than any gold-mine in the colony. "Man must drink," might have been written of the

*Sly grog shop at Hanging Rock diggings (wood engraving from* Australian Picture Pleasure Book, *W. G. Mason)*

early digger; and if he can't drink good liquor, he will drink bad, and if even that fails him, he will console himself with Worcester Sauce or Friar's Balsam.

The practice of "shouting," or treating, was then common, far commoner even than it is at the present time, and it was not unusual for a lucky digger to spend one hundred pounds, or even two hundred pounds, in "shouting," not only for his friends, but for any strangers who happened to be hanging about the bar. It is only fair to add, so extraordinary were the prices, that he received for this outlay perhaps ten pounds worth of liquor.

Thus it happened that the grog shanty—usually a large tent with a counter down the middle, the stock-in-trade on one side and the customers on the other—was generally, especially in the evening, crowded with men drinking, fighting, quarrelling, playing cards, exchanging their hard-won gold for the necessaries of life—one and all aiding the publican to pile up for himself a snug fortune. If the "rush" were large there were often three or four of these stores, but, as a rule, the impassable state of the roads and the high price paid both for stores and cartage required a large capital, and practically forbade competition.

As soon as the "rush" became an undoubted fact a post-office was established, and, though it was primitive in the extreme, and letter-carriers were, of course, unknown, it was an undoubted boon to the inhabitants. Kelly, the author of "Life in Victoria," gives the following description of the first Ballarat post-office, which bears a strong family resemblance to those on all the diggings in the colonies in the old days:—

"The St. Martin's-le-Grand of Ballarat was a very primitive establishment, contained within a moderate-sized log-cabin, the greater portion of which, even after subtracting the household corner, was devoted to general business, and the person who wanted an ounce of tobacco was attended to before the man in quest of letters. The whole exterior of the edifice was papered over with quaintly-worded and ingeniously-spelled advertisements in writing. If you could find a vacant space you were at liberty to occupy it, but woe betide you if caught either in pulling off or overriding a previously posted notice, which, under pick and shovel law, were allowed to remain till they fell off. I annex a few as a general specimen:—

"'If this should meet the eye of John Tims he will hear of his shipmate at Pennyweight Flat, next tent to the tub and cradle.'

"The sign of a store, I presume; but if not so understood, rather a vague direction in a district like Pennyweight Flat, where some thousands were at work, each party with a tub and cradle.

"'James dakin notyces the publik agin thrustin his wife.'

"'Pat Flynn calls on biddy to return to the tint forninst the cross roads.'

"'Ten pounds reward for my black mare. No questions asked nor ideas insinuated.'

"But no indication where the reward was payable.

"'For sale several householt an kulenary articles as also a numerous frackshun of odds & ends at the Tent oppsite the Frenchman's store at the Ureka.'"

Soon after the "breaking out of the gold" the Government had seen the absolute necessity of putting someone in authority to check the lawlessness of the nondescript crowd gathered together on a gold-fields' "rush," and accordingly on every diggers' camp was a Gold Commissioner, and if it were large, there were three, and sometimes four. The Commissioner's camp was invariably set on a little eminence overlooking the diggers', and presented a marked contrast to it. Down there every man was as good as his neighbour, were he poor of the realm or foul-mouthed convict from the reeking gaols of New South Wales or Van Diemen's Land; but up in the police camp the old order prevailed: each man had his well-defined rank, and the Commissioner was lord of all. In front of the camp, so as to be plainly visible to all, was the flagstaff, from which floated the emblem of British rule, the Union Jack, and facing that were the Commissioner's tents, usually four in number—a mess tent, an office tent, a bed tent, and another for his clerk. These, in contrast with the diggers', were all floored with hard wood, carefully lined with green baize, and furnished with every luxury—as luxuries were then understood. At the back were the tents of the twenty or thirty troopers in form of a square, and behind them again were the stables for the horses.

Close behind the Commissioner's quarters was the all-important gold tent, guarded day and night by two armed sentries. In it were strong cedar boxes, and here was deposited the surplus wealth of the diggers' camp. Every man brought his gold, were the quantity great or small, in a leather or canvas bag, and handed it over to be placed in the strong box. A ticket with his name on it was attached to the parcel, and he received a receipt signed by the Commissioner, who was thenceforward responsible for the safety of the gold. When sufficient quantity was collected, usually from 60 to 90 lbs. weight, the escort started with it for Melbourne. In the early days, when the roads were well-nigh impassable, all the gold had to be carried on the backs of pack-horses, and the precious metal being dead weight, and apt to give the horses sore backs, from 20 to 25 lbs. weight was considered a fair load for each horse. The gold was packed in leather bags made something after the manner of old-fashioned purses; these were carefully locked in the middle by the Commissioner himself, and then slung across the pack-saddle. The day on which the escort started was a great day in the camp, and crowds turned out to see them set off. Usually the escort consisted of from ten to twelve men. Four pack-horses—about the usual number—required a man apiece to lead them, and as these men were necessarily much hampered, six

*Gold diggers at work, 1852*

heavily-armed troopers formed a guard. The Commissioner or an officer of police commanded the escort, and was responsible for the safety of the gold, and generally there was the sergeant, twelve men in all.

*From "Gold", M. Gaunt in* Cassell's Picturesque Australasia, *ed. E. E. Morris*

While we stood in the track, gazing hopelessly over the endless heaps of clay and gravel covering the flat, a little man came up and spoke to Philip, in whom he recognized a fellow countryman. He said:

"You want a place to camp on, don't you?"

"Yes," replied Philip, "we have only just come up from Melbourne."

"Well, come along with me," said the stranger.

He was a civil fellow, and said his name was Jack Moore. We went with him in the direction of the first White Hill, but before reaching it we turned to the left up a low bluff, and halted in a gully where many men were at work puddling clay in tubs.

After we had put up our tent, Philip went down the gully to study the art of gold digging. He watched the men at work; some were digging holes, some were dissolving clay in tubs of water by stirring it rapidly with spades, and a few were stooping at the edge of water-holes, washing off the sand mixed with the gold in milk pans.

Philip tried to enter into conversation with the diggers. He stopped near one man, and said:

"Good day, mate. How are you getting along?"

The man gazed at him steadily, and replied "Go you to hell," so Philip moved on. The next man he addressed sent him in the same direction, adding a few blessings; the third man was panning off, and there was a little gold visible in his pan. He was grey, grim, and hairy. Philip said:

"Not very lucky today, mate?"

The hairy man stood up, straightened his back, and looked at Philip from head to foot.

"Lucky be blowed. I wish I'd never seen this blasted place. Here have I been sinking holes and puddling for five months, and hav'n't made enough to pay my tucker and the Government license, thirty bob a month. I am a mason, and I threw up twenty-eight bob a day to come to this miserable hole. Wherever you come from, young man, I advise you to go back there again. There's twenty thousand men on Bendigo, and I don't believe nineteen thousand of 'em are earning their grub."

"I can't well go back fifteen thousand miles, even if I had money to take me back," answered Philip.

"Well, you might walk as far as Melbourne," said the hairy man, "and then you could get fourteen bob a day as a hodman; or you might take a job at stone-breaking; the Government are giving 7s. 6d. a yard for road metal. Ain't you got any trade to work at?"

"No, I never learned a trade, I am only a gentleman." He felt mean enough to cry.

"Well, that's bad. If you are a scholard, you might keep school, but I don't believe there's half-a-dozen kids on the diggin's. They'd be of no mortal use except to tumble down shafts. Fact is, if you are really hard up, you can be a peeler. Up at the camp they'll take on any useless loafer wot's able to carry a carbine, and they'll give you tucker, and you can keep your shirt clean. But, mind, if you do join the Joeys, I hope you'll be shot. I'd shoot the hull blessed lot of 'em if I had my way. They are

nothin' but a pack of robbers." The hairy man knew something of current history and statistics, but he had not a pleasant way of imparting his knowledge.

Picaninny Gully ended in a flat, thinly timbered, where there were only a few diggers. Turning to the left, Philip found two men near a waterhole hard at work puddling. When he bade them good-day, they did not swear at him, which was some comfort. They were brothers, and were willing to talk, but they did not stop work for a minute. They had a large pile of dirt, and were making hay while the sun shone—that is, washing their dirt as fast as they could while the water lasted. During the preceding summer they had carted their wash-dirt from the gully until rain came and filled the waterhole. They said they had not found any rich ground, but they could now make at least a pound a day each by constant work. Philip thought they were making more, as they seemed inclined to sing small; in those days to brag of your good luck might be the death of you.

While Philip was away interviewing the diggers, Jack showed me where he had worked his first claim, and had made four hundred pounds in a few days. "You might mark off a claim here and try it," he said. "I think I took out the best gold, but there may be a little left still hereabout." I pegged off two claims, one for Philip, and one for myself, and stuck a pick in the centre of each. Then we sat down on a log. Six men came up the gully carrying their swags, one of them was unusually tall. Jack said: "Do you see that big fellow there? His name is McKean. He comes from my part of Ireland. He is a lawyer; the last time I saw him he was in a court defending a prisoner, and now the whole six feet seven of him is nothing but a dirty digger."

*From* The Book of the Bush, *George Dunderdale (re Ballarat, 1853)*

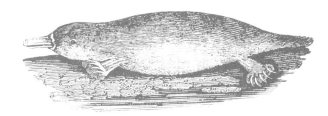

The Platypus

Every goldfield has its distinctive humours and its peculiar catch-word. The latter at the Port Curtis rush was composed of the affectionate phrase: "Oh, dearest Emma." Just after dark somebody would shout this amatory ejaculation at the top of his voice, and immediately the cry would be taken up and repeated all over the field in every varying tone of mock admiration. At first Mr Sinnett was under the impression that Emma was an actual flesh-and-blood personage running the gauntlet of playful pleasantries from the gay young diggers, but he soon discovered that Emma existed only in the realms of local imagination. It was simply an inexplicable but an established rite of the Port Curtis diggers to shout "Oh, dearest Emma," from time to time at the highest pitch of the voice. Occasionally the cry was raised during the day, but the practice was an essentially nocturnal one, lasting from seven o'clock until midnight, and attaining its maximum between nine and ten. Now and then a digger would vary the entertainment by adding to "Oh, dearest Emma," "'ow my 'art aches," but the majority contented themselves with merely apostrophising Emma. Sometimes, if tolerable quiet had reigned for half an hour, she would suddenly be addressed with startling vehemence, and the cry would then be passed on from voice to voice, until the farthest passionate appeal could be barely heard. Just as one dog beginning to bark, or one cock commencing to crow, rouses all the dogs or cocks within hearing, and sends the signal along a line of sentries for many miles, until the last answer seems but a faint and distant echo, so was it with the shouts of "Oh, dearest Emma," and "'Ow my 'art aches," at the Port Curtis rush.

*From* The Gladstone Colony, *J. F. Hogan, M.P.*

A fine body of men were the police of those days. They were all young, or at least men in the very prime of life, and though their uniform was much the same as that of the present trooper, their orderliness, their natty get-up, their well-kept horses and shining accoutrements, contrasted forcibly with the careless and ofttimes frowsy attire of the diggers in the camp below. The Gold Commissioner wore as uniform a cavalry officer's undress, namely, a dark braided frock-coat, wth a cap bound with gold lace, and, of course, the usual boots and breeches. He and his clerk were gentlemen by birth and breeding, but most of the policemen were drawn from the working classes. In the early days, however, many young men, the sons of gentlemen, came out to the colonies with the very laudable object of making their fortunes. The only question was "how?" That question was at first easily answered, "By gold digging, of course." But gold getting in theory and gold getting in practice were two very different things, and many of these young men, unaccustomed to manual labour, and with no practical knowledge to guide them, not merely found gold digging unprofitable, but in very many cases starvation absolutely stared them in the face. Glad enough, then, were they to secure a "billet" in the police force, where they were well paid and the work was not hard, or beyond their powers. These young fellows were formed into a separate body called "cadets," the only difference between them and the regular police being that they were supposed to be eligible for promotion. Some few, indeed, did rise to the rank of superintendent or inspector, but the majority, as the country became more settled, drifted away into other paths of life more suited to their status and education, while the few who remained were merged in the ordinary police force, never rose beyond the rank of senior constable or sergeant, and were fain to confess that their emigration to the "new and happy land" had in all probability ruined their lives.

*From "Bendigo," M. Gaunt in* Cassell's Picturesque Australasia, *ed. E. E. Morris*

Overweight

*Digger's wedding in Melbourne (from* Sketches of the Victoria Gold Diggings and Diggers As They Are [1852–53], *S. T. Gill)*

I was persuaded to emigrate to Australia. I arrived in Melbourne on 10th April, 1852, about six months after gold had been discovered. I did not know a soul out there then, and after a short time went on to Sydney, where I found a few people to whom I had letters of introduction.

After staying in Sydney a few months I returned to Melbourne with two mates whom I had picked up there, one a fellow-passenger I met going to Sydney. The voyage lasted seventeen days. My other mate was a runaway convict from Norfolk Island. He had been employed as workman and gardener in my other mate's family, and was a very hard-working old scoundrel. Melbourne at this time was a place to be remembered; the scenes that occurred in the streets and in the hotels would hardly be credited. The principal objects throughout the day to be seen in Collins and Bourke Streets were wedding-parties. Diggers used to come from the diggings with pounds' weight of gold, for the purpose, as they called it, of "knocking it down," and they managed to do this in a marvellously short space of time. You would hear of a man calling for two or three dozen of champagne (one pound per bottle), throwing it into a tub, and having a bath in it. Again, men would call for two slices of bread, put a ten-pound note between them and eat the note and bread as a sandwich. Hardly a day passed without seeing six or seven wedding-parties driving up and down Collins Street, dressed in most gorgeous attire. It was said the same women were married to different men over and over again. When the man had spent all his money he would go back to the diggings to make another "pile," and when he had made it he would return to Melbourne.

*From* The Last of the Bushrangers, *Superintendent F. A. Hare*

Oh, the traps, the dirty traps;
    Kick the traps when e'er you're able;
At the traps, the nasty traps;
    Kick the traps right under the table.

Quoted by James Kirby, a Victorian pioneer

Long time the Captain of Police reflected in
    despair,
At last he thought of Nicholson, De Montfort,
    and of Hare
All men inured to peril, sons of a warlike race,
Men never known to shrink from looking danger
    in the face.

*From "A Night's Walk", Anon.; a ballad about the capture of the bushranger Harry Power*

The Chinaman had no friends. Wherever he was met he was beaten and ill-treated, and at one period riots against the Chinese were common all over the colony. On the slightest pretext, or on no pretext at all, the Chinese camp would be rushed, and the unfortunate occupants driven from their tents and huts. On one occasion the diggers, among whom was a large sprinkling of the Yankee element, at a rush on the Buckland River, celebrated the glorious Fourth by an unprovoked attack on the unoffending Chinese camp. There were about 800 Chinamen and not a quarter as many white men; but the Celestials made little or no attempt to defend their household gods, and fled out into the bush, pursued for some distance by the valorous diggers. Word of the state of affairs at the Buckland was soon brought to the nearest Gold Commissioner, about ninety miles away. He at once came down with twenty troopers at his back. He was too late, however, for many of the Celestials. As the little band of troopers rode through the bush on that bitter July night, they came across unfortunate Chinamen lying alone, dead and dying, wantonly murdered by the drunken rioters. Some were hidden away in the scrub, shivering with cold and fright, too terrified almost to move, while others, in little parties, crouching round a handful of fire, endeavoured to shelter themselves from the keen winter's wind. Short and sharp was the Commissioner's justice. He and his troopers promptly reinstated the Chinamen, and if it was whispered that, in the redistribution of claims, the lion's share, or, more properly speaking, the best holes, fell to the foreigners, few will be found to blame the Commissioner now, and none dared to do so then.

*From "Gold", M. Gaunt in* Cassell's Picturesque Australasia, *ed. E. E. Morris*

*The Gold Commissioner mentioned above was Henry Gaunt. He held the post of Sub-Warden in the Beechworth district for a time, being appointed Warden of the Woolshed district in 1856. "M. Gaunt" was almost certainly his daughter Mary, one of the first women to enrol at Melbourne University (1881). She did not graduate, but became a successful novelist. Her account is probably reliable. A less reliable account is given below.*

## A Tale Of The Buckland, Dick The Digger

Dick the digger had pitched him a tent
By the side of a running creek
Where he had been told there was plenty of gold
For all who'd take the trouble to seek.
With his spade and his pick
To his work he would stick
No matter where others might roam;
Love lightened his toil
As he thought with a smile
Of the dear ones he'd left at home.

*Chorus*
And pick, pick, like a heavy old brick
He worked without dreaming of failure;
And he merrily sung, as his cradle he swung,
"Ho, a cheer for happy Australia."

But soon there rose, just under his nose,
A crowd of ugly tents;
And the masters they'd got were a sad ugly lot,
Both in manners and lineaments;
And whilst he toiled,
The water they spoiled,
And prigged all the fruits of his labours.
Dick was fain to be kind,
But it riled him to find
Them such very unneighbourly neighbours.

*Chorus*
For pick, pick, it made him sick,
To think he was getting daily, a
Heap of these accursed Chinese,
And he cried, "They'll ruin Australia."

Then up rose Dick, and seizing his pick,
Went sallying out with his mates.
Leaving the gold, these diggers so bold
Had a pick at the Chinamen's pates:
Poor John Chow Chow
Found himself in a row,
And away down the creek he ran,
Till in his place
Was left no trace,
Nor the ghost of a Chinaman.

*From* Colonial Songster, *ed. J. Hall*

*Chinesen beim goldwaschen (engraving from* Australien, *Friedrich Christmann)*

# Lambing Flat Riot
# June 1861

Meanwhile matters were approaching a crisis: fifers and drummers were obtained, and flags bearing patriotic sentiments were hoisted. Fire-arms and other weapons were procured; public-houses and booths were rushed, and plenty of Dutch courage imbibed. All these preparations and precautions were considered necessary by thousands of brave men (?) in order to successfully attack a few hundred defenceless Chinese.

The poor Asiatics made scarcely any resistance. All who could do so secreted their gold, and many of them lost their lives for refusing to tell where it was; others who were not quick enough in getting out of the holes and drives were buried alive in them—just for fun; such of the tents and goods as were not appropriated by the civilizers were collected in heaps and burned, and thus the work of murder and robbery went bravely on.

*From* Illustrated Sydney News *(5 August 1880)*

Early in 1861 there was a great roll-up of the diggers to drive the Chinese off the field, and the military were sent up from Sydney to restore order. The leaders of the riots strictly forbade robbery, and any person found stealing gold or any other property from the Chinese was to be handed over to the police; but burning the humpies, tents and other property of the unfortunate chinkies, cutting off their pigtails, beating or otherwise illtreating them, as an inducement for them to leave the field, were justifiable, if not meritorious acts.

*From* History of the Australian Bushrangers, *George Boxall*

Scene on a Bush Road.

*Notwithstanding the trouble with the Victorian authorities that culminated in the battle at the Eureka Stockade, most of the violence on the goldfields and elsewhere in the newly settled country was not anti-authoritarian. It stemmed from the notion that the coloured races were in some way inferior to the white, and could therefore be treated in the most savage and barbaric way with impunity. The shooting and poisoning of the aboriginal people to "bring them to their senses", and the often rough and sometimes fatal manhandling of the peaceable Chinese diggers speak better than words of this opinion that was so widely held.*

"The object of scouring the bush was to show the blacks that we were in some force. Occasionally, we saw dusky figures; but I would not allow any firing. Catching sight of a man, Paddy Long, raising his musket to fire at a black, I shouted to him to drop it, and told him that for the first blackfellow he shot in cold blood, I would shoot him.

"Now, Paddy Long was a very good fellow, who would not, as the saying is, 'harm a fly'; but his conception, doubtless, was that we were out on a shooting party, and, indeed, a raid on the blacks was, in my time, by squatters often so conceived; and in cases where the squatters' cattle have been speared, it is difficult at times to draw an ethical line, especially in districts where Her Majesty's writ does not run."

*Major De Winton, quoted in* The History of the Gladstone Colony, *J. F. Hogan, M.P.*

Chinese were reckoned fair game for a swindle by anyone who could manage it, as the following incident told by Joe Porter intimates. A local horse dealer, hearing that the market gardeners on the borders of the town wanted a horse, pulled a fast one on the local celestials. Hearing they wanted a horse to pull a dray he brought along a fair-sized animal. The yellow men inspected, and rejected him. "Him too smaw," they decided. "Wantum *big* one, Welly big one."

"Righto," said the dealer, cheerfully. "You come to-morrow. I got another one. Oh! *Very* big one."

When the Chinese arrived next day there were several horses standing the yard. One of them appeared to be a veritable giant of a horse. The Chinese were delighted.

"Ha!" they chortled gleefully. "*Him* more better. Him *welly* big fella . . . *MY WOR.*" And closed the deal forthwith, at double the price asked before.

The dealer had scouted round and borrowed all the small and weedy runts about the place to put in the yard with his exhibit.

It was the same horse.

*From* Roll the Summers Back, *Joseph Porter ("Spinifex")*

*Probably the horse did not complain about his new owners, for there was a simile I have heard my elders use when I was a child, "He's as fat as a Chinaman's horse." It is indeed strange how the Chinese excited contempt and dislike despite their industry and careful thrifty behaviour. The following extract from a serious historian of the Cooktown-Palmer River field shows the general attitude that prevailed among people who probably had no direct contact with the Chinese diggers, but reflected the general social attitude of the times.*

The far-resounding clink and clang of the sacred metal was heard throughout the world and even China heard the echo. Hordes of short, sturdy men, oblique of eye, yellow complexioned, and with plaited hair-lock, invaded the colony and crowded the white adventurers. From this irruption of Mongolians, and the angry feeling which ensued when the diggers, having exhausted the richest deposits, sought to fall back upon the half-worked ground, or poorer "wash", and discovered the Chinese, like a cloud of locusts, had stripped all bare, originated subsequent legislation which excluded men of that race from all goldfields until a certain period had elapsed from their first discovery. From this incident also ultimately resulted the present imposition of a poll tax upon every Mongolian arriving in Queensland.

*From, "Historical Sketch of Queensland",* Picturesque Atlas of Australasia, *Vol 2, ed. Hon. Andrew Garran*

*Here we see the humble coolie being blamed for daring to work the ground that had been deserted by the white diggers while they themselves cleaned out "the richest deposits".*

Crib was the most popular game among bush workers. Shearers, fencers, or stockmen would sit up for hours, shifting the little pegs up and down the cribbage-board, and striving to build up runs and flushes and fifteens.

A story is told of a Chinese cook who worked on Saltern Creek station when A. R. Brown was the manager. The boys in the hut were wont to play crib till the small hours. Sometimes there were arguments, and Ah Chong's rest was sadly disturbed. Finally he decided he'd had it, and stalked up the office to give notice. According to the story he announced his intention thus—"Fif-teen four . . . Fif-teen four . . . fif-teen fi' . . . You blully lie . . . You come ow-si' . . . I give you black eye . . . Eb-ley ni' . . . By Cli. I go 'way to-molla, Missa Brown."

And he did.

*From* Roll the Summers Back, *Joseph Porter ("Spinifex")*

*It would appear from the above extract that some "Mongolians" had a sense of pride and independence, possibly learned from the tough men they were compelled to work beside. See also the incident below, when "Tom Collins" is rescuing bullocks being impounded for trespass from a Chinese boundary rider. The Celestial remains patient and bows to the inevitable, but is not put down!*

In a couple of minutes Bunyip had settled down to that flying trot which would have been an independence to anyone except myself. After clearing the lignum, I got a back elevation of the bullocks, half-a-mile out on the plain; and, rapidly overhauling them, I perceived that I should have to pit myself against the Chinese boundary rider this time. Consequently I felt, like Cassius, fresh of spirit and resolved to meet all perils very constantly.

"Out of my way, you Manchurian leper, or I'll run over you!" I shouted gaily, as I swung round the cattle, turning them back.

"Muck-a-hi-lo! sen-ling, ay-ya; ilo-ilo!" remonstrated the unbeliever, drawing his horse aside to let them pass.

"You savvy, John," said I, suiting my language to his comprehension, while from my eye the Gladiator broke—"bale you snavel-um that peller bullock. Me fetch-um you ole-man lick under butt of um lug; me gib-it you big one dressum down. Compranny pah, John?" The Chinaman had turned back with me, and, as if he had been hired for the work, was stolidly assisting to return the cattle to the spot whence he had taken them.

"Why don't you speak for yourself, John?" I asked, thanklessly quoting from the familiar hexameter, and lighting my pipe as I spoke.

"Eulopean dam logue," responded the heathen in his blindness.

"In contradistinction to the Asiatic and the Australian, who are scrupulously honest," I observed pleasantly. "You savvy who own-um that peller bullock, John?"

"Walligal Alp," replied the pagan promptly. "Me collal him bullock two-tlee time to-molla, all li; two-tlee time nex day, all li."

"All li, John—you collar-am that peller bullock one more time, me manhandle you; pull-um off you dud; tie-um you on ant-bed, allee same spreadeagle; cut-um-off you eye-lid; likee do long-a-China; bimeby sun jump up, roast-um you eye two-tlee day; bull-dog ant comballee, eat-um you meat, pick-um you bone; bimeby you tumbledown-die; go like-it dibil-dibil; budgeree fire long-a that peller. You savvy, John?"

"Me tellee Missa Smyte you lescue," replied John doggedly. "All li; you name Collin; you b'long-a Gullamen Clown; all li; you killee me bimeby; all li." With this the discomfited Mongol turned his horse in the direction of Mondunbarra homestead, and, like a driver starting an engine when there is danger of the belt flying off, gradually worked up his pace to a canter, leaving me in possession of the field.

*The Chinese ex-miner in the United States fared no better than his Australian counterpart. There is the story of a mob who were going to lynch a Chinese for fun in a western town. They were stopped by the Marshal. When they asked him why he was a spoilsport, his reply was, simply: "If'n you hang Wong, who'll wash my shirts?" Thus the man's life was saved for a purely practical reason, no more or less.*

*Personal accounts of hold-ups by bushrangers are many, but few achieve the almost gossipy style of this story taken from Samuel Shumack's book,* An Autobiography; Tales and Legends of the Canberra Pioneers. *It has an immediacy lacking in many other accounts, and has the air of polish about it that comes from being told orally many times, as has most writing from old bushmen, men like Bill Harney and Joseph Porter. One also gets an objective view of the robbers, as Shumack himself had not been robbed and could therefore feel no resentment toward Hall and his gang. Note also that small sympathy was extended to the major victim, who "became the laughing stock of the district", probably because he was classed as a "windbag" and boaster.*

Shortly after the goldrush to the Snowy Mountains ceased, Frank Gardiner was "King of the Road"—a position he held until after the Eugowra escort robbery, when he vanished. Others then took his place. Gardiner, Ben Hall and company had a host of impersonators, and many of these were in the Queanbeyan district. Alexander Fraser at Gundaroo had several visits from these pseudobushrangers.

I can remember only one of Gardiner's gang suffering the death penalty—his name was Henry Manns. A friend of mine named William Casey was in Sydney with his team and went to see the execution. He later told me that he would never forget the awful scene—the hangman was drunk and did not adjust the rope properly. When the bolt was drawn and the victim dropped through the trapdoor the rope closed around his head above the ears and his hands came loose and he grasped the rope. The hangman kicked the struggling man's hands to make him let go, and eventually he was hauled up on to the scaffold, his hands tied, the rope shoved round his neck, and he was thrown off. The savagery of this execution raised a storm of protest which lasted for some time and the press was most vitriolic in their attack on those in authority. Several of the gang were tried for the same offence and were sentenced to fifteen years' hard labour, and the public wondered at the variation in punishment.

Ben Hall was, in a measure, Frank Gardiner's successor. My neighbours Thomas Gribble and Thomas Wells met this gang shortly after they stuck up the escort between Yass and Gundagai, when Sergeant Parry was shot dead and Inspector O'Neill surrendered. Gribble and Wells were *en*

*Gold escort attacked by bushrangers (engraving from* History of Australasia, *David Blair)*

*route* to Sydney with a load of wool when they were stuck up by the gang, and when they returned from Sydney they gave us an account of the hold-up. Gribble said,

> We had just passed the Lake Ranges on the Goulburn Road and were going up a steep hill when a horseman told us to take the team into the bush. He said he was Ben Hall and that they were waiting for the mail coach, and advised us to do as we were told in order to avoid trouble. I did as directed and some distance from the road I joined some other teams and a group of men and women. Dunn was in charge of this group and I was surprised that all seemed happy. He was relating some of the gang's exploits when he was interrupted by a cry, "Here she comes", and we then saw the Royal Mail Coach coming down the track with Hall on one side and Gilbert on the other, and there was a loud moan when we saw that the coach was full of passengers. Our storekeeper, George Harcourt, was the first male passenger to descend. All the male passengers were searched and relieved of their valuables and cash, and a large case was broken open and found to contain cherries, of which all hands were invited to partake. The mail bags were then ransacked and Ben Hall announced that they had done a good day's work and invited us to continue our journey, after which they lifted their hats and galloped away. They treated us in a very polite manner.

Our employer, William Davis, was a noted shot and had won prizes all over the State. He made a boast that if ever he met the bushrangers he would reduce their number. Ben Hall had sent Davis a message telling him that he was a boaster and that they would meet one day. In the meantime Davis ordered a new repeating rifle which had just been perfected, and he showed father his arms and the precautions he had taken to defend the station should Hall and company pay them a visit. The Ginninderra homestead was more or less a fort. All his men—about ten—were armed, and shooting practice took place daily. It was an absurdity to think that a party of three bushrangers would attack such a place. Davis knew this—but his name was in every paper and he was greatly praised. Some scribes "wished we had a few more like him and the bushrangers would soon be a thing of the past".

A short time later Mr Davis went to Picton by mail coach and then by train to Sydney, where he purchased a small arsenal which included a fifty pound shot gun, a revolver of the latest pattern and a repeating rifle. He practised with the latter at a range near Sydney in preparation for a chance meeting with the bushrangers.

About 1840 a young man arrived from England and his name was John Brown. He was employed on landing at a wage of twelve pounds per annum, later increased to seventeen pounds per annum. He was a steady young man and he prospered and was a landowner at Canberra twenty years later. In 1864 he went to Sydney on horseback to purchase a large quantity of goods which were despatched by horse team for Canberra, and he left for home on horseback with an up-to-date saddle outfit. All went well until near Collector, where he met Ben Hall and three of his men, who told him to turn off into the bush. Here he saw several others bailed up like himself. Hall took his watch and said, "Well, well, I am surprised to see a 'swell' like you with such a common timepiece, but it is better than none—I expect a splendid one from a passenger on the mail coach, and if I am not disappointed I will return you this one."

Although the bushrangers were well mounted, Dunn had a bridle made of greenhide and his saddle was little more than a wreck. Less than twenty-four hours previously they had had a brush with the police and Dunn lost horse, saddle and bridle. He now confiscated Brown's new outfit, which he replaced with his own, saying, "There—old 'Brusher'—fair exchange is no robbery."

Hall interrupted and said, "She will be here in a minute—come, Johnny", and he and Gilbert went away leaving Dunn in charge of about twenty persons who were not visible from the road. Soon after the mail coach appeared in the distance and stopped at the foot of a hill, where a passenger alighted. After a brief delay the coach moved off followed by the passenger—William Davis. When about half way up the incline he was astonished to hear, "Throw up your hands, you blowing windbag, or we will scatter your brains!" He then saw Hall and Gilbert—one on each side of the track. Davis was well covered and had no option but to throw up his hands. Hall relieved Davis of his revolver and Gilbert directed the coach off the road into the bush where the group were standing. The passengers alighted and Hall relieved Davis of his fifty-guinea watch and a purse containing ten pounds. Gilbert took the repeating rifle and mockingly thanked Davis for his thoughtful kindness in bringing them such a splendid weapon. Hall now addressed Davis. "There," he said, "is the 'swell' windbag who was going to give us hell if ever we appeared before him; however, we have made a good day's work today so you can have the gun, Johnny, and you, 'old Brusher', can have your watch as I was not disappointed", and he returned the watch to Brown. He then told Davis what he thought of his boasting and warned him against any repetition. The ladies were not molested. Whilst Hall ransacked the mail bags, Gilbert amused the crowd with tales of their exploits and during a temporary lull one of the female passengers, a widow named Charlotte Sidley whom Davis had hired as cook, had a few words to say: "Ye are very bad men, you know, very wicked men, you know, and if you don't give up this wicked life, you know, you will all go to that place, you know, where the devil will have ye, you know."

Here Dunn interposed: "Shut up, you ugly old devil—good looking men like us don't go to bad places like that—only old devils like you go there—it is full of ugly old things like you." A general laugh followed and Hall, having emptied the mailbags, bade them "good day" and the gang rode away. Father and mother went to see Mr Davis when he arrived home and he gave them a full account of the matter. He said, "I had no chance as my revolver was in my belt."

"If you had had it in your hand do you think you could have done anything?" asked Robert Kilby.

"No, they had me covered before I saw them and I was powerless with surprise. Hall asked me about remarks I had made about him and his gang—I made them at my dinner table and would like to know how he obtained the information."

This question is easily answered because his remarks were common knowledge. I met John Brown years later and he gave me an account of the hold-up and Davis's humiliation at the hands of Ben Hall. Charlotte Sidley married Thomas Wells eighteen months later. Davis had few sympathizers and for a time was the laughing stock of the district.

An Up-country Coach

The bushranging mania was now rife in both New South Wales and Queensland, and for some months in 1866 we were in continual dread of a visit from one styling himself "The Wild Scotchman," as well as from a German named "Biermaster." Both these men were prowling about the country. The latter had stuck up the Maryborough Mail, while the former, though often seen on our run, never molested us further than sticking up our Mail and opening our letters. The black police and their officers were frequently on our station on the lookout for them.

On New Year's night, 1867, one of my men returning late to the homestead, told me that he felt certain that the Scotchman was camped in a gully near the house. We were now all excitement to effect his capture. The moon was shining brightly, and we considered the best plan to adopt was to wait until midnight, when the man was likely to be asleep, and then pounce upon him.

When midnight arrived, I and several gentlemen who were spending the evening with us, dressed ourselves in dark clothes, these being less conspicuous than our white coats in the bright moonlight. We armed ourselves with revolvers and sallied forth. At the place mentioned we found the supposed bushranger rolled in his blanket, asleep. We rushed upon him, and seizing his arms, made him prisoner. Pulling off the blanket which covered his face, we discovered our captive to be a stockman from a neighbouring station. The poor man was almost frightened to death at the strange proceedings. We soon explained the thing to him, however; whereupon a general laugh ensued. We returned to the house, he none the worse for his New Year's night's adventure, and we rather crestfallen. The ladies greatly enjoyed the mistake, being no longer anxious about our safety.

Biermaster was, I think, slightly out of his mind. He had been arrested by the police, from whom he had escaped. One of my black-boys informed me that he had seen a man answering to his description, on the run, about six miles from the homestead. He was carrying a double-barrelled gun. I gave the black-boy a revolver, as he was a good shot. Taking one also with me, we started in pursuit (my wife being terribly anxious this time). We were not long before we came on his tracks, and caught sight of him at a turning of the road. Being a magistrate, I had given the black-boy orders that when I challenged him in the Queen's name to throw down his gun, if he did not immediately obey, or if he presented it at us, he was to cover him with his revolver. As yet he had not seen us, although we were only a couple of hundred yards behind him. Spurring our horses we galloped up to him. The moment I challenged him, he dropped his gun without the slightest hesitation. Covered by the black-boy's revolver, he submitted to have his hands fastened behind him with a coat strap, and thus we marched our bushranger to the homestead. During all this time he never spoke a word.

How to keep him securely until the police arrived from Gayndah puzzled me. I could not at once send information to them, as the town was fifty miles distant—under eight hours—and it would take them the same time to arrive. As there was no lock-up on the station, I could only chain him to the verandah post of the store. I did this by padlocking one end of a horse trace-chain round his neck, fixing the other end to the post in the same way, and never losing sight of him. It was weary work, this constant watching for over sixteen hours, though he endured no hardships, for he was quite comfortable, and in the shade. An amusing incident occurred. On my wife telling the cook to take him some dinner, she appeared greatly shocked at my wife's kindness, and asked if she should put salt, pepper, and mustard, on his plate? On being told to do so, she went off thoroughly disgusted that the bushranger should be so treated, and particularly that he should have *mustard*. At length the police arrived, and this time he was safely conveyed to prison. He was sentenced to fifteen years with hard labour. I had no further experience with his class; indeed, he was nearly the last of the Queensland bushrangers.

*From* Leaves from a Squatter's Note-book, *Thomas Major*

*Alpin Macpherson, or "the Wild Scotchman" as he preferred to be known, had a remarkable career as a bushranger, and his exploits rival some of those of the Hall gang and the Kellys. He is largely forgotten, perhaps because he was not very successful financially, and I doubt if he ever killed anybody. He was an intelligent young migrant from Scotland, who was apprenticed to a Brisbane stonemason. When tales of the doings of the Hall gang were prominent in the newspapers, his Celtic blood was apparently aroused, and he left Brisbane, vowing to join Hall and "fight a duel with Sir Frederick Pottinger". He did go to the Lachlan diggings, and he is supposed to have exchanged shots with Sir Frederick on one occasion. Hall is reported to have been a little worried by the young fellow's recklessness, and to have told him to get back north of the border.*

*When he returned to Queensland he seems to have operated in the Burnett district, but as there had not been a major gold find in the State at that time (Gympie was still in the future) he and some companions were content to hold up travellers for whatever they might have upon them at the time. Their favourite target seems to have been squatter members of Parliament on their way to Brisbane for sittings of the house. Three of his gang were captured by the police, but the Scotchman himself escaped. He carried on alone for a while, but was eventually captured on Monduran station, by a number of men who recognized him.*

*He was taken to Rockhampton for extradition to Sydney to stand trial for his nefarious activities in that State, and strangely enough it was at this time that Sir Frederick Pottinger was killed on his way to Sydney. In fact, one of the reasons he was on his way to Sydney (apart from the reasons mentioned elsewhere in this book) was to give evidence at Macpherson's trial.*

*Macpherson was returned to Queensland to stand trial in that State, for his further misdeeds. He was in leg-irons and escorted by a constable. He must have been active in the north, for examination of the Horace Flower letter about the "Dying Stockman" song shows that he says his father knew "the Gulf bushranger", the Wild Scotchman. At the port of Mackay, the Scotchman escaped from custody, and the constable did not miss him until after the ship had sailed for Rockhampton. He got as far south as Kolonga station, about fifteen miles north of Gin Gin, and was recaptured while trying to steal a horse. He was returned to Rockhampton, and stood his trial there, receiving a sentence of twenty years for "robbery under arms". From there on he seems to have faded from the record. Some folk say that his name was McGregor, and it may well have been for at one time in Scotland the clan McGregor was proscribed by law and many of the clan changed their names in public while proudly retaining their secret title to the old identity.*

"But why this solicitude and panic over being detected in trifling trespass?" asked Willoughby. "Like most things in this country, it appears to be purely a matter of pounds, shillings and pence. Now, I have taken the liberty of totting up, in my own mind, some of your earnings. Will Thompson permit me to take his case as an illustration? I find, Thompson, that the tariff of your wool is exactly sevenpence half-penny per ton per mile. You have eight tons on your wagon at the present time. This will give you five shillings for each mile you travel. You have travelled ten miles to-day"——

"Sabbath day's journey," sighed Thompson.

——"that is two pounds ten. Now,—all things considered—an occasional penalty of, say, one pound, appears to me by no means ruinous. It is not to be mentioned in comparison with other losses which you have been unfortunate enough to sustain, yet it appears to be your chief grievance."

"Yes; that 's one way of looking at it," muttered Thompson, after a pause. The other fellows were silently and futilely wrestling with the apparent anomaly. A metaphysical question keeps slipping away from the grasp of the bullock driver's mind like a wet melon-seed.

[Yet the solution is simple. The up-countryman is decidedly open-handed; he will submit to crushing losses with cheerfulness, tempered, of course, by humility in those cases where he recognizes the operation of an overhanging curse; he will subscribe to any good or bad cause with a liberality excelled only by the digger; he will pay gambling debts with the easy, careless grace which makes every P. of W. so popular in English sporting circles—in a word, the smallest of his many sins is parsimony. But the penal suggestiveness of trespass-penalty touches the sullen dignity of his nature; and the vague, but well-grounded fear of a law made and administered solely by his natural enemies makes him feel about as apprehensive as John Bunyan, though certainly more dangerous. Of course, Willoughby, born and bred a member of the governing class, could n't easily conceive the dismay with which these outlaws regarded legal seizure for trespass—or possibly prosecution in courts dominated by squatters.]

*From* Such Is Life, *Joseph Furphy ("Tom Collins")*

"Well, mate," said William, "I thought it out,
An' I sez to myself, sez I:
There's not much hope for the rouseabout,
As the rousy can testify.

"So I'll drink the honey of Freedom's Cup,
An' do as it pleases Brown;
I'll roll me swag when the sun gets up,
An' I'll camp when the sun goes down.

*From "Bill Brown", Edward S. Sorenson*

Rose early, according to my custom, and surveyed my new dwelling with a particular sort of satisfaction. "No rent to pay for you," said I; "no taxes, that's pleasant, no poor-rates, that's a comfort; and no one can give me warning to quit, and that's another comfort; and it's my own, thank God, and that's the greatest comfort of all." I cast my eyes on the plain before me, and saw my flock of sheep studding the plain, with my working bullocks at a little distance. . . . As we sat at breakfast that morning in my rude cottage, with the bare walls of logs of trees and the shingle roof above us, all rough enough, but spacious, and a little too airy, I began to have a foretaste of that feeling of independence and security of home and subsistence which I have so many years enjoyed.

*From* Tales of the Colonies, *Charles Rowcroft*

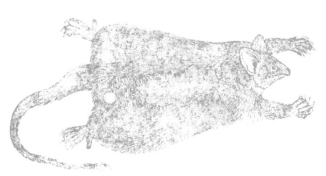

The Flying Opossum of New South Wales

*Station hands at billiards (engraving from* Australasian Sketcher, *21 May 1881)*

Clear cold night, slight breeze from the east, day beautifully warm and pleasant, Mr. Burke suffers greatly from the cold, and is getting extremely weak; he and King start tomorrow up the creek to look for the blacks: it is the only chance we have of being saved from starvation. I am weaker than ever although I have a good appetite and relish the nardoo much, but it seems to give us no nutriment, and the birds here are so shy as not to be got at. Even if we got a good supply of fish, I doubt whether we could do much work on them and the nardoo alone. Nothing but the greatest good luck can save any of us; and as for myself, I may live four or five days if the weather continues warm. My pulse is at forty-eight, and very weak, and my legs and arms are nearly skin and bone. I can only look out, like Mr. Micawber, "for something to turn up": but starvation on nardoo is by no means very unpleasant, but for the weakness one feels, and utter inability to move oneself, for, as far as appetite is concerned, it gives me the greatest satisfaction. Certainly, fat and sugar would be more to one's taste, in fact, these seem to be the great stand by for one in this extraordinary

Continent; not that I mean to depreciate the farinaceous food, but the want of sugar and fat in all substances obtainable here is so great that they become almost valueless to us as articles of food, without the addition of something else.

*From W. J. Wills's Journal, the last entry.*

"Now, Mosey," said Willoughby, courteously but tenaciously, "will you permit me to enumerate a few gentlemen—gentlemen, remember—who have exhibited in a marked degree the qualities of the pioneer. Let us begin with those men of whom you Victorians are so justly proud,—Burke and Wills. Then you have——"

"Hold on, hold on," interrupted Mosey. "Don't go no furder, for Gossake. Yer knockin' yerself bad, an' you don't know it. Wills was a pore harmless weed, so he kin pass; but look 'ere—there ain't a drover, nor yet a bullock driver, nor yet a stock-keeper, from 'ere to 'ell that could n't 'a' bossed that expegition straight through to the Gulf, an' back agen, an' never turned a hair—with sich a season as Burke had. Don't sicken a man with yer Burke. He burked that expegition, right enough. ''Howlt! *Dis*-MOUNT!' Grand style o' man for sich a contract! I tell you, that (explorer) died for want of his sherry an' biscakes. Why, the ole man, here, seen him out beyond Menindie, with his——"

"Pardon me, Mosey—was Mr. Price connected with the expedition?"

"No (adj.) fear!" growled Price resentfully. "Jist happened to be there with the (adj.) teams. Went up with stores, an' come down with wool."

Willoughby, who probably had wept over the sufferings of Burke's party on their way to Menindie, seemed badly nonplussed. He murmured acquiescence in Price's authority; and Mosey continued,

"Well, the ole man, here, seen him camped, with his carpet, an' his bedsteed, an' (sheol) knows what paravinalia; an' a man nothin' to do but wait on him; an'—look here!—a cubbard made to fit one o' the camels, with compartments for his swell toggery, an'—as true as I'm a livin' sinner!—one o' the compartments made distinctly o' purpose to hold his bell-topper!"

"Quite so," replied Willoughby approvingly. "We must bear in mind that Burke had a position to uphold in the party; and that, to maintain sub-ordination, a commander must differentiate himself by"——

"It's Gord's truth, anyhow," remarked Price, rousing his mind from a retrospect of its extensive past. And, no doubt, the old man was right; for a relic, answering to Mosey's description, was sold by auction in Melbourne, with other assets of the expedition, upon Brahe's return.

*From* Such Is Life, *Joseph Furphy ("Tom Collins")*

A Bushman's Hut

# A Reminiscence of The Fifties

In the fifties things were done, in Victoria, in a free-and-easy, unconventional way. The writer remembers staying at Murphy's Castlemaine Hotel when the sessions were on, and at the dinner-table, along with the judge on circuit, his associate, the crown prosecutor, and a number of barristers, were several persons charged with criminal offences, but out on bail. Among these were two young men from Smythesdale, who were to take their trial for tarring and feathering a man. After dinner, at the suggestion of bibulous little barrister McDonough (known as John Phillpott Curran), the table was removed. Quinn, a surveyor, produced his fiddle, and soon was presented an astonishing spectacle, judge, men on the jury list, solicitors, barristers and offenders, whooping around in jig, and reel, and polka, and waltz, until the morning hours, when broiled bones and whisky-punch finished up the saturnalia.

Next day every peg fitted into its proper place. The people on bail gave themselves up. The judge sat. The crown prosecutor thundered his charges against men with whom he had hobnobbed the night before. And the two young fellows tried for tarring-and-feathering got three years "hard."

As G. V. Brooke (one of the company) observed, "They never did it better in Ireland."

*From "Aboriginalities", the* Bulletin

# Twelve Years' Experience by a Queensland Prospector

I arrived at the Twenty-mile during the time of the rush from the Cape River to the Gilbert. I spent about three weeks at this place, and prospected the country round for twenty miles and found payable gold in many places, but nothing to give me a "rise." My next prospecting was at Black David, where I found that every one was on payable gold. Around this place I prospected for about a fortnight, and was very well satisfied. The greater portion of the diggers were making from 1 oz. to 1½ oz. per week. The place received the name of Black David after the man who opened this and many other gullies throughout the North of Queensland. I then had four weeks "dry fiddling" on the Gilbert, and made on an average 4 ozs. per week. After this I started with four men prospecting out as far as Morrison's and Thompson's stations, getting indications of gold all along eighty miles. Returned to the Gilbert and commenced dry fiddling again. Here I laid twenty or thirty men on to gold. I may mention that an old miner came to me one day and said he could not get any gold. I happened to be very lucky at the time, so as I knew where I could get another good claim I gave him up mine, on condition that if he struck the reef I was to have a show. I was away one day when he turned up a 22 oz. nugget, besides a lot of smaller pieces. Hearing that Messrs. M'Gregor and Moran were out prospecting on the Delaney and Western Creek watersheds, I made a start from the Gilbert by myself, and prospected the Granite Creek, and so on to the Percy River, with my galvanized mare (? animated skeleton). I got gold on the Percy, but not payable. If it were in another country, and provisions cheap, it would pay. When I arrived at the Robinson River there seemed to be any quantity of niggers about, and plenty of horseshoe tracks. I followed these tracks to the Quartz Blue Mountains, and camped there all alone. I remained here for three or four days and prospected the country round, and some days got 3 to 4 dwts. At last I saw blacks on the other side of the river, and having no company I pushed down the river again, and pulled up at the junction of Oakey Creek and the Robinson. Here I found that parties had been prospecting previously; I believe it was Mr.

Daintree's party. During the night the blacks attacked me when I was asleep, and I had to fly for my life. I went down the Robinson for two miles, and found some fresh horse tracks crossing the river. I followed the tracks up to Mosquito Creek, as I afterwards found it was called. Got on to Tabletop and crossed Moran's Gully, but was not lucky enough to find Daintree, although he was getting gold within half a mile of where I crossed the gully. I got good indications of gold at Tabletop in one or two gullies. There I was camped a few days, and saw large numbers of horse tracks in the direction of the Delaney. As the blacks were very bad, and had surrounded me, I made up my mind to make towards the Gilbert again. I arrived at the Percy once more, not having met any white men the whole time. Whilst camped here I only got payable prospects, and then started to the Gilbert, where I made up a party of four to go back to the Percy. I showed Mr. Commissioner Hackett the gold I had got. We got to work on the Percy and it was all right, and very soon a rush followed from the Gilbert. When we were found out I went and opened another gully, and these were the first two gullies opened on the Percy on the crossing to the Robinson. Next, my three mates and I started for Cape Creek; we prospected all the way to the Robinson, and thence to Cape Creek, getting gold which would have been payable in any more civilized part of the country. At last we pulled up at Western Creek, and found innumerable prospecting parties. We got here 38 ozs., and as some shanty keepers had set up, we had a jollification, a fight all round, and parted.

I then started bush work, and in five weeks managed to earn two horses and a rig-out. As soon as I was fitted out I made from the lower township to Sandy Creek. In this place I spent a week prospecting about, and got good tucker gold; thence prospected up as far as Edwardstown, and from there to Cradle Creek, where I got payable gold in several gullies. At the head of Cradle Creek got 4 dwts. per day. I then returned to the Palmer River, where I found crowds of men getting provisions to start for supposed new rushes, which were on in all directions.

After getting beef and every other necessary, three of us started for one of these supposed rushes; my mates were S. M'Cann and Richard Petersen. The first gold we got was on Purdie Creek. Here we spent a few days; found gold in many places, but nothing to make a rise. Prospected across on to the

Sandy Creek and Stony Creek; on the former we got payable gold, 3 to 4 dwts. to the dish. After prospecting about a week we separated in the camp. There was no one digging in Sandy Creek in those days. The next prospecting was done up towards Oakey Creek; everything there seemed very exciting when we arrived. There was a rush of shanties and packers. Everything was very dear: boots, One pound fifteen shillings per pair; flour, two shillings per lb., and everything else in proportion. I got a claim in Man's Creek, where I made from 1 to 3 ozs. some days. Then I shifted up the left-hand branch of Oakey Creek, where 2 ozs. per day for a few days. When this was done I prospected further up the creek, and struck good gold. I named this creek the Gall, or Snider Gully. I set to work here and got from 1 oz. to 1 lb. weight to the dish, and in ten days had 300 ozs. of gold. One month and two

days' work in the gully gave me 375 ozs. Previous to going I sold a half share for one hundred pounds, and in a day and a half took out two hundred pounds worth more gold. I have been prospecting nine places not before mentioned; the Dry River is one;—eventually a good reef will be got here.

I now conclude this portion of my wanderings in the search for gold over Northern Queensland, but I shall commence a further recital soon.

THOMAS SMITH,

Flying Prospector G. Y., or King of the North; one who has persevered more than any miner in the North, and who has prospected as much as any man from the time of the Cape River rush to the present.

*Quoted in* Old Colonials, *A. J. Boyd*

*In a Queensland bar*

The great vice of the bush is drinking. Not that as a rule bushmen drink when at work, but it only too often happens that at periods varying from two months to a year they obtain a cheque for the full amount of their earnings, ride into the nearest township, hand their cheque to the publican, and remain in a state of intoxication until that worthy declares that their money is exhausted and pushes them out into the street, or, as an exceptional favour, allows them to sleep off the effects of the poison upon the tap-room floor. This is called, in bush vernacular, "a spree." As soon as his "spree" is over, the bushman will return to his work, and for the next six months touch nothing stronger than tea. What makes these orgies the more injurious is the poison supplied to the unfortunate men. Provided that it burns the palate and intoxicates the brain, the bushman is not very particular as to the taste of his drink, and no stuff is too vile to use for the laudable purpose of emptying his pockets. In the absence of other liquor he has been known to "spree" on "Pain-killer." The intelligent reader may perhaps infer from these remarks that the bush publican is not, as a rule, a model member of the commonwealth, and in this surmise he would be tolerably correct. Yet the rule is not without its exception, and many bush hotels are conducted as decently and honestly as need be. Bush publicans sometimes make large fortunes, turn squatters, and become eminently respectable members of society; but more often they themselves succumb to the vice upon which they have thrived, and die in poverty.

*From "Daily Life in the Bush", O. Sawyer, in* Cassell's Picturesque Australasia, *ed. E. E. Morris*

Pething a Bullock

Amongst other things ordered was a five-hundred-gallon tank, and Mr. Bibulus, thinking it a pity that this should come up empty, gave orders that it should be filled with rum. On its arrival, a general orgie of all hands took place, until the liquor was exhausted. A friend of the writer chanced to call at the station the day after its arrival, and was greeted by the proprietor—"Oh, come in, Mr. Blank —come in. Delighted to see you! I'm drunk, my brother's drunk, the overseer's drunk, and all the men are drunk; and still the station pays!" Generally, however, the squatter, at all events when at home and at work, is a most sober and temperate man, rising early, and generally eating the bread of carefulness; for in spite of the boast of the hero of the above story, backed by the popular idea of the enormous profits of squatting, it is only by the greatest energy, care, and economy, that station properties nowadays can be got to pay, and even then the risk from drought and other causes is considerable.

*From "Daily Life in the Bush", O. Sawyer in* Cassell's Picturesque Australasia, *ed. E. E. Morris.*

View of Brisbane

The Ellis brothers, known as the three Honourables, though neither remittance men nor impostors, succeeded in winning considerable notoriety during their meteoric career in Central Queensland.

Arriving from "the old country" with one hundred thousand pounds between them they purchased a station in the Peak Downs district and set about getting rid of their combined bank-roll as speedily as possible. Amazing stories were told of their care-free hospitality, their eccentric behaviour, and their complete disregard for business principles.

As all were equal partners in the venture any one of the brothers engaged or discharged employees without bothering to consult the others—a circumstance to which the Weary Willies of the west soon woke up. Having seen the Honourable George or the Honourable John ride away from the homestead the artless swagman would trudge along to the station and announce to the Honourable James that he'd just been fired by one of the brothers aforementioned and had come to get his cheque.

"Very well, my man," the Honourable James would reply. "How long have you been working here, and what wages were you getting?"

"My man" would put the figures as high as he dared, probably volunteering the information that he'd had some tobacco and matches from the store, just to make it look good. After a square feed he'd wander on his way with his tucker-bag filled and a cheque in his pocket to reward him for the toil he hadn't done.

In those days all station supplies came by horse-team or bullock-team from Rockhampton—over two hundred miles away. Roads were practically non-existent, so it was advisable to make full use of every available inch of space on the wagons. The Ellis brothers had ordered further supplies to be sent to the station, and part of one proposed load consisted of a square four hundred gallon iron tank. In view of the space it would take up the agents thought it would be a good idea to fill it with goods of some kind.

They wrote to the three Honourables with a suggestion to that effect, and asked for instructions as to the class of goods with which it should be filled. Back came the reply: "Splendid idea. Fill it with rum."

The order was filled. So was the tank; and when, in due course, the tank arrived at its destination, so were the three Honourables and all those who chanced along to enjoy their hospitality.

Though the brothers appear to have got on well together during their sojourn in Queensland they had their little differences, but these were settled without undue rancour. The Honourable John was extremely fond of riding and shooting. Naturally he was the possessor of a very fine horse, and an equally fine gun. The Honourable George was rather fond of kangaroo-hunting. He, too, had a very fine horse and a magnificent dog (a staghound) *and* a very fine gun.

One morning, when the Honourable John was mounting his very fine horse the magnificent dog came frisking around. The startled horse reared and plunged, depositing his honourable master none too gently in the dust. The fallen aristocrat arose smartly and scanned his attire with disfavour. To the waiting menial he gave an order.

"Bring me my gun!" he said curtly.

The gun was brought. The Honourable John raised it to his shoulder with practised ease and shot the dog stone-dead. Some little time later the Honourable George arrived.

"Who shot my dog?" he asked, indignantly.

"The Honourable John, sir," said the faithful servitor.

"Oh! . . . He *did* . . . Did he? . . . Bring me my gun" he said, in tones as curt as those of his honourable brother. The gun was brought. The Honourable George sauntered around to the stables where his brother's very fine horse was gazing out over the paddocks. The Honourable George raised his gun . . . with practised ease.

BANG ! ! ! ! ! Down went the horse. The Honourable John rushed forth.

"Who shot my horse?" he demanded, truculently.

"I *did!*" said the Honourable George, with a languid air. "You shot my dog. I shot your horse."

The Honourable John thought it over.

"That's fair enough," he said. "Let's have a drink."

The Honourable James also had a hobby, of a different nature. He was something of a naturalist, and specialized in reptiles, especially snakes. He could handle them with the facility and confidence of a professional snake-charmer. Nothing pleased him better than to potter around with an assortment of venomous reptiles in his capacious pockets.

After a year or so the eccentricities of the brothers had seriously depleted the one hundred thousand pounds they'd started with, and bank officials were displaying signs of reluctance when asked to cash their cheques. In Rockhampton, when one presented by the Honourable James seemed likely to bounce, he sought an interview with the manager.

Carefully seating himself in a strategic position near the door, the *only* door, he presented the cheque. The manager eyed it distastefully, and cleared his throat.

"I'm afraid, Mr. Ellis," he began. Then he looked up and realized he was speaking the simple truth. His visitor was fondling a large and venomous-looking serpent. He was also smiling hopefully.

The manager swallowed hastily, and cleared his throat once more.

"Er . . . certainly, Mr. Ellis!" he gulped, as he hastily O.K.-ed the cheque.

Not a great while after that the station changed hands, and the three Honourables, who had done so much to entertain their neighbours, faded, for ever, from the scene.

*From* Roll the Summers Back, *Joseph Porter ("Spinifex")*

*Mustering cattle (engraving from* Australasian Sketcher, *21 February 1874)*

It is high noon at Wilcannia. A yellow haze stretches away to the burnished horizon, and on the plains clouds of dust rise, telling of sheep on the march. Making towards the River Darling is a herd of nine hundred cattle. They have come a thousand miles over the plains of Thargomindah and beyond in Queensland. They must cross the river. The cattle seemed to know that a stranger was at hand, and began to stamp impatiently. One broke out of the bunch, and came over to inspect the alien. Others moved wildly, and threatened a stampede. But at that moment the horses were sent ahead to lead the cattle to the river, and on they all go. But on the very banks of the stream they begin to ring.

There is danger in this. Should they ring in the river hundreds will be drowned. Round and round they go in a painful centripetal motion, a wheel of horns upon a heaving base of brown and red and grey. But the stock-riders force their horses in, and break the ring, with many a sharp call, and snap of whip, and sharp expletive. Then into the river the cattle plunge, following the horses, first with a tremor and snort of fear, and then with a rush. It was a forest of horns, where shaggy manes tumbled and tossed in the swift current; a mêlée of floating heads, warring and waggling. The current at first carries them down. Then they begin to ring again. The spectator is thrilled by the struggle. The stock-riders thrust in, and the stock-whip cuts the air like a knife. Some steers floated down, but struck out bravely and were caught in the trees on the bank, where they were held fast, for the water was flowing among the branches of the gums. A forlorn hope at last made straight after the horses for the shore. They ranged into line; they swam shoulder to shoulder; their heads became motionless; they put forth their utmost strength; they reached the solid ground. And after that, in phalanxes the herd fought its way across, and the great feat of the long travel was over. The Darling was crossed, and with only half a dozen cattle lost.

"Thus far into the bowels of the land
Have we marched on without impediment,"

said a lithe-limbed stock-rider, bearded like a pard, as he lit his pipe—the bushman's only friend. And this was once a Fellow of St. John's, Cambridge. Such are the fortunes of the gentle as the rude. And there, beside a clump of sandal-trees, they cooked their chops, and made their damper, and drank their quart-pot tea, and the world went very well then, whatever its errant course had been.

*From* Round the Compass in Australia, *Gilbert Parker*

At the present date of writing [1892, Ed.] Australia may be fairly said to be in a flourishing condition. The indications of increasing prosperity and a growing spirit of independence are marked and unmistakable.

Formerly we used to import all our criminals from England, but now we have developed our resources and manufacture our own, and competent judges—in ermine, too—have pronounced the manufactured equal, and in some points superior, to the imported article. If further evidence of an advancing civilization be required, it can be produced without difficulty.

We shall for a moment drop our own style of writing and adopt that of Messrs. Allan and Cornwall, authors of the elementary geography from which our earlier impressions of Australia and most other countries were imbibed. Their style is pleasing and familiar, and, if deficient in the gaudier flowers of the garden of literature, is at least concise, perspicuous, and to the point. Thus:—

*Exports.*—Wool, hides, tallow, gold, silver, copper, Colonial produce (whatever that is), cricketers, parvenus, and *delirium tremens.*

*Imports.*—Wine, beer, spirits and tobacco, machinery, manufactured goods of every description, soap, sugar, small-pox, Ethiopian serenaders and servant girls, lords, laundresses, fools of families, authors, actors, poets, pianos, old maids, dudes, missionaries and Chinamen.

*Flora and Fauna.*—We may as well admit candidly that we don't know anything about flora—scarcely enough to tell a cabbage rose from a cabbage-tree hat.

*Fauna.*—Kangaroos, wallabies, opossums, insurance agents, wombats and C.M.G.'s, dingoes, native bears, aboriginals, editors, sharebrokers and syndicates.

*Religion.*—Marsupial. That is, most of us have pouches and a wonderful knack of keeping them well lined.

*Climate.*—But the elementary geographies scarcely do justice to the Australian climate. Allan and Cornwall never lived in a country where it is necessary to pile a couple of thermometers one on top of another in order to ascertain how many degrees of fiery torture, incandescent misery, and mosquito-bite go to make up a cubic foot of average shade.

There is a good deal of climate in Australia; as much, perhaps, to the square mile as in any country in the world. There is considerable variety of it, too. You can have a foot of snow in the streets of Kiandra in July; the damp, foggy drizzle of Devon in Sydney; an Italian sirocco in Melbourne or Sandhurst, Vic.; an African sand storm, a London fog, Egyptian darkness, and the "glorious light of the Southern constellations" (with the Aurora Australis and the electric light thrown in) if you only choose the right times and localities in your search for them. Oh! and we forgot—thunder of the best Olympian quality, chain-lightning that would illuminate the Pit of Acheron, and hailstones bigger than bantams' eggs.

If this is not a climatic menu sufficiently varied to satisfy the most exacting meteorological enthusiast, he must get a climate built for him. We can't cater for persons whose meteorological tastes are morbid.

The changes of temperature are rapid and startling till you get used to them. You go out in the morning "a thing of beauty" in your pith helmet,

*Gully at Woolongong (Skinner Prout, from* Australia, *ed. Edwin Carton Booth)*

white pants, canvas shoes and a gossamer coat of airy nothingness—thermometer 103 in the shade. In three hours the wind has veered to the South, a yellow haze rises slowly from the horizon in that direction, a "southerly buster" is coming up. The air darkens. The shadow of the black wings of the storm spreads and spreads, and with a howl, a rush, and an icy, eddying swirl it is upon you. In two minutes your face is black with impalpable dust; your eyes, nostrils, and pockets hold sand enough to start a miniature Sahara; while shingles, sheets of galvanized roofing iron, literally "out on the loose," and other unconsidered trifles float on the wings of the shrieking blast at a mean rate of 60 miles an hour. Then comes the rain. The pith hat speedily becomes pulp, the shoes paste, and your airy costume tightens round you like a fish skin. The freezing blast eats into your flesh and coils itself in an icy embrace round your spinal cord, and the bonier portions of your anatomy, until, with shivering limbs and a heart heavy with curses, which your chattering teeth cut into infinitesimal and ineffectual fragments, you yearn to creep inside a Newfoundland dog or beneath the wings of an archangel, or anywhere else that is woolly, and warm, and sheltered.

But it is on the limitless salt-bush plains and arid sand-hills that lie in the more central portions of this vast continent that the Australian climate "comes out of its shell," so to speak, and asserts itself in a way that flying European visitors, who come to us for a few months, interview a reporter or two, excursionize a hundred miles or so inland, and depart to criticize the hash of our restaurants and the political principles of our legislators, have little idea of. It is there that the thermometer sometimes gets up on its hind legs and reaches out its mercurial paw till it touches 120 degrees of Fahrenheit in the shade; and there it is that the swarthy stockman, hobbling out his parboiled Bucephalus, and stretching himself for a noontide siesta in the meagre shadow of a stunted myall, hath his mental vision tantalized by a delusive mirage of iced "shandy-gaff" and whisky squash; and the far central editor obtains a foretaste of that still warmer climate whither his tendency to lie in his local column, to vacillate in his political one, and to print impossible snake stories among his general news will infallibly lead him.

And there it is, but less frequently than formerly, that the ill-starred traveller who has lost track and bearings, heart and hope, in that waterless desert realizes all that is implied in the simple phrase, "lost in the bush," and, with starting eye-balls and swollen, blackened tongue gasps his last prayer, or curse, and dies. A little while, and crow and wild dog, ant and eagle-hawk will have completed their foul rites, leaving but a pile of bleached bones and a name scrawled on a battered pannikin. Sad record of an awful doom. A startling sermon for the reckless "boundary rider" who perchance may find them—an unwritten epitaph, eloquent of a fate that may be his own. The carrion crows of Central Australia could prate strange truths if their gory beaks could give the ghastly chronicle to the world.

But Australia to-day is not by any means the Australia of Governor Phillip's time; it even differs widely from the Australia of twenty years or so ago, and the romance of the early days of pioneer squatting, gold discovery, and bushranging is as dead as the chivalry of the middle ages. The pastoralist and the miner—twin pioneers of civilization whom no obstacle can stay, no dangers daunt—have won foot after foot, mile after mile, from the unknown desert, doing well and thoroughly the first labours of exploration and settlement—preliminary processes by which the wilderness is hereafter to be induced to blossom as the rose.

Even the Barrier Ranges (a chain of low sand-hills and stony ridges near the western border of New South Wales), which were to the early settler as the Hartz mountains to the German charcoal-burner—a terra incognita of myth and mystery, thirst and terror—have been turned upside down and inside out by prospectors, and are now haunted by silver mining syndicates instead of gnomes and spirits; and the only demon to be dreaded, and, if possible, avoided, is the fiend who has "scrip" to sell and wants to "lay you on to a good thing." Truly the conditions of life in Australia have changed mightily.

It is no longer possible to start a sheep-station with two gallons of rum, a bag of flour, twenty flukey merinoes and a wall-eyed black gin shepherdess, and sell out in five years for twenty thousand pounds.

The modern method is to start with a capital of twenty thousand pounds, and, after three dry seasons, find that your earthly possessions consist of an unliquidatable bank overdraft and a four-bushel bag full of unpaid station accounts.

Bushranging is no longer recognized as a profession; cricket and football have superseded

*The squatter's first home ( I. W. G., hand-coloured lithograph, from* Scenes in the Bush of Australia, *by a Squatter)*

throat-cutting as a recreation; and diggers do not, habitually, play poker with revolvers in their belts and twelve-inch bowies in their fists.

The modern station hand wears a coat, often a collar, and frequently canters into town for the mail in a pair of elastic-side boots and a necktie!

O tempora! O mores! the Australian stockman no longer wears a red shirt, cabbage-tree hat, crimson sash, and boots reaching higher than his aspirations after immortal glory; but these articles (essential to complete the costume of the typical stockman of the past) have taken such a hold upon the minds of men that no artist, in this country or out of it, can be induced by bribes or threats to depict one without them.

The bullock-driver, another typical Australian, popularly supposed to consist principally of boots, beard and blasphemy, has been so toned down as to have become almost useless for the purposes of sensational anecdote or blood-curdling melodrama. The boots have disappeared, or nearly so, but, take heart, my brother, the profanity remains, and time, which has decapitated his boots and shortened his beard, has but mellowed his curse and enlarged his vocabulary. We once knew a member of Parliament—no, not in this country—who was a painstaking liar and a gifted blasphemer. His curses meandered along in a rippling rivulet of dreamy profanity and then "broke from the off" with sudden and deadly precision, very much in Jonah's best style on a wet wicket—we mean when denouncing a particularly hard-shelled and unrepentant Ninevite—but, with all the advantages of natural ability and careful training, he never attained the *élan*, the fervour, the inspired fluency of the apostle of green-hide.

The genuine black soil "bull-puncher" with his team well bogged in a bad crossing can hold his own with the mate of a Yankee whaler and curse a Thames bargee into—despondency and an early grave.

This is not flattery. It is but a just and simple tribute to his merits.

The changes referred to are, however, but a few of the most noticeable. Scarcely anything is done in the way it used to be. Even sheep are shorn by machinery, and there are so many new ways of swindling one's fellow-travellers through this vale of tears that we feel we are behind the age in choosing such an old-fashioned method of doing it as writing a book.

*From the Introduction to* Ironbark Chips and Stockwhip Cracks, *G. H. Gibson ("Ironbark")*

" . . . But let us change the subject."

"Yes; do," said Cooper cordially. "I hate argyin'. Fust go off, it 's all friendly;—'Yes, my good man.'—'No, my dear feller.'—'Don't run away with that idear.'—'You 're puttin' the boot on the wrong foot.'—'You got the wrong pig by the tail.'—an' so on, as sweet as sugar. But by-'n'-by it 's 'To (sheol) with you for a (adj.) fool!'—'You 're a (adj.) liar!'—'Who the (adj. sheol) do you think you 're talking to?'—an' one word fetchin' on another till it grows into a sort o' unpleasantness."

*From* Such Is Life, *Joseph Furphy ("Tom Collins")*

Hail our Australia,
Girt by the sea;
Sons of the summerland,
Brothers are we.
Ring out our battlecry!
March at its call,
"Each for the Commonwealth,
God for us all."

*From "Federation"*, The Federation Cantata, *G. F. Chinner.*

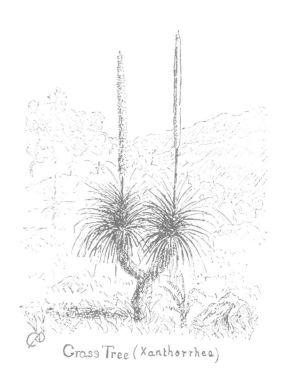

Grass Tree (Xanthorrhea)

# Section 11

# Traditional Songs

"Whilst we are sitting here singing folksongs in our Folksong Club, the folk are somewhere else—singing something different."

*Tony Davis*

"This is what a folksong realy is the folks composes there own songs about there own lifes and there home folks that live around them."

*Aunt Molly Jackson (American singer)*

# Introduction to Section II

This book is not intended as a work of scholarship, but rather as an introduction to song, story and history of our country. Consequently I have not included fragments of songs which are interesting in that they are versions. The songs included are songs that are designed for performance rather than for purposes of scholarship. There are many excellent books available for those who wish to study the growth and development through field collection. Probably the best one of all is the *Overlander Song Book* of Ron Edwards. With the possible exception of John Meredith, my brother Alan Scott, and Wendy Lowenstein, Ron has done more actual field collection than anybody else in Australia, and he has continually published his results. At the end of this section I include a bibliography of titles that the earnest student should acquire for his own library if possible, or seek in libraries.

The songs herein are those which have been performed at the Folk Centre in Brisbane for many years. Many of them were collected by members of the Queensland Folklore Society, or members of the old Moreton Bay Bush Music Club. The two major collectors were Stan Arthur and Bob Michell, though John Callaghan, Garry Tooth, Evan Mathieson and myself helped in one way and another from time to time. The accent on our collecting has always been for propagation of the songs, rather than merely stockpiling of material, so most of them have been performed widely at social events or at the Folk Centre, which is the oldest existing folk coffee shop in Australia (having been opened in 1964) and which still operates three nights a week in Brisbane—largely due to the dedication of Stan Arthur and his wife, Kath.

So these versions are composite in many cases, versions smoothed and polished by actual performance, and should not be regarded as actual collected items. A glance at the notes of "The Canecutter's Lament" will show how an actual field collection became modified to suit public performance, with some surprising results. In other words, these are songs that should be sung, and are ready to be sung, with many of the awkwardnesses of diction on the part of the (often elderly) informant smoothed and rounded by the substitutions made during actual performance. I have mentioned some specific cases of interpolation in notes to various songs for students of such things. These songs are intended for Everyman, not the small number of people who have an academic interest in the music.

The songs are arranged alphabetically by title rather than grouped by trade or period of composition.

*The emigrants—a story without words (from an early illustrated paper)*

What is a folksong, anyway? I once heard them described as a song everyone knew a bit of, and the endless variations described as the result of a lot of blokes with bad memories singing to one another. Let us not become too serious about this pleasant pastime of singing old songs. The blokes who wrote them were concerned with having a good sing; entertainment, in other words. It is a fact that folksongs flourish in an atmosphere where people are compelled to provide their own entertainment. Hence the cheerful bawling of bawdy, frankly ironic songs that was a feature of almost every wet canteen during the war years. Mention the words "One-Eyed Reilly" or "The Harlot of Jerusalem" to any ex-serviceman and you'll get a grin and probably a quote despite the years that have elapsed.

I think that the main thing is that the good songs will be remembered and the bad ones will die, and who the hell cares which is which at the moment. It's just that the purists can't abide a composer of topical songs calling them "folksongs" when they are not strictly so. But where can one draw the line about what will remain and what will wither? I am sure that in a hundred years time, blokes sitting round a keg late at night will still sing the "Derby Ram" and "Down Mobile" and "The Fireship" and "Crusher Bailey". At least I hope so.

*Bill Scott in a letter to* Australian Tradition, *November 1964*

The broadside tradition still exists among bushmen in regard to the "giving" of songs, though, of course, these broadsides are not printed; and this is often forgotten when the business of "oral transmission" is mentioned. It is surprising how many old-timers still have yellowing, handwritten copies of verses that they always keep with

*Concert on the diggings (engraving from* Illustrated Sydney News*)*

their belongings, and these verses, when being "given" to someone, are often given in written form, either the original paper, or a copy.

Somewhere or other a man will compose a song or a recitation, and if it is a fairly long one, he will often write it down. When he decides to give it to someone he will simply give them the broadside rather than having to repeat the words over and over till the other has them parrot fashion. The tune, of course, will have to be memorized.

Once the recipient has committed the words to memory, the paper is of no further use, and so when he in turn wants to pass the song on, he may let the other copy out the words, or even give him his own copy. In time a song may pass through many hands this way, but even though it is in written form, it will still be getting altered, as when a singer makes a new copy from his own memory, having given his written copy away.

I recently received one of these broadsides on paper that was so old and brittle that it was almost falling to pieces where it was folded. The verses had been written with a blunt pencil, one line running after the other across the page, so that it looked like unpunctuated prose rather than verse. I spent some time sorting it back into recognizable form, and for a short time thought I had come across a new ballad.

Then I realized that what I actually had was a poem of Ogilvie's, but one altered almost to the point of being a new work. In the course of being copied and re-copied in the light of stockmen's fires, all the unnecessary trimmings had been discarded, words had been altered, and the end result told the same story in about a third of the space, and probably told it just as well.

This passing around of copies helps explain the number of different tunes that come to be attached to a particular set of words. A recent informant put it this way: "Sometimes I'd be given a copy of a song, and sometimes the bloke had such a bad voice I wouldn't know what tune he was using, so I'd just put on a tune of my own."

A similar attitude was shown by another old-timer, who said, "I'll give you a good song now. I can't remember the tune, but here's how it goes!" Then he sang it straight through, using a tune from his memory that happened to fit the words.

The general attitude seems to be that the tune is of no great account, the story or sentiment being the important thing. This is borne out by another informant who said, "If a bloke had a crook singing voice, or couldn't remember the tune, he would always recite the songs." In this way, a song could lose its tune while being passed on, and have another one grafted on by a later recipient.

As I said earlier, the singer was quite un-selfconscious about any ethics involved in these alterations; he learnt a song in order to entertain himself and his mates, not with any idea of preserving historical relics. If he was a singer, he would put tunes to poems, if he preferred re-citations he would drop the tunes from songs.

*From "Songs and Singers", Ron Edwards,* National Folk, *Number 33*

# Across the Western Plains

Chorus

*This is an Australian version of an old English seafaring song called "Across the Western Ocean". In both cases the singer has spent his accumulated wages on a spree, and is compelled to seek employment once again. Several books have versions of it; the closest to the original English detailing of how the singer lost his possessions is in the* Overlander Song Book. *The words we sing are very close to the composite version in* Old Bush Songs, *and these words were almost the same as those used by A. L. Lloyd on a recording he made for Wattle Records in the 1950s.*

Well, I'm stiff and stony broke, and I've parted
    with my moke
And the sky is looking black as flaming thunder.
So's the Boss of the shanty, too, for I haven't
    got a sou,
That's the way you're treated when you're out
    and under.

*Chorus*
So it's oh for my grog, the jolly, jolly grog.
Hooray for the beer and tobacco.
I've spent all my tin in this shanty drinking gin,
Now across the western plains I must wander.

I'm crook in the head for I haven't been to bed
Since first I hit this shanty with my plunder.
I see centipedes and snakes, and I'm full of aches
    and shakes,
So I'd better make a push out over yonder.

*Chorus*

So I'll take to the Old Man Plain, criss-cross it
    once again
Until the track my eye no longer sees, boys.
For my beer and brandy brain seeks balmy sleep
    in vain,
And I feel as though I've got the Darling Pea[1],
    boys.

*Chorus*

Oh, repentance brings reproof, so I sadly pad
    the hoof.
All day I see the mirage of the trees.
When my journey's at an end I will reach the river
    bend
And hear again the sighing of the breeze.

*Chorus*

Then hang the jolly grog, the hocussed shanty
    grog[2]
And the beer that's loaded with tobacco.
Working humour I am in, and I'll stick the peg
    right in
And settle down again to some hard yakka.

*1. The Darling Pea is a bush that grows on the western plains country, known in Queensland as Poison Pea. Animals grazing on it have their vision affected, and often die.*
*2. The "hocussed shanty grog"; Mick Ryan told me once about a pub near the Parragundy Gate on the Queensland-New South Wales border that was called "The Stiffeners" because the publican actually poisoned some travellers with his homebrew. His explanation was that he usually tried the mixture on an Aborigine first, but this time the cheque men had arrived before he'd had a chance to test it, for the local tribe was away on walkabout.*

Scene on a Bush Road.

# Another Fall of Rain

*John Neilson, father of the much better known John Shaw Neilson, was a versifier of some talent, winning prizes at the occasional eisteddfod for his poems. The Brisbane author James Devaney, in his book on the younger poet, tells how the father would occasionally go off to shear and do other bush work to keep the selection going and the grocer's bills paid when the family were trying to farm in the western district of Victoria. This appears to be his only poem that is still extant as a song, for it was fitted to the tune brought from America, "The Little Old Log Cabin in the Lane", a tune that was used a lot for parodies of the original words as well as other sets of words. Another Australian song in this book to use this tune is "The Freehold on the Plain". A number of collectors have found versions of the song. John Meredith collected one from Leo Dixon in Sydney and Earl Loughlin knew it, or parts of it. Ron Edwards tracked down the original poem, and gives two additional verses in the Overlander Song Book.*

The weather had been sultry for a fortnight's
    time or more,
And the shearers had been driving might and main,
And some had got the century that never
    had before
But now all hands were wishing for the rain

*Chorus*

For the Boss is getting rusty and the ringer's
    caving in,
His bandaged wrist is aching with the pain,
And the second man, I fear, will make it hot for him
Unless we have another fall of rain.

A few had taken quarters and were coiling
    in their bunks
When we shore the six-tooth wethers from
    the plain.
And if the sheep get harder then a few more men
    will funk
Unless we get another fall of rain.

*Chorus*

But the sky is clouding over, and the thunder's
    muttering loud,
And the clouds are driving eastward o'er the plain,
And I see the lightning flashing from the edge
    of yon black cloud
And I hear the gentle patter of the rain.

*Chorus*

So lads, put on your stoppers, and let us to the hut.
We'll gather round and have a friendly game.
While some are playing music, and some play
    ante-up,
And some are gazing outward at the rain.

*Chorus*

But now the rain is over, let the pressers spin
    the screw,
Let the teamsters back their wagons in again.
And we'll block the classer's table with the way we
    put them through,
For everything is merry since the rain.

*Final chorus*

And the Boss, he won't be rusty when his sheep
    they are all shorn,
And the ringer's wrist won't ache much
    with the pain
Of pocketing a season's cheque for fifty pounds
    or more,
And the second man will press him hard again.

*Shearers will not shear wet sheep, of course. In fact, Duke Tritton says they sometimes voted sheep "wet" in dry weather, for the same reason as the men in this song were praying for rain, to get a spell from hard shearing. Six-tooth wethers were hard going, as were rams. I think the best rendition of this song I have ever heard was Garry Tooth's. He used to join two verses together between choruses, and it speeded up the song considerably.*

At the Dam.

# Augathella Station (Ladies of Brisbane)

*There is little doubt that the original set of words for this song were written by Saul Mendelsohn, a storekeeper at Nanango, but the words and melody suffered a bush change and the original chanty tune, "Ladies of Spain", was replaced by this more haunting melody. The words changed and were more polished. The track described was the old stock road from the Burnett to the Brisbane saleyards, and Bob Michell and others have retraced the route. The framework of the old stone house is still standing, and all the other places mentioned have been identified. John Manifold discusses this song in his book,* Who Wrote the Ballads? *It is a favourite among Brisbane singers.*

Farewell and adieu to you, Brisbane Ladies,
Farewell and adieu to the girls of Toowong.
We've sold all our cattle and cannot now linger
But we hope we'll be seeing you again before long.

*Chorus*
We'll rant and we'll roar like true Queensland drovers,
We'll rant and we'll roar as onward we push,
Until we return to the Augathella Station
But it's flaming dry going through the old Queensland bush.

The first camp we'll make, we shall call it the Quartpot,
Caboolture, then Kilcoy and Colinton's hut,
We'll pull up at the Stonehouse, Bob Williamson's paddock,
And early next morning we'll cross the Blackbutt.
Then it's on to Taromeo and Yarraman Creek, lads,
It's there we will make a fine camp for the day,
Where the water and grass are both plenty and sweet, lads,
And maybe we'll butcher a fat little stray.
*Chorus*

Then it's on to Nanango, that hardbitten township,
Where the out-of-work station hands sit
   in the dust,
And the shearers get shorn by old Timms,
   the contractor,
And I wouldn't go past there but I flaming
   well must.
The girls at Toomancie, they look so entrancing,
Like young bawling heifers, they're out for
   their fun,
To the waltz, the polka, and all kinds of dancing,
To the old concertina of Hen-er-ee Gunn.

*Chorus*

Then fill up your glasses, let's drink to the lasses,
We'll drink this town dry, then farewell to you all.
And when we return once again from Augathella
We'll always be willing to pay you a call.

*Chorus*

*A back blocks post office (engraving from* Australasia Illustrated, *ed. Andrew Garran)*

# The Banks of the Condamine

*There are almost as many versions of this song as there are of the "Wild Colonial Boy" and "The Old Bark Hut". We usually sing this version as a duet, male and female voices alternating. A Women's Lib. friend of mine calls it "the M.C.P. song"! But life was different in those days, and shearers went out into the wilds to make a living for the family, much as sailors have always had to do.*

Male:
Oh, hark the dogs are barking love, I can no
 longer stay,
The men are all gone mustering and it is nearly day.
I must be off by the morning light before
 the sun doth shine
To meet the Sydney shearers on the banks
 of the Condamine.

Female:
Oh, Willy, dearest Willy! Please let me go with you.
I'll cut off all my auburn fringe and be a shearer too!
I'll cook and count your tally, love, while
 ringer—O you shine
And I'll wash your greasy moleskins on the banks
 of the Condamine.

Male:
Oh, Nancy, dearest Nancy, with me you can not go.
The squatter has given orders, love, no woman
 may do so.
Your delicate constitution is not equal unto mine
For to stand the constant tigering on the banks
 of the Condamine.

Female:
Oh Willy, dearest Willy, then stay at home
  with me.
We'll take up a selection and a farmer's wife I'll be.
I'll help you husk the corn love, and cook
  your meals so fine,
You'll forget the ram-stag mutton on the banks
  of the Condamine.

Male:
Oh when the shearing's over, I'll make of you
  my wife.
I'll get a boundary rider's job and settle down
  for life.
And when the day is over and the evening star
  doth shine
We'll talk about those bygone days on the banks
  of the Condamine.
So Nancy, dearest Nancy, please do not hold
  me back,
Out there the boys are waiting and I must be
  on the track.
So here's a goodbye kiss love, back home I
  will incline
When we've shore the last of the jumbucks
  on the banks of the Condamine.

*There are numerous variations, as I said. In some
epics, the man is a horse-breaker; in others, such as the
one John Meredith collected in Sydney, the action
took place on the "Banks of the Riverine". But all
cases agree that the lady is prepared to cut her long
hair and assume men's clothing to go along, but is
frustrated and forced to remain at home.*

*Australian shepherd's hut (Skinner Prout, from* Australia, *ed. Edwin Carton Booth)*

# Bellbottom Trousers

*I learned a version of this song while serving in the Navy in the early 1940s, and it was printed in the journal* Singabout *in the issue of Vol. 3, number 1. However, when I was singing with the Moreton Bay Bushwackers' Band in the late 1950s, Stan Arthur taught me a better version he had learned while on loan to the British Navy about the same time I was learning mine in Australian waters. His is obviously closer to the original, and is much more interesting musically, so that was the one we adopted for performance, and it is the one given here.*

I was a serving maid, down in Drury Lane,
My mistress she was good to me, my master was
   the same.

When along came a sailor, ashore on liberty,
And oh, to my woe, he took liberties with me.
*Chorus*
Bellbottom trousers, coat of navy blue,
And let him climb the rigging like his daddy
   used to do.
Bellbottom trousers, coat of navy blue,
Oh! Let him climb the rigging like his daddy
   used to do.

It was at a ball I met him, he asked me for a dance.
I knew he was a sailor by the way he wore his pants.
His shoes was nicely polished and his hair
   was neatly combed.
After the ball was over he asked to see me home.
*Chorus*
He asked me for a candle to light his way to bed,
He asked me for a handkerchief to tie
   around his head.
And I, like a silly girl, and thinking it no harm,
Jumped into bed beside him to keep
   the sailor warm.
*Chorus*

He may have been a sailor but that night he
　　went to town,
He laid me on the bed there till my blue eyes
　　turned to brown.
Then early next morning, the sailor he awoke,
And reaching in his pocket, pulled out a two
　　pound note.

*Chorus*

He said, "Take this, my darling, for the damage
　　I have done,
Soon you will be having a daughter or a son.
If it be a daughter, just bounce her on your knee.
If it be a son, send the bastard off to sea."

*Chorus*

So all you young maidens, a warning take by me,
Don't ever let a sailor an inch above your knee.
For I trusted one once, and he took liberties
And left me with a pair of brats to jounce
　　upon my knee.

*Chorus*

*A version of this song has reached the hit parade since I learned it, and I cannot say how surprised I was to hear it from a passing transistor radio for the first time. The impact was much the same as when I first heard a group of children singing a cleaned-up version of the "One-Eyed Reilly". Many bawdy songs of considerable antiquity have been given a bit of a scrub-up and put on to the popular market, usually with considerable success. Ah, well, as General William Booth is reported to have said, "Why should the Devil have all the good tunes?"*

The "Lady Nelson" entering Port Phillip (engraving from
Picturesque Atlas of Australasia, *ed. Andrew Garran*)

# Bill Brinks

*A. L. Lloyd sang a version of this song, called "Bluey Brink", on one of his early Wattle recordings. This one, with a different and I think better tune, was collected by Stan Arthur from a seafaring person in a bar in Brisbane.*

There once was a shearer by name Billy Brinks,
A devil for work and a demon for drink.

He could shear his two hundred a day without fear,
And drink without winking four gallons of beer.
*Chorus*
He stayed far too late and he came far too soon,
At morning, at evening, at night and at noon.

Now, Jimmy the barman who served out the drink,
He hated the sight of this here Billy Brinks.
With his shouting and fighting and screaming
   for grog,
And his whiskers stuck out like an old native dog.
*Chorus*

*In the men's hut (engraving from an early illustrated paper)*

One morning as Jimmy was cleaning the bar
With sulphuric acid he kept in a jar,
Old Billy came yelling and bawling with thirst,
Saying, "Come along, Jimmy, and serve
   to me first!"

*Chorus*

Now it's not down in history, not down in print,
But that shearer drank acid with never a wink.
Saying, "That's the stuff, Jimmy, Lord strike me
   stone dead,
It'll make me the ringer of Stevenson's shed!"

*Chorus*

Now all the long day as he served out the beer
Poor Jimmy was shaking with trouble and fear,
Too worried to argue, too anxious to fight,
Thinking the shearer a corpse in his fright.

*Chorus*

But early next morning when he opened the door,
In came old Billy, and asking for more.
With his eyebrows all singed and his whiskers
   deranged,
And holes in his hide like a dog with the mange.

*Chorus*

Said the barman, "And how did you like
   the new stuff?"
Said Billy, "It's fine but I've not had enough.
It gives me great courage to shear and to fight,
But why does that stuff set my whiskers alight?

*Chorus*

"I thought I knew drink, but I must have
   been wrong.
That stuff that you gave me was properly strong.
It sets me to coughing, and you know I'm no liar,
But every cough sets me whiskers on fire!"

*Chorus*

# Billy Sheehan

*My brother David, who is a railwayman, sent me the words of this song from Hughenden in the middle 1950s, I think. It is, of course, a parody of an American song called "Steamboat Bill", which itself used the tune of the American railroad ballad, "Casey Jones". (Incidentally, "Casey" was the nickname of the driver involved, and was derived from his home town, Kansas City, or K.C. for short.) That is beside the point. Billy Sheehan's story follows closely the story of Steamboat Bill, even to the bet in mid-air; and some of my older readers may remember the old 78 recording that was popular in the late 1930s. Billy Sheehan could only have been a Queenslander; C 16 locos were early on the scene and wore themselves out in shunting yards round the State after larger and more powerful locos were introduced for the distance hauls. There was still a C 17 "tanky" shunting in the Roma Street and Mayne Junction yards in the 1930s, though.*

Grass Tree (Xanthorrhea)

Out on the forty-pound rails[1] steamed a C 16,
Commanded by its driver, Mister Billy Sheehan,
The G.M.[2] gave him orders on the strict Q.T.
To run a faster schedule than the Spirit of P.[3]
"Keep that regulator open, watch the black
   smoke roll,
Pile on all the floorboards if we run out of coal.
If we don't break that record," Billy said
   to his mate,
"Send my memos care of Peter at the Golden Gate

*Chorus*
Billy Sheehan, ran a faster schedule,
Billy Sheehan, a mighty man was he;
Billy Sheehan, ran a faster schedule,
Out to break the record of the Spirit of P.

His fireman was a punting boy from Narrabeen,
He said, "I'll lay the odds against the C 16."
Billy flashed a roll of notes that was a bear,
The boiler then exploded, blew them both
   in the air.
Said Billy to his fireman as they left the wreck,
"I dunno where we're going but we're neck
   and neck!"
The fireman then said "Billy, I'll tell you
   what I'll do,
I'll bet another fifty I go higher than you!"

*Chorus*
The wife of Driver Sheehan was at home in bed
When the railway wired that old Bill was dead.
She called her children to her, said, "Listen,
   honey lambs,
The next old man you get'll be a Guard in the van!"
The railway's all in mourning now for Billy
   Sheehan,
No more we'll hear the puffing of his C 16.
There's crepe on all the locos, both the goods
   and mails,
From Ingham and Mount Isa down to New South
   Wales.

*Chorus*

*1. Rails weighing forty pounds a yard length. Very light rails, and hence easily distorted and unsafe.*
*2. General Manager presumably of the Northern Division, from the locality of the song.*
*3. Spirit of Progress was the express that ran from Albury to Melbourne, and made the best times in Australia. It was replaced by the Southern Aurora.*

# The Black Ribbon Band

Chorus

This is a version of the more familiar "Black Velvet Band", collected in Brisbane by Stan Arthur from the singing of Margaret Edmonds. The song is a transportation ballad, and was well known in England and in Ireland as well as in Australia.

It was in the town of Tralee, an apprentice
    to trade I was bound,
With plenty of bright amusement, to see
    the days go round.
Till misfortune and ruin came over me, which
    caused me to stray from my land,
Far away from my friends and companions,
    to follow her black ribbon band.

*Chorus*
Her eyes they shone like diamonds, you
    would think she was queen of the land,
With her hair thrown over her shoulders,
    tied up with a black ribbon band.

As I went down the Broadway, not intending
    to stay very long,
I met with a ticklesome damsel, as she
    came tripping along.

A watch she pulled out of her pocket, and slipped it
    right into my hand,
And the very first day that I met her, bad luck
    to her black ribbon band.

*Chorus*
Before judge and jury next morning we both
    of us did appear,
And a gentleman swore to the jewellery,
    and the case against us was clear.
For seven long years transportation, right
    into Van Diemen's Land,
Far away from my friends and relations, to follow
    her black ribbon band.

*Chorus*
Before all you young Irish lads, a warning
    take from me,
Beware of them ticklesome colleens that are
    hanging around in Tralee,
They'll treat you to whisky and porter, until you're
    not able to stand,
And before you have time to leave them, you're
    into Van Diemen's Land.

*Chorus*

# Bold Jack Donahue

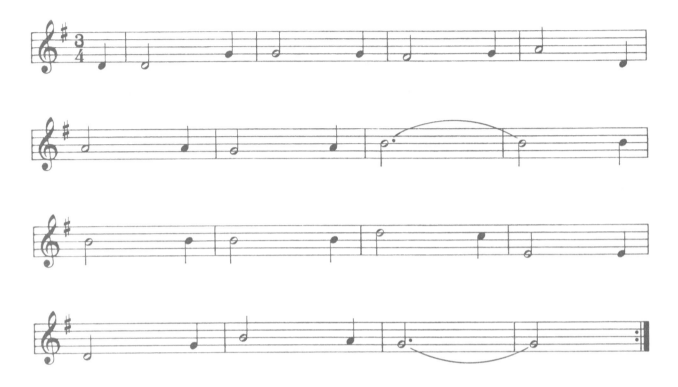

*Jack Donahue was a convict who "bolted" from Sydney and set up in business as a bushranger in the Parramatta, Liverpool Plains and Windsor districts in 1829-1830. He was shot to death by Private Muckleston on 1st September 1830. Walmsley and Webber, who were with him at the time, escaped, but Webber was hung and Walmsley shot to death within a few months. John Underwood hid for a time, but was killed in 1832, also by shooting. During their career as a gang, their victims included the Reverend Samuel Marsden, the "Flogging Parson"; and the explorer Charles Sturt, though Donahue refused to rob Sturt after he recognized him, for he respected him and his accomplishments. He did challenge Sturt to try to catch him, and no doubt Sturt tried, for he was a Magistrate.*

*Private Muckleston said, at the inquest into Donahue's death, that when challenged, Donahue waved his hat in the air three times, threw it away, and called out, "Come on, you —— ——— , we're ready, if there's a dozen of you!"*

In Dublin Town I was brought up, that city
  of great fame,
My decent friends and parents they will tell
  to you the same.

It was over a sum of five hundred pounds I was sent
  across the main,
For seven long years in New South Wales, to wear
  a convict's chain.

I had not been six months or more
  upon the Australian shore
When I took to the highway as I often had before.

There was me and Jacky Underwood,
  and Webber and Walmsley too,
These were the true associates of bold
  Jack Donahue.

One day as he was riding, the mountainside along
A-listening to the little birds, their pleasant
  laughing song,

When a Sergeant of the horse police discharged
  his carabine
And called aloud on Donahue to fight or to resign.

"Resign to you, you cowardly dogs, a thing I
    never would do,
And I'll fight this night with all my might!"
    cried bold Jack Donahue.

"I'd rather roam these hills and dales like wolf
    or kangaroo
Than work one day for the Government,"
    cried bold Jack Donahue.

He fought three rounds with the horse police,
    until that fatal ball
That pierced his heart and made him start, caused
    Donahue to fall.

And as he closed his mournful eyes, and bade
    the world adieu,
Saying, "Convicts all, both great and small,
    remember Donahue."

*At the inquest, he was described in the official report
as, ". . . a native of Dublin, twenty-three years of
age, five feet four inches in height, brown freckled
complexion, flaxen hair, blue eyes, and a scar under
the left nostril . . ."*

*Mounted police, gold escort guard (from* Sketches of the Victoria Gold Diggings and Diggers As They Are *[1852–53],
S. T. Gill)*

# Botany Bay

*Along with "Click Go the Shears" and the "Wild Colonial Boy", this is one of the best known Australian folksongs. It began life as a broadside ballad, was changed to make a stage performance in a play called "Little Jack Sheppard" and survives to this day. Hugh Anderson has researched it and comments on its history in his book* Farewell to Old England, *the title of which comes from this song.*

*Ron Edwards has some interesting observations on this song in the* Overlander Song Book, *where he presents no less than four versions of it!*

Farewell to old England forever,
Farewell to my rum-culls as well,
Farewell to the well-known Old Bailey
Where I used for to cut such a swell.

*Chorus*
Singing tooral-i ooral-i addity,
Singing tooral-i ooral-i ay.
Singing tooral-i ooral-i addity,
And we're bound for Botany Bay.

There's the Captain as is our commander,
The bosun and all the ship's crew;
The first and the second class passengers
Knows what we poor convicts goes through.

*Chorus*
It aint leaving old England we cares about,
'Taint 'cause we miss-spells what we knows.
It's just that us lightfingered gentry
Hops around with a log on our toes.

*Chorus*

*The First Fleet entering Botany Bay (engraving from*
Picturesque Atlas of Australasia, *ed. Andrew Garran)*

It's seven long years I've been serving,
And seven long more have to stay.
For bashing a cop in our alley,
And stealing his truncheon away.

*Chorus*

Oh, If I had the wings of a turtle-dove
I'd soar on my pinions so high,
Slap-bang to the arms of my Polly-love,
And in her sweet bosoms I'd die.

*Chorus*

Now, all you young dookies and duchesses,
Take warning from what I do say.
Mind all is your own as your toucheses
Or you'll join us in Botany Bay.

*Chorus*

*Captain Phillip's first sight of Port Jackson (engraving from*
Picturesque Atlas of Australasia, *ed. Andrew Garran)*

# The Broken-Down Squatter

*One night the Bushwackers' Band was playing for a
group dinner at Lennon's Hotel in Brisbane when the
local branch of the Country Party was also celebrat-
ing on the same floor. The sound of the music brought a
number of country fellows into the room, and one of
them asked the Bushwackers where they learned their
songs. The quick reply was "From fellows like you!"
The enquirer was so pleased that he agreed to sing his
repertoire of bush songs for us, and the following
Saturday he did so. When he sang "The Broken-
Down Squatter", he was asked where he learned it.
"That's Charlie Flower's song", he replied. His name
was Earl Loughlin, and he sang a number of other
songs for us, including "The Goondiwindi Song".
Investigation showed that C. A. Flower had come to
Queensland from Victoria in the late 1870s and had
established Durham Downs station on the Dawson in
the early eighties. The song, which was written about
that time, was strangely prophetic, for in the huge
droughts of the turn of the century, Flower was forced
to abandon Durham Downs, though he later re-
established himself on another property called Gar-
rabarra, on Bungil Creek, between Roma and Surat.
He wrote a number of songs that have survived,
including "The Cabbage-Tree Hat" in this section,
and also probably "A Thousand Miles Away".*

Come, Stumpy, old man, let us shift while we can
For your mates in the paddock lie dead.
Let us bid our farewells to Glen Eva's sweet dells
And the place where your lordship was bred.
Together we'll roam from our drought stricken
    home,
It's hard that such things have to be,
And it's tough on a horse when he's naught
    for a boss
But a broken-down squatter like me.

*Chorus*

For the banks are all broken, they say,
And the merchants are all up a tree.
When the big-wigs are brought to the
    Bankruptcy Court
What chance for a squatter like me.
No more will we muster the river for fats
Or spiel on the fifteen-mile plain;

Or rip through the scrub by the light of the moon
Or see the old stockyards again.
Leave the slip panels down, it don't matter
    much now,
There's none but the crows left to see;
Perching gaunt on yon pine as though longing
    to dine
On a broken-down squatter like me.

*Chorus*

When the country was cursed by the drought
    at its worst
And the cattle were dying in scores;
Though down on my luck, I kept up my pluck,
Thinking justice might temper the laws.
But the farce has been played, and Government aid
Ain't extended to squatters, old son.
When my money was spent, they doubled the rent,
And resumed the best part of my run.

*Chorus*

It was done without reason, for, leaving the season,
No squatter could stand such a rub.
And it's useless to squat where the rents are so hot
That you can't earn the price of your grub.
And there's not much to choose twixt
    the Banks and the screws
When a fellow gets put up a tree.
No odds what I feel, there's no court of appeal
For a broken-down squatter like me.

*Chorus*

They have left us our hides and but little besides,
You have all I possess on your back.
But Stumpy, old sport, when I boil my next quart
We'll be out on the Wallaby Track.
It's a mighty long ride till we cross the Divide
And the plains stretching out like a sea,
But the chances seem best in the far away west
For a broken-down squatter like me.

*Chorus*

# The Buffalo Shooter's Song

*Keith Willey, the author, taught me this song after he had returned from an expedition back to the Territory; a trip he ably recorded in his book,* Crocodile Hunt. *There are some popular songs that seem to lend themselves to parody, and "Galway Bay" from the film* Going My Way *is one of them. The Clancy Brothers sing a vulgar Irish one that has the virtue of being very funny, that was written by an Irishman in Dublin. It ends with the classic final verse:*

*On her back she has tattooed a map of Ireland*
*And when she has a bath on Saturday,*
*She rubs the Sunlight soap around by Claddagh*
*Just to see the suds run down by Galway Bay.*

*This version from the Northern Territory reflects deplorable racial attitudes, but is undoubtedly funny, and gives a true picture of the beliefs of some of the people who live there. I once heard Ted Egan sing a version that was very similar, in words and sentiments.*

*Sundowners (engraving from* Australasian Sketcher, *26 April 1881)*

If you ever go up north among the buffalo
Then maybe at the closing of the day
You can sit and listen to them flaming mozzies
And see the moon go down in Fanny Bay[1].

Just to hear again the crying of the curlews
With the lubras in their nagas, salting hides.
Just to sit beside a campfire in the moonlight
And listen to those shooters telling lies.

Oh, the gins come down from Oenpelli Mission
And they're all wrapped up in Jesus
    when they come;
But they bloody soon forget the Ten
    Commandments
When you hit 'em with a snort of O.P. rum.

Oh, the strangers came and tried to pinch
    our lubras,
And we just lay and laughed, and watched the fun;
For they might as well have tried to kiss a dingo
Or catch a flaming emu on the run.

And if you chance to meet a piccaninny,
The chances are he ain't entirely black;
For the shooters like their little bit of nonsense
Along the Alligator River track.

1. *Fanny Bay was the old Darwin gaol.*

# The Bullockies' Ball

*I have never been fortunate enough to collect this or any part of it in the field, though when John Meredith collected it in Sydney, the two ladies who sang it for him said they had learned it from their father, who had picked it up in the Gulf Country (see* Folk Songs of Australia, *Meredith and Anderson). It was the backing for the best-selling 78 recording of the "Drover's Dream" recorded for Wattle Records by the Sydney Bush Music Club in the 1950s, and it is a rollicking good song. The tune is the Irish "Finnegan's Wake", and, like that song, a revel turns into a free-for-all. Ron Edwards mentions that he found a fellow called Sam Long who recalled hearing it in his youth, and who thought it was written around Port Douglas. This is a possibility for Port Douglas was the outlet for the Etheridge mineral fields before the railway was built to the Atherton Tableland and the teams used to battle up the range through Julatten and Cassowary to Mareeba, and inland from there.*

*There has been some speculation about "Wallow-man Doughy Roley Foley" in the final verse. I have wondered if it might not be a corruption of either "Wooloowin", a Brisbane suburb, or "Wallaman", a waterfall on the Herbert River system outside Ingham.*

Pethinga Bullock

The teams were camped along the gullies,
Soon the news flew round about.
Plans were worked out by Pat Scully,
We gave the boys a grand blow-out
We had an awning of tarpaulins,
Kegs and casks came quickly rolling,
Then the boys and girls came strolling
To have a burst at the bullockies' ball.

*Chorus*
Oh, my hearties, that was a party, help yourself,
    free gratis all,
Lots of prog and buckets of grog to swig away
    at the bullockies' ball.

First came Flash Joe, but Jimmy was flasher,
Hopping Billy, the one eyed boss,
Brisbane Sal and the Derwent Slasher,
Billy the Bull and Paddy the Hoss.
Nanny the Rat, the real May Cassa[1]
Brisbane Bess and Mother May Call,
All came rolling up together
To have a burst at the bullockies' ball.

*Chorus*

Soon pint pots began to rattle,
The cry was, "Pass the rum this way,"
The boys began to blow their cattle,
The ladies, of course, must have their say.
Sal said she'd take cheek from no man,
And down to a dish of hash did stoop.
She'd got a smack in the eye with a doughboy,
Put her sitting in a bucket of soup.

*Chorus*

Oh then boys, there was the ructions,
Man the tucker and let fly,
Brisbane Bess with a hunk of damper
Caught Flash Joe right in the eye.
Nanny the Rat, the real May Cassa
With a frying pan a dozen slew,
She got a clip with a leg of mutton,
Took a dive in a bucket of stew.

*Chorus*

There was Wallowman Doughy Roley Foley
Said he'd put them to the rout,
Seized a chunk of roly-poly
But a poultice of pigweed stopped his mouth.
This raised his old woman's dander
And into an awful tantrum flew,
"Fair play!" cried she to a bleeding overlander,
"You pumpkin-peeling toe-rag coot!"

*Final chorus*
Oh, my hearties, that was a party, help yourself,
    free gratis all.
Blackened eyes and broken noses, that wound up
    the bullockies' ball.

*1. "The real May Cassa": the real macassar, i.e. the dinkum oil?*

*I have always thought that this might have been an actual incident. Mother May Call could well have been a Mrs McCall, for instance, and certainly the Derwent Slasher was an historical personality, a boxer called Thomas Davis, who fought in the 1840s in Sydney. Did he finish his days at Port Douglas?*

# Bullocky-Oh!

*This is song from the Numinbah Valley west of the Gold Coast in southern Queensland. The original singer was a fellow from Nerang, who gave Stan Arthur many songs. His name was Cyril Duncan. One of the fellows mentioned in the song, Hugh Guinea, is alive still and living near Nerang. The A.B.C. recently made a television programme about the old-time timber-hauling bullockies featuring Mr Guinea. A great pity they had not heard about the song at the time they made the programme.*

Well, I draw for Speckle's Mill[1], bullocky-oh,
  bullocky-oh,
And it's many the log I drew, bullocky-oh.
I pull cedar, beech and pine, and I never get
  on the wine,
I'm the king of bullock drivers, don't you know,
  bullocky-oh,
The king of bullock drivers, bullocky-oh.

There's Wapples, now, he brags, bullocky-oh,
  bullocky-oh,
Of his fourteen rawboned stags, bullocky-oh.
I can give him a thousand feet, axe them square
  and never cheat,
I'm the king of bullock drivers, don't you know,
  bullocky-oh,
I'm the king of bullock drivers, bullocky-oh.

There's Guinea and Anderson, too, bullocky-oh,
    bullocky-oh,
It's many the log they drew, bullocky-oh.
And I say it is no slander when I reckon I get
    their dander,
When they hear the crack of my whip,
    bullocky-oh, bullocky-oh,
When they hear the crack of my whip,
    bullocky-oh.

*Wool drays (engraving from* The Australian Sketchbook,
*S. T. Gill)*

*1. My friend Pat Briody assures me that this should read "Smeckle's
Mill". He did not know the song, but he knew the Valley.*

# The Cabbage-Tree Hat

*This is another of C. A. Flower's poems that picked up a tune. Charles Flower, Jr, speaking to me of his father, told me that "the old Boss used to get his cabbage-tree hats made by another old fellow outside Sydney. He always wore a cabbage-tree hat for as long as he was still able to get them." The tune is the well-known Irish song, "Rosin the Bow", which seems to have picked up many sets of words in its travels, including "Men of the West", an I.R.A. song, and "Acres of Clams" in the west coast States of America.*

*Carrying goods in the ranges (detail, engraving from* Picturesque Atlas of Australasia, *ed. Andrew Garran)*

Old hat, though I may want a new one,
I can't bear to throw you aside,
For you've been a friend and a true one
On many a blazing hot ride.
Each dent in your crown tells a story
Of gallops on mountain and flat,
Your brim is all covered with glory,
My gallant old cabbage-tree hat.

You have streaked it by moonlight, old fellow,
When the cattle were going like smoke.
You have heard the scrub bull's ringing bellow
From his stronghold of brigalow and oak.
You've been soaked in the floods on the Dawson,
Rolled over, and nearly tramped flat
By the bullocks that broke at the crossing,
My gallant old cabbage-tree hat.

Though your crown has been patched up
    with leather
And I've sewed you with horsehair and string,
No more will we foot it together
When the mustering starts in the spring.
Your troubles are over, lie peacefully there
And I hope when my time comes for that,
I trust I will go with a record as fair
As you, my old cabbage-tree hat.

# The Canecutter's Lament

*When I was cutting cane and working on mill locos around Innisfail in 1947, there was a couplet often recited by blokes in public bars that went*

> *"Never again will I cut cane*
> *On the banks of the Johnstone River."*

*I had a fair idea that there must be a song or poem around this, for it was extant throughout the cane-growing areas, only the name of the river being changed to suit local conditions. However, I was never successful in tracking it down. Then, in 1959, when Stan Arthur was on holidays in Childers, he heard two blokes singing in a bar about ten o'clock one night, about how they would never again cut cane. Stan joined them, of course. The fellows' names were Arnie Warren and Norm Barnes, two canecutters, and the song was carefully picked out by Stan and noted down before he went to bed (these were the days before tape machines simplified field collection).*

*When he returned to Brisbane, Stan called on me and we went together to the home of John Callaghan, for John had one of the new-fangled tape machines, and Stan sang the song on to tape. Unfortunately, there were some phrases that made it unsuitable for public performance in those more strait-laced days, so, as resident writer-in-attendance, I altered these words to make them suitable for the platform. It was this cleaned-up, bowdlerized version we recorded on the record "Folksongs from Queensland" in 1959, to celebrate the State Centenary. Since then the song has been reprinted in a number of collected versions, but the odd thing is that one or another of the changes I made to the text then are in the collections being made now and since that time. This is a good example of how readily people accept what they hear or read as being Gospel, and is a good example of the potential unreliability of field collection, for one has only the word of an informant as to the source of their knowledge.*

How we suffered grief and pain
Up in the Isis, cutting cane.
We sweated blood, we were black as sin
For the ganger, he drove the spur right in.

The first six weeks, so help me Mike
We lived on cheese and half boiled rice,
Doughy bread and cats-meat stew,
And corn beef that the flies had blew.

The Chinese cook with his cross-eyed look
Filled our guts with his corn-beef hashes,
Damned our souls with his halfbaked rolls
That'd poison snakes with their greasy ashes.

The cane was bad, the cutters was mad,
The cook had a hob-nailed liver,
And never again will I cut cane
On the banks of the Isis River.

Now I'm leaving this lousy place,
I'll cut no more for this hungry bugger,
He can stand in the mud that's red as blood
And cut his own blasted sugar.

*Strange are the ways of some collectors. My brother Alan and his friends had a similar experience when they completed a version of "Charlie Mopps". Also, an incomplete verse I collected for "The Dying Stockman", and filled in the missing two lines rather than discard them, is frequently heard now on a recording. I am not complaining, just showing how easily a single person can alter an authorized version and not be noticed. I feel that if the song is improved, and thus be more likely to be sung, performances can be changed so. I am not talking now about the documentation of items as originally collected. These should remain inviolate.*

*The sugar industry, Richmond River (engraving from* Picturesque Atlas of Australasia, *ed. Andrew Garran)*

# The *Catalpa*

A noble whaleship and commander, called
  the *Catalpa*, they say,
Came over to Western Australia, and stole
  six poor Fenians away.

*Chorus*
So come all you screw warders and gaolers,
  remember Perth Regatta Day,
And take better care of your Fenians
  or the Yankees'll steal them away!

Now all the Perth boats were out racing,
  and making short tacks for the spot,
When the Yankee came into Fremantle and took
  the best prize of the lot.

*Chorus*
The *Georgette,* well armed with bold warriors,
  went out the poor Yanks to arrest,
But she hoisted her star-spangled banner, saying,
  "You will not board me, I guess!"

*Chorus*
For seven long years they were serving,
  and seven long more had to stay,
For defending their country, old Ireland,
  for that they were banished away.

*Chorus*
You kept them in Western Australia, till their hair
  began to turn grey,
When a Yank from the States of America came
  out here and stole them away.

*Chorus*
Now remember those Fenians colonial,
  and sing o'er these verses with skill,
Remember the Yankee that stole them, and
  the home that they left on the hill.

*Chorus*
Now they've landed safe in America, and there
  will be able to cry,
"Hoist up the green flag and the shamrock,
  Hurrah! for old Ireland we'll die!"

*Chorus*

*This song was written in Western Australia about the
rescue of six convicts by an associate of theirs, John
Boyle O'Reilly, who had escaped himself a couple of
years previously. Below are some notes I wrote for the
song that were published in* Australian Tradition *in
October 1972.*

Re Sue Bunting's story about the *Catalpa,* in the last issue, there is no doubt that John Boyle O'Reilly was a colourful character indeed. According to one of my references, he was already a Fenian at the age of eighteen when he was instructed to enlist in the Hussars, the purpose of the exercise being to spread alarm and despondency and foment trouble in the ranks of that regiment. Incidentally, my reference is that he joined in 1862, not 1863. He seems to have been a particularly inept and naive propagandist. He pinned patriotic emblems to his saddlecloth and in the mess sang patriotic songs and advised his comrades to hamstring their horses for the greater glory of old Ireland. After a while even the British officers woke up to him and he and some of his friends were charged with "sedition and conspiracy", found guilty and sentenced to be shot. He and a group of fellow exiles were landed at Fremantle on 10 January, 1868. The name of the priest concerned in helping him escape was Father McCabe. Incidentally, another man saw him making his way to the *Gazelle* and insisted on being taken along and O'Reilly had no choice, though the fellow was universally disliked by his fellow convicts. Must have been an Englishman! The fellow's name was Bowman. He met disaster later in the voyage when the *Gazelle* was stopped by a Royal Naval vessel who had word of the escape. O'Reilly hid in the bilges while Captain Gifford calmly handed over Bowman to the Navy and told them O'Reilly had died on the voyage! After his being landed in Liverpool and then smuggled to the United States, he did a lecture tour speaking to large audiences, and made quite a considerable sum of money from the activity. On the strength of his early experience on the newspaper, he was given a job as a reporter on an Irish newspaper in Boston, where he also wrote and published books. He went along as official War Correspondent with the Fenian Army that invaded Canada from the States. This was in 1870, only a year after his escape from Western Australia.

Not all the money for the rescue attempt was raised in the United States by O'Reilly and Devoy. After the arrival of "Smith and Collins" in Sydney, they were joined by two men from Ireland called McCarthy and Walsh. These may or may not have been their real names. Over three thousand pounds (an awful lot of money for those times, but gold was king at the time, and Irish diggers were sympathetic, no doubt) was collected in Australia. The six who were to be rescued were named Wilson,

Cranston, Harrington, Dassagh, Hogan and Hassett. The plot was successful. Out on a working party from Fremantle jail, they dashed into the scrub, mounted the waiting horses and galloped to Rockingham Bay. So many people saw them and there were so many conflicting reports that for a while Authority was convinced that the Fenians were invading West Australia from the sea.

O'Reilly became a fairly popular and well known (among the Irish in America) poet, and continued writing savage and stirring (to Irishmen) poetry until his death in 1890 from an inadvertant overdose of sleeping tablets. Rather an anticlimax for a man after such a stirring youth!

*Ron Edwards quotes a song called "The Fenians Escape" in his book* Australian Folk Songs, *and gives its source as being a book called* More Irish Street Ballads *by Colm O'Lochlainn, Dublin, 1968. According to the notes, he says, the song comes from a broadside of the time. Could this be one of O'Reilly's poems, gone home to Ireland from Boston? Russel Ward published a version of "Catalpa" in his book* Three Street Ballads. *It is certainly a well-known song and deserves more performances than it has received. Of course, folk in Australia may have been embittered by the attitude adopted by extremists on both sides in the civil disturbances that are taking place in Ulster at present, and this may be the reason for the current lack of performance.*

*Shearing at the Yanko, New South Wales (engraving by Samuel Calvert, from* Illustrated Sydney News, *18 February 1869)*

# Click Go the Shears

Chorus

*This is certainly the best known Australian folksong with the exception of Waltzing Matilda, and yet it has gained its popularity only in the past couple of decades. The words are obviously homegrown, but the tune is an overseas import, from a song called "Ring the Bell, Watchman". Strangely enough, I knew a verse of an indelicate song from my Naval days that used the same tune, long before I ever heard of "Click Go the Shears".*

Down by the catching pen the old shearer stands,
Clasping his shears in his thin bony hands.
Fixed is his gaze on a bare-bellied yoe,
Glory, if he gets her, won't he make the ringer go.

*Chorus*

Click go the shears, boys, click, click, click.
Wide is his blow and his hands move quick.
The ringer looks around and is beaten by a blow,
And curses the old snagger with the bare-bellied yoe.

In the middle of the floor in his cane-bottomed chair
Sits the boss of the board, with his eyes everywhere,
Noting well each fleece as it comes to the screen,
Paying strict attention that it's taken off clean.

*Chorus*

The tar-boy is there and waiting on demand,
With his blackened tar-pot in his tarry hand.
Sees an old yoe with a cut upon her back.
This is what he's waiting for, "Tar here, Jack!"

*Chorus*

The Colonial Experience Man, he's there,
    of course,
Shiny boots and leggings, boys, just off his horse.
Casting round his eyes like a flaming connoisseur,
Shaving cream and brilliantine and smelling
    like a whore.

*Chorus*

Shearing is all over and we've all got our cheques,
Roll up your swags, boys, we're off along the track.
The first pub we come to we'll all have a spree,
And everyone that comes along it's, "Have
    a drink with me!"

*Chorus*

Down in the bar, the old shearer stands,
Grasping his glass in his thin bony hands.
Fixed is his gaze on a green-painted keg.
Glory, he'll get down on it before he stirs a leg.

*Chorus*

There we leave him standing, shouting
    for all hands,
While all around him the other shearers stand.
His eyes are on the keg which now is lowering fast.
He works hard, he drinks hard, and goes to hell
    at last.

*Chorus*

*Ron Edwards is of the opinion that this song may be of recent date (1910-1920) but one of John Meredith's informants claimed to have learned a song with much resemblance in the 1890s. This was Jack Luscombe of Ryde.*

*Sheep shearing in Victoria (engraving from* Wood Engravings in Victoria*)*

# The Death of Willy Stone

*Numbers of Australian sportsmen are remembered in song, Les Darcy the fighter for instance, and Alex Robinson the jockey from Victoria. The Queensland Folklore Society collected this song about a local jockey from a number of people in Brisbane and did considerable research on it. For full details, if the reader is interested, see* Australian Tradition, *April 1967. Although almost a hundred years have passed since this rider was accidentally killed in Brisbane, his memory still lives in the song. Bob Michell was the man who did most of the investigation into the facts behind the song.*

They'll tell it far and wide, for the lad we love
  has died,
His mission on this earth is at an end.
My eyes are wet and dim, for tonight I think of him,
The one I was so proud to call my friend.

*Chorus*
Now, mother, dry those tears, stop weeping,
  sisters three,
Weeping for your brother who's at rest;
Come, father, dry those tears, stop grieving,
  brother dear,
It's God's decree, and He alone knows best.

You jockeys on this earth of the thundering land
  of turf,

Of our grieving and our sorrows take a share.
You sportsmen, one and all will regret his fatal fall
For the loss of such as he is hard to bear.

*Chorus*

With the coffin and the wreath they've laid him
  down to sleep
And the lilies will be growing o'er his grave.
In the graveyard at Toowong where the river
  rolls along,
Sleeps Willy Stone, so trusty, true and brave.

*Chorus*

Oh, trusty friend of mine no other could outshine,
His cleverness, his courage in a race;
Where silken jackets flash, how bravely he
  would dash
Courageously through every open space.

*Chorus*

Now, right and round-about, "Come on, Willy
  Stone!" they'd shout,
And the horse would feel steel spurs in his side,
Oh, the horse would do its best, and the rider
  do the rest,
And ride as only clever jockeys ride.

*Chorus*

# Dennis O'Reilly

This song is a representative of the enormous number of songs throughout the English-speaking world that are known as the "Roving Journeyman" series. The feature of this series, apart from the related tunes, is the incidents in the story, where a girl tells her mother that she will go with the travelling man, and the mother remonstrates with her daughter. There are a number of these in the United States, two of the best known being "The Guerilla Man", from the Civil War period, and "The Gambling Man". The series almost certainly originated in the British Isles, and there are a number of variants there. The cycle has another variant in Australia, a song called "With My Swag All on My Shoulder", and a comparison of the two makes the family resemblance obvious, and another variant is called "The Union Boy". I have never collected any of these, but Stan Arthur found "Dennis O'Reilly".

My name is Dennis O'Reilly,
From Dublin Town I came.
To travel the wide world over,
I sailed the Australian main.
With my pack upon my shoulder
And a blackthorn in my hand,
I'll travel the bushes of Australia
Like a true-born Irishman.

When I arrived in Melbourne town
The girls all jumped with joy,
Saying one unto another
"Here comes my Irish boy."
With his pack upon his shoulder
And a blackthorn in his hand,
He'll travel the bushes of Australia
Like a true-born Irishman.

"Oh, daughter, dearest daughter,
What do you intend to do?
To fall in love with an Irishman,
A man you never knew!"
"Oh mother, dearest mother,
I'll do the best I can.
I'll travel the bushes of Australia
With my true-born Irishman.

"So mother, dearest mother,
I'll do the best I can.
If ever you see me coming back
I'll be with my Irishman.
With his pack upon his shoulder
And a blackthorn in his hand.
I'll travel the bushes of Australia
With my true-born Irishman."

*Ah, Phil my hearty, are that you?* (*from* Sketches of the Victoria Gold Diggings and Diggers As They Are [1852–53], *S. T. Gill*)

# The Digger's Song
## (Dinky-di)

*This set of words to the old English tune, "Villikens and His Dinah", was written during World War I, and was very popular with members of the first A.I.F. It would be approved by most of the troops, I am sure; as well as expressing the emotions of many folk who come into contact with the petty bureaucratic mind.*

He came up to London and straightaway strode
To the Army Headquarters in Horseferry Road,
To see all the bludgers who dodge all the strafe
By getting soft jobs on the Headquarters staff,

*Chorus*
Dinky-di, Dinky-di,
For I'm an old digger and can't tell a lie.

A lousy Lance-Corporal said, "Pardon me, please.
There's mud on your tunic, there's blood
    on your sleeve.
You look so disgraceful that people will laugh!"
Said the lousy Lance-Corporal on the
    Headquarters staff.

*Chorus*

The digger then shot him a murderous glance.
He said, "I'm just back from the trenches in France
Where the whizz-bangs are flying and comforts
    are few,
And brave men are dying for bastards like you."

*Chorus*

"We're shelled on the left and we're shelled
    on the right,
We're bombed all the day and we're bombed all
    the night,
And if something don't happen, and that
    pretty soon,
There'll be nobody left in the bloody platoon."

*Chorus*

The story was brought to the ears of Lord Gort,
Who gave the whole matter a great deal of thought;
Then awarded the digger a V.C. and two bars
For giving that Corporal a kick in the a——— .

*Chorus*

*Port Stephens (Skinner Prout, from* Australia, *ed. Edwin Carton Booth)*

# The Drover's Dream

*John Callaghan and self collected a version of this song with a variant tune from a fellow called Albert Stacey, of Cloncurry; who said he learned it from a shearer's cook called "The Pelican", "before they sang it on the wireless". He was, of course, referring to the recording mentioned before, in the notes on "The Bullockies' Ball". Other songs Bert sang for us included "Paddy McGinty's Goat" and a version of "Patsy Fagan". The words and music given here are those used on the old Wattle recording, from the Sydney Bush Music Club.*

One night while travelling sheep, my companions
    lay asleep,
There was not a star to illuminate the sky,
I was dreaming, I suppose, for my eyes were
    nearly closed,
When a very strange procession passed me by.
First there came a kangaroo with his swag
    of blankets blue,
A dingo ran beside him for a mate,
They were travelling mighty fast, and they shouted
    as they passed,
"We have to jog along, it's getting late."

The pelican and the crane, they came in
    from off the plain,
To amuse the company with a Highland Fling.
Then the dear old bandicoot played a tune
    upon his flute
And the native bears sat round all in a ring.

The possum and the crow sang us songs
    of long ago,
While the frill-neck lizard listened with a smile,
And the emu, standing near, with his claw up
    to his ear,
Said, "The funniest thing I've heard for quite
    a while!"

Some frogs from out the swamp where
    the atmosphere is damp
Came bounding in and sat upon some stones.
They each unrolled their swags and produced from
    little bags,
The violin, the banjo and the bones.
The goanna and the snake and the adder
    wide awake
With an alligator danced "The Soldier's Joy";
In a spreading silky-oak the jackass cracked a joke
And the magpie sang "The Wild Colonial Boy".

Some brolgas darted out from the tea-trees
    all about
And performed a set of Lancers very well,
While the parrots, green and blue, gave
    the orchestra its cue
To strike up "The Old Log Cabin in the Dell".
I was dreaming, I suppose, of these entertaining
    shows,
And it never crossed my mind I was asleep;
Till the Boss beneath the cart woke me up
    with such a start,
Yelling, "Dreamy, where the hell are all
    the sheep?"

*A sheep drover's camp (engraving from* Illustrated Australian News, *1 September 1890)*

# The Dying Stockman

Chorus

Oh the 5th of November, 1959, I received a letter from the late Horace Flower, part of which read as follows:

The Dying Stockman — The words of this were written by my dear father, when I was five years of youth, and he was Manager of the Queensland National Bank Ltd in Gatton, in 1892. He had quite a good voice for ballads, and loved the bush ballads which his brother wrote, which he set to his own music that he twanged out on his banjo. He was Horace Alfred Flower, born two years ahead of Charles, and had lived in the early eighties in Roma and Charleville; then at Burketown and Port Douglas, (where my first three years were spent), and he had known most of the pioneers and men such as old Jimmy Tyson and the Wild Scotchman, a Gulf bushranger.

He often sang us to sleep with his banjo on his knee, singing the songs of Stephen Foster, or with "Wrap me up in my stockwhip and blanket".

He it was, (Horace A. Flower) who wrote these words in Gatton in 1892 and used to sing them as a duet with Walton Kent (one of the Kents of Jondaryan station, who lived in that area of Gatton way, and often dined with us). My father knew the old English hunting song, "Wrap me up in my tarpaulin jacket", etc. having hunted in England when over there to finish his education, (from fourteen to nineteen years of age). . .

Whatever the authorship, this haunting song has lived on and still has a telling effect when sung "straight". Unfortunately, for its serious rendition, there are a number of bawdy parodies on it which seem to affect the audience with mirth when a serious singer tries to render it. I have heard it sung often, and it certainly travelled widely across the land, for it has been collected in all the eastern States of Australia.

A strapping young stockman lay dying, his saddle
　　supporting his head,
His mates all around him were crying, as he
　　raised on his elbow and said,

*Chorus*

Wrap me up in my stockwhip and blanket,
　　and bury me deep down below,
Where the dingoes and crows won't molest me,
　　in the shade where the coolibahs grow.

Then cut you two stringybark saplings, place one at
　　my head and my toe,
Carve on them crossed stockwhips and saddle,
　　to show there's a stockman below.

*Chorus*

Then bury me deep in some gully, where
　　the sweet-scented kurrajongs wave,
Where the breeze from the bush can blow o'er me,
　　and the wildflowers grow on my grave.[1]

*Chorus*

Oh, had I the flight of the bronzewing, far over
　　the plains would I fly,
Straight to the land of my childhood, and there
　　I'd be willing to die.

*Chorus*

Hark! There's wail of a dingo, watchful and weird;
　　I must go.
For he tolls the death knell of a stockman,
　　in the gloom of the scrub down below

*Chorus*

There's tea in the battered old billy, put
　　the pannikins out in a row,
And we'll drink to the next merry meeting
　　in the land where the good stockmen go.

*Chorus*

And oft in the shades of the twilight when
　　the soft winds are whispering low,
And the darkening shadows are falling, sometimes
　　think of the stockman below.

*Chorus*

1. *I inserted this line in the song. The first line was given to me at a barbecue in Cloncurry at a farewell to a local schoolteacher, and I added the second line with a couplet from Gordon's "Sick Stockrider" in mind.*

*Bushing it—camped for the night (engraving from an early illustrated paper)*

# Euabalong Ball

*John Manifold has some interesting things to say about the transformation of this song from the original poem written by "Vox Silvis" to the oral versions collectors have found extant. See his book,* Who Wrote the Ballads?. *(For the words of "Wooyeo Ball", see Stewart and Keesing,* Old Bush Songs.*)*

Oh, who hasn't heard of Euabalong Ball,
Where the lads of the Lachlan, the great
   and the small,
Come bent on diversion, from far and from near,
To forget their troubles for just once a year.

Like stringy old wethers, the shearers in force
All rushed in the bar as a matter of course.
While waltzing his cliner, the manager cursed,
Someone had caught him a jab with his spurs.

There were sheilas in plenty, some two or
   three score,
Some weaners, some two-tooths, and some
   maybe more,
Their fleeces all washed, so fluffy and clean,
The finest damn sheilas that ever you've seen.

The boundary riders was frisking about,
But the well-sinkers seemed to be feeling
   the drought.
If the water was scarce, the whisky was there.
What they couldn't swallow, they rubbed
   in their hair.

There was music and dancing and going the pace,
Some went at the canter, some went at the race.
There was bucking and gliding, pigrooting
  and sliding,
When they varied the gait, there was couples
  colliding.

Euabalong Ball is a wonderful sight.
The rams danced the two-tooths the whole
  flaming night.
And many there'll be who'll regret to recall
Of the polkas they danced at Euabalong Ball.

*Convivial diggers in Melbourne (from* Sketches of the Victoria Gold Diggings and Diggers As They Are [1852–53], *S. T. Gill)*

# The Eumerella Shore

Chorus

*Stewart and Keesing, in their* Old Bush Songs, *say that this was originally published as a poem in the* Launceston Examiner, *and that it was probably written by a disgruntled squatter. Certainly, there were many verses written on both sides of the Lands Act question (see "Stand Back" in the ballad section of this book). This one was enthusiastically taken up by bushmen, and has been collected widely.*

*For this song, each verse is followed by a different chorus.*

There's a happy little valley by the Eumerella shore
Where I've lingered many happy hours away.
On my little free selection I have acres by the score,
And when I unyoke the bullocks from my dray—

*Chorus*
To my bullocks I will say, "It don't matter where
    you stray,
For you'll never be impounded any more.
You'll be running, running, running
    on the duffer's piece of ground,
Free-selected on the Eumerella shore."

When the moon has climbed the mountains
    and the stars are shining bright
We will saddle up our horses and away,
And we'll yard the squatter's cattle in the darkness
    of the night
And have the calves all branded by the day.

*Chorus*
Oh, my pretty little calf, at the squatter we
    will laugh,
For he'll never be your owner any more.
You'll be running, running, running
    on the duffer's piece of ground,
Free-selected on the Eumerella shore.

When we find a mob of horses and the paddock rails
    are down,
Though before that they were never known
    to stray,
How quickly we will drive them to some distant
    inland town
And we'll sell them into slavery far away.

*Chorus*
To Jack Robertson we'll say, "Now we're on
    a better lay,
And we'll never go off droving any more.
For it's easier duffing cattle from the squatters
    round about,
Free-selecting by the Eumerella shore!"

*A home in the bush (from a photograph, engraved by J. Saddler, from* Australia, *ed. Edwin Carton Booth)*

# Flash Jack from Gundagai

*This version comes from Paterson's* Old Bush Songs. *An acquaintance of mine, Ms Zita Denholm, who was researching some history of properties in the One Tree Plain area, came up with the theory that the "old Tom Patterson" mentioned in the song, and for whom the singer has such obvious affection, was in fact not a station owner but a shanty keeper. If this is so, it would certainly explain why this man had such a respect for Patterson, and why he was keen to return to his place. "Banjo" Paterson, in a note on the expression, "pinked 'em with the Wolseleys", says that this means that the man shore so close with machine shears that the pink skin of the jumbuck showed through the stubble. Might I suggest, on the other hand, that he cut them so they bled. In fencing with swords it certainly had that meaning, and in the prize ring, to make a man bleed was to "draw the claret", or "pink him". Paterson should certainly have known, but he was a cattleman.*

I've pinked 'em with the Wolseleys and I've
    rushed with B-bows too,
I've shaved 'em in the grease, my lads,
    with the grass-seed showing through,
But I never slummed a pen, my lads,
    no matter what it contained
When shearing for old Tom Patterson on the One
    Tree Plain.

*Chorus*

I've been whaling up the Lachlan and I've
    dossed on Cooper's Creek,
And once I rung Cudjingie shed and blued it
    in a week.
But when Gabriel blows his trumpet, lads,
    I'll catch the morning train
And I'll head for old Tom Patterson's on the One
    Tree Plain.

*Chorus*

*Sheep shearing (lithograph, from* History of Australasia, *David Blair)*

I've shore at Burrabogie and I've shore
    at Toganmain,
I've shore at big Willandra, and upon
    the Coleraine;
But before the shearing was over, I've wished
    myself back again,
Shearing for old Tom Patterson on the One
    Tree Plain.

*Chorus*
All among the wool, boys, all among the wool,
Keep your blades full, boys, keep your blades full,
I can do a respectable tally myself if ever I like to try
And they know me round the blackblocks
    as Flash Jack from Gundagai.

I've shore at big Willandra and I've shore
    at Tilberoo,
And once I opened blades, my boys,
    upon the famed Barcoo,
At Cowan Downs and Trida, and as far
    as Moulamein
But I was always glad to get back again to the One
    Tree Plain.

*Chorus*

# The Flash Stockman

*This is another "boasting" song like Flash Jack. They were not meant to be taken seriously, and the singer was usually laughing at himself. "Widgeegoara Joe" is another perfect example of the "boasting" song. There are variants of this from Victoria to the gulf, where Ron Edwards collected a very strange version of it. The tune used here is not the one used on the Lloyd recording, but a version of "The Little Ball of Yarn", a bawdy song, much sung in fo'c'sles.*

I'm a stockman, yes, I am, and they call me
    Ugly Sam,
I'm old and grey, an' I've only got one eye.
In a yard I'm good of course, but just put me
    on a horse
And I'll go where lots of young-uns daren't try.

I can ride 'em through the gidgee, over country
    rough and ridgy,
I can lose 'em in the very worst of scrub.
I can ride both rough and easy, on a jumper
    I'm a daisy,
And a flamin' bobby-dazzler in a pub.

You should see me use a whip, I can give
    the tailers gyp,
I can make the bloody echoes roar and ring,
With a branding iron, oh, hell! I'm a perfect
    flamin' swell
In fact, I'm duke of every blasted thing.

You should see me skin a sheep, it's so lovely you
    could weep,
I can act the silver-tail as if me blood was blue,
You can strike me pink or dead, if I stood
    upon me head,
I'd still be good as any other two.

There's a notion in me pate that it's luck,
    it isn't fate,
That I'm so far above the common run,
For in everything I do you can split me fair in two
For I'm far too bloody good to be in one.

*Near Lake Tyers (engraving from* Picturesque Atlas of Australasia, *ed. Andrew Garran)*

# Frank Gardiner,
# He Is Caught At Last

*This version of the words and tune came from the singing of Bill Berry, who sings it better than anyone else I have ever heard. John Meredith and Nancy Keesing collected it originally, I think, from Mrs Popplewell. Ron Edwards says the tune is a variant of the Irish air, the "Shan Van Vocht", which was a rebel song from the troubles after the Boyne. One line of this went "Oh, Boney's on the sea, says the Shan Van Vocht", which places the composition of the words in the early nineteenth century. It probably was brought to Australia by Irish exiles and acquired new words here.*

Frank Gardiner, he is caught at last, and now in Sydney gaol,
For wounding Sergeant Middleton and robbing the Mudgee mail.
For plundering of the gold escort, and the Carcoar mail also,
And it was for gold they made so bold, and not so long ago.

His daring deeds surprised them all throughout the Sydney land,
For on his friends he gave a call and quickly raised a band,
And fortune always favoured him until the time of late
Until Ben Hall and Gilbert met with their dreadful fate.

Young Vane he has surrendered, Ben Hall's got his death wound,
And as for Johnny Gilbert, near Binalong was found,
He was all alone and lost his horse, three troopers came in sight,
And he fought the three most manfully, got slaughtered in the fight.

Farewell, adieu, to outlawed Frank, he was
    the poor man's friend.
The government has secured him, their laws he
    did offend,
He boldly stood his trial, and answered in a breath,
"Do what you will, you can but kill, I have
    no fear of death!"

Day after day they remanded him, escorted from
    the Bar,
Fresh charges brought against him from
    neighbours near and far,
And now it is all over, the sentence they have
    passed.
They sought to find a verdict, and "Guilty!" was
    at last.

When lives you take, a warning boys;
    a woman never trust.
She will turn round, I will be bound,
    Queen's evidence the first.
He's doing two-and-thirty years, he's doomed
    to serve the Crown,
And well may he say he cursed the day he first met
    Mrs Brown.

*Gardiner did not serve his sentence of "two-and-thirty years". An account of his reprieve and exile is to be found in* The Pictorial History of Australian Bushranging, *by Wannan and others. Gardiner spent the last years of his life in California.*

*Portrait of Gardiner, the bushranger (engraving from* Illustrated Australian News, *25 April 1864)*

# The Freehold on the Plain

Chorus

*This song is set to the tune of "The Little Old Log Cabin in the Lane", and was one of the numbers sung by the Moreton Bay Bushwackers on the recording "Folksongs from Queensland" in 1959. It can be compared with the Charles Flower song, "The Broken-down Squatter". So far as I know, these are the only two songs about pastoralists who have failed in their business from drought and for other reasons.*

I'm a broken-down old squatter, and my cash it is
   all gone.
Of troubles and bad seasons I complain;
My cattle are all mortgaged, of horses I have none,
And I've lost that little freehold on the plain.

*Chorus*
For the stockyard's broken down and the
   woolshed's tumbling in,
I've written to the mortgagees in vain.
My wool it is all damaged, it is not worth a pin,
And I've lost that little freehold on the plain.

I started as a squatter some twenty years ago
When fortune followed after in my train,
But I speculated heavy, and I'll have you all
   to know
That I've lost that little freehold on the plain.

*Chorus*

I built myself a mansion, and chose myself a wife;
Of her I have no reason to complain.
For I thought I had sufficient to last me all my life
But I've lost that little freehold on the plain.

*Chorus*

And now I am compelled for to live a drover's life,
Driving cattle through the sunshine and the rain,
And to leave her there behind me, my own dear
   loving wife,
We were happy in that freehold on the Plain.

*Chorus*

*Harpers Hill, Hunter River (Skinner Prout, from* Australia, *ed. Edwin Carton Booth)*

# The Free Selector's Daughter

Chorus

*This parody on the old London street song, "The Pretty Little Ratcatcher's Daughter", is equally amusing, and possibly had a foundation in fact. Some suffering swain certainly put feeling into the line about feeling sorry for Annie Laurie! Wasn't it G. B. Shaw who reviewed a concert once by simply saying, "The —— Orchestra played Bach last night. Bach lost!"*

Not long ago near Penrith Town lived a free
    selector's daughter,
She wasn't born in Penrith Town, but t'other side
    of the water.
Her father was read in wondrous books,
    and he visited every quarter,
And the young men round all cast sly looks
    at the free selector's daughter.

*Chorus*
De dum di, de dum di, de dum de dum do.

Now, being new to her roguery, I was to her house
    invited,
Just for a social cup of tea, and her Ma was
    quite delighted.
I looked to the right, I looked to the left,
    no escape seemed in that quarter,
And my heart as I sat went pit-a-pat, for the free
    selector's daughter.

*Chorus*

Now after tea, her mother said, "You haven't
    heard our pianner,
My daughter plays, 'Those Happy Days
    upon the Banks Of Banna'."
When she did scream out "Love's Young Dream"
    you could hear her down this quarter,
And I felt sorry for "Annie Laurie" with
    the free selector's daughter.

*Chorus*

152

She's laid on the shelf quite long enough
  till few now care to behold her,
And the young bucks think she's getting tough,
  or else they'd be much bolder.
Her affected air would make you stare, though
  her figure makes a slaughter,
And her mother booked that I was hooked
  on the free selector's daughter.

*Chorus*

If ever I marry in New South Wales, it will be
  no girl so affected,
My future bride shall scorn such pride, or by me
  be neglected.
All you young men that's got some pelf, go visit
  in that quarter,
If you want beauty on the shelf, try the free
  selector's daughter.

*Chorus*

*Gladstone, Queensland (J. Carr, from* Australia, *ed. Edwin Carton Booth)*

# The Gilliatt Mug

*Stan Arthur collected this song from the late Mr T.
Gleeson of Townsville. I have commented on it in the
notes to the poem "The Boxing Kangaroo". This song
was collected in 1957; and in 1966 I called on Mr
Gleeson myself, with a tape recorder and got a lot
more from him. He remembered parts of the "Ship
That Never Returned", "Wild Colonial Boy" and
others, also two verses and chorus of a song called
"Cardigan, the Fearless", about the charge of the
Light Brigade. Mr Gleeson was also an accomplished
musician on accordion, mouth organ and fiddle; and
often performed at the local Pensioners' Club. He had
played for bush dances all his life.*

He's slabsided, lean, and lanky, with a sunburned
   hard old dial,
Sometimes cheerful, sometimes cranky,
   working points to make his pile.
You will see him white and floury in some
   shady little nook,
Whether cloudy, fine or showery, the Gilliatt
   Mug's the cook.

Stroll along in any weather if your teeth are
   strong and good,
For the meat is tough as leather and the damper
   cuts like wood;
If a knife and fork's not handy, well, just grab it
   in your dook,
You'll see things to knock you bandy when
   the Gilliatt Mug's the cook.

Come along, my dear old maties, with your
   appetites immense,
Here's plenty beef and praties scrambled
   through the barbed wire fence.
Try the jam tart from the ashes if you're
   feeling rather crook,
Watch him while the steak he slashes,
   for the Gilliatt Mug's the cook.

Bring along your pills and potions, Epsom's salts
    and castor oil,
Any new ideas or notions that'll make
    your belly boil.
If you are inclined to doubt it, well, just come
    and take a look.
All the blooming swagmen shout it, "Gilliatt
    Mug's the blanky cook!"

*Tea and damper (drawn by J. Davis, coloured wood engraving from the Supplement to* Australasian Sketcher, *4 June 1883)*

# The Goondiwindi Song

*I have already mentioned Mr Earl Loughlin, who sang "The Broken-down Squatter" for us, and identified C. A. Flower as the author. This is another of the songs he sang for us, and it is not surprising that he knew it for his property was near the town of Goondiwindi. Stan and I used to sing it as a duet, taking alternate verses, and we altered a few words in one verse to suit the performers. It was a private joke. The origin of the tune remained a mystery to me until one night I was listening to the Overseas Service of the B.B.C., when they played it (at about half speed compared to the Goondiwindi version) as a folkdance tune, and gave it the name, "The Rose Garden". There are many versions extant.*

Snowflake Willy are my name, and the Welltown
    are my station,
It's no disgrace, the old black face, it's the colour
    of my nation.

*Chorus*
Oh, it's bindi-eye and mind your eye,
    and don't kick up a shindy,
And we'll all hop in and collar a gin,
    and dance around in the bindi.

Oh, the Big Pontoon, you all know him, we'll
    take him to the dances,
We'll dance him around barefoot on the ground,
    that's how the poddy prances.

*Chorus*

I'm the boy from Welltown, the cause of many
    a shindy,
Got sixteen sweethearts in St. George, and ten
    in Goondiwindi.

*Chorus*

Mister Stan is a very nice man, and so is
    Mister Willy,
We send a piccaninny down each day to boil
    their flaming billy.

*Chorus*

Snowflake Willy are my name, and the Welltown
    are my station,
I'm black in the face, it's no disgrace, it's
    the colour of my nation.

*Chorus*

*Australia; News from home (George Baxter, after an oil painting by Harden S. Melville)*

# I'm Tomahawking Fred, The Ladies' Man

*Stewart and Keesing reprinted a text of this song without music from* The True History of the Australian Bushrangers *by Jack Bradshaw. Edgar Waters notes in* Australian Tradition, *May 1965, that it is a parody of an English music hall song called* Fashionable Fred, *and quotes the original chorus as being*

> *Yes, I'm just about the cut for Belgravia,*
> *To keep the proper pace I know the plan,*
> *Wire in, and go ahead, then, for I'm*
> *Fashionable Fred,*
> *I'm Fashionable Fred, the ladies' man.*

*The relationship is quite obvious, though the original writer may have been a little startled to see what happened to his lyrics when they went outback!*

Now, some shearing I have done, and some
  prizes I have won,
Through my knuckling down so close
  on the skin,
But I'd rather tomahawk every day and shear
  a flock,
For that's the only way I make some tin.

*Chorus*

For I'm just about to cut out for the Darling,
To turn a hundred out I know the plan.
Give me sufficient cash and you'll see me
  make a splash,
I'm Tomahawking Fred, the ladies' man.

Put me on the shearing floor, and it's there I'm
  game to bet
That I'd give to any ringer ten sheep start.
When on the whipping side, well, away from
  them I slide,
Just like a flaming bullet or a dart.

*Chorus*

Of me you might have read, for I'm
  Tomahawking Fred,
My shearing laurels famous near and far.
I'm the don of Riverine, 'midst the shearers cut
  a shine,
And our tar-boys say I never call for tar.

*Chorus*

Wire in and go ahead then, for I'm
  Tomahawking Fred,
In a shearing shed, my lads, I cut a shine.
There are Roberts and Jack Gunn, shearing
  laurels they have won,
But my tally's never under ninety-nine!

*Chorus*

*The black faced or heath ram (from* 1800 Woodcuts by Thomas Bewick and His School, *ed. Blanche Cirker)*

# Jack Lefroy

Chorus (2nd time)

*Once again, the collector is Stan Arthur. This bushranging ballad is something of a mystery to me, for I have never been able to trace a bushranger by that name. Perhaps some interested reader may have access to files of executions or something similar that will enable us to discover something more about him. While it is highly unlikely that a fellow called Lefroy wrote the ballad on the eve of his execution, it was a common practice for ballad-writers and broadside sellers to have a poem or ballad printed ready for execution day, to be sold in the streets on the morning of the execution, purporting to have been written by the condemned in his cell the previous night. I have always suspected the Donahue poem to be a case of this sort. But as to Jack Lefroy, apart from the song, I know nothing of the man and why he was being hanged. For the chorus of this song, repeat the last four lines of the music.*

Coaching by Night

Come all you lads and listen, for a story
   I would tell,
Before they take me out and hang me high.
My name is Jack Lefroy, and life I would enjoy,
But that old judge has sentenced me to hang.
My mother she was Irish, and taught me
   at her knee,
But to steady work I never would incline,
As a youngster I could ride, any horse was wrapped
   in hide,
And when I saw a good one, he was mine.

*Chorus*
So all young lads, take warning, and don't be
   led astray,
For the past you never, never can recall.
While young your gifts enjoy, take a lesson
   from Lefroy,
Let his fate be a warning to you all.

"Go straight, young man!" they told me when my
   first long stretch was done,
"If you're jugged again, you'll have yourself
   to thank!"
But I swore I'd not be found hunting nuggets
   in the ground,
When the biggest could be picked up in the bank.
Well, I've stuck up some mail-coaches
   and I've ridden with Ben Hall,
And they never got me cornered once until
A pimp was in their pay gave my dingo-hole away,
And they run me down to earth at Riley's Hill.

*Chorus*

"Come out, Lefroy!" they called me, "Come out,
   we're five to one!"
But I took my pistols out and stood my ground.
For an hour I pumped out lead, till they got me
   in the head,
And when I awoke they had me bound.
It's a pleasant day to live, boys, a gloomy one to die,
A-dangling with your neck inside a string.
How I'd like to ride again down the hills
   to Lachlan Plain
But when the sun has risen, I must swing.

*Chorus*

# Jacky-Jacky Was a Smart Young Feller

I had been singing bush songs at a social gathering at a Writers' Week function at the Adelaide Festival when Roland Robinson, that good poet, came up to me and asked me if I would sing "Jacky-Jacky". I had never heard it, so we sat quietly in a corner while he taught it to me. He said it was a favourite with many of his Aboriginal friends. I asked Kath Walker about it when I returned to Brisbane, and she had also heard it, though with slightly different tune and words, of course. As Ron Edwards also collected it in Cairns from an Aboriginal friend, who had also heard it sung in the Northern Territory, you can see it has a wide distribution among the original inhabitants.

Jacky-Jacky was a smart young fellow, full of vim
    and en-i-gy,
He was thinking of getting married, but his girl
    run away, you see.

*Chorus*
Crickita bubbla, will dee ni-ah, Billy ni-ah,
    gingerrie wah.

Jacky used to go out hunting, with his spear
    and waddy too,
He's the only one can tell you what the emu said
    to the kangaroo.

*Chorus*

The hunting days was Jacky's business till
    the white man came along,
Put his fences across the country, now the hunting
    days are gone.

*Chorus*

White fellers have to pay all taxes to keep
    Jacky-Jacky in clothes and food.
Jacky don't care what becomes of the country,
    white man's tucker, him very good.

*Chorus*

*The above words may not be exactly the ones I learned, for what with one thing and another my memory is somewhat hazy about the end of that day, but the above is as close as I can remember now, some ten years later. Aboriginal people certainly swap songs and have excellent memories; I remember "Uncle" Willy MacKenzie singing corroborees for John Callaghan and myself that he had learned when working in Western Queensland in the 1920s. But then, a people without writing would tend to develop remarkable memories, wouldn't they?*

# Jim Jones at Botany Bay

*While many transportation ballads are laments for past happinesses, and singers express a wish to return to their "native shore", this one is much more in the spirit of the wild colonial boys. Its mention of the bushranger Donahue as being still at large dates its composition to the late 1820s.*

Come listen for a moment lads, and hear me
  tell my tale,
How o'er the sea from England's shore I was
  compelled to sail.
The jury said, "He's guilty, sir," then said
  the Judge, said he,
"For life, Jim Jones, I'm sending you
  across the stormy sea.
But take a tip before your trip to join the iron gang.
Don't be too gay in Botany Bay, or else you're
  sure to hang.
Or else you'll hang," he said, said he, "And
  after that, Jim Jones,
High up upon a gallows pole, the crows will
  pick your bones."

"You'll get no chance for mischief there,
  remember what I say,
They'll flog the poaching out of you when you
  get to Botany Bay!"
The wind blew high upon the sea, the wind blew
  up in gales,

I'd rather drown in misery than go to
  New South Wales.
The wind blew high upon the sea, and the pirates
  came along,
But the soldiers in our convict ship, they were
  three hundred strong.
They opened fire and very soon drove
  that pirate ship away.
I'd rather have joined that pirate's crew than go
  to Botany Bay.

Where night and day the irons clang, and like
  poor galley-slaves,
We toil and moil, and when we die we fill
  dishonoured graves;
But later on I'll break my chains, into the bush
  I'll go,
And join the bold bushrangers there,
  Jack Donahue and Co.
And some dark night when all around is quiet
  in the town,
I'll shoot the bastards one and all, I'll shoot
  the floggers down.
I'll give the law a little shock, remember what I say.
They'll yet regret they sent Jim Jones in chains
  to Botany Bay.

# Jimmy Sago, Jackeroo

*This piece of advice to embryo squatters was written with the tongue firmly in the cheek. Station hands didn't think much of a "Colonial Experience" man, as a quick look at the appropriate verse in "Click Go the Shears" will show. The jackeroo was normally a young man of good family and some means who was employed on a station to gain experience before either obtaining a station of his own or applying for a job as manager of an existing property. This wry song advises them how to "get on".*

If you want a situation, I'll just tell you the plan,
To get on to a station, I am just your very man.
Pack up the old portmanteau, and label it "Paroo",
With a name aristocratic—Jimmy Sago, jackeroo!

When you get on to the station, of small
  things you'll make a fuss,
And in speaking of the station, mind, it's "we"
  and "ours" and "us".
Boast of your grand connections, and your
  rich relations, too,
And your own great expectations, Jimmy Sago,
  jackeroo.

They will send you out on horseback,
  the boundaries for to ride,
But run down a marsupial, and rob him of his hide.
His scalp will fetch a shilling and his hide
  another two,
Which will help to fill your pockets, Jimmy Sago,
  jackeroo.

When the Boss wants information, on the men
    you'll do a sneak,
And don a paper collar on your fifteen bob a week.
Then at the lamb-marking, a boss they'll make
    of you.
Now, that's the way to get on, Jimmy Sago,
    jackeroo.

A squatter in the future, I've no doubt you may be,
But if the banks once get you they will put you
    up a tree;
To see you humping bluey, I know, would
    never do,
'Twould mean goodbye to our new-chum,
    Jimmy Sago, jackeroo.

*A new-chum's first Christmas (engraving from* Illustrated Australian News, *26 December 1884)*

# Lazy Harry's

Chorus

*The very first commercial recording of Australian folksong to be made in Queensland for general release was an odd record indeed. It was called the "Billy-Goat Overland", and was only the size of a 45 recording but was intended to be played at 33 r.p.m. The two fellows involved were Bill Scott and Stan Arthur, and the songs were more significant for the vigour of their performance and their gusto than for their musical excellence. They were rough but infectious, in other words. One of the songs on the record was "Lazy Harry's", and I am as fond of it today as I was in 1958. John Callaghan taped the songs on his old Byer 66 with home-made pre-amp. equipment. The record was made and distributed by Wattle Records, of nostalgic fame.*

Oh, we started down from Roto when the sheds
    had all cut out
With a three spot cheque between us that we meant
    to knock about.
And we humped our blues serenely, we had
    Sydney in our eye,
Till we came to Lazy Harry's, on the road
    to Gundagai.

*Chorus*
We came to Lazy Harry's on the road to Gundagai,
The road to Gundagai, the road to Gundagai,
We came to Lazy Harry's on the road to Gundagai.

We crossed the Murrumbidgee near the Yanko
    in a week,
And we passed through old Narrandera and we
    crossed the Burnett Creek,
But we never stopped at Wagga, we had Sydney
    in our eye,
Till we came to Lazy Harry's on the road
    to Gundagai.

*Chorus*
Well, we strolled into the parlor, threw our swags
    upon the floor,
And we ordered rum and raspberry,
    and a shillingy[1] cigar,
But the girl that served the poison, well, she
    winked at Stan[2] and I,
So we camped at Lazy Harry's on the road
    to Gundagai.

*Chorus* So we camped at . . . etc.

I've met a lot of girls, my boys, and drunk
    a lot of beer,
And met with some of both, my boys, that left me
    feeling queer.
But for grog to knock you sideways and for girls
    to make you sigh,
You should camp at Lazy Harry's on the road
    to Gundagai.

*Chorus* So we camped at . . . etc.

In a week the spree was over and the cheque was
    all knocked down,
So we shouldered our Matildas and we turned
    our backs on town.
And the girls they stood a nobbler as we
    sadly waved goodbye,
Then we tramped from Lousy[3] Harry's on the road
    to Gundagai.

*Chorus*
So we tramped from Lousy Harry's on the road
    to Gundagai,
The road to Gundagai, the road to Gundagai,
We tramped from Lousy Harry's on the road
    to Gundagai.

*1. Originally "a shilling each cigar". This version is courtesy my brother Alan.*
*2. Originally "Bill". I substituted "Stan" as when Stan and I sang this song, I used to sing that particular verse.*
*3. I am grateful to my brother Alan for many things, but for nothing more than the suggestion of the substitution of "Lousy" for "Lazy" the last three times.*

# The Limejuice Tub

*Yet another shearers' song, to send up the new-chums and reassure themselves of their own skill and toughness. It is a most engaging song, though the history of its collection and piecing together would take some time to tell. But it sings very well in the version below, and it's a good song.*

When shearing comes, lay down your drums, step on the board, you brand new-chums,
With a rah-dum, rah-dum, rub-a-dub-dub, we'll send you home in a limejuice tub.

Here we are in New South Wales, shearing sheep with daggy tails,
And a rah-dum, rah-dum, rub-a-dub-dub, we'll send them home in a limejuice tub.

Because you crossed the briny deep, you reckon you can shear a sheep,
With a rah-dum, rah-dum, rub-a-dub-dub, we'll send you home in a limejuice tub.

There's immigrant coves and cocky's sons, they fancy they can shear great guns,
They reckon they can shift the wool, but the buggers can only tear and pull.

The very next job they undertake is to press the wool, but they make a mistake,
They press the wool without any bales; oh, the shearing's hell in New South Wales.

When the sheep with tar is black, roll up! roll up, you'll get the sack,
Once more, once more on the wallaby track, once more to look for the shearing-oh.

When we meet upon the road, from off your back throw down your load,
Then at the sky we take a look, and, "I reckon it's time to breast the cook!"

We camp in huts without any doors, sleep upon the dirty floors,
With a pannikin of flour and a sheet of bark, we can wallop up a damper in the dark.

You cockatoos, you never need fret, for to pay you out I'll never forget,
For I'm the man who's willing to bet, you're up to your eyes, heels-first, in debt.

You're up to your eyes, your neck as well, your daughters wear no crinolines,
Nor are they bothered with boots and shoes, for they're wild in the bush with the kangaroos.

Home, it's home I'd like to be, not humping my drum in the sheep country.
Over a thousand miles I've come, to march along with a blanket drum.

# Look Out Below

*This is one of the songs of the "inimitable Thatcher", as he was known. An unsuccessful digger, he made his pile on the diggings as an entertainer, both in Australia and later in New Zealand. He wrote many songs that have survived among old-timers; like "Where's Your Licence?" and "The Green New-Chum". I have a recording of this song sung most expressively by Marion Henderson.*

A young man left his native shores, for trade was
    bad at home;
To seek his fortune in this land, he crossed the
    briny foam; ·
And when he got to Ballarat, it put him in a glow,
To hear the sound of the windlasses and the cry,
    "Look out below!"

Wherever he turned his wondering eyes, great
    wealth he did behold,
And peace and plenty in the land by the magic
    power of gold.
Said he, "I am both young and strong, to the
    diggings I will go,
For I like the sound of the windlasses and the
    cry, 'Look out, below!'"

Among the rest he took his chance, and his luck
    at first was vile;
But he still resolved to persevere, and at length
    he made his pile.
Said he, "I'll take my passage home, to England
    I will go,
And I'll say farewell to the windlasses and the
    cry, 'Look out, below!'"

Arrived in London once again, his gold
    he freely spent
And into every gaiety and dissipation went.
But pleasure, if prolonged too much, oft causes
    pain, you know,
And he missed the sound of the windlasses and
    the cry, "Look out, below!"

And thus he reasoned with himself, "Oh, why
    did I return?
For the digger's independent life I now begin
    to yearn.
Here, purse-proud Lords the poor oppress, but
    there, it is not so;
Give me the sound of the windlasses, and the cry,
    'Look out, below!'"

So he started for this land again with a charming
    little wife,
And he finds there's nothing to compare with a
    jolly digger's life.
Ask him if he'll go back again, he'll quickly
    answer, "No!"
For he loves the sound of the windlasses and the
    cry, "Look out, below!"

# Maggie May

Chorus

*I learned a version of this song in the early 1940s when I first went to sea, but the best set of words I know came from an A.B. on the* Cape Leeuwin *who himself came from Liverpool. There are many versions, but this is my favourite.*

Gather all you sailors, and gather all you whalers
And when you hear my tale you'll pity me;
For I was a goddam fool in the port of Liverpool
The first time that I came home from sea.

*Chorus*
Oh, Maggie, Maggie May, they have taken you
   away
To slave upon that cruel Van Diemen shore.
But you robbed so many sailors and you robbed
   so many whalers
You won't never walk down Lime Street
   any more.

I paid off in the hold of a ship called the
   *Marigold*–
Two pound ten a month, it was my pay.
I landed on the quay, and waiting there for me
Was a lady by the name of Maggie May.

*Chorus*

Next morning I awoke, alone and stony broke,
I found that she had gone and left me there.
She took my clothes to pawn, and left me
   there forlorn,
But what was worst, she didn't seem to care.

*Chorus*

To a policeman on his beat at the corner
   of the street,
To him I went, to him I told my tale;
And then they went and found her, a-robbing
   of a homeward-bounder,
And took her off and clapped her into gaol.

*Chorus*

*The Derwent, Tasmania (Skinner Prout, from* Australia, *ed. Edwin Carton Booth)*

# Moreton Bay (Lament for the death of Captain Logan)

## The Melancholy Fate of Captain Logan

On the 9th of October, 1830, Captain Logan, accompanied by his servant and five Prisoners, proceeded from Brisbane Town to the neighbourhood of Mount Irwin and the Brisbane Mountain, with a view of completing his Chart of this part of the Country. Captain Logan on his return Home on the 17th of October, when, not far from the foot of Mount Irwin, left the party, desiring them to proceed to a place he pointed out, and where he said he would join them in the Evening.

From some unfortunate Misunderstanding, however, he was unable to do so; and the next day, the party, believing he would proceed immediately to the Lime Stone Station, took their departure also for that place, where they arrived the following Evening. Finding that Captain Logan was not there as they expected, and having seen many Natives on the day previous, their fears were naturally excited, and three of them immediately returned to the place where Captain Logan had left them, while the others went on to Moreton Bay to announce the distressing intelligence.

It was naturally concluded that Captain Logan had fallen into the hands of the Natives. Parties were sent out in every direction to endeavour to meet them: while, in the meantime, his servant and party found his Saddle, with the stirrups cut off as if by a Native's Hatchet, about ten Miles from the place where Captain Logan had left them, in the direction of Lime Stone Station. Near to this place also were the marks of his horse having been tied to a Tree, of his having slept upon some Grass in a Bark hut, and having apparently been roasting Chestnuts, when he had made some rapid strides towards his Horse as if surprised by the Natives. No further traces could however be discovered, till the 28th, when Mr. Cowper discovered the dead Horse sticking in a Creek, and not far from it, at the top of the Bank, the body of Captain Logan, buried about a foot under the ground. Near this also were found papers torn in pieces, his boots and part of his waistcoat stained with Blood.

From all these circumstances, it appears probable that, while at the place where he had slept for the Night, Captain Logan was suddenly surprised by the Natives, that he mounted his Horse, without Saddle or bridle, and, being unable to manage him, the Horse, pursued by the Natives got into the Creek, where Captain Logan, endeavouring to extricate him, was overtaken and foully Murdered.

*From the letter from Captain Clunie to the Colonial Secretary, A. McLeay, published in the* Sydney Gazette *of 25 November 1830*

One Sunday morning as I went walking,
  by Brisbane waters I chanced to stray,
I heard a convict his fate bewailing, as on the
  sunny riverbank he lay.
"I am a native of Erin's island, but banished
  now from my native shore,
They stole me from my aged parents, and
  from the maiden that I do adore."

"I've been a prisoner at Port Macquarie,
  at Norfolk Island and Emu Plains,
At Castle Hill and at cursed Toongabbie, at all
  these settlements I've worked in chains.
But of all places of condemnation, and penal
  stations in New South Wales,
To Moreton Bay I have found no equal,
  excessive tyranny each day prevails."

"For seven long years I've been beastly treated,
  heavy irons on my legs I bore,
My back with flogging was lacerated, and
  oft-times painted with my crimson gore.
And many a man from downright starvation,
  lies mouldering now beneath the clay,
For Captain Logan, he had us mangled,
  on the triangles at Moreton Bay."

"Like the Egyptians and ancient Hebrews, we
  were oppressed under Logan's yoke,
Till a native black, lying there in ambush, did
  deal our tyrant with his fatal stroke.
My fellow prisoners, be exhilarated, that all such
  monsters like death may find,
And when from bondage we're liberated, our
  former sufferings will fade from mind."

*Brisbane, from South Brisbane (from a photograph, engraved by J. C. Armytage, from* Australia, *ed. Edwin Carton Booth)*

# Nine Miles from Gundagai

*This song needs little introduction to most Australians, for almost everyone knows what the dog actually did in or on the tucker box near Gundagai, whether it was five, six, nine or ten miles away. The words given here are from a* Bill Bowyang Reciter, *and the tune is widely known.*

I'm used to punching bullock teams across
    the hills and plains,
I've teamed outback this forty years, in blazing
    droughts and rains.
I've lived a heap of troubles down
    without a blooming lie,
But I can't forget what happened me nine miles
    from Gundagai.

'Twas getting dark, the team got bogged,
    the axle snapped in two.
I lost my matches and my pipe, oh, what was I
    to do.
The rain came on, 'twas bitter cold, and hungry
    too was I,
And the dog, he sat in the tucker box, nine miles
    from Gundagai.

Some blokes I know has stacks of luck, no matter
    how they fall,
But there was I, Lord love a duck, no blessed
    luck at all.
I couldn't make a pot of tea, or get my trousers dry,
And the dog sat in the tucker box, nine miles
    from Gundagai.

I can forgive the blinking team, I can forgive
    the rain,
I can forgive the dark and cold and go
    through it again,
I can forgive my rotten luck, but hang me till I die
I can't forgive that plurry dog, nine miles
    from Gundagai.

*Native encampment (Skinner Prout, from* Australia, *ed. Edwin Carton Booth)*

# Oh! T.I.

## (also Old T.I. and Old P.I.)

Verses Two and Three

This song is widely known in North Queensland, the Torres Strait and the Northern Territory in a number of forms. "T.I." is of course Thursday Island, the old centre of the pearl and trochus fishing industry in the Torres Strait, and, as far as Ron Edwards has been able to discover, the song was composed there in 1936 aboard the lugger Pearl by a fellow called Jarfar Ahmat. It became instantly popular, and travelled widely among coloured people through the north, and changed its words and tune a bit as it went, as is normally the way of such things. I had learned it from Ron Edwards, who learned it from Charley Ahmat, Jarfar's brother, in 1965. I tried to sing it in unison with Ted Egan who had learned it from a friend in Darwin, and we found that there was a significant difference in words and music, enough to make the songs different versions.

Australian Aboriginals called the song "Old P.I." after the Palm Island native settlement east of Ingham, but there is no doubt, I think, that it was originally a Torres Strait song, but it seems to have kept closer to the original composition among the Island folk. This is the version given by Ron in his Overlander Song Book.

Why are you looking so sad, my dear,
Why are you feeling so blue?
I'm thinking of someone so far away
In that beautiful place called T.I.

Chorus
Oh, T.I., my beautiful home,
That's the place where I was born.
Where the moon and stars they shine,
    make me longing for home,
Oh, T.I., my beautiful home.

Take me across the sea,
Over the deep blue sea,
Darling won't you take me
Back to my home T.I?

Chorus

T.I. beautiful home,
T.I. my home sweet home,
I'll be there forever,
The sun is setting, farewell.

Chorus

# The Old Bark Hut

*Probably a shepherd's or hut-keeper's song orig-inally, this remains a humorous reminder of what it was like to be an employee on rations, working on a station before the unions demanded and eventually got better conditions for the men they represented. There is a ring of verity about the conditions depicted, though with the greatest good humour apparent. There are many sets of tunes and words, and these are my favourite ones.*

Oh, my name is Bob the Swagman, and I'll have
  you understand,
I've had lots of ups and downs while travelling
  through the land.
I once was fairly well-to-do, but now that's all
  gone phut,
And I'm forced to go on rations in an old
  bark hut.

*Chorus*
In an old bark hut, in an old bark hut,
I'm forced to go on rations in an old bark hut.

Ten pound of beef, ten pound of flour, some
  sugar and some tea,
That's all they feed a hungry man until the
  seventh day.
Unless you're mighty sparing, boys, you'll go
  with a hungry gut—
That's one of the great misfortunes in an old
  bark hut.

*Chorus*
In an old bark hut, in an old bark hut,
That's one of the great misfortunes in an old
  bark hut.

The bucket I wash my feet in has to cook
  my tea and stew,
They'd say I was getting mighty flash if I should
  ask for two.
The table's just a sheet of bark, God knows
  when it was cut,
It was blown from off the rafters of the old
  bark hut.

*Chorus*
Of the old bark hut, of the old bark hut,
It was blown from off the rafters of the old
  bark hut.

On stormy days the rain comes in just like
  a perfect flood,
Especially through the big round hole where
  once the table stood.
It leaves me not a single place where I can lay
  me nut,
For the rain is sure to find me in the
  old bark hut.

*Chorus*
In the old bark hut, in the old bark hut,
Oh, the rain is sure to find me in the old
  bark hut.

Of furniture, there's no such thing was ever
  in the place,
Except the chair I sit upon, and that's an old
  gin case.
I've a billy and a pint pot and a broken-handled
  cup,
And they all adorn the table in the old bark hut.

*Chorus*
In the old bark hut, in the old bark hut,
And they all adorn the table in the old bark hut.

In summer, when the weather's warm, the hut
  is nice and cool,
You'll find the gentle breezes blowing in
  through every hole.
You can leave the old door open, or you can
  leave it shut,
There's no fear of suffocation in the old bark hut.

*Chorus*
In the old bark hut, in the old bark hut,
There's no fear of suffocation in the old bark hut.

Beside the fire I lay me down, wrapped up
  in two old rugs;
It doesn't make for comfort, for it seems to lure
  the bugs.
And all I've got for company's me poor old
  collie pup.
So I use him for a pillow in the old bark hut.

*Chorus*
In the old bark hut, in the old bark hut,
Oh, I use him for a pillow in the old bark hut.

And now I've sung my little song as nicely
  as I could.
I hope the ladies present didn't think my
  language rude.
And all you handsome boys and girls around me
  growing up,
Remember Bob the Swagman, and his old
  bark hut.

*Chorus*
His old bark hut, yes, his old bark hut,
Remember Bob the Swagman and his old
  bark hut.

# The Old Bullock Dray

*Another song from the 1860s for it mentions John Robertson. There are different words and tunes, but once again I have included my personal favourites.*

Now the shearing is all over and the wool is
coming down
And I mean to get a wife, me boys, when I get
into town.
Everything stands a chance that presents itself
to view
From a little paddymelon to a bucking kangaroo.

*Chorus*

So it's roll up your blankets, and let us make
a push.
I'll take you up the country and show you
the bush.
I'll be bound such a chance you won't get
another day
So roll up and take possession of me old
bullock dray.

Well, yes, of beef and damper, I reckon we've
enough,
And we'll boil in the bucket such a whopper
of a duff;
And my mates they will all dance to the honour
of the day
And the music of the bells around my old
bullock dray.

*Chorus*

Now, we'll have lots of tucker; for good living
I'm your man,
We'll have leatherjacks, johnnycakes, and fritters
in the pan.
And if you'd like some fish, I'll catch you
some soon,
For we'll bob for barramundis on the banks
of a lagoon.

*Chorus*

Oh, we'll have lots of children, now, you musn't
mind that,
There'll be Buckjumping Maggie and
Leatherbelly Pat,

There'll be Stringybark Sue and Greenhide
  Mike,
Oh, yes! My Colonial! As many as you like.

*Chorus*

Oh we'll stop all immigration, we won't need it
  any more,
We'll have young colonials, kids by the score.
And I wonder what the hell Jacky Robertson
  will say
When he sees 'em promenading round me old
  bullock dray.

*Chorus*

*Cockatoo Island (Skinner Prout, from* Australia, *ed. Edwin Carton Booth)*

# The Old Keg of Rum

*There were two versions of the words of this song extant, one in Paterson's* Old Bush Songs, *a farmer's-harvester's song, and the other from Vance Palmer's collection, where the celebrants are shearers. It was the second one we learned first, so it is the second one that is included here. As in "The Old Bark Hut", the Chorus repeats the last line of the preceding verse.*

My name is old Jack Palmer, and I once dug
    for gold,
And the song I'm going to sing to you concerns
    the days of old,
When I'd plenty of mates around me and the talk
    would fairly hum,
As we all sat together round the old keg of rum.

*Chorus*
The old keg of rum, the old keg of rum,
We all sat together round the old keg of rum.

There was Bluey Watt the breaker, and old
    Tommy Hines,
And little Joe, the ringer, who now in Glory
    shines;
And many more hard doers who are gone to
    Kingdom Come,
We were all associated round the old keg of rum.

*Chorus*

When shearing time was over in the sheds along
    the Bree,
We'd raise a keg from somewhere and we'd all
    have a spree.
We'd sit and sing together till we got that blind
    and dumb
That we couldn't find the bunghole of the old
    keg of rum.

*Chorus*

There were some who'd last the night out, and
    some who'd have a snooze;
And some be full of fight, me boys, and all be full
    of booze.
And sometimes in a scrimmage I'd to cork it with
    me thumb
For to keep the life from leaking from the old
    keg of rum.

*Chorus*

And when the spree was over, and we'd wake up
    from our snooze,
For to give another drain, the old keg would
    refuse.
We'd rap it with our knuckles, though it sounded
    like a drum,
For the spirit had departed from our old
    keg of rum.

*Chorus*
And now my song is over, and I've got
    to travel on,
Just an old buffer skiting of days that's dead
    and gone;
And you youngsters who now hear me will
    perhaps in years to come,
Remember old Jack Palmer and his old
    keg of rum.

*Chorus*

*Digger on the tramp (lithograph, from* History of Australasia, *David Blair)*

# The Old Palmer Song

*Perhaps the best popular history of the Palmer River goldrush is* River Of Gold *by Hector Holthouse. The discovery and opening up of the Palmer field is a fascinating bit of our history, and a wealth of poems and ballads celebrate the event. There are some of these quoted in the ballad section of this book. But the tune and words that were most popular proved to be this song. Set to the English tune, "Ten Thousand Miles Away", the words were probably composed either prior to boarding or on board a vessel bound for Cooktown. There is that fine air of expectation about the sentiments expressed that is characteristic of diggers before disappointment set in.*

Oh, the wind is fair and free, my boys, the wind
   is fair and free,
The steamer's course is north, my boys, and the
   Palmer we will see.
The Palmer we will see, my boys, and
   Cooktown's muddy shore,
Where I've been told there's lots of gold, so stay
   down south no more.

*Chorus*
So blow, ye winds, heigh-ho, a-digging we
   will go,
We'll stay no more down south, my boys, so let
   the music play.

In spite of what I'm told, I'm off in search
   of gold,
And we'll make a push for the brand new rush,
   a thousand miles away.

They say the blacks are troublesome, they spear
   both horse and man,
The rivers all are deep and wide, no bridges
   them do span.
No bridges them do span, my boys, and so you'll
   have to swim,
But never fear the yarns you hear, and gold
   you're sure to win.

*Chorus*
So let us make a move, my boys, for that new
   Promised Land
And do the best you can, my boys, to lend
   a helping hand.
To lend a helping hand, my boys, where the soil
   is rich and new,
In spite of the blacks and the unknown tracks,
   we'll show what we can do.

*Chorus*

# On the Queensland Railway Lines

*The words of this song were composed by joint effort at John Manifold's home one night as an effort by the Realist Writers' Group of Queensland. The tune is from a German folksong, I think, about a peasant who wanted to take his goat on the train with him. The whole thing proves that it is possible to create something very entertaining from the most unpromising material, in this case the Long Distance Trains Timetable supplied from the Queensland Railways Department. The awful details about the availability of provisions and ablution facilities were correct at the time of composition, and I shouldn't be too surprised if they were not true today as well. The Queensland Railways are essentially a conservative body. The names of the stations quoted in the chorus are no longer entirely valid, for a number of branch lines have been closed since the song's composition. For instance, I think you must now go by road if you want to visit Wonglepong.*

On the Queensland Railway Lines
There are stations where one dines,
Private individuals
Also run refreshment stalls.
*Chorus*
Bogantungan, Rollingstone,
Mungar, Murgon, Marathon.
Guthalungra, Pinkenba,
Wanko, Yaamba, ha-ha-ha.

Pies and coffee, baths and showers,
Are supplied at Charters Towers,
At Mackay the rule prevails
Of restricting showers to males.
*Chorus*

Males and females, high and dry,
Hang around at Durikai,
Booramugga, Djarawong,
Giligulgul, Wonglepong.

*Chorus*

Iron rations come in handy
On the way to Dirranbandi,
Passengers have died of hunger
During halts at Garradunga.
*Chorus*

Let us toast, before we part,
Those who travel, stout of heart,
Drunk or sober, rain or shine,
On the Queensland Railway Lines.
*Chorus*

# One of the Has-Beens

Chorus

*This rather sad and pensive little ditty is sung to the tune of "Pretty Little Polly Perkins" and "Cushy Butterfield". It is not a complaint, just a statement of an older man who is no longer capable of the hard driving of shearing that he could accomplish when he began as a youngster. It is best sung in a meditative quiet way, I feel.*

I'm one of the has-beens, a shearer I mean,
I once was a ringer, boys, and I used
   to shear clean.
I could make the wool roll off like the soil
   from the plough,
But you may not believe me, for I can't do it
   now.

*Chorus*
For I'm as awkward as a newchum, and I'm used
   to the frown
That the Boss often shows me, saying, "Keep
   them blades down!"

I've shorn with Paddy Hogan, Bill Bright and
   Jack Gunn,
Charlie Fergus, Tommy Layton, and the great
   roaring Dunn.
They brought from the Lachlan the best they
   could find,
But there was never one among them, boys, could
   leave me behind.

*Chorus*

But it's no use complaining, I'll never say die,
Though the days of fast shearing for me have
   gone by.
I'll take the world easy, shear slowly and clean,
And I merely have told you just what
   I have been.

# The Overlander

*The tune I give here is not the better known one, but I have a preference for a rollicking version of a song if it is available, and this one certainly moves along much better than the one usually sung. Ron Edwards quotes three variants of the song in his* Overlander Song Book *and those interested could see his notes for details. The song seems to have been originated by a Queenslander, though possibly not in that State.*

There is a trade you all know well, it's bringing
    cattle over.
I'll tell you all about the time that I became
    a drover.
I wanted stock for Queensland, to Kempsey did
    I wander,
And picked up a mob of "duffers" there and
    became an overlander.

*Chorus*
Pass the bottle round, boys; don't just let it
    stand there.
For tonight we'll drink the health of every
    overlander.

When the cattle were all mustered and the outfit
    ready to start,
I saw the boys all mounted and their swags
    all in the cart.
I found I had all sorts of men, from Germany,
    France and Flanders.
They're a well mixed pack, both white and black,
    the Queensland overlanders.

*Chorus*

From the route I fed them out where the grass
    was green and young,
When a squatter, with an awful shout, told me to
    move along.
I said, "Old man, you're rather hard, but don't
    you raise my dander,
For I'm a regular knowing card, and a
    Queensland overlander."

*Chorus*

It's true we pay no licence and our run is
    rather large,
It's not often they can catch us, so they cannot
    lay a charge.
They think we live on store beef, but I'm no
    flaming gander,
If a fat little stray should come our way,
    "He'll do!" says the overlander.

*Chorus*

Now, I would scorn to steal a shirt, as all my
    mates can say,
So if we chance to pass a town upon a washing
    day,
Those little brats of kids, my boys, they quickly
    raise my dander,
Saying, "Mother, dear, bring in the clothes,
    here comes an overlander!"

*Chorus*

In town we drain the wine cup, and go to see
    the play,
And never think to be hard up, or how to pass
    the day,
For each one has a sweetheart there, dressed up
    in all her grandeur—
Dark eyes and jet-black flowing hair, "She's
    a plum!" says the overlander.

*Chorus*

A little girl in Brisbane Town, she said "Don't
    leave me lonely!"
I said, "It's sad, but this old prad was built for
    one man only!"
So now I'm headed west again on a steed that's
    quite a goer,
I'll pick up a job with a crawling mob on the
    banks of the Maranoa.

*Chorus*

*Cattle drovers (engraving from an early illustrated newspaper)*

# The Ribuck Shearer

I learned this song from my brother Alan many years ago. It is another shearer's boasting song, and is not intended to be taken seriously. The Australian bushman was not much of a boaster. Tradition has preserved some of the boasts of the American river-men, who were often, according to their own witness; "half horse, half alligator and the rest wildcat". The Australian, on the other hand, was ironic even in his cups, and these songs, as represented in this collection by "Widgeegoara Joe", "The Springtime It Brings on the Shearing", "The Limejuice Tub", and this one, show that even when he boasted of his capabilities, he was, in part at least, laughing at himself. The word "Ribuck", or "Rye-buck", is an obsolete slang expression capable of two interpretations. It could be used, as in this case, as an adjective, to signify that something was the real thing, and not a counterfeit. On the other hand, if used in reply to a question, it signified agreement, the modern equivalent being, "OK, I'll go along with that." Readers of The Sentimental Bloke by C. J. Dennis, will remember that when the Bloke asks the fellow who works

> *"In that same pickle found-ery. ('E boils*
> *The cabbitch stalks, or somethink.)"*

for an "intro" to Doreen, "'E says, 'Ribuck.'"

I come from the south and my name is Field,
And when my shears are properly steeled
It's a hundred or more I have very often peeled
And of course I'm a ribuck shearer.

*Chorus*
If I don't shear a tally before I go,
My shears and stone in the river I'll throw;
And I'll never open Sawbees[1] to cut
    another blow[2],
To prove I'm a ribuck shearer.

There's a bloke on the board, and I heard
    him say
That I couldn't shear a hundred sheep in a day,
But one fine day, I'll show him the way,
And prove I'm a ribuck shearer.

*Chorus*

Yes, one fine day, but I'm not saying when
I'll up off my tail and I'll into the pen,
While the ringer shears five, I'll shear ten,
And I'll prove I'm a ribuck shearer.

*Chorus*

There's a bloke on the board, and he's got
    a yellow gin,

A very long nose and a wart on the chin,
And a voice like a billygoat spitting on a tin,
And of course, he's a ribuck shearer.

*Chorus*

But if I don't beat his tally before I go,
My shears and stone in the river I'll throw,

And never open Sawbees to cut another blow,
And prove I'm a ribuck shearer.

*1. "Sawbees" were hand shears, possibly a corruption of the brand name, "Salisbury's". "B-bows" was also another name for hand shears, from the shape of the spring steel handles. "Stoppers" were leather keepers into which the shears were slipped when not in use, to prevent rust and keep the edge of the blades.*
*2. A blow, a cut and a drive were strokes with the shears when shearing.*

*Tailing (detail, engraving from* Australasian Sketcher, *21 October 1882)*

TAILING

# The Sheep Washer's Lament

*Before the days when wool scours were built, men were employed on contract rates to wash the sheep in creeks to get the worst of the bulldust out of the wool before shearing. There is a description of the operation in* The letters of Rachel Henning. *This explains the number of watercourses called "Washpool Creek" one encounters when driving through the districts of early settlement. The words of the song given here are those published by John Manifold in the* Penguin Australian Song Book. *I don't know where John collected this version, but it is certainly an improvement on the longer and rather rambling lyric quoted by Paterson, in his* Old Bush Songs.

When first I took the western tracks,
    many years ago,
No master then stood up so high, no servant
    bowed so low.
But now the squatters, puffed with pride, do treat
    us with disdain,
Lament with me the bygone days that will not
    come again.

I had a pair of ponies once, to bear me
    on my road.

I earned a decent cheque at times, and blued it
    like a lord.
But lonely now, I hump my drum, in sunshine
    and in rain,
Lamenting on those bygone days that will not
    come, again.

Let bushmen all in unity, combine with heart
    and hand,
Till bloody cringing poverty is driven
    from our land.
Let never Queensland come to know the tyrant's
    ball and chain
And washers all in times to come their vanished
    rights regain.

# The Springtime It Brings on the Shearing

*As I mention in the note on Overbury's poem, "The Wallaby Track", part of it picked up a fine tune. This is the song referred to, and if any of my readers think he can include more of the poem in the song, let him go ahead by all means.*

Oh, the springtime, it brings on the shearing, and it's then you will see them in droves
To the west country stations come steering, and seeking a job of the coves.

*Chorus*
With a ragged old swag on my shoulder, and a billy quart-pot in my hand,
Well, I'll tell you we'll 'stonish the newchums, to see how we travel the land.

And after the shearing's all over, and the wool season comes to an end,
It's then you will see the flash shearers making johnny-cakes round in the bend.

*Chorus*

*Drawing out the sheep (detail, engraving from* Australasian Sketcher, *21 October 1882)*

# Stir the Wallaby Stew

Chorus

*A record of the vicissitudes of a family of no-hopers after Father got caught cattle-duffing, and was sent to prison. In New South Wales, he was accommodated at "Maitland Gaol", but in Queensland, it was "Boggo Road" that rejoiced in his unwilling patronage. Dad must certainly have been the guide and mentor of his little flock, for they certainly went to pieces in his absence!*

Poor Daddy got five years or more, as
    everybody knows;
And now he lives in Boggo Road, broad arrows
    on his clothes.
He branded all Brown's cleanskins, and never
    left a tail,
So I'll relate the family's fate, since Dad got
    put in gaol.

*Chorus*

So stir the wallaby stew, make soup with the
kangaroo's tail.
I tell you things are pretty crook since Dad got
put in gaol.

Our sheep all died a month ago, not rot, but
flaming fluke.
Our cow was boozed last Christmas Day by my
big brother, Luke;
And Mother has a shearer cove forever
within hail,
The family will have grown a bit when Dad
gets out of gaol.

*Chorus*

Our Bess got shook upon a bloke, he's gone, we
don't know where.
He used to act around the sheds, but he ain't
acted square.

I've sold the buggy on my own, the place is up
for sale.
That isn't all that won't be junked when Dad
gets out of gaol.

*Chorus*

They let Dad out before his time to give us
a surprise.
He came and looked around the place, and gently
damned our eyes.
He shook hands with the shearer cove, and said
he thought things stale,
So he left him there to shepherd us, and battled
back into gaol.

*Chorus*

*Coffee tent, six miles from Bush Inn (from* Sketches of the Victoria Gold Diggings and Diggers As They Are *[1852–53],
S. T. Gill)*

# The Stockman's Last Bed

*This song, like "The Dying Stockman", celebrates the same story as the American song, "The Streets of Laredo". The tune and words below are from the singing of Sid Davis originally, who learned this version of the song in his youth near Maryborough. While some of the words are rather mawkish and sentimental, and some of the lines awkward verse, the song can be sung with very telling effect, for the tune is pleasantly mournful.*

Be ye stockman or no, to my story give ear,
It's all up with poor Jack, and no more will
    we hear,
The crack of his stockwhip, his steed's lively trot,
His clear "Go ahead!" and his jingling quartpot.

*Chorus*
For we've laid him where the wattles their sweet
    fragrance spread,
And the tall gumtrees shadow,
The tall gumtrees shadow,
The tall gumtrees shadow the stockman's
    last bed.

While drafting one day he was horned by a cow.
"Alas!" cried poor Jack, "It's all up
    with me now.
I never will swing to the saddle again
Or chase the wild breakaways over the plain."

*Chorus*

His whip is now silent, his dogs they do mourn,
His horse looks in vain for its master's return.
No friends to bemoan him, now silent he dies,
Save the wandering myalls none know where
    he lies.

*Chorus*
Now, stockmen, if ever on some sunny day
While tailing a mob, you should happen that way,
Tread light by the mound in the tall gum
    tree's shade,
For it may be the spot where our comrade is laid.

*Chorus*

197

# The Streets of Forbes

*This song about the death of the bushranger Ben Hall seems to have been written very soon after his death at the hands of the police party at Coobong Creek, and some say it was written by "John McGuire, Hall's brother-in-law". It was certainly written by a sympathizer. A good account of the incident is given in* A Pictorial History of Australian Bushranging, *by Wannan and others, published by Lansdowne Press.*

Come all you Lachlan men, a sorrowful tale
   I'll tell,
Concerning a bold hero, who through
   misfortune fell.
His name it was Ben Hall, a man of great renown,
Who was hunted from his station, and like a dog
   shot down.

Three years he roamed the highway, and had
   a lot of fun.
A thousand pounds was on his head, with Gilbert
   and John Dunn.
Ben parted from his comrades, and the outlaws
   did agree
To give up their bushranging and cross
   the briny sea.

Ben went to Goobang Creek, and this was his
   downfall,
For riddled like a sieve was valiant Ben Hall.
It was early in the morning upon the fifth
   of May,
When the police surrounded him as fast asleep
   he lay.

Bill Dargin, he was chosen, to shoot the outlaw
   dead,
The troopers fired madly, and filled him full
   of lead.
They threw him on his horse, and strapped him
   like a swag,
Then led him through the streets of Forbes, to
   show the prize they had.

*Scene of Ben Hall's capture and death, near Forbes, New South Wales (engraving from* Illustrated Melbourne Post, *22 May 1865)*

# Ten Thousand Miles Away

*This old fo'c'sle song was popular afloat in the ships of the English-speaking seafarers, and the tune must have been familiar to Australians, for there are two sets of words for it written locally. Both of these are included herein, but this is the original song.*

Sing ho, for a brave and gallant ship, and a fair
   and favouring breeze,
With a bully crew and a captain too, to carry me
   over the seas.
To carry me over the seas, my boys, to my true
   love far away,
I'm taking a trip on a government ship ten
   thousand miles away.

*Chorus*
Then blow, ye winds, hi-ho, a-roving I will go,
I'll stay no more on England's shore to hear the
   music play.
I'm off on the morning train, across the raging
   main,
I'm taking a trip on a Government ship, ten
   thousand miles away.

My true love, she was beautiful, my true love she
   was young.
Her eyes they shone like diamonds bright, and
   silvery was her tongue.
And silvery was her tongue, my boys, but now
   she's far away,
And doing the grand in a distant land, ten
   thousand miles away.

*Chorus*

Oh, dark and dismal was the day when last I seen
   my Meg,
She'd a Government band around each hand and
   another one round her leg.
And another one round her leg, my boys, and
   fifty pounds they weigh,
"Farewell," said she, "Remember me, ten
   thousand miles away!"

*Chorus*

The sun may shine through a London fog and the
   river run quite clear,
Or the ocean brine be turned to wine, or I forget
   my beer,
Or I forget my beer, my boys, or the landlord's
   quarter-day,
Ere I forget my own sweetheart, ten thousand
   miles away.

*Chorus*

I wish I was a bosun bold, or even a bombardier,
I'd take a ship and away I'd trip, and straight for
   my true-love steer;
Straight for my true-love steer, my boys, where
   the dancing dolphins play,
And the whales and sharks are having their larks,
   ten thousand miles away.

*Chorus*

Government House Sydney

# A Thousand Miles Away

*The words for this song were attributed to C. A. Flower by Mr R. C. Lethbridge in a letter to Stewart and Keesing when they were compiling their expanded version of Paterson's* Old Bush Songs. *Paterson had included it in his original book. Flower could have written it, for he was employed on the railroad when it was being built from Roma to Mitchell. He was Accountant for Frazer, McDonald and Company, who were building the line under contract to the Queensland Government. He was familiar with the western cattle country, for he travelled widely through the far west for about six months after he left the railroad job in 1883.*

Hurrah for the Roma railway! Hurrah for Cobb
    and Co.!
And give me a horse, a good stockhorse, to carry
    me westward-ho!
To carry me westward-ho, my boys, out where
    the cattle stray,
On the far Barcoo and the Flinders, too,
    a thousand miles away.

*Chorus*
Then give your horses rein across the open plain,
We'll ship our beef both sound and sweet, nor
    care what some folks say.
And frozen we'll send home those cattle that
    now roam,
On the far Barcoo and the Flinders too,
    a thousand miles away.

Knee-deep in grass they've got to pass, for the
    truth I'm bound to tell,
How in six months those cattle get as fat as they
    can swell;
As fat as they can swell, my boys, and a thousand
    pounds they weigh,
On the far Barcoo and the Flinders too,
    a thousand miles away.

*Chorus*

No Yankee hide e'er grew outside such beef as we
    can freeze.
No Yankee pasture grew such stock as we send
    overseas,
As we send o'er the seas, my boys, a thousand
    pounds they weigh,
On the far Barcoo where they eat nardoo,
    a thousand miles away.

*Chorus*

*Shipping, Circular Quay (engraving from* Picturesque Atlas of Australasia, *ed. Andrew Garran)*

# Van Diemen's Land

*There are many variants of this song that have been collected both here and also in Ireland. The text in Stewart and Keesing comes from an Irish collection of street ballads, but the song has been collected in Australia. A. L. Lloyd sings a version of it on the old Wattle record, "Convicts and Currency Lads". A note enclosed with that record states "One historian says that in only three years, (from 1827), eight thousand men and boys were convicted under the Game Laws (for poaching), and many of them were sentenced to transportation."*

Come all you gallant poachers that ramble
    void of care,
Who walk out on a moonlight night, with gun and
    dog and snare;
While the hare and lofty pheasant you have
    at your command,
Little thinking of the dangers upon Van Diemen's
    Land.

Poor Thomas Brown from Nenagh town, Jack
    Murphy and poor Joe,
They were three of them gallant poachers
    as the county well did know.
One night they all were captured by the keepers
    hid in sand,
And for fourteen years transported, unto Van
    Diemen's Land.

The first day that we landed upon that
    fatal shore,
The planters, they came round us; some twenty
    score or more.
They ranked us up like horses and sold us
    out of hand,
And yoked us to the plough, my boys, to plough
    Van Diemen's Land.

The houses that we live in are built
    with clods of clay;
With rotten straw for bedding, we dare not
    to say nay.
Our cots we fence with fire, my boys, and
    slumber when we can,
To drive off wolf and tigers, upon Van
    Diemen's Land.

There was a girl from Nenagh town, Peg Brophy
    was her name,
For fourteen years transported, for playing
    of the game.
Our planter bought her freedom, and married
    her out of hand,
And she gives to us good usage, boys, upon Van
    Diemen's Land.

And oft when I am slumbering, I have
    a pleasant dream,
And with my sweetheart sitting, all by a purling
    stream.
Through Ireland I am roaming, with my true
    love close at hand,
But I waken brokenhearted, upon Van
    Diemen's Land.

Oh, if I had a thousand pounds, all laid out
    in my hand,
I'd give it all for liberty, if that I could command.
Again to Ireland I'd return and be a happy man,
And say farewell to poaching, and to Van
    Diemen's Land.

*Plough gang, Port Arthur (from* For the Term of His Natural Life, *Marcus Clarke)*

# The Wallaby Brigade

Chorus

*This song is the antithesis of the one above, and reflects the buoyant spirit of the Currency Lad, the itinerant worker, who knew his power as well as his limitations, and looked no further than the life he was leading on the track.*

Now you often have been told of armies brave
    and bold,
But we are the finest ever made,
We're called the rag-tag band and we rally in
    Queensland,
We're the members of the Wallaby Brigade.

*Chorus*
It's tramp, tramp, tramp across the border,
The swagmen are rolling up, I see.
When the shearing's at an end, we'll go whaling[1]
    in the bend,
And hooray for the Wallaby Brigade!

When you are leaving camp, you must ask
    some brother tramp,
If there are any jobs to wield the blades;
Or what sort of a shop that station is to stop,
For a member of the Wallaby Brigade.

*Chorus*

You must ask if they need men, you must ask
    for rations, then;
If they don't stump up, a warning should
    be made.
And to teach them better sense, burn down their
    bloody fence[2]!
That's the war-cry of the Wallaby Brigade!

*Chorus*

Now the squatters thought us done, when they
    fenced in all the runs,
But a prettier mistake was never made;
You've only to flash your Dover[3], and knock
    a monkey[4] over,
That's cheap mutton for the Wallaby Brigade.

*Chorus*

And when the shearing's in, then our harvest
    will begin,
Our swags then for a spell down will be laid;
And when our cheques are drained we will take
    the road again,
Lime-burners[5] in the Wallaby Brigade.

*Chorus*

*1. "Whaling": camped in the bend of the river fishing for cod and yellowbelly.*
*2. The threat of firing the fence could be delicately implied; see Henry Lawson's story about Mitchell begging rations from a station.*
*3. "Dover": a brand of knife favoured by bushmen.*
*4. "Monkey": cant phrase for a sheep.*
*5. Lime-burning was a very dry occupation, hence a man whose skin was cracking for a drink could be described as a "lime-burner"; now obsolete slang.*

# Widgeegoara Joe

*Another shearer's boasting song, first collected by Russel Ward from the singing of "Hoopiron" Jack Lee, retired shearer of Sydney. It is one of the songs first brought to prominence by its use in the musical show* Reedy River *in the 1950s.* Reedy River *had much to do with the re-awakening of interest in Australian folksong. This is intended to be a facetious song, and not to be taken seriously.*

I'm only a backblock shearer, as easily can
    be seen,
I've shorn in most of the famous sheds on the
    plains of the Riverine;
I've shorn in most of the famous sheds, and I've
    seen big tallies done,
But somehow or other, I don't know why, I never
    became a gun.

*Chorus*
Hooray, me boys, me shears are set, and I feel
    both fit and well;
Tomorrow you'll see me at my pen when
    the gaffer[1] rings the bell.
With Hayden's Patent Thumb-guards fixed,
    and both of my blades pulled back,
Away I'll go with my sardine blow, for a century
    or the sack!

I've opened up the wind-pipe straight, I've
    opened behind the ear,
I've shorn in all the possible styles in which
    a man can shear.
I've studied all the strokes and blows of the
    famous men I've met,
But I've never succeeded in plastering up those
    three little figures[2] yet.

*Chorus*

When the Boss walked on to the board today,
    he stopped and stared at me,
For I'd mastered Moran's great shoulder-cut,
    as he could plainly see.
And when he comes round tomorrow, me boys,
    I'll give his nerves a shock
When he discovers that I have mastered Pierce's
    Rangtang Block[3].

*Chorus*

And if I succeed as I hope to do, then I intend
    to shear
At the Wagga demonstration, that's held there
    every year.
It's there I'll lower the colours, the colours of
    Mitchell and Co.,
Instead of Deeming you will hear of
    Widgeegoara Joe.

*Chorus*

*1. "Gaffer": English slang, contraction of "grandfather", meant the boss of the board. Now obsolete in Australia, though still extant in England for the overseer on a job.*
*2. One hundred sheep in a day was a good tally with hand shears.*
*3. "Pierce's Rangtang Block": obviously a shearing blow invented by someone called Pierce. Block is probably poetic licence for the word "blow". Many expressions used by blade shearers were forgotten when machine shears were introduced and new techniques were developed for handling them.*

*A shearing shed in 1883 (engraving from* Sydney Mail, *15 December 1883)*

THE BOSS SHEARER

IN THE SHEARING SHED

# The Wild Colonial Boy

*This early folksong from our country has aroused almost as much discussion about its possible origins as the much debated "Waltzing Matilda". It is not my purpose to enter into this discussion here, merely to present a version collected by Stan Arthur in Brisbane. Stan and I recorded this tune on a recording for distribution to schools by Jacaranda Press in Brisbane to help sales of one of their poetry anthologies for high school students.*

Absit Omen!

'Tis of a wild colonial boy, Jack Doolan was
    his name,
Of poor but honest parents who lived in
    Castlemaine.
He was his father's only hope, his mother's pride
    and joy,
And dearly did his parents love their wild
    colonial boy.

*Chorus*
So come, all my hearties, we'll roam the
    mountains high,
Together we will plunder, together we will ride.
We'll scour along the valleys and gallop
    o'er the plains,
And scorn to live in slavery, bound down
    with iron chains.

He was scarcely sixteen years of age when
    he left his native home,
And through Australia's sunny clime
    a bushranger did roam.
He robbed those wealthy squatters, their stock
    he did destroy,
And a terror to Australia was the wild
    colonial boy.

*Chorus*

In sixty-one this daring youth commenced
    his wild career,
With courage all undaunted, no foeman
    did he fear.
He stuck up the Beechworth mail-coach and he
    robbed Judge McEvoy,
Who, trembling cold, gave up his gold, to the wild
    colonial boy.

*Chorus*

He bade the Judge "Good morning," and told
    him to beware,
That he'd never rob a hearty chap who acted
    on the square.
And never to rob a mother of her son and
    only joy,
Or else he might turn outlaw like the wild
    colonial boy.

*Chorus*

One day as he was riding the mountain side
    along,
A-listening to the little birds, their pleasant
    laughing song;
Three mounted troopers rode along, Kelly, Davis
    and Fitzroy,
With a warrant for the capture of the wild
    colonial boy.

*Chorus*

"Surrender now, Jack Doolan, you see
    we're three to one,
Surrender in the Queen's name, you daring
    highwayman!"
He pulled a pistol from his belt and waved
    the little toy,
"I'll fight but not surrender!" cried the wild
    colonial boy.

*Chorus*

He fired at Trooper Kelly, and brought him
    to the ground,
But in return from Davis received his mortal
    wound.
All shattered through the jaws he lay, still firing
    at Fitzroy,
And that's the way they captured him,
    the wild colonial boy.

*Chorus*

# The Wild Rover

*I had always thought that this song was an Australian composition, until in 1965 I collected it from the singing of Mr Hay, of Yeppoon in central Queensland. Mr Hay is the father of Bob Hay, the Rockhampton poet. He is a Scottish miner, now retired, who came to Australia at the beginning of the Depression years to work at the open cut mine at Blair Athol, and he told me that the song was well known in Scotland. Since then I have found versions of it in books of song from the British Isles. The version of the words given below seem to me to be a composite of two songs, or two versions of the same song, one called the "Wild Rover" and the other called the "Wild Boy". This may be drawing too fine a distinction, but these are the words Stan Arthur has always sung, and so I present them without too many apologies. The combination (if indeed it is one) is fitting enough, and the song is a good one.*

Well, I've been a wild rover this many a year,
And I've spent all my money on whisky
   and beer,
But now I'm returning with gold in great store
And I never will play the wild rover no more;
*Chorus*
And it's no, nay, never,
No, nay, never no more,
Will I play the wild rover,
Nay, never no more.

I went to a shanty I used to frequent
And I told the landlady my money was spent;
I asked her for credit, she answered me "Nay!"
"Such custom as yours I can get any day!"

*Chorus*

Then I pulled from my pocket ten sovereigns
   bright
And the landlady's eyes opened wide with delight.
   Said she, "I have whisky and wines of the best
And the words that I told you were only in jest!"

*Chorus*

There was Margaret and Kitty and Betsy
   and Sue,
And two or three more who belonged
   to our crew.
We'd sit up till midnight and make the place roar,
I've been a wild boy, but I'll be so no more.

*Chorus*

And then as a prisoner to Cockatoo[1] sent,
On a bed of cold straw for to lie and lament.
At last then I got what so long I'd looked for
And I never will play the wild rover no more.

*Chorus*

I'll go home to my parents, confess what
   I've done,
And I'll ask them to pardon their prodigal son;
And if they will do so, as often before,
Then I never will play the wild rover no more.

*Chorus*

*1. This is undoubtedly a reference to the old convict prison on Cockatoo Island in Sydney Harbour.*

Snakes!

# Reference Books

Australian Bush Ballads, *Douglas Stewart and Nancy Keesing, Angus & Robertson, 1955*
Colonial Ballads, *Hugh Anderson, Cheshire, 1955*
Farewell to Old England, *Hugh Anderson, Rigby, 1964*
Favourite Australian Bush Songs, *L. Long and G. Jenkin, Rigby, 1964*
Folk Songs of Australia, *John Meredith and Hugh Anderson, Ure Smith, 1967*
Goldrush Songster, The, *Hugh Anderson, Ram's Skull Press, 1958*
Index of Australian Folksong, 1857-1970, *Ron Edwards, Ram's Skull Press, 1971*
Old Australian Bush Ballads, *Vance Palmer and Margaret Sutherland, Allan, 1951*
Old Bush Songs, *A. B. Paterson, Angus & Robertson, 1st edn 1905*
Old Bush Songs *(enlarged and revised from the collection of A. B. Paterson), Douglas Stewart and Nancy Keesing, Angus & Robertson, 1957*
Overlander Song Book, *Ron Edwards, Rigby, 1971*
Penguin Australian Song Book, *John Manifold, Penguin, 1964*
Penguin Book of Australian Ballads, *Russel Ward, Penguin, 1964*
Who Wrote the Ballads? *John Manifold, Australasian Book Society, 1964*

# Magazines

Australian Tradition *(replacing* The Gumsucker's Gazette*) Folklore Society of Victoria and the Victorian Folk Music Club, beginning March 1964*
Northern Folk, *later* National Folk, *Ram's Skull Press, beginning March 1964*
The Queensland Bush Telegraph, *Queensland Folklore Society, irregular intervals beginning 1956*
Singabout, *Sydney Bush Music Club, beginning Summer 1956*

# Section III

# The Tall Story

As a matter of fact, Australia's true embodiment of Puck is neither a jolly old Punch nor a folksy old Uncle Remus. He's a lethal old prankster called the Bastard from the Bush. (And, for grim pleasantry, it would be hard to beat the much-quoted comeback: "'Will you have a cigarette, mate?' said the Leader of the Push. 'I'll have the flamin' *packet!*' said the Bastard from the Bush.")

Unfortunately, this sharp, hard-bitten and highly individual attitude was obscured, only too often, by images of dying stockmen, tipsy drovers and sentimental swaggies—who all looked more or less like colonial caricatures of Wordsworth's Old Leech Gatherer.

*From "The Melancholy of Lennie Lower", Alexander Macdonald in* The Best of Lennie Lower, *ed. Cyril Pearl and W. E. Pidgeon*

# Introduction to Section III

I suppose spoken humour can be divided into three parts, like Gaul. There is the joke, which can be as simple as a question and response or a mere statement. There are cycles of such stories which appear from nowhere, are ubiquitous for a time, and then are forgotten. Older readers may remember Little Audrey, who laughed and laughed, for instance. A good example of the one liner is the series about "Confucius, he say—". The simple statement leads to the punch line, usually a pun or a play on meaning.

The second type of spoken joke is the anecdotal type. These can vary enormously in length, from the mere question and response to the rambling "shaggy dog" story which can last for as long as the narrator chooses. I had a friend who told such a story which lasted for about four beers, and concerned a man who caught a small fish, of a kind he had never seen before, which started to grow bigger as soon as it was taken from the water. He took it ashore and asked a professional fisherman what it was. "That's a rarie, I've never seen one of those before," says the fisherman. The fish continues to grow. It is transferred to a utility, and then a ton truck and taken to a museum for identification. The ichthyologist admits that it is indeed a rare specimen, and that he cannot identify it. By this time the fish has grown to such an extent that it needs a low loader to transport the corpse, which is beginning to offend the noses of all who come near. The enormous stinking carcass, still growing, is eventually tipped into a river and towed out to sea by two tugs, where it is eventually abandoned. The payoff after this twenty minute dialogue, delivered with great emphasis was, "It's a long way to Tipperary!" There is a similar story about a little bull that went a long way. Cycles of these stories come and go in the folk tradition of our nation, and not only of our nation—I once wrote a short account of some current folk tales for a magazine and received a letter from a student of such things in the United States who assures me that some of the stories I mentioned in the article were known and were widespread in that country.

There is a wonderful grapevine, a bush telegraph for good stories, that sends them on their way with great rapidity. They spread from Cairns to Wyndham around the coast with a speed that is frightening and mysterious. For me the best kind of spoken humour is that of the tall story; Walter Blair described tall stories as ". . . exuberant combinations of fact with outrageous fiction". Strangely enough, they seem to flourish best in Australia and the North American continent, and indeed could be said to replace the myths, fairy tales and legends of the gods that exist in lands with a longer written history. Who is to say that Paul Bunyan of the American logging camps with his double-bitted axe or the hairy man from Hannigan's Halt with his shovel are not relatives (albeit of lesser antiquity) of Thor of the hammer or Jove of the thunderbolt? Given a thousand years or so, without the pervasive media of television and the newspaper, they might well have developed into just such deities.

The greatest early repository of these anecdotes was in a section of the Sydney *Bulletin* called "Aboriginalities" where paragraphs were contributed by men from all over the Commonwealth. This continued until the paper was remodelled about fourteen years ago. There was also a distaff side in another magazine for women published by the same Bulletin Newspaper Company. It was called *Between Ourselves,* and invited letters from readers. The tall story did not intrude much into these rather frilly effusions; in fact it seemed to be rather a male province. The tradition has been carried on in recent times by Bill Wannan who edits a page in the *Australasian Post.*

*Ballarat Post Office and township from Government Enclosure (engraving from* Victoria Illustrated, *S. T. Gill)*

# On Bush Liars

It is difficult to interestingly write up the lies one hears "Out Back," the blanky having to be omitted, and a bush "mulga" without the blanky is as a damaged ginger-bread. In order to have "a night of it," you must strike a camp of four or six men (not more, or things are confused and none have a chance to "settle down to it" properly), and, when supper has been despatched and pipes filled, just start the ball with a record suited to the gathering. After that the bush lie grows all round you without further assistance.

For instance, as to fencing—you knew a man who put up one hundred and thirty-five, in black soil; but, bless you, it's beaten in three places inside four seconds. The winning number is usually about two hundred, "an' ground as 'ard as bell-metal." Boring six inch hardwood posts (six holes), comes to a standstill at two hundred and thirty-four, with a rider to the effect that the narrator "'eard as some on 'em was a bit fuzzy."

Weight-lifting and carrying is a prolific topic. One saw three bags of flour carried fifty yards. Win? Not a hope! Billjim promptly swears that he knew Billjack to "hump" five bags one hundred yards and back—"though, mine yer, three on 'em was tied tergether" (a concession not always admitted).

It's hard on such occasions to find a man who was not present when "Black" Andy supported the half-ton case of iron—not to mention the "frill" that they attach to the performance.

*Les colons de Queensland (engraving from a collection of cuttings from French periodicals in the Rex Nan Kivell Collection)*

"'E 'umped it from ther boat up ther bank, steep as that (throwing arm into almost perpendicular position), an' tossed it inter ther waggon like nothin'."

You are safe also to hear of the German "cockie" whose habit it was to carry a bag of flour from the township to his selection—"seven-an'-alf measured miles" without a "spell."

"Met 'im myself one day, an' 'ad a bit of a 'pitch' ter 'im, an' after 'e'd bin spoutin' 'bout ten minutes I says ter 'im: 'Ain't yer goin' te' put ther flour down fer a bit?' an' 'e says:

"'Oh, der flure! Dat am right—it vos nuthin'—I vos vorgot.'" Sometimes if it's a "warm" night, the German's forgetful way is described as crossing ranges and skirting yawning precipices where one false step means smash. Extremes in this lie are not often necessary, however.

It's in the matter of riding that liars, even the champions, have to put their best yarn forward.

"I saw Dick Martin, a white man, mind yer, on Kickerebel, ride a big upstan'ing bay 'orse called 'Playboy,' an' 'e turned clean over—none o' yer rolling bucks, mind—but fair over in ther air, an' then never shifted 'is man. An' Dick in a 'untin saddle, too, not wedged in behind eight-inch pads! S'truth, 'e could ride, that bloke."

As for distances ridden "between suns," it's never safe to speculate as to what the "record" will be.

If time permits, and there's plenty of firewood, or the mosquitoes are not too bad, dogs are reasonably certain to be on the tapis ere the meeting breaks up. You'll hear of the "coming" dog—the dog that would muster a ten mile block "on his own," and the tyke that would cut out a marked sheep from a flock of ten thousand. You'll also be told about the dog that could round-up one particular blow-fly in a ten acre paddock. And when you get to that dog it is about time to go to bed.

*From "Aboriginalities", the* Bulletin

On my way to the locality I met the slide man, who informed me that a terrible accident had taken place; that, while proceeding down the range,

having a hogshead of rum on his slide, the horse swerved, brought the slide against a rock, the result being that the hogshead slipped off and rolled down the mountain. On reaching a prominent point it bounded and lodged directly on the miner's hut, demolished it, and exploded with a terrific report, resembling the discharge of a cannon. We went to the hut, expecting to find the miner dead, but found he had marvellously escaped, and had succeeded in saving a bucketful of rum. On seeing us, he remarked, "It is a bad wind that does not blow fair for somebody."

He was a man of fine physique, about 50 years old, well-set, good-looking, and of a military cast. There was a sapling resting on two uprights in front of the wrecked hut, from which were suspended about forty dead snakes of various colours and sizes. After a brief conversation as to his narrow escape from the rum fiend, I asked where he got so many snakes.

"I killed them, and a number of others, during my two months' encampment here. I have been in the British Army in India; have been mining in California, where I have seen thousands of reptiles, but I have never seen so many snakes as I have on this mountain. Look at this one," pointing to a peculiar brown snake about twelve feet long; "it's like a large gutta-percha tube. See, it has a prominent ligament from the head to the tail, along the ventral side. This snake is known as the Rota Anguis, probably the most dangerous of all."

"Where did you get it?" I inquired.

"I killed it this morning close by, at very great risk. While going up the mountain, I saw what I thought was a cask-hoop, but soon discovered it was a hoop snake. I endeavoured to strike it with my sapling, but failed. I saw from the gyrations it made that my position was serious, and ran down the declivity to an ironbark-tree, when lo! I heard the whizzing of the wheel serpent, which I saw was almost upon me. I moved beside the tree, and, just as it glanced the ironbark, I struck it with my sapling and fractured the vertebra. There is sure to be another of the class about, and, as my hut is now demolished, I think it is a good omen for me to leave, and I will do so this afternoon, and go to Crown Flat. I have now had two marvellous escapes, and I think these are sufficient for one day."

*From* Reminiscences of the Goldfields and Elsewhere in New South Wales, *Martin Brennan*

*View on the Yarra, near Dight's Mill (engraving from* Victoria Illustrated, *S. T. Gill)*

*I had heard of the hoop snake in a roundabout way in casual conversation over the years, there being two variants of the story, one in which the snake swallowed itself and vanished in a puff of smoke when frustrated; in the other the snake lived in mountainous country, and attacked by seizing its tail in its mouth and rolling downhill at its prey. These were nothing but casual parts of the bush menagerie to me, some of the other inhabitants of this strange and little encountered fauna being the sidehill dodger and the mooncaller. I have discovered since that these animals thrive in Paul Bunyan country in the northern United States, along with other strange creatures not found here, the axe-handle trout and the behinder which no one had ever been able to describe because it crept up from the rear and its attack was invariably deadly. Imagine my delight when I discovered this reference to the hoop snake, with its Latin name and all. Evidence at last!*

## Something Like a Snake

I once worked a reefing-claim lone-handed, and camped in a solitary old hut, with a fourteen-feet carpet snake as my only mate. Jumbo was very useful in keeping mice and 'possums away, and he used to lie and watch me at meals, ready to snap up any meat I threw at him. He had only one fault — a startling habit of climbing unexpectedly up and licking both sides of the back of my neck with his forked tongue.

One day I slithered nearly down the shaft, which was fifty feet deep and only the first twenty laddered, when the rope broke, and although not hurt, I was imprisoned. I coo-eed, but there was no one within miles, and my efforts to gad holes in the side of the shaft were unsuccessful. Long after dark I heard a noise, and struck a light, to find that it was Jumbo hanging from the last set.

221

*Diggers on way to Bendigo (from* Sketches of the Victoria Gold Diggings and Diggers As They Are [1852–53], *S. T. Gill)*

The old boy seemed to size up the trouble, and nearly turned himself inside out trying to communicate some idea he had. At last he hauled himself up to the set he was hanging from, took a turn with his head part round the timber, and let his tail drop in my direction. Then I grasped his notion, climbed up him, and got on the timber, and this performance we repeated until I reached the ladders.

I've often shuddered to think what my fate would have been if someone, taking Jumbo for a mere ordinary snake, had killed him when he was making to find me. The poor begger was so stiff for weeks afterwards that he used to creak every time he coiled himself up.

*From "Aboriginalities", the* Bulletin

*Many people in the bush kept carpet snakes as pets in the feed shed, to keep down rats and other vermin. At least, they did not disturb them if they did take up residence in the rafters of the barn. My old friend Joe Rinkevich at Innisfail had a beauty that lived in the shed where he kept the fowl feed, and on one occasion we found it disposing of a venomous brown snake. But I cannot guarantee the above story. The tale of the pumpkin, below, is a good instance of a story that flourished in America as well as Australia, and probably originated there. I think the story about the soil being so fertile that the farmers had to mount the little pumpkins on little four-wheeled trolleys to keep them from being worn out as the vines dragged them along the ground might be a local, though.*

# A Simple Story of a Pumpkin

A farmer told his son one day, in my presence, to get his axe and chop a four-horse-load off the pumpkin for market. I said, "If there's more than one load in a pumpkin it must be a big one."

"Rather," says the farmer, with a broad grin. "I shoved the ladder against it and got on top to chop a load off last week. At the first lick I dropped the axe into the hole, so I lowered the ladder and went down inside to look for it. While walking about I lost my way and met a man who asked me what I was doing. I said, 'Looking for my axe.' 'No use, ole feller,' he replied; 'I lost my team of bullicks here yesterday, and I bin lookin' for 'em ever since.'"

*From "Aboriginalities", the* Bulletin

# The Champion Bullock-Driver

*Lance Skuthorpe*

We were sitting outside old Tallwood cattle station, in our white moleskin trousers, elastic-sided boots, and cabbage-tree hats, watching two stockmen shoe a very wild brumby mare. We were all slaves to the saddle and bridle, and there was nothing too heavy or hard. The boss squatted on a new four-rail fence. There were twenty panels of this fence, big strong ironbark post-and-rails. The first rails were mortised into a big ironbark tree, and there were four No. 8 wires twisted round the butt, passed through every post and strained very tightly to the big strainer at the other end. There was a big bullock-whip standing near the ironbark and sixteen yokes and bows lying alongside the fence and the chains were rusty.

As though he had dropped down from the sky there appeared on the scene a very smart-looking young man carrying a red blanket swag, a water-bag, tucker-bag and billycan. He put them down and said, "Is the boss about, boys?"

We all pointed to the man on the fence. The new chap took his pipe out of his mouth and walked up, a bit shy-like, and said:

"Is there any chance of a job, boss?"

"What can you do?" asked the boss.

"Well, anything among stock. You can't put me wrong."

"Can you ride a buckjumper?"

"Pretty good," said the young man.

"Can you scrub-dash—I mean can you catch cattle in timber on a good horse before they're knocked up, and keep the wood out of their feet?"

"Hold my own with the best."

"Have you got a good flow of language?"

The young man seemed to hesitate a bit, so the boss said:

"I mean, can you drive a rowdy team of bullocks?"

"Just into my hand," said the young man. "Why often when driving a team through the scrub I've seen the stringy-bark saplings catch on fire."

The boss jumped down off the fence when the young man said that and walked towards him. But the young man stepped backed and said:

"Er, the little ones, I mean."

"Them tales is alright," said the boss. "I've heard a lot of them. But it's no use you saying you can drive a team of bullocks if you can't." And pointing to a little graveyard he added, "Do you see that little cemetery over there?"

The young man pulled his hat down a bit over his eye, looked across, and said, "Yes."

"Well," continued the boss, "there are sixteen bullock-drivers lying there. They came here to drive this team of mine."

I watched that young man's face when the boss said that to see if he would flinch. He showed no sign of flinching, but a little smile broke away from the corner of his mouth, curled around his cheek and then disappeared in his earhole, and as the effect of the smile died away he said, "They won't put me there."

"I don't know so much about that," said the boss.

"I'll give you a trial," the young man suggested.

"It would take too long to muster the bullocks," said the boss. "But take that bullock-whip there, and say for instance, eight panels of that fence were sixteen bullocks, show me how you would start up the team."

"Right," said the young man.

Walking over he picked up the big bullock-whip

and very carefully examined it to see how it was fastened to the handle. Then he ran his hand down along the whip, examining it as though he were searching for a broken link in a chain. Then he looked closely to see how the fall was fastened to the whip. He ran his hand down the greenhide fall till he came to a silk cracker, red, white and blue. "Aha!" he said, "you use silk crackers on bullock-whips here, do you? They don't use them where I come from; but it will do me for this fence." Then he stepped back and gave a cheer.

First he threw the whip up to the leaders then he threw it back to the polers. He stepped in as though to dig the near-side pin-bullock under the arm with the handle of the whip, then he stepped back and swung the big whip round. He kept on talking and the whip kept on cracking until a little flame ran right along the top of the fence. . . And he kept on talking and the whip kept on cracking until the phantom forms of sixteen bullocks appeared along the fence — blues, blacks and brindles, some with blue tongues and tan muzzles and horns like native spears. And he kept on talking and the whip kept on cracking till the phantom forms of sixteen bullock-drivers appeared on the scene. And they kept on talking and their whips kept on cracking till the fence started to walk on, and pulled the big ironbark tree down.

"That will do," said the boss.

"Not a bit of it," said the young man, "Where's your wood-heap?"

We all pointed to the wood-heap that stood near the old bark kitchen.

And they kept on talking and their whips kept on cracking till they made the fence pull the tree right up to the wood-heap.

We were all sitting around on the limbs of the tree, and the young man was talking to the boss, and we all felt sure he would get the job, when the boss called out, "Get the fencing gear, lads, and put that fence up again."

"Excuse me for interrupting, boss," said the young man, "but would you like to see how I back a team of bullocks?"

"Yes, I would," said the boss.

So the young man walked over and picked up the big bullock-whip again. He swung it around and called out:

"Now then, boys, all together!"

And the phantom forms of the sixteen bullock-drivers appeared on the scene again; and they kept on talking and their whips kept on cracking, till

every post and rail burst out into flame, and when the flame cleared away each post and rail backed into its place, and the phantom forms of the sixteen bullock-drivers took off their cabbage-tree hats to the young man, and they backed and they bowed, and they bowed and they backed right into their graves, recognizing him as the champion bullock-driver.

*This is, to my knowledge, the first of the really literary tall stories. Its author, Lance Skuthorpe, was a famous roughrider, and took a travelling show around the Eastern States for many years. Between acts he would regale the ringside with stories about bush happenings, but I don't know if he wrote any more down. Henry Lawson did write a story about being attacked by Aborigines in the 1890s, but it was almost a direct copy of an earlier American story, about Plains Indians and a buffalo shooter. I consider the "Aboriginalities" series to be incidents rather than stories as such, amusing as they may be.*

*There is also the story of the three teams who were travelling together for company and assistance. Two of them successfully negotiated a creek crossing but the third bogged. The other drivers unhooked their teams and hitched on to the third, and the three teams all heaved together. After they had gone about fifty yards, and should have been clear, one of the drivers looked back and then yelled, "It's no good boys, we'll have to unload her. They're pulling the creek along with them!" Old timers will show you the bend they pulled in the creek.*

*Paul Bunyan, the Logger, once pulled a river straight in North America with his ox, Big Blue, in the same manner. It had been very twisty before that. Paul was a good business man, and took the lengths of river left over from the straightening job and sold them to farmers in desert country as irrigation canals.*

An Up-Country Coach

# Holy Dan

*Anon.*

It was in the Queensland drought;
And over hill and dell,
No grass—the water far apart,
All dry and hot as hell.
The wretched bullock teams drew up
Beside a water-hole—
They'd struggled on through dust and drought
For days to reach this goal.

And though the water rendered forth
A rank, unholy stench,
The bullocks and the bullockies
Drank deep their thirst to quench.

Two of the drivers cursed and swore
As only drivers can.
The other one, named Daniel,
Best known as Holy Dan,
Admonished them and said it was
The Lord's all-wise decree;
And if they'd only watch and wait,
A change they'd quickly see.

'Twas strange that of Dan's bullocks
Not one had gone aloft,
But this, he said, was due to prayer
And supplication oft.
At last one died but Dan was calm,
He hardly seemed to care;
He knelt beside the bullock's corpse
And offered up a prayer.

"One bullock Thou has taken, Lord,
And so it seemeth best.
Thy will be done, but see my need
And spare to me the rest!"

A month went by. Dan's bullocks now
Were dying every day,
But still on each occasion would
The faithful fellow pray,
"Another Thou has taken, Lord,
And so it seemeth best.
Thy will be done, but see my need,
And spare to me the rest!"

And still they camped beside the hole,
And still it never rained,
And still Dan's bullocks died and died,
Till only one remained.

Then Dan broke down—good Holy Dan—
The man who never swore.
He knelt beside the latest corpse,
And here's the prayer he prore.

"That's nineteen Thou has taken, Lord,
And now You'll plainly see
You'd better take the bloody lot,
One's no damn good to me."
The other riders laughed so much
They shook the sky around;
The lightning flashed, the thunder roared,
And Holy Dan was drowned.

*"Holy Dan" is a well-known ballad, like "Scotty's Wild Stuff Stoo", but I have chosen it rather than the other because it shows pure genius in the past tense of the verb to pray. Also, it is a better poem as a poem, to my taste, showing skill in construction and imagination, especially in the last four lines.*

Grass Tree (Xanthorrhea)

# When "Bullicks was Bullicks"

"Yes," said Old Barney, "bullicks *was* bullicks them times. I remember one wet day goin' up the Big Range lookin' fur a tree fur shingles. I was walken' along the top of the Range when I turns round and sees a big red bullick stalken' me. I makes down the mountain side, and he after me as hard as he could lick. I sees a big holler log, and runs for it, and just as I crawls inter it down he comes 'Whooh!' and takes the sole of me boot with his near horn. I crawls up the log fur about fifteen foot, and I hears him walken' round and sniffen'. I gets me eyes to a crack and looks out, and sees him looken' in at me through the same crack, that close that if I could 'a got me knife I could 'a jabbed his eye out; but the log was too tight' I was wonderin' what he meant to do next, when I hears him hooken' his horn under the log, and away me and it goes rollen' down the side of the mountain and the bullick after us. It was steep, and we (me and the log) must 'a rolled three miles in a little more 'n three minutes, the bullick racin' close behind,

when bump we goes ag'in a big stringy bark; the log breaks in two near the middle, and one half goes down one spur, and the other half, with me in it, down another; and the last I sees of that bullick he was chasin' the wrong half. Presently my half stops at the foot of the range, and I crawls out. Didn't look any more for good-splitten' timber that day."

*From "Aboriginalities", the* Bulletin

*The "bullicks" paragraph has a family relationship to the "Bob Bloodwood" poem, "The Wild Bulls Of The Speewah", that used to "muster up the men". In my prospecting days we were occasionally almost surrounded by Herefords, peering into the gully where we were working. They were not vicious, and if you waved your hat, yelled and ran at them they would head for the ridges.*

*It was while prospecting that I tried only once to make a damper (my mate was a good cook). The resulting mass of gutta-percha-like material hung about the gully for the rest of the time we were there. The possums had a go at it, the kangaroo rats chewed it up a bit, but it defeated their attempts. It may still be there, for all I know.*

*Cattle branding (from* The Australian Sketchbook, S. T. Gill)

# A Record Damper

Humping bluey once from Aramac to Georgetown (Q.), pulled up at a bullocky's camp, and first thing I noticed was what I took to be a reduced pipeclay cast of Maoriland, with Cook's straits filled in, leaning against waggon float rail. "Yes," said the bullocky, "that'll tell you 'bout dam cooks. Could'nt find my polers 'smorning', an' had to go back to Culloden Downs after 'em, leavin' this joblot Irisher to bake a damper. On'y had about thirty pound of flour to carry me to Hughenden, an' he goes an' tips in 'bout half of it, an' spreads half-a-bucket o' water over it, an' of course drowns the miller; shoves in lot more flour, gets it too dry, then drowns the miller again, an' at last uses up all the flour, an' then has it so wet that he has to pour it into the ashes. Has his fire on the side of the only rise within fifty miles, an' of course the wet dough runs down the hill, an' he keeps follerin' it up with ashes. Anyhow, when I gets back he has a damper sixteen feet four inches. Measured it. That's only half you're lookin' at, the other half's on the other side of the waggon. Had to chop it in two before I could up-end it."

*From "Aboriginalities", the* Bulletin

# Bill and the Bear

A drunken circus camped in our paddock last night. Was ignorant of the fact until I stumbled on to a warm, heaving mass that was chained to the post. I apologised vigorously, but the warm mass grumbled from its innards, implying that it wasn't taking any, and hit me a cushion-like punch on the back. Struck a match and faced a number one sized brown bear rocking at the end of its chain. Tame, of course, but . . . I put in a lot of decent footwork between the bear and house. It appeared that everyone at home had carefully walked into Bruin. Mother was slightly hysterical.

"Never mind," said father, "Bill ain't home yet."

Nobody suggested hanging out signals to warn Bill. We were all anxious to see what effect Bill would have on the bear. We listened and we listened. Then father listened.

"Hear that?" he said, suddenly.

The noise of a terrific struggle reached us, a weird, three-cornered sound that was full of bear-growl and our Bill. Father got up and stated that the bear was getting what for.

"And serve it right, too," said mother.

Just then Bill appeared through the back window looking as though he'd been fighting a man with nine arms and a gun.

"Fine night, Bill," said father, carelessly.

"Yes," said Bill, wiping his forehead, "splendid weather."

Father lit his pipe. "Anything wrong, Bill?" he asked steadily.

"No," said Bill, "on'y that thear Brian Mullins is camped in our paddock, drunk as usual. Didn't want to scrap, so I kicked him in th' face. Can't y' hear him swearin' to hisself in Irish? I hate fightin' Mullins; he crawls all over ye an' stinks awful." Bill spat into the fire reflectively. "Never mind, I'll go down when he's asleep an' pinch his overcoat."

*From "Aboriginalities", the* Bulletin

*This little story always makes me think of Alice In Wonderland, when Alice is too big in the White Rabbit's house, and is waiting for Bill the lizard to make his way down the chimney. It has the same air of tension, though a very different outcome.*

At the Dam.

*The punt, Echuca (from a photograph, engraved by J. C. Armytage, from* Australia, *ed. Edwin Carton Booth)*

# Further Evidence
## *In Re* Cods

Re yarn about the fish on the Murrumbidgee camping in hollow logs (5th March, '08). During the late drought the Warrego was quite dry. Having been down South for a spell, I had lost the healthy sole-leather colour, and was mistaken by two bushmen for a newchum when travelling up the Warrego from Charleville. On a long stage the water-bags gave out, and my new companions, think to take a rise out of me, suggested when a big bottletree hove in sight, that I should tap it and fill the bags and billy while they fixed up the other things. As I had an axe to grind, I fell in with their proposal. My luck was in, for, besides filling the bags and billy, I drew out of the opening I had made two fine, big catfish, which had evidently left the river when it ran dry. They were A1 eating.

*From "Aboriginalities", the* Bulletin

*No collection of stories would be complete without a couple of fish stories. Ananias was a fisherman, probably. The fish from the bottletree is an old timer. Dal Stivens, on the other hand, is also an old timer, and he combines grace and imagination in his writing. Incidentally, he won the Miles Franklin Award for a novel a couple of years ago, and his short story/fable, "The Gentle Basilisk" is worthy of the late James Thurber. I first found an instalment of the adventures of Ironbark Bill in a copy of the* Listener *or* John O'London's Weekly, *I forget which, in the 1950s. It was his story of Bill's encounter with some giant mosquitos. But of all Ironbark Bill's adventures, the Snoring Cod has a great appeal for me. The only fault I could pick with Bill was that he preferred a Jno. Baker knife to a Dover brand one. The Americans preferred a Barlow knife, traditionally. See the things Tom Sawyer received for letting others paint the fence for him, and consider the lines of "Blackeyed Susie" —*

> *"I asked her to be my wife,*
> *She came for me with a Barlow knife.*
> *Hey, Blackeyed Susie, . . ."*

*The Hawkesbury, at Wiseman's Ferry (engraving from* Picturesque Atlas of Australasia, *ed. Andrew Garran)*

# The Snoring Cod

*Dal Stivens*

Ironbark Bill was a keen fisherman, and the time he was shipwrecked off the Queensland coast would have been the best in his life but for the snoring cod.

What Ironbark was doing on that little island on the Great Barrier Reef isn't quite clear. Some of the old-timers say that Ironbark shipped on board a Darling River paddle steamer during the big floods and was washed over the Great Dividing Range.

Ironbark had a grand time on that Barrier Reef island until the big cod that snored turned up. He was a mad fisherman, and the fish on that part of the Barrier Reef were so thick they grew gills on the slant so they could breathe up and down instead of sideways. Ironbark had to walk about fifty yards on their backs before he found enough water to drop his hook in.

For a line Ironbark, of course, used a greenhide, which will hold anything. The only trouble was that, being wet, it stretched so much that by the time Ironbark got the fish in they were dead of old age. Ironbark caught some electric eels, put them in a pool, and connected them up to the greenhide. The current warmed it and made it contract so quickly the fish were gutted and smoked by the time they swished up on the sand, and sometimes when the electric eels were very lemony with Ironbark the fish arrived already cooked.

Later Ironbark used electric rays for the job. They had a habit of standing up on their tails and looking like railway signals. Ironbark's cattle-dog, Bluey, came nosing round one day, sniffed one of the rays, yelped, and took such a header into the sea that Ironbark had to make three big jumps to reach him. Ironbark could leap a good sixty yards, but when he saw he was going to fall short he turned round in mid-air and jumped back on the island. He shoved his foot on purpose in the ray pool and with the shock and pain leapt a good thirty yards farther, reached Bluey, yanked him up by the collar just as a couple of sawfish were going to snaffle him, and jumped back, just wetting the soles of his bluchers.

Up to now Ironbark had done only handline fishing, but now he thought he would try a rod. The coconut palms were too thick even for a bloke as strong as Ironbark, and he was thinking of taking a

*Baines River, Northern Australia (T. Baines, from* Australia, *ed. Edwin Carton Booth)*

*Townsville, Queensland (J. Carr, from* Australia, *ed. Edwin Carton Booth)*

swordfish down for his stinger when he had a big idea. He stepped out the island and found it was fifty-four poles by thirteen. He reckoned he could spare one even if it did make the island a bit narrow.

With the rod Ironbark caught so many fish that after a month his stomach used to rise and fall with the tide and he had to give up shaving because the scales blunted his razor.

It was about then that the big cod that snored turned up. He was such a whopper that Ironbark had to take two looks to see him fully. He was black as molasses and had a mouth as big as the door of a barn. Like most of the big cod on the Barrier Reef he was very inquisitive and goggled at everything Ironbark did, coming in close to the island, standing on his tail almost out of the water, with his eyes sticking out like oversize organ stops.

Ironbark soon got fed up and threw a bait near him. The cod grinned and swallowed the hook right down. Ironbark reckoned he had him then, but the big cod nonchalantly turned himself inside out and chucked the hook before Ironbark could link up with the ray pool. Then the cod turned himself outside in until he was himself again, opened his big mouth, and cackled all along his

tombstone teeth as though he was playing a xylophone.

Well, Ironbark tried a few more times and the same thing happened. He gave it up for the day, but he hadn't heard the last of the big cod. The fish settled down for the night in a large hole near the island and began to snore. Ironbark said afterwards that a shearers' camp on Christmas afternoon had nothing on it. That big cod gulped in for five minutes and snorted out for seven; the coconut-trees shook and the rays tried to jam their spikes in their ears.

About midnight Ironbark got desperate, swam over to the big cod, and dropped the hook in. The fish inhaled and took most of the greenhide and then turned himself inside out in his sleep and threw the hook. The greenhide came out tied in a true lover's knot and the cod stayed inside out and snored worse than before, in three keys.

Ironbark did his block and threw his concertina into the cod's mouth, reasoning that if he had to listen to sounds for the rest of the night they might as well be musical ones.

The cod played "Rocked in the Cradle of the Deep", and Ironbark was able to drop off, congratulating himself. He was a little too quick because the cod's music ruined the fishing. All the fish sat around listening to the music next day, mooning and unconscious of anything else.

Ironbark was so hopping mad when they wouldn't take a hook he hitched the line up to the ray pool first and threw it near the big cod, which was awake but hadn't bothered to turn himself right side out. The cod took the bait, shrieked, and jumped clean out of the water and started chasing his tail round and round in the water. He played "Life on the Ocean Wave" now, but on a harmonium. He shimmied up to the island on his tail and came ashore.

Ironbark reckoned it was time to go for a swim and he and Bluey took a header. The cod started wrecking everything on the island and would have kicked most of it into the sea if he hadn't put a fin in the ray pool. He got such a double charge the concertina now became an electric cinema organ and the cod threw a sixer back into the drink. The shock of the cold water brought him to his senses; he turned himself right side out and threw the hook and the concertina.

After that he took himself off to his hole and sulked for a couple of days, being careful to sleep on his side.

During this time Ironbark took up his fishing again. He had always reckoned the fishing away from the island looked better, so he built himself a boat. Ironbark was right. Some of the fish he caught on the first day were so big he couldn't haul them into the boat. He had to pull the boat down to them.

On the third day the cod got up to his tricks again. He had been stickybeaking around with his eyes popping out like hat-pegs, and when Ironbark was hauling himself down to a big one the cod decided to be a nark and swam in and nipped through the line. Of course, Ironbark's boat sank to the bottom then.

Now Ironbark was so crooked on the big cod he chewed off the ends of his moustaches thinking out a way to fix him. While Ironbark was churning things over in his think-box, the sea got up a bit and the island started to rock about. The big cod had loosened its roots. That and the fact that the pole he used for fishing was the lightest he had ever handled gave Ironbark the notion that if he could cut the island free he'd be able to float about, fix the stickybeak cod, and sail to civilization, though taking his time about it.

A school of sawfish came round the island and Ironbark reckoned he'd soon put them to work. They wouldn't look at the hook, though Ironbark tried baiting it with everything about the place. But when Ironbark and Bluey went for a dip the sawfish beetled through the water after them, sucking through all their teeth with hunger. Ironbark was looking thoughtfully at Bluey when he got a better idea. He melted down all the coconuts and tipped the oil round the island.

Then he dived in and swam out towards the sawfish. As soon as they started for him, swishing their saws, Ironbark headed for the shore. When they hit the oil the sawfish couldn't stop and went hurtling up on the sand. The only catch was that Ironbark used to skedaddle up, too, and the gravel rash he got was nobody's business. His skin was never the same afterwards and used to wrinkle twice a day with the ebb tides.

While Ironbark was doing this the big cod was so agog with curiosity he was standing out of the water on the tip of his tail and his eyes stuck out like telescopes.

When Ironbark had caught fifty sawfish in this way he yanked all their saws hard over to the right before letting them go. With the tilt he had given them the sawfish went in clockwise circles and once in every while they'd bump into the island and saw through a bit of its roots.

After about a month, during which the cod took to snoring again, Ironbark's island floated free. Ironbark was now ready to put paid to the big cod. First Ironbark took off his flannel shirt and dungarees and hitched them to the trunk of the biggest palm as sails. He hitched up the rays and froze the biggest one stiff for use as a rudder. Then he started to sail round the stickybeak cod. To add to the show Ironbark and Bluey turned Catherine-wheels and the cod nearly fell over on his back into the water with excitement.

Ironbark did a full circle around the rubber-nose cod, who turned his head round to follow what Ironbark was doing. Ironbark did a few more turns, throwing in somersaults as well as reels. If anything the big fish's eyes were sticking out farther than ever, but that might have been because his windpipe was getting a bit twisted. After another half-dozen turns Ironbark heard what he had been listening for. There came an almighty crack as the big cod's neck snapped.

Ironbark sailed down the coast to Brisbane after

*The Quay, Hobart Town (from a photograph, engraved by J. J. Crew, detail, from* Australia, *ed. Edwin Carton Booth)*

that, stopping whenever he saw a good fishing spot. He had a little trouble near Rockhampton when a mob of sucker fish hooked on to his island and held it up. Ironbark had to freeze the water under the island. The sucker fish got chilblains and when they wiggled their toes the island went ahead faster than before.

*From* Ironbark Bill, *Dal Stivens*

# John the Yabby

Years ago my Uncle Arch was sitting in his humpy in the Goodnight Scrub when he thought he'd like to do a bit of saltwater fishing. He decided he'd go down and visit a couple of mates of his who lived at the mouth of the Kolan River, on the coast. He didn't have a horse at the time so he walked. When he got tired of walking he ran for a bit. He came east through Mount Perry and Gin Gin and Bungadoo and Bullyard and those places and then he struck north until he came to the river and followed it down to the coast. That's where his two mates lived. They were called John the Yabby and Mulletgut Olaf.

Now, down in the antarctic south of Australia, along the Murrumbidgee and the Ovens and Murray and other such shivering streams they have a little crustacean they call a yabby, but he's only a sort of freshwater lobster. We have them in Queensland, too, but they grow bigger up here. For instance, you've never heard of those southern ones digging their own waterholes, have you? But that's beside the point. The point is, as any Queensland fisherman can tell you, that a yabby is a sort of small saltwater crayfish with claws that looks as though someone has stepped on it. They have one huge enormous claw for fighting one another and a little skinny claw for eating with. They live in little holes they dig in the tidal mudflats, and the whiting love them. In fact you can even see whiting come out of the water at low tide and run round on the mud trying to catch them. At least you could at the mouth of the Kolan River forty years ago, Arch reckons. If you had a good blue cattle dog you didn't even have to throw a line into the water. But that's beside the point.

They used to call Arch's mate John the Yabby because he fell into a circular saw in a pine mill once when he was full, and lost the best part of his left arm. His right arm had got very powerful in consequence. He had an old dinghy he used to scull round one-handed like the Chinese do in Hong Kong, and he only used the crook arm to feed himself and to gaff fish with. He had a big shark hook with the barb filed off he used to strap to the stump. Of course John had got Worker's Compensation for losing his arm after the accident. Arch says he asked him once how much he got, but he didn't know. He reckoned it must have been a fair cheque because it took him and all his mates three weeks to drink it out.

Mulletgut Olaf came from one of them square-head countries where they can't say J but they use it a lot in their spelling to confuse outsiders. One of his cousins had come to Australia on a wool clipper once, and took home a case of Bundaberg rum, with which he had proceeded to make something of a name for himself in his home district. Even the aurora borealis was lit up better that year, they reckon. Olaf had got a whole bottle to himself, and after drinking it reckoned he'd found what he'd been looking for for a long time, so he shipped out on the next available ship to live near the place where they made it. He was a short barrel-chested bloke with skinny legs. He said he got that build from rowing boats round the fjords.

Well, these two blokes welcomed Arch, first because they liked him, and second because he brought three bottles of Bundaberg rum with him. They opened a bottle straight away to give them strength to go out and pump some yabbies for bait, so they could go fishing that night. When the bottle was empty they went and pumped for the yabbies, and got lots of them, big muscular ones, full of fight. There was one big one in particular, with a green stripe round his fighting claw, that all the others seemed a bit windy of. This big one sat in a corner of the bait box and scowled, while all the others argued and fought all over the rest of the box and didn't get too close to him.

"Yee whiz, Yonnie, dot vun must be Irish yabby," said Olaf. "Look at dem udders yoompin avay von him."

"Ah, shut yer gob, yer an eel-eatin' wreck," said Johnny.

Arch says Olaf used to like eels to eat, and he used to catch them and skin them and smoke them in an old tank till they looked like surcingles; and Johnny couldn't stand the sight of eels.

Well, they covered the yabbies with salt water, and put them away for the afternoon, then they all laid down under some sea-oaks and cracked the second bottle. Then they had a feed of black duck that Johnny had caught by his patent method, but I'm not going to tell you how you catch black ducks with a stone, two foot of nylon fishing line and one or two other things, or I'll have the R.S.P.C.A. or somebody after me. Then they laid down again and waited for sundown. Arch says he must have drifted off to sleep or something about this time, because the next thing he knew it was dark and the hurricane lamp was alight and the other two were shaking him awake to find where he'd planted the

*Arrival of the mail bag (engraving from* Illustrated Sydney News, *6 September 1879)*

third bottle. Arch says he'd been too cunning to leave it where they'd be able to find it too easy, in case they might drop it or break it or something while he was unconscious.

At any rate the three of them collected their gear and the bottle and the yabbies and piled the lot into Johnny's old dinghy, and Johnny sculled down to a channel he knew near the bar. Then they dropped the kellick and had a drink and caught a yabby each out of the bait box. Then they chucked their lines into the water. They caught a few whiting but nothing startling. Then Olaf baited a big line with a whole whiting and pulled in four big Queensland blue mudcrabs with claws like multigrips that he brought inboard with a landing net, and then left to scuttle round the bottom of the boat. Arch went crook a bit about this, but Olaf said if you didn't moof your veet dey vould dink dey vos a sdone, so Arch sat there growling and very carefully not moofing his veet.

Johnny said they had better move to the deep hole just inside the bar and try there. He said that there was not enough wind, or too much, or something. So Olaf pulled up the pick, and they sculled to a place about a hundred yards off the bank and anchored again. Then they all had another drink, and Olaf caught two of them little knot eels that tie knots in themselves, and pitched them into the bottom of the boat in spite of Johnny going crook. The two knot eels didn't know they were going to finish up being smoked in an old tank, so they quietly tied their tails together in a reef knot and went to sleep. Then Johnny caught a ten pound wire-netting cod, and then Arch pulled in a four and a half pound flathead, and knocked the bottle of rum over, so about a pint spilled into the inch of bilgewater that was slopping round the bottom of the boat.

The others couldn't complain too much about this accident, because after all, it was his rum. Johnny did mention that his grandfather had been a ham-fisted elbow-fingered stumblebum and that Arch reminded him of him in some ways, but that was all. Then Olaf got this tremendous bite on the big line he had left trailing over the side.

"Gum here!" he roared, standing up and hauling. "Gum do Poppa! Ach, Yeesus, Yonny, sdop yerkin' de boat!"

Before they could stop him he pulled a five foot conger eel, all snapping jaws and slimy thrashing coils, into the dinghy, into the slippery mess of lines, yabbies, mudcrabs, cod, flathead, whiting, rum and bare feet that covered the bottom of the dinghy. The hurricane lamp fell over and went out. Johnny took a header over the side, closely followed by Arch. They both reckoned they weren't fit enough to rassle with a conger eel in the dark under those circumstances. Olaf was more optimistic for about ten seconds, but then even he left. They all swam miserably ashore and sat on the mudbank until morning in their wet clothes. Word got round among the mozzies and sandflies that there were three human bar-rooms stranded nearby, so they were all pretty near sobered and bloodless by the time the sun poked its bloodshot eye up over the eastern horizon. Johnny abused Olaf all night, but Olaf was happy.

"Pluddy beaut, dot eel!" he remarked. "Like de pluddy Midgard Serpent, yet!"

They swam out to the dinghy and peered over the side. They were delighted to find that everything was under control, though all the rum and bilgewater was gone, drunk by the boat's inhabitants.

The big conger eel had passed out. It was stretched full length on the bottom boards with its head pillowed on the heap of anchor rope. The cod was telling the flathead it loved it. The four mudcrabs were neatly tied up and helpless, as they had apparently got stroppy and started to pick on the knot eels, who quietly tied them all up and then went back to sleep with their tails neatly fastened together in a double sheet bend. But it was the big yabby that really surprised them, said Arch. He'd made all the other yabbies untangle their lines and roll them up neatly on their proper empty bottles. He saluted them gravely as they clambered over the side, them collapsed snoring in the bilges, worn out by his sense of duty and Bundaberg rum. Johnny was speechless for once, and he just pulled up the pick and started sculling for home.

Arch asked me to write it all down, so if any of you blokes ever pump a whopping big yabby with a green stripe round his fighting claw, don't use him for bait, will you? Just put him back into his hole on the mudflat, and apologise.

*From* Some People, *Bill Scott*

# The Chinese Way

*Archer Whitworth*

We were discussing in the local rubberty the Oriental method of getting a fish breakfast by putting a ring round the neck of a deluded cormorant or shag and sending the bird down to capture a small fish. The Character was an interested listener, but we could see that he was eager to have his say in the matter, so we were not altogether surprised when he set down his glass with a thump on the bar, wiped his mouth with the back of a leathery hand, and held forth.

"All this talk of fishing with birds," said he, "reminds me of old Pelican Joe who used to live in a little shack all by himself on the banks of a mangrove creek some miles south of a little town on the nor-west coast. Old Joe was a well-known identity along the waterfront in those days, although thought to be not quite the full bottle—what some of you learned blokes might term a little eccentric. One acknowledged gift he did have, and that was his strange kinship with seabirds.

"Joe was friends with every gull, shag, heron and crane for miles around. His shanty was always surrounded by a screaming cloud of birds, which would swoop in to be fed from his hand, or perch on his arm or shoulder until it seemed Old Joe would be buried in feathers. Joe would tend to their wants, care for any sick or injured birds and share with them his daily tucker which was mainly fish anyway.

"Now, Joe's constant companion at all times was a big black and white pelican known as 'the Bosun'. Rumour had it that Joe had reared the bird from almost a fledgeling, and certainly the bird was devoted to the old man. It always occupied a place of honour on the bow thwart of the dinghy and used to follow Joe round like an affectionate pup. Guess one of the most popular camera shots for tourists on the steamer run up the coast from Perth was that of old Joe in his bare feet, strolling along the main street, and the Bosun bringing up the rear with the week's groceries stowed in the capacious pouch under his big bill. Looked quite a picture, it did!

"But, coming to this fishing business, Joe had the cunning Chinese beat a mile. He was more up to date in every way. As Joe was getting a bit long in the tooth to be pushing the dinghy for miles over banks in search of the big schools of diamond-scaled mullet, he used to send out the Bosun to do some spotting first.

"The Bosun was a bit slow and undignified in the take-off, but once he got those big wings fairly flapping, he would soar up into the blue until he could take in every detail below him; every mangrove creek and sandbank from the Beacon to Yoondoo Creek and south almost to Bush Bay. Nothing missed his sharp eyes, and soon he had every school of fish pin-pointed. Then he'd spiral down to old Joe, and croak and wave his bill and flap his wings until Joe knew what was going on and just which school to have a crack at first.

"Now, that last may sound a bit overdone to you, mates, but old Joe and the Bosun had been mates for years and knew each other very well. Joe even entertained hopes of teaching the Bosun to talk, and rumour had it that he was succeeding, too.

"When Joe made up his mind as to the school of fish he was after, he'd put the net on the boards across the stern of the dinghy—not haphazard, like, but in proper order, the Bosun piling the corkline while Joe coiled down the leads. Then Joe would stand up and lean his weight on the oars, and away they'd go, with the Bosun perched on the nose, until they could see the dark mass of mullet, with an occasional big fellow playfully lifting out of the water and falling back on his silver side.

"Joe would drop one end of the net with the Bosun to hold it and ring the school, enclosing the fish in a circle of mesh. Then in would go the Bosun, striking every way with his long bill, tossing fish into the dinghy right and left and scaring the others into meshing themselves before they could hurdle the corkline. Finally, they'd haul the net 'on the rowlock', and complete the job until the bottom of the boat was a shining heap of sea mullet, and the net was free of fish.

"Back at the shack, hanging the net was a comparatively simple operation and the Bosun would detail a couple of terns to cleaning the wiregrass out of the mesh. Then the Bosun would load up his pouch with a couple of dozen mullet, and take off for the township. To assist his take-off, Joe had built a steeply inclined ramp of mangrove logs, covered with ironhard sun-baked salt mud, and up this the Bosun would hop until he sprang over the upper edge and was airborne. This idea had been mutually adopted after Joe had built a catapult model out of 'T' Ford rubber tubes,

which, however, was not a success and caused the Bosun to prang in an undignified heap of feathers and fish.

"The Bosun would fly high above the little humpy, and then plane the long distance over the swamps into the town to deliver his cargo to the local pubs. He knew the price of fish, too, and once side-swiped the publican with a blow of his mighty wing for attempting to give him shark prices instead of mullet. When paid, the Bosun would load up with a couple of bottles of beer and fly back to base, continuing with his shuttle service, until all the fish were placed.

"Oh, old Joe and the Bosun had fishing down to a fine art, all right. The only time they fell out was when the Bosun got a crush on a young female pelican that blew in from down Hamelin Pool way, and couldn't keep his mind on his work. He was getting his deliveries so mixed up that customers began to complain. 'Course, Joe overlooked the time the Bosun accepted a few drinks in town (Christmas, I think it was) got nicely tight and hiccupped his next load of fish all over the township, Mrs Tonkin being laid low by a falling flathead right in front of the Post Office in the main street.

"But things worked smoothly enough until the day old Joe stepped on a stonefish (they call 'em devilfish up that way) and passed over to the Happier Fishing Grounds.

"They tell me the Bosun was inconsolable for a long time after, but I did hear that after that he set up in business on his own account, bought a controlling interest in the local fish freezing works and was pretty prosperous generally. His only complaint was that his high taxation was ruining him and soon he wouldn't have a feather to fly with!

"And so", concluded the Character, "you can see, gentlemen, that the Chinese are not the only experts in the game. You agree?"

Mutually, we agreed.

*The late Archer Whitworth was Clerk of Court in the West Australian town of Geraldton, and his tall stories of the fishing industry on the northwest coast reflect his marvellous sense of humour and his wonderful warmth of feeling for the odd characters who live in that isolated part of Australia. This story was quoted in* The Scream of the Reel, *Jack*

*Easter pedestrian tourists; noonday halt at the Black Spur (engraving from* Australasian Sketcher, *23 April 1881)*

Pollard's collection of Australian and New Zealand fishing stories, published by Lansdowne Press. His tales of the crayfishing industry (following) were transcribed from a tape he recorded for Wendy Lowenstein when she made her epic "around Australia" tour recording folk material. It was Wendy who actually typed up the crayfishing stories from the tape.

# Folk Stories of the Crayfishing Industry

*Retold by Archer Whitworth*

The Abrolhos Islands of Western Australia stretch, in their various groups, some 60 miles in a north-south line with the closest island, the Hummock, in the Southern Group, almost 30 miles west of Geraldton. They are the site of a seasonal crayfishing industry worth many millions of export dollars to the Australian economy. In early March of each year, nearly 200 fishermen leave their homes in Geraldtown and, together with all necessary gear, take up residence in tiny camps on the little rocky isles, there to remain for five months, baiting, setting and lifting craypots from their small craft. The catch is brought back alive and kicking in bags stacked deep on the decks of larger carrier vessels that contract to transport the crayfish from each island group to the processing factories on the mainland at Geraldton. According to my informant, a local hard-bitten fisherman and colourful character, known throughout the islands as Diabolical Dick, the industry is not without its hazards and handicaps.

Take the octopus position, for example. Not that any crayfisherman would refer to an octopus by its right name. An octopus is merely an ocky, more than one are ockies. Dick informs me that in the Pelsart Island area in the Southern Group, one should never set a line of craypots too close to one another, as the medium-sized ockies get one tentacle-cum-foot in each and wear out the pots stamping around the rough sea bottom.

Dick put steel bottoms in all his pots, but the ockies then came ashore on moonlit nights which they made hideous by clanking up and down the long eastern rocky foreshore of Pelsart. All this nocturnal activity began to seriously disturb the nesting terns, countless thousands of which lived on the island, and resulted in quick protest from the Fisheries and Fauna Department. Dick was counselled to put barbed wire around the throat of his pots and peace returned to the islands.

An unusually large crayfish is known along the coast as a jumbo. A jumbo of seven or eight pounds in weight is not unusual in mainland waters but, according to Diabolical Dick, he found a patch of much bigger ones off Beacon Island. These crays were too large to enter the pots and were biting the ends out of the latter to get at the bait. Dick was

getting nowhere at all with them until he hit on the idea of festooning the pot with several 10-fathom, trailing loose-footed ropes, so entangling the crayfish. It was but little trouble after that to rig sheer legs and swing each jumbo individually aboard with a stout block and tackle.

The normal-sized holding crates were useless for jumbos and special one three times larger had to be built, with additional metal straps to further strengthen the wooden planking. The majority of the big crays would then fit singly, even if a little tightly, into such a crate which was constructed with a hinged side to get the jumbo out again when required. On loading days, it was necessary to put a sugar bag over each eye-stalk to quieten the cray and, finally, four deckhands would lash each jumbo down to specially fitted ringbolts on the deck of the carrier boat.

There was quite a to-do in the mainland factories when jumbo crays began to arrive for processing. The Geraldton Fishermen's Co-operative was believed to be making quite a good thing out of supplying the empty tails to the Volkswagen people for car bodies, but this may have been only a rumour. However, a mate of Dick's had a Volksie that shuddered violently every time he brought an ockie near it, and also used to back into just about everything, so there might have been some truth in in the story. The hollow legs of the big crays were much in demand amongst the fishing fraternity for downpiping into their rainwater tanks on the islands.

The processing factories finally jacked up on the jumbos. The reasons were in the main economical. The factory might have a whole shift working on one cray when the knock-off whistle went. They could not knock the shift off work when partly through a cray so had to pay penalty overtime rates to finish the job. The unusually tough and highly elastic gut string was another determining factor. Processors worked in rubber boots on wet, slippery concrete and, if an unlucky operator slipped, he might be jerked violently back into the crayfish. Apart from the immediate difficulties of extraction, the company was liable to be sued for an exorbitant figure for "consequent pain and humiliation suffered" by its employee.

There was another and more direct practical disadvantage to setting pots in a jumbo area. Fishermen watch the recording needle on their echo sounders until the sudden lift and dip betrays the small coral lump on the sea floor. These tiny

*A Bendigo mill (from* Sketches of the Victoria Gold Diggings and Diggers As They Are [1852–53], *S. T. Gill)*

reefs or lumps are the home of the crays and around them the set pots bring their best results. A jumbo cray on the wide smooth 22-fathom flat showed up on the echo sounder identical to a smooth coral lump with craggy sides, and the uninitiated might be taken in thereby. One fisherman, in his craft with a rather boastful name of "Maid Marion", chased a "lump", vainly throwing pots at it, half-way back to the mainland. Besides being frustrating and nerve-wracking, this conduct also occasions much loss of gear.

Geraldton is noted for its strong prevailing southerly winds, these being particularly con-centrated at the islands. I am informed that the fishermen build their camps long and rectangular, with the sides of lesser width at the north and south ends. A chap Dick knew disregarded all proffered advice on this subject and built his camp with the opposite orientation. A strong southerly gale caught the camp on the tiny coral islet one day. The wind blew his islet from near Post Office in the Southern Group, right up past the Wallabis, and if he had not stranded on the reef at North Island, he would have undoubtedly finished in Java. How-ever, the next northerly storm blew him back again.

Big, slow-curling breakers that lift out of a

smooth sea above some hidden reef or bank and suddenly crash down with terrific power and frightening roar, taking with them all in their path, are a constant menace, and fishermen take too many deliberately calculated chances. These big swells roll all the way from Africa. Diabolical Dick was pretty fearless and once laid a whole string of pots up the side of a big breaker and then, by half an hour's solid steaming due west, got over the crest before it broke. He never got his pots back, but one, with ropes and floats bearing his boat registration number, brought down a big boomer half-way to the Warburton Ranges shortly after, so it must have been thrown quite a way. This is, however, not a common occurrence, as few pots land east of Meekatharra in these circumstances, although they are listed as air navigational hazards by M.M.A. pilots.

The Western Australian jewfish, a cousin of the pearl perch of north eastern waters, is the topline eating fish of the West. Sold under the trade name of dhufish, it brings the highest prices. During the off season for crays, on occasionally brightly moonlit evenings throughout the season when the crays are off the crawl, the cray fisherman might supplement his living by line-fishing for jewies, drifting quietly through the night with long lines out, heavy sinkers bumping over the broken sea bottom. Diabolical Dick was a most intrepid jewie fisherman and went deep and a greater distance west over the continental shelf than any other boat. Other fishermen often gave him up for lost. Once Dick was so far west that he nearly got picked up by the Lorenzo Marques Customs launch as a likely smuggler. Another time, he came back with a great load of jewies but with a couple of nasty looking assegais and some arrows embedded in the wheel-house.

Crayfish poisoning is a painful and serious complaint in the Abrolhos. The crayfish comes into contact with the roughened hands of the fishermen when being pulled from the pot or tipping box on deck and, more so, when taken from the crates prior to loading. The hide of an island fisherman did not inspire the well-known cosmetic advertisement "Lournay's Lasting loveliness". The crayfish develops poisoning and has a high mortality rate en route to town. There is no known cure according to Diabolical Dick.

*From* Australian Tradition *(December 1969)*

*Dray (from* 1800 Woodcuts of Thomas Bewick and His School, *ed. Blanche Cirker)*

# A Tale of Tooth

*Henry E. Horne*

Big Billy Bull
   Of Bungendore,
He used to pull
   Our teeth before
The railway come;
And strike me dumb,
   And dead,
   Your head
'Ud fairly hum,
When Billy's pincers grabbed your gum,
   While cross your chest
   His weight he prest
And pushed your 'pendix outer plumb.

But once a bloke
   Named Johnny Jupp
Came down and broke
   Our blacksmith up.
It turned him grey:
He tried all day
   To lift
   And shift
One tooth away;
Until, at last, in his dismay,
   What does he do
   But ties it to
The tailboards of me new spring dray.

And then we got
   Into the cart,
And at a trot
   We made a start;
The bloke behind,
He didn't mind,
   Becos
   It was
Intended kind;
Though, till he sorter grew resigned,
   He yelled, of course,
   To stop the horse,
And cursed us black, and blue, and

So by the tooth,
  Along the dust,
We dragged that youth
  Till something bust;
And then we swore
And chucked it, for
  There hung
  And swung
Our tailboard, or
The most of it, to Johnny's "jore"
  Which snapped at us
  With vicious cuss,
And said, "You crimson cows, no more!"

From Australian Bush Ballads, D. Stewart and N. Keesing

*Traditional methods of tooth extraction seem to have been to tie a string around the tooth and the door handle, and then slam the door; or an old Irishman once told me that where he came from in Ireland his father removed their teeth when they were children by slipping the end of the doorkey over the offending molar and removing it with a quick twist. Smacker may have been familiar with this poem when he told the story that follows hereafter, but if he was he embroidered it to some effect.*

. . . Smacker lived in a humpy he had built for himself from materials he accumulated in any way that would cost him nothing. This provided him with a single-roomed establishment, roofed with corrugated iron from the rubbish dump, hammered on to bush timber. The walls were built from all sorts of things, including enamelled advertising signs; and the northern end of the humpy advertised both Billy Tea and Bournville Cocoa. He was a short, thin, wiry man of indeterminate age, probably in his middle fifties, and he had come to Flying Fish Point from somewhere in the Northern Rivers district in New South Wales. When his guard was down his accent was that of an educated man, so you could not guess at his antecedents.

When asked why he had come to the North he invariably told you a good story, though rarely the same one you had heard before. His most impressive effort along these lines was that he had been a dentist, and that a very tough dairy farmer had asked him to pull one of his molars. There being little anaesthetic available, the farmer had suggested that Smacker wait until the following Saturday evening to do the job, as there was a football match on in the afternoon, and he intended to get full after the game.

"You can ask the Sergeant to drop me off for a while when he's taking me down to the peter in a wheelbarrow when the pub closes. He can pick somebody else up while you're doing the job, and I won't feel anything," he is reported to have said.

All went as planned. The farmer passed out, and the police delivered him to Smacker's surgery for the operation, en route to the cooler. Smacker had tried all his conventional instruments to remove the offending tooth from the man's jaw, but to no avail. All he did was to lift him out of the chair. So he fitted his biggest clamp to the tooth, bolted the chair to the floor, and roped the farmer firmly into the seat. He got a block and tackle from the blacksmith's shop, hooked one pulley to a ringbolt in the ceiling and the other to the clamp. Then he led the end of the rope out the window and hitched it to the back of a swingle bar of a two-horse team, which he then drove away down the street. To his joy he felt something give, but imagine his horror on returning to his primitive surgery when he discovered he had pulled the man's skeleton completely out of its fleshly envelope, which remained roped to the chair while the grisly bones swayed from the rafters.

Smacker said that he was terrified of being charged with murdering the man, so he hastily grabbed what money he had, stuffed the bones into a sugar bag and caught the midnight train out of town. He had weighted the bag with a brick, and he tossed it from the window of the carriage as the train crossed a deep swift river. He had kept on heading north until he came to Innisfail. He had been hiding there for about seven years when he was startled at being greeted by an acquaintance from the little town where he had had his practice. This man told him that the farmer was so tough that he had not even missed his skeleton, and that he had lived on for another four years without it until he was eventually killed by blood poisoning after trimming one of his corns with a pair of bolt cutters. He said that the farmer had always wondered why Smacker had never sent him a bill.

Not all Smacker's stories were of this standard, but he had a fertile wit, and when we lazed on the beach of broken coral and reddish sand below his humpy under the palms we would sometimes ask him, "Why did you come to the North, Smack"? Then we would wait in anticipation as a grin crinkled the whiskery cheeks, and he would invent yet another reason for his hurried flight.

*From an unpublished manuscript about the Innisfail district in 1947, Bill Scott*

*A bush barber (engraving from* Australasian Sketcher, *5 August 1882)*

# A Veracious Story of a Ram

My special ram began life as a little, white, woolly lamb of unimaginable innocence, beloved by a township, and grew suddenly into a large, lusty, ravening animal that literally possessed the place, and butted himself into the position of a bloated and unquestioned autocrat. When the spirit moved Jack, he would butt anybody, from a lady to a red-gum stump, but he loved best a fat small boy, or a big metal washtub. The latter he would steal from a back yard, and butt into a mangled ruin, driving it through Waddy with the rattle and clamour of an oldtime battery. Jack was a terror and a joy to the boys of Waddy. Where there was a means of escape it was the juvenile custom to bash the riotous jumbuck on the forehead with clods of dry earth. When this was repeated two or three times, Jack went butting mad, and would butt a new track clean through the township if nothing immovable intervened. This is how he was cured: One day the boys found the hub of a cartwheel, and ran a stout rope through it, and suspended it from the top rail of a fence. The bottom rails were missing, and hub swung about eighteen inches from the ground. Then Jack was inveigled into the trap with green vegetables, and his enemies worked him up by bombarding him with clods, and he fell. The ram went for the swing-hub, and his first drive caught it "fair," so that it whirled clean over the rail, and took him in the rear with a fearful boost, that drove him all of a heap. Can you understand the surprise and the fury of that ram? He gathered himself up again, and went forth to war. Rearing up he dropped the hub another hot 'un, and it came back at him unexpectedly, and knocked his chin in with an uppercut. But Jack was game, and there and then commenced the world's record catch-as-catch-can butting match. The whistle sounded, and the innocent children were called to school, when the fight raged most furiously. Two hours later they rushed out again to the battle-ground, and found Jack spread out, utterly done up. The hub lay at a distance, the inch rope having worn through under the ram's attack. Jack did not stir from that spot for three days, and then moved feebly and in great dejection, and he could never be induced to butt anything again, even under pressure of the most grievous abuse.

*From "Aboriginalities", the* Bulletin

*This is the sort of story Alexander Macdonald was talking about when he wrote the extract that opens this section. It is ruthless enough, God knows, and may well be true in most essentials. I know the Bastard from the Bush would find it funny. His humour was, and is, ruthless.*

# Flying Kate

It makes us old hands sick and tired to hear
    Them talk of their champions of today,
Eurythmics and Davids, yes, I'll have a beer,
    Are only fair hacks in their way.

Now this happened out West before records were
      took,
    And 'tis not to be found in the guide,
But it's honest—Gor' struth, and can't be
      mistook,
    For it happened that I had the ride.

'Twas the Hummer's Creek cup, and our mare,
      Flying Kate,
    Was allotted eleven stone two;
The race was two miles, you'll agree with me
      mate,
    It was asking her something to do.

She was heavy in foal, but the owner and me
    Decided to give her a spin,
We were right on the rocks, 'twas the end of a
      spree,
    So we needed a bit of a win.

I saddled her up and went down with the rest,
    Her movements were clumsy and slow,
The starter to get us in line did his best,
    Then swishing his flag he said, "Go!"

The field jumped away but the mare seemed
      asleep,
    And I thought to myself, "We've been sold,"
Then I heard something queer, and I felt I could
      weep,
    For strike me if Kate hadn't foaled.

The field by this time had gone half-a-mile,
    But I knew what the old mare could do,
So I gave her a cut with the whip—you can
      smile,
    But the game little beast simply flew.

'Twas then she showed them her wonderful
    speed,
  For we mowed down the field one by one,
With a furlong to go we were out in the lead,
  And prepared for a last final run.

Then something came at us right on the outside,
  And we only just scratched past the pole,
When I had a good look I thought I'd have died,
  For I'm blowed if it wasn't the foal.

*From a* Bill Bowyang Reciter

*No collection of this kind would be complete without
some reference to horses and horsemen, as witness the
fellow who wrote the essay on bush liars that opens this
section. Neither poem deals with "distances ridden
between suns", but the true spirit of the bush is there.
The best "horse lie" poem to be written in recent times,
to my way of thinking, is John Manifold's poem
"Incognito". It repays trying to find this poem, for it
is a lot of fun. It not only ridicules the dreadful
sentimentality of much bush verse about little broken-
down ponies that once saved the squatter's
wife/honour/child etc., but also gently sends itself up
as well.*

# The Outlaw and the Rider

*Anon.*

He had come to Umarella when the drought
    of '98
Had made Monara Plains a sea of sand,
And the philanthropic super., taking pity on his
    state,
Had given him a start as extra hand.

No doubt he'd been a wonder, for at night
    he'd sit for hours,
And boast of marvellous feats he'd seen and
    done,
How he'd won the Axeman's Trophy at the Show
    in Charters Towers,
And had killed a Syrian hawker just for fun.

How he rung the shed at Blackall, beating Howe
    by thirty sheep,
He'd broken outlaw horses in at night,
And in seven rounds at Gympie put O'Sullivan
    to sleep
With a blow for which he had the patent right.

Now we had a horse, an outlaw, bred on
    Umarella run,
No fiercer colt had ever stretched the reins,
He had thrown Monara Billy and the station
    breaker, Dunne,
And was reckoned bad throughout the southern
    plains.

The Skipper came down strolling—we had
    planned the joke of course—
"I've letters here, must catch the mail," he said;
"You had better take them, Jimmy, you can ride
    the chestnut horse,
But mind him or he'll have you on your head."

Now, Jim threw on the saddle and the colt stood
    like a sheep
One moment and we thought our joke would fail,
But Jim was barely seated when the colt he gave a
    leap,
And went at it like a demon through the rails.

Down the lane we followed and we opened wide
    our eyes
To see Jim like a perfect horseman sit,
He would fetch the stockwhip round him every
    time the colt would rise,
And would tease him with the spurs whene'er he
    lit.

245

*"I'll trot you to the house for a bottle . . . Done !"  (George Lacy, watercolour)*

We made a rush for horses, down the lane we
    followed fast,
To see our outlaw thrashed was something new,
But when we reached the clump of trees where
    we had seen him last,
Both horse and man had disappeared from view.

For miles the track we followed, and for days we
    sought in vain,
All was bustle, horsemen riding here and there,
From the cattle camp on Kindra to the farms on
    Little Plain,
We searched the rugged country in despair.

The days to weeks had lengthened, still no
    tidings came to hand,
We felt all hope of finding them was lost,
Till a party searching eastward saw some
    footprints in the sand,
Showing plainly that a horse had lately crossed.

So we tracked along the hoof-marks where once
    deep grasses grew,
And on a flat hemmed in by gorges deep
We found that chestnut bucking still for all he
    ever knew,
And Jim was there astride him, fast asleep.

*From* Australian Bush Ballads, *D. Stewart and N. Keesing*

*So we arrive at the masterpiece of the literary bush
tale. It could not have been written anywhere else in
Australia besides Kalgoorlie, perhaps, and certainly
no other writer had the technical knowledge combined
with the gentle skill to perpetrate it so successfully. In
spirit it resembles the famous steelworker's tale of Joe
Magarac, from Pittsburgh, which is told in Benjamin
A. Botkin's* Treasury of American Folklore; *but the
air and flavour, the grittiness and sense of things just a
little larger than life, are pure Hannan's Find. Gavin
Casey may have written better literary works; his
collection of short stories,* It's Harder for Girls, *for
instance, has many fine tales included. But they are
outside the scope of this collection, whereas the tale of
Polish Joe and the Hairy Man are a target for liars of
the future to approach with caution and surpass if
they can. If at any time I feel an attack of vanity
coming on about my own efforts along these lines, it is
sufficient to take this story and read it over once
again, in the sure knowledge that I'll never make it up
there.*

# The Hairy Men
# from Hannigan's Halt

*Gavin Casey*

Polish Joe was seven feet high. Scientific instruments and mathematical calculations were needed to estimate his width. He was ageless, mature without being old, in full vigour without being young. He was a roarer and a swaggerer, but he never offended anybody worth not offending by his wild, joyous, noisy enthusiasm for himself and his mates. There were a thousand and nine stories about him, seventy-four newspaper articles, and five pieces of poetry.

He was the hero of the single-handed rescue on the Dublin Luck, when a winch on the eight hundred foot level had failed, and he had hauled Dutchy Schmall hand over hand up a forty-foot winze before the shots Dutchy had set at the bottom went off. He was the man who had drunk Potter Beer, the thirsty whisky traveller, under the table at the Slag and Slimes Hotel, and then consumed a bottle and a half of a different brand to get the taste of Potter's inferior rubbish out of his mouth. He brought an old-fashioned light into the wild eye of Mother Suggs, of the Slag and Slimes, whenever she saw him, and at the same time melted the defences of Gloria Glasson, the fancy blonde behind the bar at the Railway, so thoroughly that she would only go out with mine managers and machinery travellers with big expense accounts when Polish Joe didn't need her.

Joe was a gambler who bellowed with delight, win or lose, so loudly that it should have brought the hot scones from five miles away. He was the human crane-cum-tractor who had discovered Ekker McLennan, the gold-buyer, bogged to the axle fifteen miles along the Border Road, had heaved and hauled his car out of the mud, and had towed motor and driver to town behind his push-bike. He was an oversized human shape built out of steel and springy wire cable, with the urgent strength of a gelignite explosion and the slow power of the soft, irresistible steam that quietly revolves the giant drums of winding-machines. But he was no dumb ox. He was the man who carried Springy Turf's horse-trough to the top of the Horseshoe Dump.

That time it all happened in the dusk of a great drinking afternoon of a Saturday short shift, when two hundred muscled men were bellowing and arguing about anything and everything in and around the bar of Springy's Tramstop Pub. Suddenly, about twenty of the men discovered they were arguing about Polish Joe's strength, and that Springy was disparaging it. The score of men flew into a real rage immediately, and a hundred more caught on and got ready for some knuckle-work without the slightest idea of what it was all about. Polish Joe drank his beer, and didn't say much, because none of them and no combination of them could have hurt him, anyway. But when it began to look as though they might wreck the bar, from which he would need more beer for several hours, he took a hand.

"Mister," Polish Joe said to Springy. "Would y' reckon I was a bit strong if I could pull that horse-trough outside out of th' ground?"

"I seen men who coulda did that," said Springy, challengingly.

"Would it prove anything if I could put it on me back, an' carry it?" Joe asked, softly.

"You wouldn't be so bad, if you done that," Springy admitted. "Not that I couldn't o' done it meself, when I was your age."

All the men who could see through the doors of the pub looked at the great iron-and-timber trough and roared with disbelief and indignation, but Polish Joe quietly drank two more pint pewters of beer, and then said, "What if I hoisted it on me back an' took it up to th' top o' th' Horseshoe Dump?"

There was a gasp, and then a silence, because the Horseshoe Dump was the highest and the steepest on the whole Golden Mile, and it took an ordinary man all his time to scramble to the top of it without carrying anything. It was half a mile from the Tramstop Pub, but even at that distance it towered over the little pub like a statue of surly wrath. Looking at it make Springy's eyes light up, and he said, "No stops between here and th' top?"

"No stops, mister, if you got two quid that says I can't do it," Polish Joe agreed.

Then there was an outbreak of chatter among the mob, and a lot of side-wagering, because that was something few thought even Polish Joe could do. They watched while he carried out the easy part of it, which was merely tearing the six-by-six legs of the trough out of eighteen inches of packed and sun-baked earth, and their own bones ached in sympathy when Polish Joe's great thigh-muscles burst both legs of his dungarees for eighteen inches as he crouched his vast frame under it and rose with it on his shoulders. They followed along with him over the flat, shouting encouragement and singing, and still betting, and after a hundred yards eight of them ran back for pints of beer, because Polish Joe would certainly get thirsty on the way, and wouldn't be allowed to stop until he reached the top of the Horseshoe Dump.

At the foot of the dump most fell back, and the few who tried to climb with him soon lost their footholds through beer and excitement and came rolling and tumbling to the bottom. But Polish Joe went on, with his great boots kicking toeholds in the earth like rockdrills biting into the stone underground. There was a moment of suspense when the lace of his left boot broke, with a crack like an overloaded main cable, and he stumbled. He fell forward with the half-ton iron cape on his shoulders and he could not have let go with his hands or it would have fallen. So he bit into the Horseshoe Dump with his teeth, and steadied himself, and when he turned around and spat out the mouthful of dirt those below were spattered with mullock as though the Horseshoe Dump had erupted into a volcano. When he was half-way up, and silhouetted against the darkening sky, he looked bigger than the dump, bigger than the mines around, and the pub and the shops and the town, the biggest thing in the world.

When Polish Joe came down he was pleased and very thirsty, and the drinking started in earnest, and the less reliable characters who had seen him carry the trough to the top of the Horseshoe Dump immediately started making up stories about the affair that were exaggerated. Springy Turf did a dazzling trade until midnight, but he was a mean man, and was never satisfied, and it occurred to him that he now lacked a horse-trough. He asked Polish Joe when he was going to bring it down and put it in place again, and Joe said he wasn't. When Polish Joe said that the laughter from the pub made afternoon-shift surface workers on the mines think there was a fall of earth somewhere. Then Springy offered Polish Joe one pound to bring his trough back, and lost his temper nine times bidding it up to a tenner. But Joe still said no, and at that stage Springy said, "To hell with the lot of you! I'd

rather get a new one than pay a penny more."

After that they wrecked the Tramstop Pub bar and moved off to the Slag and Slimes and made a night of it. And next day the management of the Horseshoe Mine saw the humour of the situation, and ordered Springy Turf to remove his rubbish from the top of their dump. Before it was all over, Springy employed three men and two horses for two days and had to pay the cost of a horse which broke its legs and had to be destroyed; one man with a caterpillar tractor for a week during which he never succeeded in getting more than one third of the way up the Horseshoe Dump; and finally one old man with an auger and plugs of gelignite, who blew the horse-trough into small, untraceable pieces. So Springy had to buy a new trough, and the total cost must have been one hundred times the two pounds he had bet Polish Joe, and twenty times the ten pounds at which he had stopped bidding for Joe to bring his property down and put it in its place again. Everybody laughed for a month, and Polish Joe himself laughed so loudly that the Chamber of Mines sent him an official request to stop, because the tumultuous vibrations of mirthful sound were cracking the concrete foundations that carried the poppet-legs of the mines.

With Polish Joe a man like that, you wouldn't think anybody would argue with him or about him. But apart from the fact that the beer from the Golden Mile Brewery makes five-foot men feel like six-foot men and six-foot men feel like skyscrapers, even a sober goldfielder feels much larger and more combative than most people. Polish Joe was a bogger, a man who shifted unbelievable quantities of dirt away from the face from which it had been blown, and into trucks for dumping in the underground bins each day.

When the promoters of the St. Patrick's Day sports decided that if towns in the timber country could have their log-chops at their annual shows, then the goldfields should have periodical competitions at shifting broken stone with a shovel, all the betting was on Polish Joe. But there was no lack of bogologists who thought they could beat him, even if nobody else did. Every mine had at least one man in training, and they all swung their "banjoes" so hard that production costs dropped in a way that delighted the managements and made them regard Bogger's Championships as the best idea anybody had had since the rock-drill. As the men trained and managed to shift more and more earth their mates got enthusiastic about them, and kidded themselves that Polish Joe mightn't win after all. After a while there was some money available to back others, and the pubs were full of men telling lies about how many trucks Fancy Larsen and Pimply Horace Griller and Loop McGallick and Ostrich O'Hara had filled in an eight-hour shift.

By the time St. Patrick's Day arrived half the people had lost interest in the bike-races and the billygoats, and the Irish Dancing and the sprinters, and there had been fifty-three fights, two divorces, and a libel action resulting from high feelings about the boggers. The shrewd money was still on Polish Joe, in spite of the short odds, but from sheer patriotism the Irish made a solid block for a man called O'Flaherty, and the Great Boulder was alleged to have a dark horse in a short, square, evil-tempered man called Lobb. Polish Joe was so confident that he spent the prize-money, and the winnings from most of his bets on himself, in advance, buying drinks for his cobbers. But being the man he was, he didn't make anybody hate him because of his exuberant self-confidence, not even the Irish.

The day before the sports the tracks for the runners were laid out, and the platform for the dancers, and at the same time big trucks came in and out of the Recreation Ground and dumped a ton of good, rough, underground stone on each of a dozen quarter-inch steel plates. There were eight plates for nominations already accepted, and four in case there were any post-entries at double fees. The plates and the stone were just beside the main grandstand, and by the time the stand was looking as green as the lawn on the football field because of all the ribbons people were wearing, there were nine men with shovels ready to shift the dirt into trucks the height and size of mine trucks. The soulless people among the crowd were watching the bikes swooping around the track, or getting drunk in the bar, but the sensitive and intelligent ones had got drunk earlier, and were crowded around the boggers, mostly hammering Polish Joe on the back, or laughing at the ninth man, the only post-entry.

The man who had slapped his money down and pulled his shovel out at the last moment was from the outback. He was from Hannigan's Halt, where there was only one mine worth the name, and he was an old, lean, stiff-limbed, hairy man who looked ridiculous alongside Polish Joe or any of the other competitors. Joe shone with health and vitality, his big, eager moustache bristling, and his laugh echoing, and his enormous chest bare and bulging with muscle. He wore a wide, showy leather belt, and his trousers were underground dungarees, but they were washed into bleached beauty and ironed into creaseless perfection. He was full of beer, like all the other competitors, but that was the proper way to be, because the sluggish liquid of the beer would sweat out of them in the first five minutes, and the strength and goodness of it would stay in their vitals.

The hairy man from Hannigan's Halt had a leather belt, too, but it was the sort they issued to soldiers in the First World War, and it clamped his pants onto his herring guts over a deplorable grey flannel singlet. All around the belt were pouches and sheaths, and anyone who was old enough knew that these contained a Boyproof watch with a kerosene-stained dial, a skinning-knife, a compass, a copy of *Such is Life* by Tom Collins, and a pint bottle of O.P. rum in case of snake-bite or exhaustion. And even the receptacles on his belt weren't enough for him. He wore a ragged waistcoat, with a pipe in one pocket, a plug of villainous tobacco in another, a machine for reboring and decarbonising the pipe in the third, and an extra bottle of O.P. rum in case of snake-bite or exhaustion in the fourth. He was a sad, aged, rheumaticky-looking man, with a lot of hair on his face and none worth worrying about on his head, and among the crowd were a wild, hairy crew of his friends from Hannigan's Halt, looking much like he did, except that some were longer and some were shorter, and some were narrower and some were wider, and some carried three or four bottles of O.P. rum, because they were cautious. They were not cautious with their money, though, and the bookies chuckled richly as they took vast wads of it wagered on their creaky old cobber to win the Bogger's Championship.

When the event started, Polish Joe tossed shovelfulls of ore twenty feet into the air, and every last grain of it fell square in the centre of the truck he was filling. Every sixth shovelfull he paused for three-fifths of a second, while he swallowed a pint of beer, and after each pint six shovels would go into the truck, dead centre, so fast that you couldn't see his arms move, and the stone sprayed in a high arc, like water out of a fountain. The thunder of the rock from Polish Joe's shovel falling on the iron bottom of his truck was so loud that nobody could hear any announcements over the public-address

*Night scene in the diggings (Skinner Prout, from* Australia, *ed. Edwin Carton Booth)*

system, and they had to abandon the rest of the programme until the Bogger's Championship was finished, and soon the whole crowd was clustered around the iron plates, or craning over the northern side of the grandstand, trying to watch the men with the "banjoes".

They were all watching Polish Joe, and telling each other stories about the other things he had done. Except the hairy men from Hannigan's Halt, and somewhere underneath their wild whiskers these regrettable characters started to grin. Nobody except them noticed their aged, creaky cobber, but he had a shovel you could shave with, and he used it well. When he slid it over his iron plate and under the stone, it tumbled the rocks neatly onto its blade. There was never a pebble too many, that might fall off when he swung the contents into his truck, and there was never one too

few, to destroy the perfect symmetry of the pyramid of stone he was sending to where it belonged. Every time he threw his joints groaned, but every shovelfull went into the truck, and the bottom grain of each just grazed the side on the way. The judges had nothing to criticise, and the crowd had nothing spectacular to watch, but the old, sunburned man from Hannigan's Halt was doing all right. All the judges were utterly astonished when they were watching Polish Joe scrape together the last bits of dirt on his iron plate, to hear a wild yell from the hairy men, and see that their candidate's plate was as clean as a saucer of milk that has been dealt with by a starving cat. They had a conference that lasted most of the way through a five-gallon keg, but finally there was nothing they could do but award the championship to the hairy man with the waistcoat.

Polish Joe only laughed, but his supporters roared with anger, and because there were about ten thousand of them it made a considerable noise. Fights broke out everywhere, not because everybody didn't agree that what had happened was impossible, but just because the obvious way to deal with such a situation is to punch somebody on the nose. Polish Joe and the hairy man, neither of whom was Irish, ignored all the turmoil, and looked at each other with respect.

"You're pretty good, mate," said Polish Joe.

"I bin at th' game a long time," the hairy man said, apologetically.

"I'm a extra good man on a winze," Joe told him. "I got th' strength to chuck th' dirt right out until I'm about twenty feet down. I'd like to sink a winze alongside of you."

"I done a bit in me time," the hairy man admitted. "I'd like a go at you jist fer the fun of it. What about here an' now?"

They got the judges and arranged it, and all Polish Joe's backers were much encouraged by the way he grabbed his ten by ten quarter-inch steel plate, and slung it aside as though it were a pocket-handkerchief to make room for the shaft-sinking contest. The hairy man had to get eight of his hairy mates to help him, and then the judges marked out spaces six feet square, and the pair went to work.

Polish Joe saved his strength, but he didn't save enough of it. He only threw the dirt ten feet in the air, and he cut his pints of beer down to one for every ten shovels. The hairy man slid his dirt over the edge of the hole like a snake coming out of the ground, and only took a suck at the spout of his old waterbag twice from start to finish. Both men signalled they were through at the same time, and the mob went mad at the prospect of a dead-heat. A bookmaker swooned and another set out for New Zealand on a racing bicycle stolen from beside the training-shed, and the best cost-accountants on the ground couldn't estimate how many fights started. But when the judges measured up the little shafts the men had dug, they found that Polish Joe's was two inches short of the agreed eight feet on the west side, and had a lump three and three-sixteenths of an inch high in the middle. The hairy man's hole was flatter than a billiard table at the bottom, and nothing but a micrometer gauge would have established the fact that it was deeper on one wall than on another. They had to announce him the winner.

The hairy man felt so good that he offered Polish Joe one of his pints of O.P. rum. Polish Joe drank the rum and crunched the bottle between his teeth, and bought a demijohn of whisky for each of them, and started to talk about tunnelling. "I got the reach fer that," he said. 'I can chuck th' dirt back so far that when I started th' thousand-foot drive on th' Star of the South they had to shift th' shaft back fifty feet t' give me room."

"I don't wanna boast," the hairy man told him, "but I done much the same at th' Drongo North before I went back t' the bush again. They took me shovel away frum me, an' made me work with a teaspoon, so that th' rest o' th' mob an' th' skips an' th' treatment plant could keep up with me."

"We could make a bit of a drive, out from th' shafts we jist dug," Polish Joe suggested.

"I'd be in that, mate," the hairy man said, eagerly, easing a rheumatic kink out of his lifting elbow.

Even St. Patrick's Day comes to an end, sooner or later, and by the time the judges had fixed rules and conditions and they had got started on their shafts, there wasn't much daylight left. The crowd was keen, but furious because nobody could see exactly what was going on down at the bottom of the holes. One man went down to see how Polish Joe was going, and Joe threw him out of the hole so high that the next thing he knew he was hanging in the air, holding onto the bannister fifteen tiers up in the grandstand. One of the hairy men went down to report on their competitor, and there was a moment of awed silence as first a leg and then an arm came up in shovelsfull of earth. When his head shot out of the mouth of the hole it wore a grin of triumph, and his pals felt that their man must be going well.

There were some fights going on, of course, but nothing was finally settled about that contest. Suddenly the north corner of grandstand sagged six feet, and while the people in it were still yelling Polish Joe came out of his shaft shaking dirt out of his hair. Everybody suddenly realised that the tunnels had been going under the stand, and that Polish Joe's had fallen in, and there was a lot of excitement while people were rescued from the crumbling structure. Polish Joe carried people down fifteen at a time, seven and a half under each arm, and everyone was so busy that there was no time to think about the hairy man, still digging away in his waistcoat, and taking drinks from his waterbag now and again. When the confusion was over a lot of people thought he had simply climbed out of his hole, and started his 1914 Model T Ford, and gone home to Hannigan's Halt. One nearly human being was worried, though, and asked one of the hairy men.

"Aw, Tom'll be going home underground," the hairy man said, tersely. "Real miner, that bloke. He'll tunnel his way back to Hannigan's Halt before th' rest of us get home t'morrer night. On'y a hunnerd miles, y' know."

St. Patrick's Day being what it is, there was a great deal of confused thought, and even larger quantities of no thought at all, that evening. The most noticeable fact was that nobody worried less about Polish Joe's defeat than Joe, whose laughter was just as loud and gay as it was when he was a heavy loser at the two-up school and whose moustachios bristled as challengingly as ever. But, as always after St. Patrick's Day and a considerable number of other days, the time of reckoning came next morning.

Lots of Model T Fords, and four-cylinder Dodges were still parked outside the recreation ground, and a low, jubilant roar was coming from beneath the grandstand. Yellow lights were competing from the grandstand windows with the clear, colourless glare of the morning sun, and nearby residents reported to the police that something untoward was afoot. The constabulary arrived with drawn pistols and live ammunition, but not before the news of strange doings had reached the bars and bazaars, and laymen were surging about in multitudes with post-St. Patrick's Day hangovers and feeling of spite towards anybody who might prove worthy of them. The best-humoured man about the place was Polish Joe, and even he looked thoughtful when an inexperienced cop told him what had happened.

"That So-and-so from Hannigan's Halt kept on tunnelling until he was right beneath the bar, and then he put in a short rise, and there he was. All these other hairy old cows from Hannigan's got in along with him, and they've been there all night. Now we gotta get them out."

There was a great and joyous roaring and thumping from the bar under the grandstand, and when the sergeant had a look through the window the pane shattered, and a full bottle of scotch whizzed past his ear. Polish Joe reached out a big fist, caught the bottle in full flight, knocked the neck off it, and drank its contents reflectively. The sergeant used language for which he would have arrested anybody else.

"You want 'em out, boss?" said Polish Joe with an eager light in his eye. "All right, I'll pass 'em to you, a couple at a time."

Polish Joe put his shoulder against the big, locked double door of the bar, and the whole grandstand leaned over a foot, and then two, and then three, before all the hinges and the lock gave at the same time. Then he went in and rocked the place about for a while bouncing the hairy men from one wall to the other, and when he was good and ready he started throwing them out.

The first hairy man was lucky, for Polish Joe threw him so far that he landed right in his own ancient utility in the road, and he had the presence of mind to start the engine straight away and drive right to Hannigan's Halt, flat out, at nearly thirty miles an hour. After him they came fast, in ones and twos, flying through the air and being gathered up out of the dust by the policemen. When Polish Joe came to a very old hairy man he showed proper respect for age, and bounced him neatly off the sergeant's soft paunch, so that none of his poor, stringy old limbs would get broken. But he had no mercy on any who were middleaged or younger, and the bigger they were the further he threw them. Last of all, he appeared in the doorway with the hairy man who had beaten him at bogging and shaft-sinking, and then had tunnelled his way into the bar. The hairy man's whiskers were smoking and smouldering slightly, because of his breath passing through them, but there was a dreamy, satisfied, don't-care-a-damn look in his eye, and Polish Joe was carrying him with both hands, at arm's length over his head.

"Wash worth it," the hairy man told the world. "Put me down, big bloke. Can't blurry-well fight y' when I'm shtuck 'way up here." A strange look appeared on Polish Joe's face, almost as though he were afraid that the man who had beaten him twice might do it a third time. He placed the hairy man carefully upright on the grounds, and held him at arm's length. The hairy man aimed blows from every direction, but of course his arms weren't long enough for his fists to reach Joe as long as Joe held him. He cut holes in the air with hands moving so fast that anything that got into the vacuum they created behind them was dragged in their wake and flew all over the place. "Let me go, y' great ape," he bellowed. "I can't fight y' frum away over here, neither."

Polish Joe held on tight, and looked at the hairy man sadly, and said, "You was a feller I had respect for, yesterday, when you beat me at them things

*The digger's favourite recreation (engraving from* Sydney Mail, *31 July 1880)*

I'm best at, but I'm disappointed."

"Wotcha mean?" snarled the hairy man, pulling a punch so suddenly that the cuff of his coat shot down five inches past his bunched knuckles, and then snapped into place.

"Wanted t' buy y' a drink," Polish Joe told him, sorrowfully. "Couldn't find y' nowhere, an' here you was all th' time, guzzling away with them hairy mates o' yours, with never a thought for me bein' just as thirsty as yourself, on account of I'd shovelled near as dam it as fast, at the bogging and th' shaft sinking."

"Jees, I'm sorry," said the hairy man, looking truly ashamed. "Never done a thing like that before. Dunno what I coulda been thinkin' of. Anyway, if it ain't too late, we can have one now. There's plenty more back in there, an' we can have the fight after."

Then the pair of them went back into the bar like brothers, and they never got around to having the fight at all. It was five days before the police persuaded them to come out of the bar at all, and go to jail like good citizens. By then they were up for an immense amount, between them, for what they drank, and for damages, and for what all the other hairy men had drunk on the night of St. Patrick's Day. But the publican who owned the stock and the equipment in the recreation ground bar didn't worry, because he knew that when Polish Joe did anything like that he paid to the last penny. And this time he had a mate as good as himself, or maybe even a whisker better, to help him earn the money.

And sure enough, when they came out of jail they got contract work side by side on the North Kalgoorlie Deeps, and between them they earned all the money they needed, in a fortnight. In that two weeks they deepened the North Kalgoorlie shaft a thousand feet, and they took a drive at the 1800-foot level right across the border into the next State, and the two of them drank not a drop of anything except water, of which they consumed 215 gallons a day on the job, and an unknown quantity when they were off shift. They became warm friends, but the hairy man was too hairy and set in his ways to be really happy anywhere but at Hannigan's Halt, and Polish Joe couldn't be happy anywhere too far from Gloria Glasson, the fancy blonde behind the bar at the Railway.

So when they had paid their debts they spent three weeks shaking hands and having a parting drink, and the last hairy man went off out of town, and there were never any more bogging champion-ships, because it was obvious that there would be no worthwhile competition for Polish Joe unless the hairy man came back, which he never did. The only permanent results of the whole affair are the story, and the cranky lean on the Recreation Ground grandstand, where one of its corners subsided into Polish Joe's tunnel.

*From* View from Kalgoorlie, *ed. Ted Mayman, published by Landfall Press*

He learnt in the bush—in the loneliness and isolation where there was no radio and few books, and men had to create their own entertainment. Imagine a group of ringers (in Queensland a stockman is a ringer) with time on their hands. They would start talking, and as the talk would pass from the experiences of the day yarns would start. Perhaps when there was a pause, Sam would throw in his story, and some other poker faced individual in a flannel shirt would throw in his bit, and they were off and away, creating a fine, though unwritten literature. If some new chum were foolish enough to say, as I did, "You wouldn't be telling me lies, would you?" there might be a pained silence. He obviously didn't understand the rules of the game. Some old bushman would put him firmly in his place, and the talk would go on.

"What was the worst droving job you ever had?" I asked.

"Well," said Sam. "I did have one job that was a bit unusual. I brought a mob of turkeys down from the Gulf once. They got very sore-footed, and I had a terrible time with them until a mate told me to have them shod. I ran them through some coal tar, and then through a pit of sand, and I never had any more trouble with them at all! I did well out of that job."

"Sam," I said, looking at him sideways. "You won't be having me on, would you?"

"No," he answered calmly. "I never tell lies. The truth's strange enough, don't you think?"

*Wendy Lowenstein, in* Australian Tradition *(December 1970)*

Pething a Bullock

*Settlers outside a hut in the bush (Richard Daintree, photograph overpainted in oils)*

# The Darling River

Floating bottles began to be more frequent, and we knew by that same token that we were nearing "Here's Luck!"—Bourke, we mean. And this reminds us.

When the Brewarrina people observe a more than ordinary number of bottles floating down the river, they guess that Walgett is on the spree; when the Louth chaps see an unbroken procession of dead marines for three or four days they know that Bourke's drunk. The poor, God-abandoned whaler sits in his hungry camp at sunset and watches the empty symbols of hope go by, and feels more God-forgotten than ever—and thirstier if possible—and gets a great wide, thirsty, empty, quaking longing to be up where those bottles come from. If the townspeople knew how much misery they caused by their thoughtlessness they would drown their dead marines, or bury them, but on no account allow them to go drifting down the river, and stirring up hells in the bosoms of less fortunate fellow-creatures.

There came a man from Adelaide to Bourke once, and he collected all the empty bottles in town, stacked them by the river, and waited for a boat. What he wanted them for the legend sayeth not, but the people reckoned he had a private still, or something of that sort, somewhere down the river, and were satisfied. What he came from Adelaide for, or whether he really did come from there, we do not know. All the Darling bunyips are supposed to come from Adelaide. Anyway, the man collected all the empty bottles he could lay his hands on, and piled them on the bank, where they made a good show. He waited for a boat to take his cargo, and, while waiting, he got drunk. That excited no comment. He stayed drunk for three weeks, but the townspeople saw nothing unusual in that. In order to become an object of interest in their eyes, and in that line, he would have had to stay drunk for a year and fight three times a day—oftener if possible—and lie in the road in the broiling heat between whiles, and try to hang himself naked, and be finally squashed by a loaded wool team.

But while he drank, the Darling rose, for reasons best known to itself, and floated those bottles off. They strung out and started for the Antarctic Ocean, with a big old wicker-worked demi-john in the lead.

For the first week the down-river men took no notice; but after the bottles had been drifting past with scarcely a break for a fortnight or so, they began to get interested. Several whalers watched the procession until they got the jim-jams by force of imagination, and when their bodies began to float down with the bottles, the down-river people got anxious.

At last the mayor of Wilcannia wired Bourke to know whether Dibbs or Parkes was dead, or democracy triumphant or, if not, wherefore the jubilation? Many telegrams of a like nature were received during that week, and the true explanation was sent in reply to each. But it wasn't believed, and to this day Bourke has the name of being the most drunken town on the river.

*Henry Lawson*

A Squatter's Home.

*As with Gavin Casey's story, this is probably the funniest of all bush verse written to be read aloud, and it was written in the last twelve years. I have read it on many occasions, to audiences ranging from those at folklore festivals to city schoolchildren; and the response is guaranteed. For sheer sustained fun it beats even the oldtimers at their best. Graham Jenkin is a South Australian, and by being alive and writing as well as this, he confounds those critics who have been writing the bush off. Perhaps here is a poet who has not forgotten the people, because when they hear the poem, the people do not forget the poet. I might add, for those of the younger generation, 1963 was the year Sir Donald Campbell broke the world land speed record for a piston-engined motor car on Lake Eyre.*

# The Ballad of the Birdsville Drover

Oh come all you wild young bushy blokes and
    listen unto me
And I'll tell youse all about them floods they had
    in 'sixty-three.
I've been droving down that Birdsville Track
    since I was just a lad,
And it'd take a book to tell youse all the narrow
    scrapes I've had:
I've been in that many rushes now it's just a
    flaming bore
When I see the dust cloud gather and I hear the
    hoof beats roar.
I've swum across that many rivers boys with
    cattle, prads and sheep
I've been known to cross the Cooper in
    flood—and wake up sound asleep.
I've done me share of duffing boys: in nineteen-
    twenty-four,
I beat old Harry Redford by a thousand head or
    more
When I duffed two thousand scrubber micks up
    there orf Brunette Downs
And drove 'em acrorst the desert there (avoiding
    all the towns)
And took them down to Melbourne, but on stock
    exchange advice
I drove 'em on to Launceston and got a better
    price.
Now I see you want to interrupt, and I know
    what you want to say;
How did I get them across Bass Strait? Well I
    didn't go that way!
Yes I've worked within and without the law, I've
    druven from sea to sea
And whenever a cove wants a tough job done he
    usually comes straight to me.
I've druven mutton and beef and goat,
I've druven things that walk or float,
I've druven 'roos and emus too,
Though I've never druven things that flew
(Bar chooks).
I remember taking one big band
Of bloodstock roosters overland
From Burringun to Booroobrand,
I tell yer when I took me cheque
I was bloody near a nervous wreck.
But still I never lost me flair
For droving things peculiare

Till Nineteen Sixty Three.
For in 'sixty-three after years of drought
The North was nearly all washed out,
And over the pasture parched and brown
Old Hughie really sent her down.
And them that couldn't swim was drowned.
And man and beast all had to share
Them little islands here and there.
I lost me plant, I lost me cook,
Me men and all me stores was took,
I clung to a tree and watched me dray
And all that was in it sail away.
I'd an old felt hat, a tattered shirt, a belt and a
    pair of strides,
A pair of boots, a tin of weed, and beggar all
    besides.
If I'd waited there for rescue, I'd be hanging up
    there still
So I plunged into the murky mud
And swam acrorst that flamin' flood
And made for Myall Hill.
Now Myall Hill is a cattle run that's owned by
    Percy Brown—
One of them grand old cattle kings
Renowned (amongst many other things)
For sinking pizzen down.
And around the run for miles and miles
You could see these dirty great big piles
Of bottles, flagoons and even kegs,
And I thought; now if only they had legs
I'd muster 'em up and take 'em down
Cause they'd fetch a decent price in town.
But then I thought; you cranky goat
These flamin' bottles and things will float,
And it'd only take about a week
To drove 'em down on Cooper's Creek.
Old Percy said, "Yes, take 'em son
I'll be glad to get 'em orf the run."
And so we started on the job
Of mustering this peculiar mob.
Now the holding yard was off the creek in a dirty
    big lagoon
And there we mustered every bottle and counted
    each flagoon.
Twelve hundred thousand bottles there was of
    every size and shape,
Nine hundred thousand old flagoons that held
    Crow-eatin' grape,
And a thousand forty gallon kegs was all that I
    could find
So of course I used 'em as me plant and brought
    'em up behind.

And when at last they were all arranged in
glorious array
They opened up the netting gates and the leaders
moved away.
And what a magnificent sight to behold as they
moved out on the tide,
The Cooper was fifteen miles across and they
reached from side to side,
And as I brought the tailers out I tell you I felt
quite proud,
In me saddle astride of a well built keg—I waved
to the station crowd.
Now exactly just what happened next I've never
been too clear
But as soon as the mob got into the creek they
jumped clean out of gear,
And off they went like a bat out of
hell—completely out of hand—
The only mob that ever escaped from the king of
the overland.
The bottles panicked: the flagons rushed,
The kegs with all me gear were crushed,
The Cooper bellowed and crashed and swore
And whirled and swirled like never before,
And bottles was spread from shore to shore.
And as for me flamin' riding keg, well strike me
pink and blue
I've never ridden a worser moke—and I've
ridden some stinkers too.
He wouldn't answer whip nor spurs,
He wouldn't heed my fearsome curs,
He wouldn't hold: he wouldn't stand,
He wouldn't come to either hand.
He charged the flagons and dozens burst
Then he bolted for miles with his hind part first.
He ducked, he bucked; the stinking cow
He tried to swipe me on a bough.
He tried to break me flamin' legs
By bashing against the other kegs,
And then to end this little prank
The rotten lousy bludger sank.
So there I was in that avalanche
With nothing to hold but an old dead branch.
And there I clung for over a week
Swept on and on by Cooper's Creek
Until at last she dumped us there
Right in the middle of Lake Eyre.
Now I dunno if you jokers know that feeling you
sometimes get,
When you've been in a lake for months on end
and you're always hungry and wet,
Surrounded by thousands of bottles and

kegs—but never a drop of grog,
When all that keeps you from Davey Jones is a
leaky old Mulga log.
Well anyway I wasn't sad when the sun blazed in
the sky
And evaporated the water up and left us high and
dry.
So there I was in the middle of that endless salty
plain,
With a fortune's worth of bottles and kegs, but
without a truck or train
How was I going to get them down? So I stood
and thought awhile;
For days I thought and as I thought I got them in
a pile.
I was still intently thinking when I saw a tiny
speck
Appear on the horizon, and I said to myself "By
heck
Some joker's coming up here with a semi-trailer
truck—
It's time the flamin' tide was turned and I had a
bit of luck."
But as the thing grew closer there and got within
me range,
I could see it wasn't a truck at all but something
very strange.
It was sort of long and flat and blue with a tail
stuck up behind
I didn't know what the heck to do—I thought I
was orf me mind.
It was doing a hundred miles an hour—it could
have been even more.
I don't know if the driver knew or if the bludger
saw,
But before a cove could catch his eye, the stupid
bloody clot
He went clean through me flamin' mob and
smashed the bloody lot!

I tell yer boys that incident was quite enough for
me—
I've stuck to droving cattle since them floods of
'sixty-three.

From Two Years on Bardunyah Station, *Graham Jenkin*

---

*Lennie Lower is unjustly forgotten today, though in
his day he probably brought more laughter to
Australians than any other single writer, and his
prose stands the test of time in that it is still funny. I
have included two of his better send-ups here, of the*

*Public Service and the Bush. They are both included in a collection called* The Best of Lennie Lower, *edited by Pearl and Pidgeon.*

# Red Tape in the Sunset

A terrible thing has happened to the Lower family. It all comes of living in New South Wales and being a civil servant. Harold, my grandfather, joined the civil service at the age of fourteen. He is now sixty-two. And all civil servants who have reached the age of sixty are now compelled to retire in order to make way for the employment of youths! Didn't the old man go mad!

He was at his desk in the Income Tax Department when his secretary shook him and told him that his morning tea was getting cold.

"What time is it?" he asked, stretching himself.

"Time to retire," answered the secretary, breaking it gently.

"Goodness gracious!" exclaimed Harold, who was always addicted to violent language from his youth up, "I didn't know it was so late."

"I mean you've gotter snatch your time," said the secretary, a coarse youth, who had only been in the service a bare thirty years. "Put your hat on. They've put the skids under you. They're wheeling out your superannuation. Scram!"

The old man was dazed. I mean to say, he was more dazed than usual. "But what am I going to do?" he moaned. "I haven't any other hobbies."

"Sit in the park and play draughts," said the unfeeling secretary. "There's a youth outside who's a somnambulist, and he's coming this way. And," he hissed, "you know that the Government is economizing? Well, this new fellow doesn't take milk or sugar in his morning tea!"

"Then I am indeed undone," said Harold mournfully. "Where is this youth?"

The secretary produced the youth, a mere lad of about forty-two.

"What is your name, my boy?" said Harold.

"I'm afraid you're in the wrong department," said the youth mechanically. "Registrar-General's Office. Fill in a form. Go to the other counter. Inquiries on the right. Put your signature here. Call in again tomorrow. The officer who deals with these matters is out at the moment."

"You'll do," said Harold. "My boy, there is a taxpayer who owes the State one shilling and fourpence. He is BM2756813. Remember that, my boy. I have been hounding him for four years. His files are in yonder safe. I bequeath him to you. Never let up on him."

The youth's eyes moistened. "Thank you, sir, for giving me a start in my career," he said.

But the old man was asleep.

"Hey!" bawled the secretary, "didn't I tell you that you're not working here now!"

". . . be payable without fine within fourteen days," muttered Harold. They dragged him from his chair, screaming.

Life at home now is hellish. As we're all living on Grandfather's superannuation, he has taken over the management of the house. He spends most of the housekeeping money on forms. If I want a drink of water, I have to fill in form XB7, and then he rings up the Water Board and inquires how things are at the reservoir, and after that he gets on to the Weather Bureau and wants to know about the prospects for rain and if they will kindly furnish him with statistics of the rainfall as from 1890 up to the year ending June 30, 1935. Then I go next door and get a drink of water.

It is rather significant that once upon a time the State's employees used to be called civil servants. The mistake has since been rectified, and they are now called public servants. Of course, Grandfather was never really a public servant. He was only a temporary employee during the whole of his thirty-eight years of service, during which he was the mainstay of countless money-lenders, and was also the champion time-book signer of his department. At one time he was signed up two months ahead of anybody else in the State and was presented with an illuminated fountain-pen.

Talking about money-lenders, my grandfather once called a meeting of creditors, and everybody thought it was an Empire Day rally. He eventually promised to pay five shillings in the pound, but nobody would lend him the five shillings. Our home is now entirely upholstered in red tape, and our bulldog answers to the name of BM529.

And Grandfather, now that he has retired, would like to meet all his old pals at the usual place at the racecourse on Wednesdays, and he expects to see them all out at the cricket ground as soon as the big games start. If he can spare the time, he may join the Navy in order to see the Melbourne Cup next November.

*From* The Best of Lennie Lower, *ed. C. Pearl and W. E. Pidgeon*

*A shearer knocking down his cheque (from* Australasia Illustrated, *ed. Andrew Garran)*

# Where the Cooler Bars Grow

I'm only a city boy. Until a short time ago I'd never seen a sheep all in one piece or with its fur on. That's why, when people said to me, "Go west, young man, or east, if you like, but go," I went.

Truth to tell, I thought it would be safer. I had a shotgun and a rifle, and a bag of flour, and two sealed kerosene tins of fresh water in the luggage van. I thought of taking some coloured beads for the natives, but decided it was too expensive.

I forget now where it was I went to. Anyhow, it was full of wheat silos and flies, and there was a horse standing on three legs under a tree. There were no other signs of life except a faint curl of smoke coming from the hotel chimney.

When I walked into the bar there was nobody there, so I walked out the back to the kitchen and there was nobody there. I went out to the front veranda again, and saw a little old man picking burrs off his socks.

"Good-day!" I said.

"Day!" he replied.

"Where's everybody?" I asked.

"Never heard of him. Unless you mean old Smith. He's down by the crick. You're a stranger, aren't you?"

"Just got off the train. Where's the publican?"

"Do you want a drink?"

"Yes."

"Orright!"

So we went into the bar and had a drink.

"I want to book a room here," I told him.

"Don't be silly!" he replied. "Sleep out on the veranda with the rest of us if you've got blankets. They're decoratin' the School of Arts with the sheets. You going to the dance?"

"I can't dance!"

"Strike me pink, who wants to! We leave that to the women. There ought to be some good fights at this one. When I was younger there wasn't a man could stand up to me on the dance floor. Here comes somebody now."

"Day."

"Day. Don't you bring that horse into the bar! Hang it all, you've been told about that before."

"He's quiet. I broke him in yesterday. Hear about Snowy? Got his arm caught in the circular saw up at the timber mill."

"That's bad."

"Too right it is! They've got to get a new saw. Whoa there!"

"Take him out into the kitchen. The flies are worryin' him."

"Goodo. Pour me out a beer."

"Pour it out yourself."

"Go to bed, you old mummified ox!"

"I'll give you a belt in the ear, you red-headed son of a convict!"

"Give it to your uncle. Giddap!"

"One of me best friends," said the old man, as the horse was led into the kitchen.

"I suppose," said the red-headed one, returning, "it'll be all right if he eats that cake on the kitchen table? Won't do him any harm, will it?"

"That's for supper at the dance!"

"Well, I'll go and take it off him. There's a good bit of it left."

Outside on the veranda voices were heard.

"I wouldn't sell that dog for a thousand pounds."

"I wouldn't give you two bob for 'im."

"You never had two bob in your life! You ever seen a sheep dog trial? That dog has won me more prizes at the Show than ten other dogs.

"Why," he continued, "you could hang up a fly-veil, point out one particular hole in it and that dog could cut a fly out of a bunch and work him through that hole."

"Good-day!"

"Day!"

"No sign of rain yet."

"No. I heard of a swaggie who had to walk eighty miles to get water to boil his billy, and when he got there he found he'd forgotten his cup and saucer, and by the time he'd walked back for his cup and saucer there was a bushfire started in the water-hole, it was that dry."

"Don't bring your horses into the bar!"

"Don't take any notice of the old crank. Why don't you put this beer out in the sun to get cool? If it was any flatter you'd have to serve it in a plate. Going to the Show this year?"

"Of course I am. Why don't you teach that horse manners?"

"Good-day, Mrs. Smith."

"Who put that horse in my kitchen?"

"Is he in the kitchen? Well, what do you think of that!"

"Fancy him being in the kitchen!"

"In the kitchen, of all places!"

"Who could have let him in?"

"Never mind about that. Get him out at once, Jack! Wipe up that counter. I told you to cut some wood this morning. And put that dog outside and get the broom and sweep up the bar. Wash those glasses first."

By this time we were all out on the veranda.

"She hasn't found out about the horse eating the cake yet," said somebody.

"Better go for a walk somewhere, eh?"

But that was years ago. They've got radios and refrigerators in the bush now, and that's why you see me mournfully wandering about the cattle stalls at Show time. I'm thinking of the good old days before the squatters took up polo, and started knitting their own berets. When men were men, and women were useful about the farm when the plough horse took sick.

> *Wrap me up in my stockwhip and blanket*
> *And bury me deep down below*
> *Where the farm implement salesmen won't*
> *molest me,*
> *In the shades where the cooler bars grow.*

*From* The Best of Lennie Lower, *ed. C. Pearl and W. E. Pidgeon*

*Ron Edwards has said (*Australian Tradition, *December 1971), "The tall story is another matter entirely, but my own experience has been that it has more often been found in print than in the field. In all my years of collecting, and also living in country towns, I have only heard half a dozen tall stories, and I found these recitals rather embarrassing, as they seemed to be laboured re-workings of material from Bill Wannan's column in the* Australasian Post."

*My own experience has been that while he is a rare bird, the teller of tall tales is around, and he is to be treasured when found. The idea for this poem was given me while working at Hume Pipe Works, at Meeandah in Brisbane, and the following note comes from an incomplete and untitled manuscript, the same one from which I took the story of Smacker found earlier (see page 242).*

View of Brisbane

# The Queensland Dog

A stranger came from New South Wales, and he
  was tall and brown,
He lined beside us at the bar, he sank his
  schooners down,
And all the while, to pass the time, he told us
  doubtful tales
Of the country he laid claim to, remarkable New
  South Wales.
With soil so rich and fertile, so ran his line of
  talk,
That pumpkin vines fair sprinted along, as fast as
  a man could walk;
He said it took two hours, sometimes, to ride
  through the hollow logs,
For the timber grew so thick and tall. And then
  he mentioned dogs.

Little Maginnis spoke up then, arising from his
  seat.
"I don't know about them other things, but at
  dogs we got you beat.
I was boundary riding once," he said, "On a
  station Longreach way,
And lost me bearings among the hills, right at the
  end of the day.
So I let the old moke poke along and find his own
  way in the dark
Until in the distance I saw a light. And then I
  heard him bark.
Well, station dogs are mostly noise. I never took
  no heed.
I only wanted me bearings, and I could have
  done with a feed,
So I went on riding toward the light, just
  following me nose
And then I heard him bark again, but this time
  he's up close.
I needn't have worried, he's only a dog; the kind
  cow-cockies keep
That chase the dingoes away all night, then lay all
  day and sleep.
When he gets nearer he whines a bit, friendly and
  quiet and deep.

Then he stands on his hind legs to lick me face,
  and I see his gentle eye
And his dusty coat and wagging tail by the
  starlight in the sky.
And the horse I was sitting on at the time was
  seventeen hands high."

The stranger paled and admitted, with the wind
took out of his sails,
That dogs grow bigger in Queensland than they
do in New South Wales.

*From* Brother and Brother, *Bill Scott*

. . . It was not an onerous job, and smoke-ohs
were enlivened for me by a one-eyed black
Australian called Patch for obvious reasons, and his
wonderful stories of the adventures and excitement
that obtained in the Beaudesert district of southern
Queensland. There was The Cockatoo That Foiled
the Bank Robber, for instance, (though that story is
too long to tell in passing, because I am setting out
to tell how I shipped out on the strangest ship that
ever sailed the Great Barrier Reef). All this is by
way of a preliminary. I might have time to tell you
one story about the Cockatoo, though. It went
eventually to live at the pub, where it spent much of
its time walking up and down the clothes lines in
the back yard, shouting at the yardman, and
smooging to the cook, who treated it with some
diffidence and great respect.

"I don't know if you've noticed," said Patch,
"but if you get a wild mob of sulphur-crested
cockatoos and they happen on a tame one of the
same kind, they'll mob him. Kill him, if he can't get
away. Crows are the same. They seem to resent one
of their mob getting tied down in one place, like a
mob of bachelors when one of them decides to get
married. At any rate there's a mob of us in the bar
one day, and we can hear this cockatoo shrieking
and carrying on out at the back; but he does that
every time one of the maids sneaks off down to the
dunny for a smoke. You know, dobs them in to the
publican's Missus. But this keeps up this day, and
after a while we went out to see what he's making
such a fuss about, and bugger me if he isn't being
mobbed by a flock of wild birds that must have
been flying past and spotted him for a Judas. At any
rate they've got him weaving by the time we got
there and chased them away, but old Cocky was
game. He's hanging upside down on the bit of chain
they used to rig the clothes line, and he's shouting
at the top of his lungs,

'One at a time, you bastards, and I'll have the lot
of you.'"

Patch swore that this was true, and while its
veracity might be a bit in doubt I really only put it
in to give you some idea about the sort of stories he
used to tell . . .

*Accomplished tellers of bush lies are rarely found, but
when you do get one he is usually outstanding. Keith
Willey's account of the talking championship of the
Northern Territory between "Walkie-Talkie" Nelson and "Tall-Tale Tex" Tyrell at the Alice, in his
book* Eaters of the Lotus, *shows what heights can be
reached by the real professional when called upon to
do so. I met a fellow from the Territory once at Coll
Portley's house in Brisbane who left me speechless
with admiration. His name was Egan, and he has
since made something of a name for himself com-
mercially with his recordings of his own songs,
including that one called "They're a bloody good lot of
drinkers in the Northern Territory", in which he
accompanies himself on an empty stubby carton. I
shall never forget his story about the mailman who,
when he got bogged, measured the length and stickiness
of the mudhole by the number of bottles of rum he
drank while getting out. He used to talk of two and
three bottle bogs as being not too bad, and I seem to
remember hearing of a thirteen bottle bog that was the
worst he ever struck.*

*However, as the bloke said in the article early in
this section (see page 220), we have got to dogs, and so
with the next story, which has to do with such a dog,
the section closes, for it is indeed time, when you get to
that dog, to go to bed.*

# The Great Sheepdog Trials

My Uncle Arch had a sheepdog called Charles once, and it was the smartest sheepdog between Melbourne and wherever Arch happened to be at the time. It could read brands on horses. It was entirely trustworthy too. Most of the time Arch used to let Charles carry their money round with him. This saved him having to worry about paying bus conductors, but it was sometimes awkward when they were on a railway station and he needed a penny in a hurry. Charles never needed a penny. In fact Arch made this plain to me one day when we were talking. I said to him, "I expect Charlie's got a good pedigree."

"What's a pedigree?" asked Arch.

"A family tree," I said.

"Any old tree does Charles," said Arch. "And don't call him Charlie!"

He told me this story years after the dog was dead. Arch told me he missed Charles something awful. Especially as he had all the money when he died, and he passed on before he could dig it up and hand it over. But that's beside the point. The point is that Charles was waiting on the verandah of the pub that time at Muckadilla when Arch got into the argument with the three drovers that were moving this big mob of sheep down to Moree. New South Welshmen, they were. I mean, said Arch, nobody can help where they are born, but you don't have to go on living there after you know that there's a place like Queensland just a bit north. Not that I've got anything against New South Welshmen, but I wouldn't want one to marry my sister.

It turned out that these three blokes all had the smartest sheepdog in the world. They were standing arguing at the bar, and drinking raspberry in their rum, which should have warned Arch they weren't Queenslanders, and the next thing he knew he was talking to them just as though they weren't foreigners. Really, it all started out with him telling them quietly that they were all mistaken. They wouldn't believe him, and one thing led to another, as things sometimes do in bars, in places like Muckadilla. It finished up with Arch inviting them to all come out the back where the bull fed and try their luck. He was very debonair in his youth, said Arch, gay and reckless like that bloke D'Artagnan in *The Three Musketeers*, the only other bloke I know who challenged three blokes to fight him at

the same time. Well, there was old Ban Ban Jackson that time at Biggenden, but that's another story, and I doubt if anyone would ever tell it. All of it, anyhow.

So there was Arch ready to strip off his waistcoat and into these three blokes when the parson who had been listening in the parlor came running out and stopped them much to the disappointment of the dogs who had been watching from the wood-heap. This parson asked what the trouble was, and when they explained it he said, "Come, come!" and things like that. He pointed out that fighting would only settle who was the best fighter, not whose dog was the smartest. He suggested that the dogs be given a trial, youngest first, and that if they cared to put a small wager on the result, he would gladly hold the stakes as an impartial observer. That's what he said. When Arch explained all this to Charles, Charles said that he was confident that he could beat two of the other dogs after listening to them, but that there was one big old kelpie that he wasn't too sure about. Anyhow, Arch made him give him the money, and they all put up a fiver a side and gave it to the parson to hold while they put the dogs through their paces.

At straight sheep work there wasn't anything between them. They could all cut out a marked wether from the mob and yard it by itself in no time. So it came down to fancy tricks. The youngest dog went up first. The drover pretended to be asleep on the ground beside his fire. The dog fetched some kindling, blew up the coals until the fire blazed up, filled the billy from the waterbag, and woke the drover when the billy boiled. A good standard average performance, but nothing to the competition that was there that day. The second drover laughed, and then he pretended to go to sleep. His dog did the same as the younger one, only it made the tea and poured a cup for the drover before it woke him. Fair enough. Then the third drover pretended to go to sleep. His dog, the old red kelpie, did all that the others had done, only it put a spoon of sugar in the tea, carried it over to the drover, blew on it till it was cool, and then woke him up. Arch could see it would be a close go, but he needn't have worried. Charles did all the things that the other dogs had done, except that he milked a passing nannygoat as well, milked Arch's tea before he woke him, and then went back to the billy and poured out one for himself.

"Well, I don't know," said the parson. "I think we must eliminate the first two contestants. Let us

*Mustering sheep (W. Hatherell, engraving from* Cassell's Picturesque Australasia, *ed. E. E. Morris)*

proceed to a final test between the two remaining animals.''

The other two drovers wanted to argue the point about this, but Arch had the other bloke on his side this time, and they told the others to shut up. The parson went into the bar and got two old empty hock bottles that had been left there by a passing locomotive driver. These he placed side by side on the ground about three feet apart. Then he caught a blowfly out of the millions that were hanging round the publican and marked it on the back with a spot of white paint, and let it go again. Then he stood back and invited the dogs to put the fly into either of the two bottles.

The big red kelpie went first. He quartered back and forth with his belly close to the ground. He never barked. He shouldered the other blowflies aside, and when they got too thick he got up on their backs and ran across them in midair, and all the time he relentlessly droved that one marked blowfly towards the two bottles. Eventually he had it poised outside the neck of one of the bottles. He crouched motionless on the ground, menacing the blowfly. The blowfly stamped one of its forefeet at him, but it recognised its master, and turned disconsolately and buzzed into the bottle, which the dog then corked and took to its master. Even Arch could scarce forbear to cheer.

Arch was worried. He knew Charles was good, but it began to look as though he might have met his match in this big ugly red dog. The kelpie sneered at Charles and winked at the local dogs who had gathered to watch. A small lady fox terrier present was heard to remark that the kelpie was welcome to put his boots under her bed any time he felt like it. Arch looked at Charles in a worried sort of way. Charles just grinned back confidently at him and winked his offside eye. The other drovers demanded a fresh blowfly as the one that had been yarded was used to being worked by this and would be easier. The parson caught a real leggy big blowfly and barely touched it with the paint. The minute he let it go it went and sat on the big dog's head and sneered at Charles. Charles waited until the other drover had emptied the other fly from the bottle and replaced it on the ground. Then he went into action, and he was a joy to behold.

First he flew into the big red kelpie and bit him until he screamed and ran back to the camp, probably to make himself a mug of tea. This dislodged the blowfly. With deadly skill and cunning Charles worked that blowfly. He worked it in and out of the bystanders. Then he took it three times round the pub, and then over to the railway station and back through the store. He ran it till its buzz fell off. Quickly, before it could escape, he rounded up the buzz and droved it into one of the bottles, which he quickly corked. You couldn't see it, but if you put the bottle to your ear you could hear it, very faintly, through the glass. Of course the blowfly couldn't fly very well without its buzz, so it was child's play to put it into the other bottle, which he also corked. Then he droved the three drovers into an empty beer keg that was standing nearby, and drove the bung in so that they couldn't get out and cause any further unpleasantness. Then he stopped and looked proudly at Arch.

Arch said, ''Well. It looks as though Charles has won. He's a real Queensland dog.'' The parson looked a bit put out by this, and said, ''If it comes to that, I'm from across the border myself.'' Before Arch could offer to fight him, Charles droved him away too, and when he had got him into the tiny building he slipped the bolt into the latch of the door. But before he put him away, he droved the stakes from his pockets and into Arch's. Then he shot round to the front of the pub and came back leading the packhorse and the saddle horse, and Arch took the hint and got out of there before the staves of the barrel gave way. So don't mention sheepdogs when you're round Arch. He had a better one—once.

*Bill Scott*

Scene on a Bush Road.

# Section IV
# Poems & Ballads

"All human beings not utterly savage long for some information about past times, and are delighted by narratives which present pictures to the eye of the mind. But it is only in very enlightened communities that books are readily accessible. Metrical composition, therefore, which, in a highly civilised nation, is a mere luxury, is in nations imperfectly civilised almost a necessity of life, and is valued less on account of the pleasure which it gives to the ear than on account of the help which it gives to the memory. A man who can invent or embellish an interesting story and put it into a form which others may easily retain in their recollection will always be highly esteemed by a people eager for amusement and information, but destitute of libraries. Such is the origin of ballad poetry, a species of composition which scarcely ever fails to spring up and flourish in every society at a certain point in the progress towards refinement."

*Lord Macaulay*

# Introduction to Section IV

Many of the verses included in this collection have tunes to which they were sung, but I have included them here rather than in the folksong section as the two are often interchangeable. Verses from established writers often acquired tunes in the bush, good instances being Paterson's "A Bushman's Song" and his children's poem, "The Billygoat Overland"; and Lawson's "Andy's Gone with Cattle". The idea of fitting a tune to such verses as an aid to memory is as old as ballad-making itself. All the Scottish Border ballads had melodies to which they were droned, and many of these tunes crossed the seas to America and Australia to be fitted with new words. The reverse held true; songs often lost their tunes and were remembered as recitations long after the tunes were forgotten. Many of the verses in the *Native Companion Songster* have lost their tunes, though they must have been well known and popular at the time the booklet was published.

The reason for such tunes being lost, and for variations in words of collected songs, poems and ballads, is almost certainly due to two causes; bad memory on the part of the hearer (for these were almost all in the oral tradition), or the inability of the hearer to carry a tune. The Australian Broadcasting Commission recently televised a programme about Hugh Guinea, a pioneer bullock driver from the Numinbah Valley in Southeast Queensland. During the course of the programme, the old gentleman chanted what he remembered of the words of a song written about bullockies in the valley, in which he was actually named; but he could not remember either the words or the melody. Fortunately for the record, Stan Arthur had already recorded both words and music from the singing of Mr Cyril Duncan, formerly of Nerang and a fine song it is. It was recorded in 1959 on a Wattle recording called "Folksongs from Queensland", sung by Stan and the old Moreton Bay Bushwackers' Band, and thus was available. A copy of the words

and music had also been placed in the Oxley Library in Brisbane by the Queensland Folklore Society, when Bob Michell was President.

The best overall collection and anthology of Australian ballads is almost certainly Douglas Stewart and Nancy Keesing's book *Australian Bush Ballads,* published originally by Angus and Robertson in the 1950s. The editors were careful and painstaking in their research and selection, and their scholarship is outstanding when it is realized that there was not the fieldwork available for them to draw upon that is now available. Russel Ward has also edited a paperback for Penguin, with the excellent comments to be expected from such a fine historian. Anyone thinking of beginning a library of Australian ballads could not do better than to begin with these two volumes.

My own judgement in the selection of the ballads that form this collection has been largely guided by the fact that they are written in the Australian language rather than the English language. In other words there are no "literary" ballads in the chosen works. Those who prefer the works of the more established bush balladists, Ogilvie, Paterson and others, can find their work available still in print elsewhere. More than half the ballads here are of anonymous or doubtful authorship, and that is how it should be, for the bush was full of versifiers and parts of the outback still are. The marvel to me is that so many men wrote poetry, when the practice of writing verse is usually regarded with much suspicion among many Australians today. Just how common the practice was at that time is shown by the lines in the old song, "The Hut That's Upside-down".

At night we pass the hours away with
Euchre, Nap and Bluff.
Many rhyme to kill the time while others
talk and guff—

Apparently the making of verse was at that time a recognized way of passing the time in a shearer's hut at night. I will admit that when I first began versifying while serving in the navy, I was regarded rather darkly by my shipmates until the then poetry editor of the *Bulletin* accepted one of my efforts. From then on I was accepted, and though still regarded as being a bit strange, I was boasted about in my absence by my shipmates! Publication in the *Bulletin* was the ultimate accolade in 1946, so far as working men were concerned. It was a passport that let you carry on with the, by then, strange activity of writing.

After working for some fourteen years in a publishing house, I can testify that a great number of Australians still try to write verse, though few seem to buy it any more, or read much of anyone elses' works. Perhaps the poets have forgotten the people, for the people have almost certainly forgotten the poets. I trust you get some pleasure from this selection.

*Men in the bush (Richard Daintree, photograph overpainted in oils)*

# Convict Phelosiphy

*John Weachurch (?)*

My name is poor Jack.
I've done my whack
In sin and disepation.
As A gambler and thief
I have bean chief
With all its degridation.

But I hope I am one
Whoes name will be John,
Now ive seen my sin and folley.
For as gambler and thief
Has brought me to grief
In it there is nothing so jolley.

Ah the lad is A fool
That practises the rule
Of trickery and deception.
For it is sure to bring
Him an unpleasent sting
By way of A fools correction.

*Stewart and Keesing note of this poem that Weachurch's name was really John Taylor. He was hanged at Pentridge Gaol on 6 December 1875, for a murderous attack on a prison warder. He had a record of crime over a period of twenty-five years.*

Garden Island in a Fog

# The Henty Song

*Charles Gee*

Come all you English lads that have a mind to go
Into some foring Contery I would have you
    for to know
Come join along with Henty and all his joiful
    crew
For a Set of better fellows in this world you never
    knew.

*Coris*
So is hear is of to New Holland if God will spear
    our lifes
All with littel families, hower sweethearts, and
    hower wifes.

Now England is got very bad, of that you well
    doth know
Provishons they are got very dear, and little
    for to do
So join along with Henty and all his joiful crew.

Now all you I leves in England, I hope you may
    do well
But allow me for one moment your fourchon for
    to tell
You must unto your Parish go to get small relife
Weare you will be flounced and bounced about as
    if you weare a thif.

Now when we come to New Holland I hope that
    soon will be
All will send home to England, and how happy
    there wee be
With plenty of provishons boys and plenty
    for to do
So hear is health to Henty and all his joiful crew.

*The words were apparently written on board a ship called the* Caroline *on a voyage from England to Western Australia in 1829.*

*The Henty brothers (and the establishment they had recruited) intended to settle in Western Australia but later moved to Portland Bay, in Victoria, where they were discovered in possession of a fine tract of country by Sir Thomas Mitchell on one of his explorations.*

*Road to Bendigo from Forest Creek (from* Sketches of the Victoria Gold Diggings and Diggers As They Are *[1852–53], S. T. Gill)*

*The* Cyprus *was captured from Authority by convicts on board in Recherche Bay in 1829 while taking convicts to Macquarie Harbour, in Van Diemen's Land. Lieutenant Carew and others were put ashore, and the mutineers, led by William Swallow, sailed off into the blue. Some eventually succeeded in making their way to England, where two were executed. Swallow was also tried in 1830, but acquitted. Geoffrey Ingleton reprinted this poem from a manuscript copy in the Mitchell Library, in his book* True Patriots All.

# Seizure of the Cyprus Brig in Recherche Bay

*"Frank the Poet"*

Come all you sons of Freedom, a chorus join
    with me,
I'll sing a song of heroes, and glorious liberty.
Some lads condemned from England sailed to
    Van Diemen's shore,
Their country, friends and parents perhaps never
    to see more.

When landed in this Colony to different Masters
    went,
For trifling offences, to Hobart town jail were
    sent;
A second sentence being incurred we were
    ordered for to be
Sent to Macquarie Harbour, that place of
    tyranny.

The hardships we'd to undergo are matters of
    record,
But who believes the convict, or who regards his
    word?
For starved and flogged and punished, deprived
    of all redress,
The Bush our only refuge, with death to end
    distress.

Hundreds of us were shot down, for daring to be
    free,
Numbers caught and banished to life-long
    slavery.
Brave Swallow, Watt, and Davis, were in our
    noble band
Determined at the first slant to quit Van
    Diemen's Land.

Marched down in chains and guarded, on the
    *Cyprus Brig* conveyed
The topsails being hoisted, the anchor being
    weighed,
The wind it blew sou'-sou'-west and on we went
    straightway,
Till we found ourselves wind-bound, in gloomy
    Recherche Bay

'Twas August eighteen twenty-nine, with
    thirty-one on board,
Lieutenant Carew left the brig, and soon we
    passed the word

The Doctor too was absent, the soldiers off their
    guard:
A better opportunity could never have occurred.

Confined within a dismal hole, we soon contrived
    a plan,
To capture now the *Cyprus*, or perish every man.
But thirteen turned faint-hearted and begged to
    go ashore,
So eighteen boys rushed daring, and took the brig
    and store.

We first addressed the soldiers, "For liberty we
    crave!
Give up your arms this instant, or the sea will be
    your grave.
By tyranny we've been oppressed, by your
    Colonial laws,
But we'll bid adieu to slavery, or die in freedom's
    cause."

We next drove off the Skipper, who came to help
    his crew,
Then gave three cheers for liberty, 'twas
    answered cheerly too.
We brought the sailors from below, and rowed
    them to the land,
Likewise the wife and children of Carew in
    command.

Supplies of food and water we gave the
    vanquished crew,
Returning good for evil, as we'd been taught
    to do.
We mounted guard with watch and ward, then
    hauled the boat aboard;
We elected William Swallow, and obeyed our
    Captain's word.

The morn broke bright, the wind was fair, we
    headed for the sea
With one cheer more for those on shore and
    glorious liberty.
For navigating smartly Bill Swallow was the man,
Who laid a course out neatly to take us to Japan.

Then sound your golden trumpets, play on your
    tuneful notes,
The *Cyprus Brig* is sailing, how proudly now she
    floats
May fortune help the noble lads, and keep them
    ever free
From Gags, and Cats, and Chains, and Traps,
    and Cruel Tyranny.

# A Tail of a Kangaroo

*Anon.*

It wasn't on the Chinee coast, nor yet upon
   Japan,
But happened on the Sydney side, nor far from
   Marieyan—
As told me by a splitter, which his name is
   Blathering Jim,
A cove—you can't expect to get a lot of truth
   from him

*Chorus*
But there's no gammon in this yarn, for every
   word is true,
How maidens four waged deadly war with an old
   man kangaroo.

Within a hut of she-oak slabs, all roofed with
   stringybark,
Four Sydney-native ladies sat, all game for any
   lark.
Big Jane was there (Bondingie Bill, the bullock-
   driver's gal)
With Mountain Mag from Blue Lookout, and
   Parramatta Sal.

And Julia (whose bushranging brother Sam has
   come to grief)
Was cutting up and salting down a side of stolen
   beef,
While Mountain Mag was plaiting of a cracker
   for the thong
Of Jack, the boundary-rider's whip, that lives at
   Bogalong.

Big Jenny dreamt the happy hours away upon the
   bunk,
After an evening party, where no end of lush was
   drunk;
And Parramatta Sal, she blowed a tidy cloud of
   smoke,
While coiling in her possum rug, and thought
   about her bloke.

Her father, who was absent with his gully-raking
   sons,
Was busy duffing cattle on the nearest squatters'
   runs—
One of the good old colonists he was, who often
   bragged
That though he'd been quite close to it, he'd
   never yet been scragged.

'Twas thus these maidens, all alone, were
   mustered in the hut,
When on a sudden something bumped agin the
   door full butt;
Then Julia spoke, that artless maid brought up in
   nature's school,
"Don't stand there humbugging all day; come in,
   you ——— fool!"

As no one answered to their call, on looking out,
   they saw
A booming kangaroo who'd run his head agin the
   door,
And being thus knocked out of time, and anxious
   for a swim,
Was making for the water, so the girls just went
   for him.

Now Julia's just the sort of girl to ride a bucking
   colt,
Or round a mob of cattle up, if they're inclined
   to bolt,
Ride on her brother's saddle all astride, or, on a
   push,
Do any mortal kind of work that's wanted in the
   bush.

And so she grabbed a roping pole, and Maggie
   seized the adze,
With all her ringlets streaming loose with
   "Follow me, my lads!"
The propstick of a bullock-dray was all that Jane
   could find,
But Sarah waved a waddy that the blacks had left
   behind.

On coming to close quarters with those
   formidable claws,
The "old man" made for Sarah, but she hit him
   in the jaws,
As Julia gave the beggar fits, with that rentless
   arm
That cleared the shanty ballroom near the free-
   selector's farm.

Then, closing, he charged Marguerite, but
   missed her, so she placed
A stinger in the region of the middle of his waist,
And gave him such a mauling o'er the face, and
   eyes, and ribs,
As fellows do each other in these rowdy fighting
   cribs.

The boomah sought for vengeance, and grabbed
 Jenny by the skirt,
But luckily it gave, and so the lady wasn't hurt.
Though it must be confessed that she was
 terribly in dread,
Until the ladies rallied round, and knocked him
 on the head.

Thus "old men" often come to grief, whene'er
 they chance to stray
Among the rocky gullies, where the ladies stop
 the way;
Because the girls are just as smart to bail up
 kangaroos,
As their parents are to travellers who've anything
 to lose.

*This marvellous ballad of low life in the bush near
Sydney must date from after Sir John Robertson's
Land Act, for it mentions the "free-selector's farm". I
particularly like the moral drawn in the final stanza,
which is reminiscent of Burns's "Tam O'Shanter".*

The Kangaroo

# The Road to Hogan's Gap

*A. B. ("Banjo") Paterson*

Now look, you see, it's this way like—
You cross the broken bridge
And run the crick down till you strike
The second right-hand ridge.

The track is hard to see in parts,
But still it's pretty clear;
There's been two Injun hawkers' carts
Along that road this year.

Well, run that right-hand ridge along—
It ain't, to say, too steep—
There's two fresh tracks might put you wrong
Where blokes went out with sheep.

But keep the crick upon your right,
And follow pretty straight
Along the spur, until you sight
A wire and sapling gate.

Well, that's where Hogan's old grey mare
Fell off and broke her back;
You'll see her carcass layin' there,
Jist down below the track.

And then you drop two mile, or three,
It's pretty steep and blind;
You want to go and fall a tree
And tie it on behind.

And then you pass a broken cart
Below a granite bluff;
And that is where you strike the part
They reckon pretty rough.

But by the time you've got that far
It's either cure or kill,
So turn your horses round the spur
And face 'em up the hill.

For look, if you should miss the slope
And get below the track,
You haven't got the slightest hope
Of ever gettin' back.

An' half-way up you'll see the hide
Of Hogan's brindled bull;
Well, mind and keep the right-hand side,
The left's too steep a pull.

And both the banks is full of cracks;
An' just about at dark
You'll see the last year's bullock tracks
Where Hogan drew the bark.

*The station boundary (A. H. Fullwood, oil on canvas)*

*"Kimo" team in Sheridan Street, Gundagai*

The marks is old and pretty faint
And grown with scrub and such;
Of course the track to Hogan's ain't
A road that's travelled much.

But turn and run the tracks along
For half a mile or more,
And then, of course, you can't go wrong—
You're right at Hogan's door.

When first you come to Hogan's gate
He mightn't show, perhaps;
He's pretty sure to plant, and wait
To see it ain't the traps.

I wouldn't call it good enough
To let your horses out;
There's some that's pretty extra rough
Is livin' round about.

It's likely, if your horses did
Get feedin' near the track,
It's goin' to cost at least a quid
Or more to get them back.

So, if you find they're off the place,
It's up to you to go
And flash a quid in Hogan's face—
He'll know the blokes that know.

But listen—if you're feelin' dry,
Just see there's no one near,
And go and wink the other eye
And ask for ginger beer.

The blokes come in from near and far
To sample Hogan's pop;
They reckon once they breast the bar
They stay there till they drop.

On Sundays you can see them spread
Like flies around the tap.
It's like that song "The Livin' Dead"
Up there at Hogan's Gap.

They like to make it pretty strong
Whenever there's a chance;
So when a stranger comes along
They always hold a dance.

There's recitations, songs, and fights—
A willin' lot you'll meet.
There's one long bloke up there recites;
I tell you he's a treat.

They're lively blokes all right up there,
It's never dull a day.
I'd go meself if I could spare
The time to get away. . . .

The stranger turned his horses quick.
He didn't cross the bridge;
He didn't go along the crick
To strike the second ridge;

He didn't make the trip, because
He wasn't feeling fit.
His business up at Hogan's was
To serve him with a writ.

He reckoned, if he faced the pull
And climbed the rocky stair,
The next to come might find his hide
A landmark on the mountain side,
Along with Hogan's brindled bull
And Hogan's old grey mare.

# Corney's Hut

*Anon.*

Old Corney built in Deadman's Gap
A hut, where mountain shades grow denser,
And there he lived for many years,
A timber-getter and a fencer.
And no one knew if he'd a soul
Above long sprees or split-rail fences,
Unless, indeed, it was his dog
Who always kept his confidences.

There was a saw-pit in the range,
'Twas owned by three, and they were brothers
And visitors to Corney's hut—
'Twas seldom visited by others.
They came because, as they averred,
"Old Corney licked—a gent infernal";
"His yarns," if I might trust their word,
"Would make the fortune of a journal."

In short, the splitter was a "cure"
Who brightened up their lives' dull courses
And so on Sunday afternoons,
At Corney's hut they'd hang their horses.
They'd have a game of cards and smoke
And sometimes sing, which was a rum thing—
Unless, in spite of legal folk,
The splitter kept a drop of something.

If, as 'twas said, he was a swell
Before he sought these sombre ranges,
'Twixt mother's arms and coffin gear
He must have seen a world of changes.
But from his lips would never fall
A hint of home, or friends, or brothers,
And if he told his tale at all,
He must have told it as another's.

Though he was good at telling yarns,
At listening he excelled not less so,
And greatly helped the bushman's tales
With "Yes," "Exactly so," or "Jes so."
In short the hut became a club
Like our Assembly Legislative
Combining smokeroom, hall, and pub,
Political and recreative.

Old Corney lived and Corney died,
As we will, too, on some tomorrow,
But not as Corney died we hope,
Of heart-disease, and rum, and sorrow.
(We hope to lead a married life,
At times the cup of comfort quaffing;

And when we leave this world of strife
We trust that we may die of laughing.)

On New Year's Eve they found him dead—
For rum had made his life unstable—
They found him stretched upon his bed,
And also found, upon the table,
The coloured portrait of a girl—
Blue eyes of course. The hair was golden,
A faded letter and a curl,
And—well, we said the theme was olden.

The splitter had for days been dead
And cold before the sawyers found him,
And none had witnessed how he died
Except the dog who whimpered round him;
A noble friend, and of a kind
Who stay when other friends forsake us,
And he at last was left behind
To greet the rough bush undertakers.

This was a season when the bush
Was somewhat ruled by time and distance,
And bushmen came and tried the world,
And "gave it best" without assistance.
Then one might die of heart-disease,
And still be spared the inquest horrors,
And when the splitter laid at ease
So, also, did his sins and sorrows.

"Ole Corney's dead," the bushmen said;
"He's gone at last, an' ne'er a blunder."
And so they brought a horse and dray
And tools to "tuck the old cove under".
The funeral wended through the range
And slowly round its rugged corners;
The reader will not think it strange
That Corney's dog was chief of mourners.

He must have thought the bushmen hard
And of his misery unheeding,
Because they shunned his anxious eyes
That seemed for explanation pleading.
At intervals his tongue would wipe
The jaws that seemed with anguish quaking;
As some strong hand impatiently
Might chide the tears for prison breaking.

They reached by rugged ways at last
A desolate bush cemetery,
Where now (our tale is of the past),
A thriving town its dead doth bury,
And where the bones of pioneers
Are found and thrown aside unheeded—

For later sleepers, blessed with tears
Of many friends, the graves are needed.

The funeral reached the bushmen's graves,
Where these old pioneers were sleeping,
And now while down the granite ridge
The shadow of the peak was creeping,
They dug a grave beneath a gum
And lowered the dead as gently may be,
As Corney's mother long before
Had laid him down to "hush-a-baby".

A bushman read the words to which
The others reverently listened,
Some bearded lips were seen to twitch,
Some shaded eyes with moisture glistened.
The boys had brought the splitter's tools,
And now they split and put together
Four panels such as Corney made,
To stand the stress of western weather.

"Old Corney's dead, he paid his bills,"
(These words upon the tree were graven),
"And oft a swagman down in luck
At Corney's mansion found a haven."

But now the bushmen hurried on,
Lest darkness in the range should find them;
And strange to say they never saw
That Corney's dog had stayed behind them.

If one had thrown a backward glance
Along the rugged path they wended,
He might have seen a darker form
Upon the damp cold mound extended.
But soon their forms had vanished all,
And night came down the ranges faster,
And no one saw the shadows fall
Upon the dog that mourned his master.

*The two preceding poems point the contrast between
the sentimentality of the latter and the realism that
showed in the best of Paterson's ballads. Both were
valid, but Paterson saw bushmen with clarity and an
absence of the sentiment that sometimes spoils traditional material—not all traditional material, however, as the following two poems show. Noel Sligar, a
shipmate of mine, first sang "The Old Bull Stag" for
me one night in Cairns. This version of the words is
from a* Bill Bowyang Reciter.

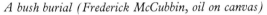

*A bush burial (Frederick McCubbin, oil on canvas)*

# The Old Bull Stag

The old bull stag leaned against the fence, he was
  too poor to walk.
As the butcher sharpened his knife the stag
  began to talk.
"Misguided man," says he, "don't perpetrate this
  crime.
Don't sell me to your customers and kid them
  that I'm prime,
Because I was thirty-two last Christmas Day, and
  bred by Johnny Rudd;
Nineteen long and happy years the pride and
  monarch of his stud.
Then I was sold and put to work with hair and
  hide flogged off me,
From Deburra across to Burke and down the
  parched Paroo,
With never a day to spare my boss kept me to my
  work.
By jingo he could swear, and roar, and tear his
  hair.

Though coming old and useless through a cancer
  in my side,
My boss swopped me to a Chow for a dog and a
  piece of hide.
Now I have cancer, bot and pleuro, I can scarce
  draw my breath,
So let me drag my bones away and die a natural
  death."
The butcher laughed his greasy laugh, and poked
  out his tongue;
"I kid them that you're lucerne fed, I kid 'em you
  are young,
These people in this town know not what they eat
God sends the like of you, old chap, to keep the
  prices down,
And if any of my customers should suffer from
  your ills
I hope it is the lousy ones that never pay their
  bills."

At that he knocked the old chap down and cut
  him into strag,
Next day he winked the other eye and dealt them
  out the stag.

*Barrossa Ranges (Skinner Prout, from* Australia, *ed. Edwin Carton Booth)*

*A fern tree valley (Skinner Prout, from* Australia, *ed. Edwin Carton Booth)*

*Matchbox trick (engraving from* Australasian Sketcher, *14 April 1883)*

# The New England Cocky

*Anon.*

'Twas a New England cocky, as of late I've been
  told,
Who died, so 'tis said, on account of the cold.
When dying he called to his children, "Come
  here!
As I'm dying I want my fortune to share.

"Dear children, you know I've toiled early
  and late,
I've struggled with Nature, and wrestled
  with Fate.
Then all do your best to my fortune repair;
And to my son John I leave a dear native bear.

"To Mary I give my pet kangaroo,
May it prove to turn out a great blessing, too;
To Michael I leave the old cockatoo,
And to Bridget I'll give the piebald emu.

"To the others whatever is left I will leave—
Don't quarrel, or else my poor spirit will grieve;
There's fish in the stream, and fowl on the lake,
Let each have as much as any may take.

"And now, my dear children, no more can I do,
My fortune I've fairly divided with you."
And these were the last words his children did
  hear—
"Don't forget that I reared you on pumpkin
  and bear."

*From* Old Bush Songs, *A. B. Paterson*

# A Drought Idyll

*George Essex Evans*

It was the middle of the drought; the ground was
  hot and bare,
You might search for grass with a microscope,
  but nary grass was there;
The hay was done, the cornstalks gone, the trees
  were dying fast,
The sun o'erhead was a curse in red and the wind
  was a furnace blast;
The waterholes were sun-baked mud, the drays
  stood thick as bees
Around the well, a mile away, amid the
  ringbarked trees.

McGinty left his pumpkin-pie and gazed upon
  the scene:
His cows stood propped 'gainst tree and fence
  wherever they could lean;
The horse he'd fixed with sapling-forks had fallen
  down once more;
The fleas were hopping joyfully on stockyard,
  path, and floor;
The flies in thousands buzzed about before his
  waving hand;
The hungry pigs squealed as he said, "Me own,
  me native land!"

"Queensland, me Mother! Ain't yer well?" he
  asked. "Come tell me how's—"
"Dry up! Dry up!" yelled Mrs Mac, "Go out and
  feed the cows."
"But where's the feed?" McGinty cried, "The
  sugar-cane's all done—
It wasn't worth the bally freight we paid for it
  per ton.
I'll get me little axe and go with Possum and
  the mare
For 'arf a ton of apple-tree or a load of prickly-
  pear."

"The prickly-pear'll kill the cows unless yer bile
  it right,"
Cried Mrs Mac, "and I don't mean to bile it all
  the night.
They tell me fer a bob a bag the brewery will sell
Their refuse stuff, like Simpson 'ad—his cows is
  doin' well.
Yer get the loan of Bampston's dray and borrer
  Freeney's nags,
And fetch along a decent load, McGinty—thirty
  bags."

McGinty borrowed Bampston's dray and hitched
    up Freeney's nags
And drove like blazes into town and fetched back
    thirty bags.
The stuff was mellow, soft, and brown; and if you
    came too near
It shed around a lovely scent till the air seemed
    full of *beer*.
McGinty fetched each feed-box out and filled it
    to the brim,
Then lit his pipe and fell asleep. That was the
    style of him!

The cows, they lurched off fence and tree and
    staggered in to feed,
The horses tottered after them—old, feeble, and
    knock-kneed.
But when they smelt that sacred stuff in boxes on
    the ground
They smiled and neighed and lowed and twirled
    their hungry tails around.
You would have walked a hundred miles or more
    to see and hear
The way McGinty's stock attacked that stuff that
    smelt like beer. . . .

"Wake up! Wake up! McGinty man! Wake up!"
    yelled Mrs Mac.
She held a broom and every word was followed
    by a whack.
McGinty had been dreaming hard that it was
    Judgment Day
And he was drafted with the goats and being
    driven away;
The Devil with a toasting fork was jabbing at his
    jaw,
He rose and yelled and fled outside—and this is
    what he saw:

The brindled cow, with spotted tail, was trying to
    climb a tree;
The spotted cow, with brindle tail, to imitate a
    flea;
Old Bally who had lost one horn engaged in
    combat stout
With the Lincoln ram whose only eye McGinty
    had knocked out;
With tails entwined, among the trees, went Bessie
    and Basilk,
Singing, "Good-bye, McGinty, we will come
    back with the milk."

McGinty, trembling, viewed the scene in
    wonderment and funk,
Then lifted up his voice and roared, "Mother,
    the cows is drunk!
Look at that bloomin' heifer with 'er head 'ung
    down the sty,
Telling the sow she loves 'er but she some'ow
    can't tell why.
Three of 'em snoring on their backs, the rest all
    on the loose—
Ain't there no policeman in these parts when
    cows gets on the boose?"

McGinty viewed the orgy with a jealousy
    profound—
Cows in various states of drunk were scattered all
    around;
But most his rage was heightened by the conduct
    of the horse
That stood and laughed, and laughed, and
    laughed—and laughed without remorse—
That horse so oft he'd lifted up and propped with
    logs and boughs
Now leant against a tree and mocked McGinty
    and his cows.

"Bring soda-water, Mother," cried McGinty.
    "Bring a tub"
(Forgetting that he lived about a league from any
    pub).
"I swear by soda-water when the drink illumes
    my brow,
And if it fixes up a man it ought to fix a cow."
But as he spoke a boozy steer approached with
    speed intense
And helped McGinty over to the safe side of the
    fence.

Regret and hate and envy held McGinty where
    he sat.
"To think," he said, "these purple cows should
    have a time like that!
For months I couldn't raise a drink—it wasn't up
    to me;
Yet every bally head of stock I've got is on the
    spree.
This comes when you forget to keep a bottle on
    the shelf."
Inspired, he rose and smote his brow and fetched
    a spoon and delf—

"My word!" he said, "It's up to me to feed on
    this meself!"

*George Essex Evans was an immigrant Englishman who wrote much verse while a public servant on the Darling Downs in Queensland. His most anthologized poem is probably "The Women of the West", but he wrote other good verse. There is a memorial to his honour at Toowoomba, and a Memorial Pilgrimage is held there each year by the Toowoomba Ladies Literary Society.*

# Jones's Selection

*G. H. Gibson ("Ironbark")*

You hear a lot of new-chum talk
Of goin' on the land,
An' raisin' record crops of wheat
On rocks and flamin' sand.

I 'ates exaggerated skite,
But if yer likes I can
Authenticate a case, in which
The land went on the man.

Bill Jones 'e 'ad a mountain block
Up Kosciusko way;
He farmed it pretty nigh to death,
The neighbours used to say.

He scarified the surface with
His double-furrow ploughs,
An' ate its blinded heart right out
With sheep an' milkin' cows;

He filled its blamed intestines up
With agricultural pipes,
An' lime, and superphosphates—fit
To give the land the gripes.

Until at length the tortured soil,
Worn out with Jones's thrift,
Decided as the time was come
To up an' make a shift.

One day the mountain shook itself,
An' give a sort o' groan,
The neighbours was a lot more scared
Than they was game to own.

Their jaws was dropped upon their chests,
Their eyes was opened wide,
They saw the whole of Jones's farm
Upend itself, an' slide.

It slithered down the mountain spur,
Majestic-like an' slow,
An' landed in the river bed,
A thousand feet below.

Bill Jones was on the lower slopes
Of 'is long-sufferin' farm,
A-testin' some new-fangled plough
Which acted like a charm.

He'd just been screwin' up a nut
When somethin' seemed to crack,
An' fifty acres, more or less,
Come down on Jones's back.

'Twas sudden-like, a shake, a crack,
A slitherin' slide, an' Bill
Was buried fifty feet below
The soil he used to till.

One moment Bill was standin' up
A-ownin' all that land,
The next 'e's in eternity—
A spanner in 'is 'and!

They never dug up no remains
Nor scraps of William Jones—
The superphosphates ate the lot,
Hide, buttons, boots, and bones.

For this here land wot Jones abused
And harassed in the past
'Ad turned an' wiped 'im out, an' things
Got evened up at last.

From this untimely end o' Bill
It would perhaps appear
That goin' free-selectin' ain't
All skittles, no, nor beer.

So all you cocky city coves,
Wot's savin' up yer screws
To get upon the land, look out
The land don't get on *yous*.

*G. H. Gibson, who contributed to the* Bulletin *under the pseudonym of "Ironbark", was a minor poet of some accomplishment and a prose writer of florid style but undoubted wit. There are three of his poems in this section, one of them still extant in the oral tradition, for I heard it recited at Mount Isa in 1947. This was his famous parody of "Sweet Alice", which is included herein. A good example of his prose style is in Section I of this book, from the introduction to his book,* Ironbark Chips and Stockwhip Cracks.

*The miners' Sunday afternoon (engraving from* Illustrated Sydney News, *4 September 1880)*

# Stand Back

*S. Lemaitre*

Ye gentlemen with sleek black coats
  And bell-toppers, pray pause awhile,
While fingering the gold and notes,
  Just think by whom you made your pile.
Thousand of miles are round you spread,
  With grass as green and sky as blue;
Don't bar the road to honest bread,
  Better step back a mile or two.

Remember, when you first came up,
  Like Shicers, innocent of gold,
Quite proud to get the bit and sup
  The digger's friendly tent foretold;
With "billy's" dangling to your back,
  Instead of J.P.'s to your name,
You followed on the beaten track,
  With little chance of wealth or fame.

Rouse up the standard to the skies!
  Shout "Freedom for the digger slaves!"
'Tis useless to repeat your lies—
  The Bendigonians "spot" the knaves.
Upon the platform, no doubt,
  You are brothers loyal, firm and true;
But when the pocket's touched, you shout
  "Diggers stand back a mile or two!"

Lords of the soil—the tyrant's hand
  But ill becomes "the Digger's friend;"
Act as you preach—unlock the land—
  Don't brave the coming storm, but bend.
Thousands of miles are round you spread,
  With grass as green and sky as blue;
Don't bar the road to honest bread,
  Better step back a mile or two.

*In the 1860s, when the big gold discoveries in Victoria and New South Wales were either ended, or the alluvial workings had turned to reefing operations; many disappointed diggers were not prepared to "follow the gold" to the new Queensland and New Zealand rushes. There was an outcry from these men that the squatters' holdings should be opened up for closer settlement. This led to the Land Acts being pushed through the Parliaments in the Colonies, first in New South Wales and later in Victoria. It is worth reading the history of the subsequent selection, for the squatters were determined to hold as much of their old territory as they possibly could. They achieved this to a degree through the process of "dummying". It was around this time that a disgruntled squatter wrote the words of "The Eumerella Shore" to the tune of "Nellie Gray" which was a popular song of the time; one of Stephen Foster's songs, I think. The words were intended as irony, but they caught on among the bush workers, and many versions of the original have been collected. The poem above was written by a sympathizer of the landless diggers, of course. An interesting feature of the song is its use of the word "shicer", which meant a worthless mining claim. It has survived in current slang in the word "shyster", meaning a person, particularly a legal person, who indulges in sharp practices. Other poems were written after the Land Acts were passed. The previous one was Victorian in origin; the one that follows hails from New South Wales.*

*A popular song among the Currency Lads early in the nineteenth century ran in part as follows.*

Oh give me a hut in my own native land,
A tent in Australia where the tall gum trees
    stand.
No matter how far in the bush it may be
If a dear native girl will but share it with me.
It's lovely to rise at the dawn of the day
And chase the wild horse on the hills far away,
They dance and they prance and they whinny
    with glee
Until they're run down by a bushman like me.

A Bushman's Hut

*I collected those words from Mrs Abbott, a near neighbour at Nudgee Beach near Brisbane about 1950. Another set of words must have been written to the tune, after the Land Act was passed in New South Wales, which ran as follows.*

Come all of you Cornstalks the victory's won,
John Robertson's triumphed, the lean days are
    gone.
No more through the bush we'll go humping the
    drum,
For the Land Bill has passed and the good times
    have come.

*Chorus*
Then give me a hut in my own native land,
Or a tent in the bush, near the mountains so
    grand.
For the scenes of my childhood a joy are to me,
And the dear native girl who will share it
    with me.

No more through the bush with our swags need
    we roam,
For to ask of the squatters to give us a home.
Now the land is unfettered and we may reside,
In a place of our own by some clear waterside.

We will sow our own garden and till our own
    field,
And eat of the fruits that our labour doth yield,
And be independent, a right long denied,
By those who have ruled us and robbed us
    beside.

*Cornstalk, of course, was the slang term for a native of New South Wales. The denizens of other States also had their peculiar nicknames. Queenslanders were Banana-landers or Banana-benders. Victorians were Cabbage-patchers (presumably from the relative size of the State), South Australians were Crow-eaters (possibly from the piping shrike featured in the coat of arms of the State), West Australians were Sand-gropers (and they, in turn lumped the inhabitants of the eastern States as "Tother-siders"), and Tasmanians were Taswegians, I can't imagine why. Most of these names are now obsolete and rarely used, though one occasionally crops up. For instance, Graham Jenkin, in his poem "The Ballad of the Birdsville Driver" refers to "old flagoons that had held Crow-eating' grape", for empty wine flagons. See the Tall Story Section in this book.*

# The Spider by the Gwydir

*Anon.*

By the sluggish river Gwydir lived a hungry
  red-backed spider
Who was just about as wicked as could be;
An' the place that he was camped in was an
  empty Jones's jam tin
In a paddock by the showgrounds, at Moree.

Near him lay a shearer snoozin', he had been on
  beer an' boozin'
All through the night and all the previous day;
An' the rookin' of the rookers an' the noise of
  showtime spruikers
Failed to wake him from the trance in which
  he lay.

Then a crafty-lookin' spieler with a dainty little
  sheila
Came along, collectin' wood to make a fire.
Said the spieler, "He's a boozer, an' he's goin' to
  be a loser;
If he isn't you can christen me a liar."

"Hustle round an' keep nit, honey, while I fan
  the mug for money
And we'll have some little luxuries for tea."
But she answered, "Don't be silly; you go back
  and boil the billy,
You can safely leave the mug to little me."

So she circled ever nearer till she reached the
  dopey shearer
With his pockets bulgin', fast asleep an' snug;
But she didn't see the spider that was ringin'
  close beside her
For her mind was on the money an' the mug.

The spider sighted dinner. He'd been daily
  growin' thinner;
He'd been fastin' an' was hollow as an urn.
As she eyed the bulgin' pocket, he just darted like
  a rocket
An' he bit the rookin' sheila on the stern.

Then the sheila started squealin' an' her clothes
  she was unpeelin',
To hear her yells would make you feel forlorn.
One hand the bite was pressin' while the other
  was undressin'
An' she reached the camp the same as she was
  born.

Then the shearer, pale an' haggard, woke, an'
  back to town he staggered
Where he caught the train an' gave the booze a
  rest;
An' he'll never know the spider that was camped
  beside the Gwydir
Had saved him sixty smackers of the best.

*The Jones Jam Company used to make the brand
I.X.L. that was so familiar in the days of my boyhood.
It was a long established company, and cases of mixed
jam formed part of the loading for many outback
stations, where, along with the ubiquitous "cocky's
joy" (treacle), it enlivened the humble damper and
Johnny cakes. The bullock teams went up with stores
and brought back the wool.*

This offsider in telling me the story said that he
never in all his life (and he had been to sea as a
midshipman—in fact, he was on the "Galatia," the
Duke of Edinburgh's ship) heard or seen anything
like this madman's behaviour with those poor
bullocks, and when the fellow put his hands
together and invoked the Almighty to engulf
himself and the team he (the offsider) said he was
afraid the prayer would be answered, so he bolted
for his bare life. This brute of a man got his deserts
in the end, for, shortly after the occurrence I have
mentioned, his strength was taken away from him,
and he became as weak as a little child. I forgot to
say that when he used to go to town for a spree he
would, when drunk, take hold of a wheel of a cab
and vomit all over it, and the driver of the cab
would be so scared of the bully that he dared not get
down to prevent him. Ah, those old bullock driving
days were very jolly at times, and, as I said before,
there were some fine fellows amongst them.

"Then roll up your bundle, and let us make a
  push;
I'll take you up the country, and show you the
  bush;
I'll make you as happy as the flowers in May,
If you'll only take possession of my old bullock
  dray."

*From* History and Adventures of a Queensland Pioneer, *E. J. Foreman*

*The night halt—teamsters preparing their camp (engraving from* Illustrated Sydney News, *30 September 1871)*

*For information on the character and outlook of bullockies it is hard to go past the first chapter of* Such Is Life *by Joseph Furphy ("Tom Collins"). There are a number of bullocky songs in the folksong section of this book. Horse teams do not seem to have aroused the same interest in bush versifiers; probably the best poem of this kind remains "How the 'Fire Queen' Crossed the Swamp", by Will Ogilvie.*

## Bullocky Bill

*Anon.*

As I came down Talbingo Hill
I heard a maiden cry,
"There's goes old Bill the Bullocky—
He's bound for Gundagai."

A better poor old beggar
Never cracked an honest crust,
A tougher poor old beggar
Never drug a whip through dust.

His team got bogged on the Five-mile Creek,
Bill lashed and swore and cried,
"If Nobbie don't get me out of this
I'll tattoo his bloody hide."

But Nobbie strained and broke the yoke
And poked out the leader's eye,
Then the dog sat on the tucker-box
Five miles from Gundagai.

*Stewart and Keesing note that this song is discussed in a pamphlet printed by the* Gundagai Independent.
*John Meredith has also discussed it, and other songs about Gundagai, in some depth in an article in the magazine* Australian Tradition *(January 1967). My father often recited the couplet:*

> *Then Nobby strained and broke the yoke, and poked out Blucher's eye,*
> *And the dog sat in the tuckerbox nine miles from Gundagai.*

*It is a long way from Gundagai to Gin Gin where he spent his boyhood, but he may have picked it up in France during World War I, of course.*

# How the Sailor Rode the Brumby

*Anon.*

There was an agile sailor lad
Who longed to know the bush
So with his swag and billy-can
He said he'd make a push.
He left his ship in Moreton Bay
And faced the Western run,
And asked his way, ten times a day,
And steered for Bandy's Run.

Said Bandy: "You can start, my son,
If you can ride a horse,"
For stockmen on the cattle-run
Were wanted there, of course.
Now Jack had strode the cross-bars oft
On many a bounding sea,
So reckoned he'd be safe enough
On any moke you see.

They caught him one and saddled it,
And led it from the yard,
It champed a bit and sidled round
And at the sailor sparred.
Jack towed her to him with a grin,
He eyed her fore and aft;
Then thrust his foot the gangway in
And swung aboard the craft.

The watchers tumbled off the rail,
The boss lay down and roared,
While Jack held tight by mane and tail
And rocked about on board.
But still he clung as monkeys cling
To rudder, line and flap,
Although at every bound and spring
They thought his neck must snap.

They stared to see him stick aloft
—The brum. bucked fierce and free,
But he had strode the cross-bars oft
On many a rolling sea.
The saddle from the rolling back
Went spinning in mid-air,
Whilst two big boots were flung off Jack
And four shoes off the mare.

The bridle broke and left her free,
He grasped her round the neck;
"We're 'mong the breakers now," cried he,
"There's bound to be a wreck."

The brumby struck and snorted loud,
She reared and pawed the air,
It was the grandest sight the crowd
Had ever witnessed there.
For Jack with arms and legs held tight
The brumby's neck hung round
And yelled, "A pilot, quick as light,
Or strike me I'm aground."
The whites and blacks climbed on the rails,
The boss stood smiling by
As Jack exclaimed, "Away she sails!"
—The brum. began to fly.

She bounded first against the gate,
And Jack cried out, "Astern!"
Then struck a whirlpool—at any rate
That was the sailor's yarn.
The brumby spun him round and round,
She reared and kicked and struck,
And with alternate bump and bound
In earnest began to buck.

A tree loomed on the starboard bow,
And "Port your helm!" cried he;
She fouled a bush and he roared "You scow!"
And "Keep to the open sea!"
From ears to tail he rode her hard,
From tail to ears again,
One mile beyond the cattle-yard
And back across the plain.

Now high upon the pommel bumped,
Now clinging on the side,
And on behind the saddle lumped
With arms and legs flung wide.
They only laughed the louder then
When the mare began to back
Until she struck the fence at last
Then sat and looked at Jack.

He gasped, "I'm safe in port at last,
I'll quit your bounding mane!"
Dropped off and sang, "All danger's passed
And Jack's come home again."
Old Jack has been a stockman now
On Bandy's Run for years
Yet memories of that morning's fun
To many still bring tears.

*It was traditional on outback stations in the early times to always try out a new hand on a "rough one". A newchum was considered fair game for any sort of legpull, and this was a favourite trick. Graham*

*Jenkin mentions it recently in his book,* Two Years on Bardunyah Station. *(Also see his poem in the section on tall stories.) For an earlier reference, Edward R. Garnsey ("Edward Kinglake"), in* The Australian at Home, *published in 1891, says: "If the new chum is, on the contrary, a good horseman, and manages to stick on in spite of the buckjumps, he will be looked on in the same light as a passenger at sea who has paid his own footing."*

# The Stockman's Tale

*Anon.*

The campfire's burning brightly, and the coals
   are glowing red,
The crackling sparks fly upwards as they vanish
   overhead.

The stockman's evening meal was over, the
   damper stowed away,
To stretch our weary limbs around the fire
   we lay;
"Put on another log, Jack, a good large
   one—that's right,
And make us up a bully fire—we'll have it cold
   tonight.

"Before you light that pipe of yours, just look in
   my valise,
You'll find a flask of good Three Star, there's just
   a nip apiece.
Come, mate, pass up your pannikin, there's
   plenty here you see."
"No thank you, Boss, I'd rather not; no brandy,
   sir, for me."

"How is it, Ned, you never drink, I've seen you
   tempted oft,
And if you chance to take a drink, it's always
   something soft?"
"I once was wild," the stockman cried, "as any
   man could be,
And many a hard-earned cheque I knocked down
   in a spree.

"But times have changed, and now on drink I
   look with dread and fear,
And were I my story to relate, it would move you
   all to hear."
To tell the story of his life, on him we did prevail

And gathered closely round the fire, to hear the
   stockman's tale.

The hardy stockman heaved a sigh, his face was
   sad and wan,
He knocked the ashes from his pipe, and thus his
   tale began:
"Three years ago or nearly so (how fast the time
   rolls by!)
We were droving on those western plains, my
   brother Ben and I.

"It is about my brother Ben I wish to speak
   the most,
A gay and manly lad was he as the country round
   could boast;
But for all his many virtues, he one great
   failing had
And that was Drink—through cursed Drink I've
   seen him raving mad.

"But soon as he had sober grown, a steady chap
   was he,
He earned his cheque and sent it home—not
   knocked it down like me.
We were in charge of a mob of cattle with other
   stockmen three,
And droving through those summer months right
   merry times had we.

"One night we camped the cattle mob upon
   some rising ground,
And when they'd steadied for the night, we built
   the fires around;
And then to have a merry time, I for the grog
   did call,
And soon I was, myself, the merriest of them all.

"My brother Ben joined in the fun, and many a
   song we sung,
We made those flying curlews scream and the
   woods with echoes rung;
But Ben he would not touch a drop although we
   pressed him hard,
To all our soft entreaties he paid not the least
   regard.

"'Come, Ben,' I said, 'don't be so mean, to stand
   the odd man out,
You know I've seen you drink your share when
   the liquor's been about!'
'But, Ned, I have not touched a drop these three
   long years,' he said,
'And well you know how crazed I go when the
   stuff gets to my head!'

"'Nonsense, man, the night is cold, you need
only have one glass!'
'One, only one,' the chorus chimed, and round
the grog they passed.
He yielded to that fatal glass which makes me sad
to think
That I the only man in this world could make my
brother drink!

"Hour upon hour, glass upon glass, we brothers
sat and drank
Till weary in the night's caress, in a drunken
sleep I sank.
How long I slept I do not know—I woke to sleep
no more,
The distant thunder broke my rest, a storm was
gathering o'er.

"I rose and stirred the dying fire, and tried to
rouse the men,
But, looking round with beating heart, I missed
my brother Ben.
Just then a vivid lightning flash lit up the gloomy
plain,
I saw Ben riding madly by, then all was dark
again.

"Aloud I cried, 'Hold hard awhile!' but his voice
came hoarse and hollow,
'Ha, ha!' he cried, 'to Death I ride; come on, you
dare not follow!'
I snatched my whip from off the ground, my
horse was standing near,
And as I to the saddle sprang my heart stood still
with fear.

"He headed for the timber-land with dark and
gloom ahead
And as I spurred with rapid strides my
maddened stockhorse fled;
I tried to grasp Ben's bridle-rein, his horse
swerved from the track
And went plunging through the midnight with a
madman on its back.

"His horse, not being used to this, tried hard his
head to free,
And, rearing back, he struck poor Ben against a
leaning tree.
Dismounting, I was on the ground and raised his
drooping head,
And as I looked into his eyes I could not think
him dead.

"But what a sight to me, alas, the coming dawn
revealed,
His blue eyes were for ever closed, his lips with
blood were sealed.
—Ah! who will break the news at home and tell
his poor old aged mother
The death of her beloved son, my one and only
brother?

"And to think that I his murderer was!—from the
ghastly thought I shrink:
Killed by lack of intellect, through the cursed
demon Drink!
On yonder sloping mountainside a lonely grave
you'll see
All covered in with grass and moss, beneath a
cedar-tree.
No marble cross or monument this lonely grave
doth mark
But we rudely carved my brother's name deep in
the growing bark."

And now, my boys, take warning all, before it is
too late,
Think of the stockman's awful tale, and his poor
young brother's fate;
Say with a will, "I will not drink" or you will
others tempt;
Pass it by as I always have with silent cool
contempt.

*As with "Corney's Hut", this poem is a sentimental
tear-jerker, but it was enormously popular at bush
concerts as a recitation, especially in Queensland
where its popularity was challenged only by such
favourites as "How McDougal Topped the Score",
"The Man from Ironbark" and the ballad of the
Queensland outlaws, "The Kenniffs".*

Screw Pine

*Reminiscences of the past—champagne nine-pins (engraving from* Illustrated Sydney News, *18 March 1882)*

# The Old Poley Cow

*Anon.*

Master came to the old hut door
And said as he had often said before,
"Tomorrow will be mustering day
So rouse up boys and all away.

*Chorus*
So early in the morning
So early in the morning,
So early in the morning,
Before the break of day.

We started a mob not far away
And brought them back without delay.
Till an old poley cow ran off the track
And Master went to fetch her back.

Now Master's horse was very free
Ran him up against a myall-tree
Threw poor Master on his head,
Broke his neck and killed him dead.

Next morning when I went to get a horse
To fetch our poor old Master's corse,
All in the morning's misty light
I got a most tremendous fright,

For there I saw old Master's ghost
Sitting in the corner on the stockyard post,
And in his mouth the same old clay
He used to smoke on mustering day.

Where e'er I go, where e'er I stay,
I'll ne'er forget that mustering day,
I'll ne'er forget old Master's ghost
Sitting in the corner on the stockyard post,
And in his mouth the same old clay
He used to smoke on mustering day.

*"So Early in the Morning" was a familiar tune at bush dances, and it was almost inevitable that words should be set to the swinging melody. The words given here are those from Stewart and Keesing's* Old Bush Songs, *though my mother and her sister Caroline sang rather different words; "Master" being replaced by "The Boss", etc. I give this version of the words as being more complete.*

# The Sandy Maranoa

*A. W. Davis*

The night is dark and stormy, and the sky is
    clouded o'er;
Our horses we will mount and ride away,
To watch the squatters' cattle through the
    darkness of the night,
And we'll keep them on the camp till break of
    day.

*Chorus*
For we're going, going, going to Gunnedah so
    far,
And we'll soon be into sunny New South Wales;
We shall bid farewell to Queensland, with its
    swampy coolibah—
Happy drovers from the sandy Maranoa.

When the fires are burning bright through the
    darkness of the night,
And the cattle camping quiet, well, I'm sure
That I wish for two o'clock when I call the other
    watch—
This is droving from the sandy Maranoa.

Our beds made on the ground, we are sleeping all
    so sound
When we're wakened by the distant thunder's
    roar,
And the lightning's vivid flash, followed by an
    awful crash—
It's rough on drovers from the sandy Maranoa.

We are up at break of day, and we're all soon on
    the way,
For we always have to go ten miles or more;
It don't do to loaf about, or the squatter will
    come out—
He's strict on drovers from the sandy Maranoa.

We shall soon be on the Moonie, and we'll cross
    the Barwon, too;
Then we'll be out upon the rolling plains once
    more;
We'll shout "Hurrah! for old Queensland, with
    its swampy coolibah,
And the cattle that come off the Maranoa."

*"The Sandy Maranoa" was sung to a fine swinging tune and has always seemed to me to be rather romantic about the hard facts of a difficult, dangerous and uncomfortable profession. I have always read or*

*sung it with the following short parody in mind, which has always seemed to reflect more of the facts of the job, which has now largely been superseded by the road trains.*

*Have you ever been droving out west,*
*Where the flies are a terrible pest,*
*The mosquitoes at night, by the Jesus they bite,*
*And the bulldog ants in your blankets at night.*
*By the Jesus you know you are earning your dough*
*When you take on droving out west.*
*(From Ron Edwards, who got it from Jack Guard, at Georgetown, Queensland. It is sung to the tune of "My Little Grey Home in the West".)*

# Where the Dead Men Lie

*Barcroft Boake*

Out on the wastes of the Never Never—
    That's where the dead men lie!
There where the heat-waves dance for ever—
    That's where the dead men lie!
That's where the Earth's loved sons are keeping
Endless tryst: not the west wind sweeping
Feverish pinions can wake their sleeping—
    Out where the dead men lie!

Where brown Summer and Death have mated—
    That's where the dead men lie!
Loving with fiery lust unsated—
    That's where the dead men lie!
Out where the grinning skulls bleach whitely
    Under the saltbush sparkling brightly;
Out where the wild dogs chorus nightly—
    That's where the dead men lie!

Deep in the yellow, flowing river—
    That's where the dead men lie!
Under the banks where the shadows quiver—
    That's where the dead men lie!
Where the platypus twists and doubles,
Leaving a train of tiny bubbles;
Rid at last of their earthly troubles—
    That's where the dead men lie!

East and backward pale faces turning—
    That's how the dead men lie!
Gaunt arms stretched with a voiceless yearning—
    That's how the dead men lie!
Oft in the fragrant hush of nooning
Hearing again their mother's crooning,
Wrapt for aye in a dreamful swooning—
    That's how the dead men lie!

Only the hand of Night can free them—
    That's when the dead men fly!
Only the frightened cattle see them—
    See the dead men go by!
Cloven hoofs beating out one measure,
Bidding the stockmen know no leisure—
That's when the dead men take their pleasure!
    That's when the dead men fly!

Ask, too, the never-sleeping drover:
    He sees the dead pass by;
Hearing them call to their friends—the plover,
    Hearing the dead men cry;
Seeing their faces stealing, stealing,
Hearing their laughter, pealing pealing,
Watching their grey forms wheeling, wheeling
    Round where the cattle lie!

Strangled by thirst and fierce privation—
    That's how the dead men die!
Out on Moneygrub's farthest station—
    That's how the dead men die!
Hard-faced greybeards, youngsters callow;
Some mounds cared for, some left fallow;
Some deep down, yet others shallow;
    Some having but the sky.

Moneygrub, as he sips his claret,
    Looks with complacent eye
Down at his watch-chain, eighteen carat—
    There, in his club, hard by:
Recks not that every link is stamped with
Names of the men whose limbs are cramped with
Too long lying in grave-mould, cramped with
    Death where the dead men lie.

*An exploring party looking for a sheep run (hand-coloured lithograph, from* Scenes in the Bush of Australia, *by a Squatter)*

*The following four poems testify to the differing attitudes of "wages men" and "contract men" in the outback in the 1880s and '90s. Shearers, being contract men, were fiercely independent. "The Rousie", being a wages man, and often taking the job to learn to shear, could not afford the independent stance adopted by the other fellow until he had mastered his trade. Old timers, working their pensions on the failing goldfields and tinfields of the Etheridge belt in North Queensland in the 1930s, would boast proudly, "I never worked for wages." (See* A Thousand Miles Away, *a history of North Queensland).*

# The Rouseabout

*Anon.*

I'm just a flamin' workin'-horse, the slavey of
    the shed,
A' chasin' up an' down the board t'earn me keep
    an' bed;
It's "Wool away!" an' "Jump back quick!" an'
    I'm a woeful name:
I grab me broom an' do me best—I'm yelled at
    just the same.
A target, me, for anyone with things to groan an'
    grouse about:
The driven, damned, demented dolt they call the
    bloomin' rouseabout.

There's wool along the shearin' board an' wool in
    every bin,
Yair, greasy, burry, stinkin' wool an' more keeps
    pourin' in;

It flutters from me mo an' beard, it's in me hair
    an' eyes—
If entered for a sheep show now I'd win the
    shornies prize,
I'm breathin' it an' sneezin' it, I'm tufted like
    a goat,
I reckon there's a bale of it gone down me achin'
    throat.

You'd think these lordly shearers owned the
    blessed countryside
The way they chuck their weight around an'
    bellow in their pride.
It's "Rousy here!" or "Lift y'r feet!" or "Clean
    the blanky board!"
I jump like I was just a dog—an' get a dog's
    reward.
From dawn to dusk I'm chivvied as a cat would
    chase a mouse about
A racin' roared an' raved-at runt, a downtrod
    blasted rouseabout.

When sore an' limp I seek me bunk an' try to get
    some sleep
I turn an' toss with nasty dreams of hordes o'
    silly sheep;
They nudge an' whisk the blankets off an' nibble
    at me toes
It's worse than what the boozer sees who's got
    the Jims an' Joes:
An' when another mornin' breaks an' cookie has
    his say,
I struggle from the haunted hut and face the
    dreadful day.

The world is full of cryin' coves who think their
   spin is bad;
They're sick or broke or sorry or the missus
   drives them mad.
They're mournin' for the things they lost, an'
   railin' at their fate,
Or weepin' in their whiskers at the woes they
   contemplate.
*By cripes, they'd all have somethin' real to shake*
   *the ruddy house about,*
*If they sweated, served an' suffered as a flamin'*
   *shearers' rouseabout!*

*This poem was sent to Bill Wannan by Mrs Alma*
*Burge, of Dubbo, New South Wales. It was given to*
*her husband some years ago. Wannan quotes it in his*
*book* A Treasury of Australian Folk Tales. *Orig-*
*inally associated with the sheds, the word has come to*
*mean any sort of "generally useful" round a homes-*
*tead or pub. See the other poem later in this section*
*also called "The Rouseabout".*

Advertising!

# Are You the Cove?

*Joseph Furphy ("Tom Collins")*

"Are you the Cove?" he spoke the words
As swagmen only can;
The Squatter freezingly inquired,
"What do you mean, my man?"

"Are you the Cove?" his voice was stern,
His look was firm and keen;
Again the Squatter made reply,
"I don't know what you mean."

"O! dash my rags! let's have some sense—
You ain't a fool, by Jove,
Gammon you dunno what I mean;
I mean—are you the Cove?"

"Yes, I'm the Cove," the Squatter said;
The Swagman answered, "Right,
I thought as much: show me some place
Where I can doss tonight."

# Beyond His Jurisdiction

*Harry Morant ("The Breaker")*

It was a Western manager, and a language-man
   was he,
Thus spoke he to the shed-boss: "Send 'The
   Rager' round to me;
I'll hie me to the office where I'll write his
   crimson cheque,
Bid him roll his dusty swag up, or I'll break his
   no-good neck."

So when the bell was ringing—when "smoke-
   oh!" time was o'er,
Says the shed-boss, "Mick, your services are
   wanted here no more."
Then "The Rager" hung his shears up, stepped
   from the shearing floor,
And went a-swapping swear-words round at the
   office-door.

For the boss began to language, and "The
   Rager" languaged back;
Says "The Rager", "There's my brother, can't
   you give him, too, the sack?"
"Your brother? D——n your brother! Yes, send
   him round here quick!"
"That narks yez," Michael answered—"he's a
   cocky down in Vic."

*"The Breaker" was executed by a British firing squad*
*in Pretoria during the Boer War, after being*
*condemned to death for shooting prisoners of war*
*while an officer in an independent company of*
*Mounted Infantry. The following account is quoted*
*from* Time Means Tucker *by Duke Tritton. His*
*informant was a man called Frank Farrell.*

Again like Ben Bridge, he had been forced to
witness the execution of Harry Morant. He said:
"They marched every available Australian soldier
into Pretoria, and lined us up where we would have
a grandstand view of how the British Army dealt
with offenders against the rules of war. Harry
refused to have his eyes bandaged, and gave the
order to fire himself. He stuck his chest out, and
said: 'Blast away, you bastards!' The only time the
British Army showed any sense was the day they
murdered Harry Morant. They disarmed us, and it
was a week before we got our rifles back."

He rose to his feet and walked away. An hour
later he came back and unrolled his blankets, and
lay down. All the next day he was morose and had
little to say.

*Cornered (engraving from* Illustrated Australian News, *25 May 1888)*

# The Shearer's Dream

*Henry Lawson*

Oh, I dreamt I shore in a shearin'-shed, and it
    was a dream of joy,
For every one of the rouseabouts was a girl
    dressed up as a boy—
Dressed up like a page in a pantomime, and the
    prettiest ever seen—
They had flaxen hair, they had coal-black hair,
    and every shade between,

There was short, plump girls, there was tall, slim
    girls, and the handsomest ever seen;
They was four-foot-five, they was six-foot high,
    and every height between.

The shed was cooled by electric fans that was
    over every shoot;
The pens was of polished ma-ho-gany, and
    everything else to suit;

The huts had springs to the mattresses, and the
    tucker was simply grand,
And every night by the billerbong we danced to a
    German band.

Our pay was the wool on the jumbuks' backs, so
    we shore till all was blue—
The sheep was washed afore they was shore (and
    the rams was scented too);
And we all of us wept when the shed cut out, in
    spite of the long, hot days,
For every hour them girls waltzed in with whisky
    and beer on tr-a-a-a-ys!

There was three of them girls to every chap, and
    as jealous as they could be
There was three of them girls to every chap, and
    six of 'em picked on me;
We was draftin' 'em out for the homeward track
    and sharin' 'em round like steam,
When I woke with my head in the blazin' sun to
    find 'twas a shearer's dream.

*The following poem of Victor Daley's was written under his pen name of "Creeve Roe". The incident took place at the big camp of striking shearers at Barcaldine in 1891. This strike, which seems to me largely neglected by historians, brought Australia much closer to a possible civil war than the Eureka Stockade, and was instrumental, among other things, for the quixotic William Lane settlement in Paraguay, and the formation of the Australian Workers Union.*

# O'Callaghan's Apple

"The matter vomited by Private O'Callaghan, of the Gympie Mounted Infantry, who was said to have been poisoned by strychnine placed in an apple given him by a unionist at Barcaldine, was forwarded to the Government Analyst for examination. His report, which has been forwarded to the Commissioner of Police, states that the Matter contained no trace of strychnine or any poison which could produce the effects described."
—*Daily Paper.*

O tame result! O'Callaghan,
   For weeks we have been thrilled
With horror of the wretch who gave
   To you an apple filled
With deadly poison. Since the Snake
   Deluded primal man
No apple-yarn made such a stir
   As yours, O'Callaghan.

No incident throughout the strike,
   Bloody, and mad, and fierce
As many were, so wrung our heart,
   So melted us in tears.
We heard with grief the deeds of men
   Splashed with that evil chrism
The shuddering daily papers name
   As the "New Unionism."

We heard that labourers who called
   Each other Bob or Jim
Seeing an Officer would cry
   Profanely "Joe!" to him:
We knew that troops had been received
   With storms of oaths and howls
While in their hearing—insult dire—
   Someone had mentioned "fowls."

We learned from various sources that
   Machiavellian plans

Were being hatched, and dynamite
   Concealed in billy-cans;
We read from documents secured,
   After a struggle tough,
The writers wished to be supplied
   With "more of the same stuff."

We heard about a scoundrel who,
   Yet roaming earth unhung,
When others cheered our Gracious Queen
   Put out his ribald tongue;
And that damned miscreant who scared
   The North out of its wits
By saying that the shearers yet
   Would give the squatters "fits".

These things were horrible, and we
   Groaned audibly to read
Of each, but your affair was of
   A more demoniac breed;
They troubled us beyond belief
   Yet nothing that we felt
Approached our anguish at your tale,
   O miserable Celt.

One afternoon, as you strode down
   The street, a joy to see,
In the full regimentals of
   The Gympie Infantry,
Some murderer a pippin on
   His coward hand outstretched,
You grabbed it and did eat thereof,
   And then, poor wretch, you retched.

You took it unsuspectingly
   And placed it in the chasm
That intersects your features, and
   Chewed on till many a spasm
Shook your great frame—we here assume
   That you are strongly built—
Then down you dropped, and up you curled,
   And out you yelled—"I'm kilt!"

They gathered round you, pale, aghast
   And trembling, one and all,
And everyone declared the deed
   Was diabolical;
"Our special correspondents" wired
   To that effect—like birds
That hunt for worms, they saw a chance
   Of several hundred words!

And some who felt the honour of
   Old Ireland was at stake
Made preparations so that you

Might have a roaring wake;
While others brought two doctors, who
    At once hauled off their coats
And emptied you with stomach-pumps,
    Filled you with antidotes.

With scientific skill they sought
    To baffle Union hate,
And searched you through for traces of
    Corrosive sublimate;
They tried for prussic-acid; then
    Believing that you might
Have, after all, been only dosed
    With modest aconite,

Prescribed for that, and, to make sure,
    For many a speci-*fic*
They gave you against cyanides,
    Nightshade, and arsenic,
And, fearing that the venom might
    Not have been one of these,
They did their best to shore you up
    Against cantharides.

They thought of digitalis, and
    For Indian hemp looked out,
"Precipitates" they grappled with,
    And quickly put to rout.
In puzzling over what had brought
    You near to Kingdom Come,
There even flashed across their minds
    The thought of Queensland rum.

But, finding that the Unionists
    Were not, with all their faults,
So fiendish as to give you *that*,
    They probed for fatal salts.
For morphia one might fairly say
    That they were "on the job,"
While strychnine at the very start
    Received one on the nob.

To show the murderer that he
    Had not to deal with flats,
They made you safe and whole against
    The fiercest "Rough On Rats;"
They slew all agents strong to slay
    Or elephants or bugs,
And pulled you through, O'Callaghan,
    With stomach-pumps and drugs.

Your comrades vowed to have revenge
    For all you had gone through,
Upon the hell-hound who had wrought
    His base design on you,

For every drachm of nauseous stuff
    You took that day, they swore
To have a fair Imperial pint
    Of his false heart's black gore.

The main camp was surrounded by
    Their most unfearing braves,
Who straightway haled before your bed
    Some guilty-looking slaves.
But all in vain; the miscreant,
    You said, was not of these—
He had escaped to perpetrate
    Yet further villainies!

Ah! well, the press might warn the world
    About the dread abysm
Society is being led
    To now by Unionism;
And well might law-abiding men
    At every failure quake,
And mutter that our liberties
    Are once again at stake!

*We* trembled then, O'Callaghan,
    But nourished still the hope
That your most fell assailant would
    Be surely brought to rope;
We knew the long arms of the law
    Would seek him far and wide
When once 'twas known what he had sought
    To place in your inside.

We waited hungrily to hear
    What devil's mixture had
Been hidden in the pippin which
    Made your poor in'ards bad,
And now we know precisely what
    Caused you to squirm and twist—
You've fooled yourself and us, but not
    The Public Analyst.

He says the apple was all right,
    And, speaking as a judge,
Declares your fearful poison yarn,
    O'Callaghan, was fudge.
You've soared to fame by a mistake,
    And made us spoil our "wipes"
With grief for—what? alack, but this—
    A Private with the "Gripes!"

*An account of a camp of striking shearers from firsthand observation (not the Barcaldine one but the second largest, at Longreach) is to be found in* Roll the Summers Back *by Joseph Porter.*

*Above, stud sheep, Mudgee (both engravings from* Picturesque Atlas of Australasia, ed. *Andrew Garran)*

*Sheep shearing (engraving from* Australian Pictures Drawn with Pen and Pencil, *Howard Willoughby)*

# I Don't Go Shearin' Now

I shore along the 'Bidgee in the good old
    roarin' days,
An' rung the shed at Tubbo, next pen to
    "Smacker" Hayes,
Oh, strike me, how I loved it, the campin' in
    the fogs,
Within hearin' of the hobble chains an' croakin'
    of the frogs,
I'd like again to face it as in the days of Jacky
    Dow,
But my bones are ancient an' I don't go shearin'
    now.

To me 'twas sweetest music, oh, the clink of
    hobble chains,
The rattle of our quart pots in our journey o'er
    the plains,

When men from cold Monaro, an' the boys from
    Dandaloo
Sought shearin' on the Bogan an' along the
    parched Paroo,
With hack an' packhorse baggage did we mooch
    along somehow,
T'was fun—that bloomin' hardship—but I don't
    go shearin' now.

Oh, yes, I am a battler of the old-time shearin'
    push,
We humped Matilda often o'er the plain land an'
    the bush,
When voices fraught with freedom came
    murmurin' through the trees,
An' gladsome shearin' tidings then were wafted
    on the breeze,
I'd love to bustle on the board with Jacky Howe,
But hang the combs an' cutters, boys, I can't go
    shearin' now.

Well, no I've never shore 'em with machine an'
    twistin' gear,
To me it's all a jumble an' a rumble mighty
    queer,
The boss, he cannot chip you 'cept he hollers in
    your ear,
An' that is not too pleasant if his voice is full of
    beer:
My tally board is empty an' there's wrinkles on
    my brow,
An' though I'd like to face it, boys, I don't go
    shearin' now.

I always go a-shearin' (in my fancy) every year,
An' can't shake off the longin' when the time is
    drawin' near,
But soon I 'spect I'll wander where the shearin'
    never ends,
Along the golden river where there's naught but
    peace attends,
But, strike me, how I'd love to strut across the
    board an' bow,
Once more to clip the wool off, but I don't go
    shearin' now.

# The Great Australian Adjective

*W. T. Goodge*

The sunburnt —— stockman stood
And, in a dismal —— mood,
Apostrophized his —— cuddy;
"The —— nag's no —— good,
He couldn't earn his —— food—
A regular —— brumby,
                  ——!"

He jumped across the —— horse
And cantered off, of —— course!
The roads were bad and ——muddy;
Said he, "Well, spare me —— days
The —— Government's —— ways
Are screamin' —— funny,
                  ——!"

He rode up hill, down —— dale,
The wind it blew a —— gale,
The creek was high and —— floody.
Said he, "The —— horse must swim,
The same for —— me and him,
Is something —— sickenin',
                  ——!"

He plunged into the —— creek,
The —— horse was —— weak,
The stockman's face a —— study!
And though the —— horse was drowned
The —— rider reached the ground
Ejaculating, "——?"
                  "——!"

*This seems to have fathered a number of poems using the great Australian Adjective. The poem following needs little introduction, but there were a number of poems extant during World War II that used the same freedom of pretended coyness at using the actual word. "The place they call ——" can be found in a number of collections, and there was a verse extant at Wewak in 1945, part of which ran:*

    *No bloody tram, no bloody bus,*
    *No one to make a bloody fuss,*
    *And no one cares for bloody us*
    *So bloody, bloody, bloody.*

*Ian Mudie in one of his collections of poems (an anthology of poems by other people), published by Rigby, included a poem called "The Man from Tumbarumba". The last two lines of the first and final stanzas of which read:*

    *Or shootin' kanga-bloody-roos*
    *At Tumba-bloody-rumba.*

*No doubt the tradition will continue of weaving what Joseph Furphy ("Tom Collins") called "the thin red line of adjective" through some of our more robust verse.*

At the Blowhard Sand-hill, on the night of the 10th, I camped with a party of six sons of Belial, bound for Deniliquin, with 3,000 Boolka wethers off the shears. Now, anyone who has listened for four hours to the conversation of a group of sheep drovers, named, respectively, Splodger, Rabbit, Parson, Bottler, Dingo, and Hairy-toothed Ike, will agree with me as to the impossibility of getting the dialogue of such *dramatis personae* into anything like printable form. The bullock drivers were bad enough, but these fellows are out of the question.

*From* Such Is Life, *Joseph Furphy ("Tom Collins")*

# The Austra—laise

*C. J. Dennis*

(To the hymn tune "Onward Christian Soldiers")

Fellers of Australier,
Blokes and coves and coots,
Shift yer —— carcases,
move yer —— boots
Gird yer —— loins up,
Get yer —— gun,
Set the —— enemy
And watch the —— run!

*Chorus*
Get a —— move on,
Have some —— sense,
Learn the —— art of
Self de —— fence.

Have some —— brains be
Neath yer —— lids
An' swing a —— sabre
Fer the missus an' the kids,
Chuck supportin' —— posts
An' strikin' —— lights,
Support a —— family an'
Strike fer yer —— rights.

Joy is —— fleetin'
Life is —— short,
Wot's the use er wastin' it
All on —— sport?
Hitch yer —— tip dray
To a —— star,
Let yer —— watchword be
Australi —— ar!

'Ow's the —— nation
Goin' ter expand
Lest us —— blokes an' coves
Lend a —— hand?
'Eave yer —— apathy
Down a —— chasm,
'Ump yer —— burden with
Enthusi —— asm.

When the —— trouble
Hits yer native land,
Take a —— rifle
In yer —— 'and.
Keep yer —— upper lip
Stiff as stiff can be,

An' speed a —— bullet fer
Pos —— terity,

W'en the — bugle
Sounds ad —— vance,
Don't be like a flock er sheep
In a —— trance.
Biff the —— foreman
Where it don't agree,
Spifler —— cate 'im
To Eternity.

Fellers of Australier,
Cobbers, chaps and mates,
Hear the —— enemy
Kickin' at the gates.
Blow the —— bugle,
Beat the —— drum,
Upper cut and out the cow
To Kingdom —— Come.

*This poem won a special prize in its initial version which was entered for the Bulletin Newspaper Competition for an Australian anthem in 1908. It was revised in 1914 and widely reprinted, and according to* Aussie, *a magazine for the A.I.F. in France during World War I, "When the First Division was in camp,* The Australaise *was to be found in almost every mess."*

Government House Sydney

*Sydney Heads from the South (engraving from* Picturesque Atlas of Australasia, *ed. Andrew Garran)*

*Mount Macedon from lagoon north of Bush Inn (engraving from* Victoria Illustrated, *S. T. Gill)*

*There is an apocryphal story that most people have heard at some time or another concerning a horseman who chased a goanna on a treeless plain, whereupon the reptile took refuge upon his pursuer's hat. I have struck it a few times, but did not know there had been a poem written about it until I found the following in one of the* Bill Bowyang Reciters. *I don't know whether the story fathered the poem or the other way round, when someone with a bad memory for verse heard the poem and started the story on its rounds. But the poem is bush versifying at its most typical.*

# The Black Goanna

On the Castlereagh some years ago
   We did not mind a buster,
And some gay old sport we used to have
   When going out to muster.
It was in the month of August,
   Tho' the ground was not too damp,
We saddled up and started out
   To put on Brigalow Camp.

And while riding across the plain
   Just in the usual manner,
When all at once we came upon
   An old man black goanna.
"Hello!" cried one. "Boys, here's a lark,
   Out here he has no shelter.
We'll down upon him with our whips
   And send him helter skelter."

Down came the whips, he stood it well,
   His hide was thick and tough,
But soon he had to do a get,
   The treatment proved too rough.
Then for the creek he doubled quick,
   And, in his headlong bolt,
The first thing he encountered
   Was Kemp upon a colt.

Now, up that colt's hind legs he went
   And large sharp claws he had.
You may talk about our wild-west shows,
   That colt went ramping mad.
But the more he bucked the more he squealed,
   They both hung on the faster,
For Kemp was the chap who bore the name
   Of being a sticking plaster.

But still he served it out in style,
   The dust he fairly skyed.
It was plain if something didn't come
   He'd surely shed his hide.
Now the crupper went, the breast plate too,
   The girths they burst asunder,
The surcingle, it snapped in two,
   And down they came like thunder.

The iguana, he was underneath,
   So Kemp was let off lightly
The goanna he was fairly squashed,
   We thought it served him rightly.
That was many years ago,
   But yet I bet a tenner
That colt and Kemp have not forgot
   That blooming black goanna.

*Mount Kiera, New South Wales (Skinner Prout, from* Australia, *ed. Edwin Carton Booth)*

*Encounter with a kangaroo (engraving from* Illustrated Australian News, *28 January 1876)*

*Anyone who has seen the tiny bush settlement of Gilliatt, near Cloncurry, might well wonder why anyone would go there, or, having gone there, would want to stay. There must have been a bush poet of some skill there at some time, however, for the following poem and the song "The Gilliatt Mug", which is also in this book, survive. This poem is also from a Bill Bowyang Reciter.*

# The Boxing Kangaroo

Away back in the Nineties when my beard was
    silky brown,
When the unemployed were scanty and no misery
    in view,
When the toilers all had money, in one little
    Gilliat town,
There lived one great big funny boxing old buck
    kangaroo.

He was taught to drink the cleanings of the beer
    at a local pub,
And he grew to have some leanings for the strong
    fermented slops,
And he'd fill himself completely—he could empty
    out a tub,
For what will blend more neatly than a 'roo full
    up of hops.

So the boxers all around there grew to love this
    kangaroo,
And the grass fighters to be found there didn't
    have it on their own,
For the 'roo was always willing when a scrap was
    put on view,
When it came to fight or swilling, well just leave
    that 'roo alone.

So one Dandy Mick was boozing, he was cuttin'
    out a cheque,
And he spied the drunken snoozing of the old
    buck kangaroo,
And he didn't think this proper so he kicked
    him in the neck,
Saying, "Now get up you flopper or I'll bust you
    clean in two."

Well, the fight was quickly started and the 'roo
    grabbed Dandy Mick,
And with claws and big toe parted all the clothes
    the boozer wore,
Poor old Dandy called on Heaven, he was feeling
    mighty sick,
And we picked up just eleven of his teeth upon
    the floor.

Well we rescued tattered Dandy and we got him
    on his feet,
With a badly needed brandy, what a sorry plight
    to view.
And he said, "I'm mighty thankful and
    nevermore I'll meet
That long-tailed beery tankful, the Gilliat's
    boxing kangaroo."

*The following poem needs no introduction from me for
any aficionado of "reciting". I first heard it at a
concert in the little New South Wales township of
Federal, at a concert where "Australia Will Be
There" was sung with the whole audience joining
enthusiastically in the chorus. It must have been about
1937, I suppose. After "The Man from Snowy
River", it was considered to be the best poem written
in Australia, and this year I was asked by a young
man from Dimbulah (not Dimboola) if I had a copy
of the "poem about the cricket match". Of course I
did!*

# How McDougal Topped the Score

*Thomas E. Spencer*

A peaceful spot is Piper's Flat. The folk that live
    around—
They keep themselves by keeping sheep and
    turning up the ground;
But the climate is erratic, and the consequences
    are
The struggle with the elements is everlasting war.
We plough, and sow, and harrow—then sit down
    and pray for rain;
And then we all get flooded out and have to start
    again.
But the folk are now rejoicing as they ne'er
    rejoiced before,
For we've played Molongo cricket, and
    McDougal topped the score!

Molongo had a head on it, and challenged us
    to play
A single-innings match for lunch—the losing
    team to pay.
We were not great guns at cricket, but we
    couldn't well say no,
So we all began to practise, and we let the
    reaping go
We scoured the Flat for ten miles round to
    muster up our men,
But when the list was totalled we could only
    number ten.
Then up spoke big Tim Brady: he was always
    slow to speak,
And he said—"What price McDougal, who lives
    down at Cooper's Creek?"

So we sent for old McDougal, and he stated
in reply
That he'd never played at cricket, but he'd half a
mind to try.
He couldn't come to practise—he was getting
in his hay,
But he guessed he'd show the beggars from
Molongo how to play.
Now, McDougal was a Scotchman, and a canny
one at that,
So he started in to practise with a paling for a bat.
He got Mrs. Mac to bowl to him, but she
couldn't run at all,
So he trained his sheep-dog, Pincher, how to
scout and fetch the ball.

Now, Pincher was no puppy; he was old, and
worn, and grey;
But he understood McDougal, and—accustomed
to obey—
When McDougal cried out "Fetch it!" he would
fetch it in a trice,
But, until the word was "Drop it!" he would grip
it like a vice.
And each succeeding night they played until the
light grew dim:
Sometimes McDougal struck the ball—
sometimes the ball struck him.
Each time he struck, the ball would plough a
furrow in the ground;
And when he missed, the impetus would turn
him three times round.

The fatal day at length arrived—the day that was
to see
Molongo bite the dust, or Piper's Flat knocked
up a tree!
Molongo's captain won the toss, and sent his men
to bat,
And they gave some leather-hunting to the men
of Piper's Flat.
When the ball sped where McDougal stood, firm
planted in his track,
He shut his eyes, and turned him round, and
stopped it—with his back!
The highest score was twenty-two, the total
sixty-six,
When Brady sent a yorker down that scattered
Johnson's sticks.

Then Piper's Flat went in to bat, for glory and
renown,

But, like the grass before the scythe, our wickets
tumbled down.
"Nine wickets down for seventeen, with fifty
more to win!"
Our captain heaved a heavy sigh, and sent
McDougal in,
"Ten pounds to one you'll lose it!" cried a
barracker from town;
But McDougal said, "I'll tak' it, mon!" and
planked the money down.
Then he girded up his moleskins in a self-reliant
style,
Threw off his hat and boots and faced the bowler
with a smile.

He held the bat the wrong side out, and Johnson
with a grin
Stepped lightly to the bowling crease, and sent a
"wobbler" in;
McDougal spooned it softly back, and Johnson
waited there,
But McDougal, crying "*Fetch it!*" started
running like a hare.
Molongo shouted "Victory! He's out as sure as
eggs,"
When Pincher started through the crowd, and
ran through Johnson's legs.
He seized the ball like lightning; then ran behind
a log,
And McDougal kept on running, while Molongo
chased the dog!

They chased him up, they chased him down, they
chased him round, and then
He darted through the slip-rail as the scorer
shouted "Ten!"
McDougal puffed; Molongo swore; excitement
was intense;
As the scorer marked down twenty, Pincher
cleared a barbed-wire fence.
"Let us head him!" shrieked Molongo. "Brain
the mongrel with a bat!"
"Run it out! Good old McDougal!" yelled the
men of Piper's Flat.
And McDougal kept on jogging, and then
Pincher doubled back,
And the scorer counted "*Forty*" as they raced
across the track.

McDougal's legs were going fast, Molongo's
breath was gone—
But still Molongo chased the dog—McDougal
struggled on.

When the scorer shouted *"Fifty"* then they knew
the chase would cease;
And McDougal gasped out *"Drop it"* as he
dropped within his crease.
Then Pincher dropped the ball, and as
instinctively he knew
Discretion was the wiser plan, he disappeared
from view;
And as Molongo's beaten men exhausted lay
around
We raised McDougal shoulder-high, and bore
him from the ground.

We bore him to McGinniss's, where lunch was
ready laid,
And filled him up with whisky-punch, for which
Molongo paid.
We drank his health in bumpers and we cheered
him three times three,
And when Molongo got its breath Molongo
joined the spree.
And the critics say they never saw a cricket match
like that,
When McDougal broke the record in the game at
Piper's Flat;
And the folk are jubilating as they never did
before;
For we played Molongo cricket—and McDougal
topped the score!

*When I went to Bathurst in 1946 to learn about prospecting for gold, which is a story I hope to relate one day, the mentor my mate had chosen refused to have anything to do with me until he was assured that I was not a "smart Alec or a Roman Catholic". This meant very little to me, save to make me wonder what it was all about, and probably until a few years ago most Australians of my generation and younger would have been in the same fix. Then there was rioting in Belfast, and we have seen the bloody business of people blown to pieces, shot and burned, mangled in explosions with such impassivity from leaders on both sides that our overwhelming impulse has been to shout, "For God's sake, stop this". But, for God's sake, they claim, it goes on, in Ulster; while in Australia this madness has sunk to rhymes chanted by children with little real animosity. Victor Daley, in his guise as "Creeve Roe", hoped for this a long time ago, and wrote this poem urging sanity on what must have been something of the same situation here. A few years ago, as I said, this poem would have meant little to me. Things have changed, now. But it was not always so, as the extract preceding the poem shows.*

Even the bush, however, is not entirely free from religious bickerings and intolerance, and this is more especially the case in the small towns, or, as they are usually called, "bush townships." There the different denominations quarrel and cavil to their hearts' content. There is more joy over one not particularly clean "cross-breed" enticed from the opposition fold, than over ninety and nine snow-white merinos that have never belonged to the heretical flock. The quarrelling, however, does not usually set in until the township has become thoroughly established and fairly prosperous; for in the first days of settlement everybody has too much on his hands to find time for it; and Presbyterian, Anglican, Wesleyan, and Jew will all unite in furtherance of the Fancy Fair to build the Catholic Church, which, a few years afterwards, some of them would be almost ready to pull down. Nor is it only in religious matters that these petty bickerings are aroused: municipal and social differences excite the wildest animosity, and politics lend a helping hand, until in some places one half of the township is not on speaking terms with the other half. It is only fair to add that a case of real distress will unite for the nonce all denominations, cliques, and political parties in the cause of charity.

*From "The Bush", O. Sawyer, in* Cassell's Picturesque Australasia, *ed. E. E. Morris*

*Playing cribbage—pegging out (from an illustrated paper, c. 1875)*

# The Glorious Twelfth at Jindabye

Came a horseman to O'Brien's, and his voice was
  stern and high;
"Mick, the Orangemen are mustherin' by scores
  at Jindabye,
And, unless the boys are gathered quick, 'twill be
  a woeful sight,
For there'll be a big procession and there won't
  be any fight."

Mick O'Brien heard the summons as he stood
  beside his gate.
He was six-foot-two in stockings, sixteen stone
  his fighting-weight.
"Pat O'Connor," he said softly, "take a dhrink
  before you go,
And thin ride and rouse the Callaghans—we'll all
  be at the show."

"Saddle up," he cried to Barney, "saddle up the
  black and bay;
Saddle up the white and roan as well—we'll have
  the divil's day!
Missus! Missus, tear yer sheets up fast as iver
  tear yez can;
We'll want bandages this evenin', or I'm not a
  Munstherman."

Then he called unto his stalwart sons: "Get up!
  Get up!" cried he.
"Now, I wonder," said Cornelius, "what the old
  man's game can be?"
But the old man's voice in thunder rose,
  "Remimber, boys, Athlone!
And remimber Byne and Aughrim, and the
  Broken Threaty Shtone!"

Then Cornelius said to Denis, "What in thunder
  does he mean?
We have heard of Boyne and Aughrim; we have
  heard of Skibbereen;
And we know that dear old Ireland of the ocean is
  the gem—
But why, why should we go breaking heads
  because of it or them?"

But their mother spake right scornfully: "And ye
  are sons of mine!
On this day me uncle, Dan O'Toole, would make
  his blackthorn shine.

He would make it shine and quiver at the mintion
  of that river,
And the batin' Billy gave us at the Battle of the
  Byne.

"Och, the Green Flag floated bravely the black
  Orangemin to spite,
And there hardly was a house widout its broken
  head that night,
And me brother, and yer father, boys—he'll tell
  you this is thrue!
Came home shtiff wid blood and glory, as good
  Irishmen should do.

"Holy Pathrick, are ye thraitors? Rise up quickly,
  Con. and Din.!
We were only lonely wimmin, but we had the
  hearts of min:
In ould Ireland, whin the Twelfth came round,
  oh faix, 'twas our delight,
For to bandage up the wounded whin they
  totthered home at night."

Then they rose and put their garments on, did
  Con., and Din., and Mick,
While young Patrick to the kitchen went to
  choose himself a stick.
"Hush!" he whispered to his sister, who was
  weeping in the yard,
"I shall *have* to stoush Bill Leaman, but I will
  not stoush him hard."

Now Bill Leaman and fair Nan O'B. were
  sweethearts on the sly,
And they took no sort of interest in mem'ries of
  July;
They were native-born Australians and had
  vowed their hands to join,
And they didn't care a hairpin for the battle of
  the Boyne.

Barney saddled up like lightning—saddled up the
  black and bay,
Saddled up the white and roan as well, and, oh!
  but he was gay;
For this old and trusty vassal of the bold O'Brien
  clan
As the devil holy water loves did love an
  Orangeman.
  ★    ★    ★

They aroused the red M'Cormacks and the Finns
  of Dooleybuck.
And the Fagans and the Hagans and the Quinns
  of Dam-the-Luck.

And these heroes swiftly sprang to horse without
  a word to say,
For they knew that fun was brewing when
  O'Brien led the way.

Mick O'Brien and Dad Hogan proudly led the
  cavalcade,
And they looked like brigand captains riding
  forth upon a raid;
And for joy of coming ructions, like a backblocks
  Taillefer,
Big M'Cormack threw his stick aloft and caught
  it in the air.

At the township's end they saw a sight madd'ning
  to behold,
All the Orangemen in trappings fine of purple
  and of gold:
There were Lyonses and Leamans there, and
  Nugents and M'Calls,
And they marched along so boldly to the tune of
  "Derry Walls."

Briggs the Sword and Bible carried—Briggs was
  always to the fore—
Sobered up for the occasion, Boozer Scott the
  banner bore,
And old Schnorinbug the Dutchman made the
  trumpet hoot and hum,
While Fat Henderson the butcher pounded
  wildly on the drum.

Mick O'Brien at the circus gazed, and his ire
  commenced to rise,
And the lurid light of war began to kindle in his
  eyes.
Old Dad Hogan, leaning over, whispered hoarse,
  behind his hand—
"Bimme sowl, now, Mick O'Brien, this is more
  than I can shtand!"

But, in spite of all, the day might still have ended
  up in peace,
Without broken heads or instruments, or work
  for the police,
If it hadn't been for Doolan's educated cockatoo
That had been for months in training for the
  Orangemen's shivoo.

On the roof of Doolan's pub, it perched and
  talked in language vile,
And, "To h—ll with old King Billy!" screeched
  in most insulting style.

"Wring its blanky neck!" cried someone, "it's a
  Papist through and through;"
And a rush was made immediately for Doolan's
  cockatoo.

Then O'Brien to Dad Hogan said—"The time to
  charge has come!
I'll lay out the banner-bearer, while you batther
  in the dhrum."
And the forces of O'Brien, that to fight were
  never slow,
With a "Whoop! remember Limerick!" rushed
  fiercely on the foe.

But the foe had seen them coming, and his
  horsemen sat in rank,
Waiting sternly to go through them with a
  counter-charge in flank.
Then the fight became Homeric, and the
  champions of each clan
Came against each other bravely—horse to horse
  and man to man.

Bull-necked Ballantyne the Blacksmith, with a
  visage fierce and grim,
Yelled around for Big M'Cormack; Big
  M'Cormack yelled for *him.*
When they met, the bold M'Cormack, with a
  polthogue mighty fine,
Made a subject for a stretcher of the valiant
  Ballantyne.
Seeing this, then, Hairy Hamilton let out a howl
  for blood,
And he charged upon Tim Fagan, and Tim
  Fagan bit the mud.
Better far for Tim had he been grubbing stumps,
  in quiet way,
On his farm at Dead Cat Gully than in Jindabye
  that day.

Sandy Armstrong, sorely battered, in his saddle
  rocked and reeled,
But he whirled his stick and scattered Cock-eyed
  Hogan on the field.
Cock-eyed Hogan was the proudest of the
  haughty Hogan race,
And they carried him to Doolan's pub, to
  straighten out his face.

But the battle-cries rose wildly, and the fight
  raged fierce and hot,
Like the fight o'er dead Patroclus, o'er the form
  of Boozer Scott—

Mick O'Brien, as he said he would, had lain him
    out all right,
But the Boozer to his banner clung and kicked
    with all his might.

"Boys, they mustn't seize our bannerman," the
    biggest Leaman cried,
And he sprang to ground with flaming eyes, the
    Boozer to bestride;
But the Boozer swore that both sides he would
    prosecute by law;
For Bill Leaman hauled him by the leg, and
    Brady by the jaw.

And the battle for the Boozer might have lasted
    through July
If the boys on either side had *not* got
    synchronously dry;
Big M'Cormack looked at Hamilton, and
    whispered, with a wink,
"If you've had enough of bloodshed, Bill, we'll
    go and have a drink."

When the fight was o'er, the battlefield a man
    might proudly scan,
Who was Irish—whether Papist fierce or furious
    Orangeman,
For there wasn't in the township any person
    to be seen
Who had not some little keepsake-scar from
    Orange side or Green.

In the gutter old Dad Hogan lay and feebly yelled
    for "Rum!"
While Fat Henderson sat weeping o'er the ruins
    of his drum;
But O'Brien into Doolan's stepped with eyes that
    proudly shone,
And a lump upon his forehead you could hang
    your hat upon.

O the night they had at Doolan's—sure its like
    was never seen!
For the Lyonses and Leamans roared "The
    Wearin' of the Green,"
And the Finns, and Quinns, and Fagans sang
    "Boyne Water" without check,
And they called each other "brother," and fell on
    each other's neck.

            ★      ★      ★

Now the moral of this yarn is—if to Jindabye
    you go,
Never aggravate a Lyons, or you'll make a Quinn
    a foe!

Never strike at an O'Brien in your very angriest
    spasm,
Or a Leaman will reduce you to organic
    protoplasm!

There are bonds of blood and marriage now these
    ancient foes between,
And the Orange is inextricably mingled with the
    Green:
And that this broad, kindly feeling should
    increase in coming time
Is the wish for Green and Orange of the writer of
    this rhyme.

*Knocking down his cheque (engraving, after Samuel Calvert, from* Australasian Sketcher, *18 November 1882)*

One day, in August 1958, I think, John Callaghan and myself were recording songs sung by a man down in Brisbane from the Northwest. There was a cold westerly wind blowing outside. We were delighted that we had found such a good source of bush songs; and the man had a tuneful voice and a good memory. He also had a tremendous hangover. He told us he was going back to the bush the following day, having blued his cheque. He always came to Brisbane for the Exhib-ition to blue his cheque. This was the relic of the old custom hallowed by time and use. It began when, back in the days of Governor King, someone said that the colony consisted of "those who sold spirits and those who drank it". The following few extracts and verses are examples of the time out of mind custom of blueing the cheque, though "lambing down" is no longer the open abuse it once was.

# The "Lambing-Down" Shop

*Anon.*

It stands on the bank of a sluggish old creek,
That oft in its running doth stop,
A filthier place you'd not find in a week—
A regular "lambing-down" shop.

It has walls of rough slabs barely shaped with
   an axe,
A veranda for loafers to lie on,
Its carpet consists of some dirty old sacks,
And its roof is of galvanised iron.

Old Grigson sits there in his cane-bottomed chair
And leers with his bleary old eye
At any poor chap that comes into his trap,
As a spider looks after a fly.

In the bar are the poisons he retails as grog.
Which is watched by his wife and his daughter,
The beastly decoctions would sicken a dog.
The only scarce liquor is water.

And Grigson has been an old lag in his time,
And a pretty hot sentence did get;
But if justice don't fail, the walls of a jail
Will hold the old reprobate yet.

By the skin of his teeth he's evaded the law
Many times and, if people don't wrong him,
He still robs the shearers of many a score,
And the police always have an eye on him.

And yet he sits there in his cane-bottomed chair,
A limb that the country should lop,
In his greasy old clothes, with his ruddy old nose,
The boss of a lambing-down shop.

The only time I saw lambing-down in operation was in 1905. When Dutchy and I were waiting for Rockedgiel to start, and with nearly a week to go, we camped with several other shearers near a pub on the Coolah-Gunnedah road. Five men had completed a ringbarking contract on Bomera, and Carson (of Winchcombe Carson) had given each man a cheque for 32 pounds.

At the pub each cheque was presented, but only two were cashed, there not being sufficient money in the house to cash the five. But the cheques were retained by the publican, and the three men were told to order what they wanted, and an account would be kept. A heavy drinking-session went on till midnight, but the next day none of the five put in an appearance. On the second day, when the mail-coach bound for Coolah pulled-up the publican led three shambling wrecks of men out, shoved them in the coach, and said to the driver, "Drop them at Coolah, Bill," and handed him a pound-note. Bill nodded, and drove off, as though it was a common occurrence.

The two men, whose cheques had been cashed had another day, but as the coach was on the return-trip to Gunnedah they were put aboard with instructions to Bill to drop them at Tambar Springs. None of the five had made any protest. The rotgut liquor, and what had been added to it, seemed to have completely robbed them of their manhood. It was the most casual and cold-blooded act I saw in my many years in the bush. One-hundred-and-sixty pounds in three days. It would have bought the pub and all the grog in it.

*From* Time Means Tucker, *Duke Tritton*

# The Big Gun Shearer

*Anon.*

The "Big Gun" toiled, with his heart and soul,
Shearing sheep to make a roll
Out in the backblocks, far away,
Then off to Sydney for a holiday.

Down in the city he's a terrible swell,
Takes a taxi to the Kent Hotel,
The barmaid says, "You do look ill,
It must have been rough tucker, Bill."

In the city he looks a goat
With his Oxford bags and see-more coat,
He spends his money like a fool, of course,
That he worked for like a bloomin' horse.

He shouts for everyone round the place
And goes to Randwick for the big horse race,
He dopes himself with backache pills
And talks of high tallies and tucker bills.

And when it's spent he's sick and sore,
The barmaid's looks are kind no more,
His erstwhile friends don't care a hoot,
He goes back to the bush per what?—Per boot.

Back in Bourke where the flies are bad
He tells of the wonderful times he's had,
He tells of the winners he shouldn't have missed,
And skites of the dozens of girls he's kissed.

He stands on the corner cadging fags,
His shirt tail showing through his Oxford bags,
He'd pawned his beautiful see-more coat,
He's got no money—oh, what a goat!

He's got no tucker and he can't get a booze,
The soles have gone from his snakeskin shoes,
He camps on the bend in the wind and rain
And waits for shearing to start again.

All you blokes with a cheque to spend
Don't go to the city where you've got no friends.
Head for the nearest wayside shack,
It's not so far when you've got to walk back.

*From a* Bill Bowyang Reciter. *I have sung this to the tune of the Canadian folksong, "The Winnipeg Whore". It fits nicely if you repeat the last line of each verse.*

A stranger cannot fail to notice the prodigious number of public-houses in this place, and, judging from general appearances, I fear they are only too well supported, and receive the greater part of the earnings of the lower classes, among whom habits of intemperance are unhappily very prevalent. The advocates of the temperance and tee-total societies have, I believe, effected considerable good, but much more remains to be done. . . .

The universality of this vice is most dreadful to contemplate, and far worse to witness and endure. Almost the only exceptions among the lower classes are the families of English emigrants, who, accustomed to poor living and hard work at home, continue sober and industrious, thankful for the many hitherto unknown comforts and luxuries they can enjoy, and carefully and fearfully abstaining from all excess. Of this class I have known excellent examples, both old and young, male and female, and can only hope that in time their better and wiser course may be appreciated and emulated by other portions of this now numerous population.
population.

*From* Notes and Sketches of New South Wales, during a residence in that Colony from 1839 to 1844, *L. A. Meredith*

*The only time I have heard of shearers getting the better of a publican in a shanty was the yarn Mick Ryan told me in Cooktown about the Lake Eliza Pub in New South Wales. Some shearers came in with cheques, and the publican put them off with the same story mentioned by Duke Tritton and quoted before. They drank for a day and a night, when one of the more sober of the men suggested a race to be run on their pushbikes over a course of ten miles. They were to compete with waterbags and swags up. The publican was to act as starter and judge. They lined up and wobbled into the heat haze, and the publican waited for them to return. He is still waiting, and he found when he gave up and went back into the bar that their cheques had gone with them. Mick later told the story in his book,* Black Man, White Man.

Absit Omen!

# Our Ancient Ruin

*"Crupper D."*

The new-chum leaned against the bar
And tapped his boot and tipped his beer,
Then, looking round, remarked: "Er—ar—
One thing you chaps don't have out here!

"You've churches, chapels, pubs and halls—
Er—er—and such and so-and-so;
But you've no ivied abbey-walls,
No ancient ruins, don-cher-know!"

Then Jack the Shearer left the bar
(It might have been to dodge his shout!)—
They filled 'em up with Dick's three-star,
And scarcely noticed him go out.

He came back, lugging by the hair
Old Ned the Cook, all rags and beer—
"Er—er!" the joker said. "Er—air—
"We've got *one* ancient ruin here!"

# The Rouseabout

*Jim Lawson*

I am the Rouseabout,
the Generally Useful
a social microbe
of no status whatever.
I am the first and last
ambidextrous yes-man.
I swing the axe at roots
of ironbark
reducing them
to kindling.
I groom, milk, and feed the bloody pigs
and stop the dog
from biting the Chinaman.
I clean the knives and polish up
the lawn.
Boots, too,
and stinkin' pans.
Anon
I stand dumbfounded
at reproof
or
meekly contrite,
solemn, looselipped,
excuse myself.
Again,
aeroplanic, seven things at once
"Yessir!" "Yessum!"

when whistled to
abnormally willing
AND obliging,
smiling into the shark jaws
of provocation. . .

But on payday,
(30 bob)
let nobody bark at me.
I'm on me dig,
full of nails
and Triple Star.
King of the dyke,
arguing the point,
looking for lash
until—
the thirty bob
is flown,
vamoosed,
swallowed down,
spewed up,
non est.
Next day at sparrow fart
back on the job,
vigilant,
Argus eyed,
Pro-Bono Publico.
Busy with the sanitary clout,
scrubbing the bar,
emptying slops,
swinging the axe,
shaving the goat,
licking the pot,
Billy the Blot,
Sammy the Slot,
the dog's understudy—
that's me.

Shirt hanging out
8 stone
flyblown
poor bloody rouseabout.

*My brother David, who is a locomotive driver for the Queensland Government Railways sent me this poem which he had copied from another handwritten copy, from Hughenden, about 1960. I have never been able to trace the "Jim Lawson" to whom the poem was ascribed, but I stand in admiration of his talent. If this meets his eye, I would apologize for quoting his poem without permission, and assure him that I did try to find him to ask same. The poem is too good not to quote.*

*Sticking up the Mudgee mail (coloured lithograph, from the Supplement to* Illustrated Sydney News, *June 1874)*

## A Curious Reminiscence

*Alexander Montgomery*

Of all the bloomin' awful things, the awfullest
    I've known
In the five-and-sixty years I've bin alive,
Took place at Paddy Doolan's on the old Jerilda
    road,
'Way back in 'Sixty-four or 'Sixty-five.

Old Doolan had a handy man, a useful sort o'
    chap,
But a real, right-down tiger for his rum;
An', one day, bein' tipsy, why he tumbles from a
    trap,
And cracks his skull, an' goes to kingdom come.

Well, they sends an' tells the trooper, an' the
    trooper rides across,
"An'," says he, "I'll have to let the 'Crowner'
    hear;"
So they stretches out old Jerry in the place he
    used to doss—
A tumbledown old shanty at the rear.

I was trampin' down from Bulga, an' had just run
    out of grub;
Rainin', too, till every rag on me was soaked;
So, you bet, I wasn't sorry to pull-up at Doolan's
    pub
On the evenin' of the day that Jerry croaked.

Well, I'd had my bite o' tucker an' a glass or two
    o' beer
An' was sittin' there a-fillin' of my pipe,
When in comes Mad Macarthy an' Long Jim of
    Bundaleer,
An' my word! but they was well upon the swipe.

Two strappin' big six-footers, an' as strong as
    bullocks, both;
An' ripe for any devilment, as well;
The man that interfered with 'em, you just might
    take your oath,
Stood a pretty lively chance of catchin' hell.

Well, they drank an' laughed an' shouted, an'
    they swaggered an' they swore,
Till Macarthy took a notion in his head

That they'd make old Jerry drunker than he'd
    ever bin before;
"Yez can't do that!" says Doolan—"Jerry's
    dead!"

"Dead drunk, you mean!" says Jimmy. "No,"
    says Doolan, "no begob!
He's as dead as he can be—without a lie!
For he tumbled out of Thompson's trap, right
    fair upon his nob."
Says Macarthy, "Come, old man, that's all my
    eye!"

"Bedad!" says Pat, "Then take a light an' go
    yerselves to see.
Sure he's lyin' in the shed forninst the gate."
So my nobles get a candle an' they tips a wink to
    me,
An' out they goes to see if it was straight.

Well, sir, back they comes directly an' a-laughin'
    fit to split,
And behind 'em Mother Doolan cryin' "Shame!"
And well she might, for there, between the pair
    of 'em, was *it*—
The clay that used to answer Jerry's name.

With its head a-hangin' forward and its legs a-
    draggin' loose,
You can bet it was a dreadful sight to see!
And I started up to stop 'em, but says Doolan,
    "Where's the use?
They could smash a dozen chaps like you
    an' me!"

So they humped their fearsome burden to a
    corner of the bar,
And propped it on a cask agin the wall;
"What will *Jerry* drink?" says Jimmy, and
    Macarthy says, "Three-star!
For we won't be mean with Jerry—damn it all!"

Well, sir, Doolan fills three nobblers, an'
    Macarthy collars one,
And slaps it down before the senseless clay;
Then they bobs their heads to Jerry, an' says
    they, "Old man, here's fun!"
And punishes their liquors right away.

Then 'twas, "Fill 'em up again, Pat—fill 'em
    right up to the brim!"
Till they'd swallered half a dozen drinks a head;
Then Macarthy stares at Jerry's glass, an' then he
    stares at Jim—
"By the Lord!" says he, "old Jerry *must* be dead!

"For it's five-an'-twenty minutes he has had his
    pizen there,
And he's never tried to touch a bloomin' drop!
So you're right for once, old Doolan! Have a
    drink, an' let us square.
For it's nearly gettin' time for us to hop."

So they humped old Jerry back again to where he
    was before—
Mother Doolan still a-scoldin' them in vain;
Then they staggers to their horses that was
    standin' at the door
An' gallops off like madmen through the rain.

# Walks Like This

*G. A. P.*

He was dry as Georgie's poodle and was
    quickly growing worse,
But he didn't hold the boodle—'twas a fact that
    made him curse—
But he was a man of mettle and was not exactly
    dumb,
So he walked into McPherson's bar and
        called
            for
                rum.

So they handed him the bottle and he made that
    rum look queer,
Swigged it off and asked politely: "Is Jim Smith
    a-staying here?—
A peculiar sort of feller but a decent, Jimmy is,
And he's got a gammy left leg and he
        walks
            like
                this."

Then he limped (as his friend Smith did) to the
    door and did a git,
And McPherson, realizing that he hadn't paid his
    bit,
Cursed until the glasses rattled and the beer-
    machine got jammed,
Then he wound up with a homely phrase of:
        "Well,
            I'm
                damned!"

Now, the chap who "had" McPherson thought
   the joke too good to lose,
So he told a friend of his'n, who was dying for a
   booze,
How he'd scored his cheap refreshment—though
   he didn't tell him where—
And that friend he struck McPherson's and he
      called
         for
            beer.

And they drew a quart of swanky—it was in a
   pewter pot—
And he downed it with a single gulp, and said,
   "It's mighty hot!
Is Tommy Brown a-stayin' 'ere? 'E's whiskers on
   his phiz,
An 'e's kind o' wooden-legged and he
      walks
        like
          this."

Then McPherson waxed wrathy, there was
   murder in his gloat
As he leapt him o'er the counter, seized that joker
   by the throat;
And he shouted, "Brown's not staying here, I
   don't know who he is,
But McPherson's pretty handy, and he
     *kicks!*
       *like!!*
         *this!!!"*

*From "Aboriginalities", the* Bulletin

# Humping the Drum

*Anon.*

I humped my drum from Kingdom Come
To the back of the Milky Way,
I boiled my quart on the Cape of York,
And I starved last Christmas Day.

I cast a line on the Condamine
And one on the Nebine Creek;
I've driven through bog, so help me bob,
Up Mungindi's main street;

I crossed the Murray and drank in Cloncurry
Where they charged a bob a nip.
I worked in the Gulf where the cattle they duff,
And the squatters let them rip.

I worked from morn in the fields of corn
Till the sun was out of sight,
I've cause to know the Great Byno,
And the Great Australian Bight.

I danced with Kit, when the lamps were lit,
And Doll, as the dance broke up;
I flung my hat on the myall track
When Bowman won the Cup.

I courted Flo in Jericho,
And Jane at old Blackall,
I said farewell to the Sydney belle
At the doors of the Eulo hall.

I laughed aloud in the merry crowd
In the city of the plains;
I sweated too on Ondooroo
While bogged in the big bore-drains.

I pushed my bike from the shearers' strike
Not wanting a funeral shroud;
I made the weights for the Flying Stakes
And I dodged the lynching crowd.

I've seen and heard upon my word,
Some strange things on my way,
But spare my days, I was knocked sideways
When I landed here today.

One forenoon, about ten o'clock, while we were busy, peacefully digging and puddling, we heard a sound like the rumbling of distant thunder from the direction of Bendigo flat. The thunder grew louder until it became like the bellowing of ten thousand bulls. It was the welcome accorded by the diggers to our "trusty and well-beloved" Government when it came forth on a digger hunt. It was swelled by the roars, and cooeys, and curses of every man above ground and below, in the shafts and drives on the flats, and in the tunnels of the White Hills, from Golden Gully and Sheep's Head, to Job's Gully and Eaglehawk, until the warning that "Joey's out" had reached to the utmost bounds of the goldfield.

*From* The Book of the Bush, *George Dunderdale*

*The first Commissioner Hardy collecting licences, and diggers evading (George Lacy, pen and wash drawing)*

# Catching the Coach

*Alfred T. Chandler*

At Kangaroo Gully in 'Fifty-two
The rush and the scramble was reckless and
 rough;
"Three ounces a dish and the lead running true!"
Was whispered around concerning the stuff.

Next morning a thousand of fellows or more
Appeared for invasion along the brown rise,
Some Yankees, and Cockneys and Cantabs of
 yore
And B.As from Oxford in blue-shirt disguise.

And two mornings later the Nugget saloon,
With billiards and skittles, was glaring with signs,
A blind fiddler, Jim, worried out a weak tune,
Beguiling the boys and collecting the fines.

Then tents started up like the freaks of a dream
While heaps of white pipeclay dotted the slope,
To "Dern her—a duffer!" or "Creme de la
 creme!"
That settled the verdict of languishing hope.

And bustle and jollity rang through the trees
In strange combination of humankind traits;

With feverish searchings and gay levities
The fires of excitement were fully ablaze.

Well, three mornings after, the stringybark gums
All rustled their leaves with further surprise;
They'd seen old stagers and limey new-chums,
But here were galoots in peculiar guise:

With nondescript uniform, booted and spurred,
A fierce-looking strap on the underneath lip,
An ominous shooter, a dangling sword,
A grim leather pouch above the right hip!

And maybe a dozen came cantering so,
All clanking and jaunty—authority vain—
When down through the gully rang out the word
 "Joe",
And "Joe" was sent on with a sneering refrain.

There was hunting for "rights", and producing
 the same,
Or passing them on to a paperless mate,
Or hiding in bushes or down in the claim—
Such various expedients to baffle the State.

Then "Who put him on?"—"Twig his illigant
 seat!"
"Cuss me, but it's purty!"—"The thing on the
 horse!"

323

"His first dacent clothes!"—"What surprise for his
   feet!"
Such volleys as these were soon fired at the
   Force.

But duty was duty. Just then through the scrub
A digger made off—he a culprit no doubt!
"Dismount you then, Wilson!" roared Sergeant
   Hubbub;
"Quick! follow the rascal and ferret him out."

The sapling cadet, with budding moustache,
Then sprang to the ground in dauntless
   pursuit
And, filled up with zeal and a soldier-like dash,
He felt a true hero of saddle and boot.

The gully quick echoed with taunts that were
   real,
Keen chaff of defiance allied to revolt,
Such sharp wordy weapons as might have been
   steel
From skirmishers laughing on hillock and holt.

Away went the fugitive, spurred on by haste,
Escaping the undergrowth, leaping the logs,
Yet ne'er looking back—did he know he was
   chased?
Said Wilson, "He's one of the worst of the dogs!

"Some greater misdeed must have blackened his
   hand;
I'll have him—promotion! Stop there, or I'll
   shoot!"
The other ahead didn't hear the command
But sprang on unheeding o'er dry branch and
   root.

The chase settled down to a heavy set-to;
They ran o'er the hill and across the clear flat;
And Wilson was chuckling—the villain he knew
Was making a bee-line for jail—Ballarat!

"I'll follow the rogue safely into the trap—
Confound him, he's speedy: I can't run him
   down;
But there, quite unconscious of any mishap,
I'll fix him up neatly in gay Canvas Town!"

Then over a creek where a line of sage-gums
All flourishing grew, then away to the right;
Their loud breathings mingled with strange
   forest hums,
And wallabies scampered with terror and fright.

And cockatoos screeched from the loftiest trees,
The minahs and magpies all fluttered and flew,

The drowsy old possums were roused from their
   ease,
The locusts and lizards quick stepped out of
   view.

But on went the pair, never noticing this,
For both had a serious business in hand.
With one there were feelings that prophesied
   bliss,
The other saw capture and glory so grand.

O'er hillside and creek, beyond hollow and spur,
Through brief strips of woodland, they hurried
   on still;
The trooper lost ground, but he wasn't a cur;
Besides, they were nearing on Bakery Hill.

Then suddenly broke on each sweltering sight
The thousand of tents in the city of gold;
And straight to the thick of them ran with delight
The chased and the chaser—what luck for the
   bold!

The coach was just starting for Melbourne that
   day
As Wilson rushed eagerly on to his man.
"I'll put you with care where you won't be so
   gay,"
The trooper in triumph already began.

"You've led me a dance in a lively hour's sun;
Now trip out your licence, or waltz off to jail!
What! got one? Oh, ho! Why the —— did you
   run?"
"To post this here letter for Nell by the mail."


Melbourne, 26 Sept., 1856

Sir,

I have the honor to report that I have this day
sentenced Constable Richard Stewart to 3 days'
imprisonment in Richmond Depot Prison for
being absent from barracks without leave and
found Drunk at 10 minutes past 12 o'clock last
night. As he has upwards of 30 reports against him,
many of them for drunkenness and other serious
offences, I beg respectfully to recommend his
dismissal from the service as he is useless as a
constable.

Signed J.E.F.
Chief Commissioner of Police.

*Quoted in* Police Life (*15 November 1969*)

# A Yarn of Lambing Flat

*Anon.*

"Call that a yarn!" said old Tom Pugh,
"What rot! I'll lay my hat
I'll sling a yarn worth more nor two
Such pumped-up yarns as that,"
And thereupon old Tommy "slew"
A yarn of Lambing Flat.

"When Lambing Flat broke out," he said,
"'Mongst others there I knew
A lanky, orkard, Lunnon-bred
Young chap named Johnnie Drew,
And nicknamed for his love of bed,
The Sleeping Beauty too.

"He sunk a duffer on the Flat
In comp'ny with three more,
And makin' room for this and that
They was a tidy four,
Save when the eldest, Dublin Pat,
Got drunk and raved for gore.

"This Jack at yarnin' licked a book,
And half the night he'd spout,
But when he once turned in, it took
Old Nick to get him out.
And that is how they came to cook
The joke I tell about.

"A duffer-rush broke out one day,
I quite forget where at—
(It doesn't matter, anyway,
It didn't feed a cat)—
And Johnnie's party said they'd say
Good-bye to Lambing Flat.

"Next morn rose Johnnie's mates to pack
And make an early shunt,
But all they could get out of Jack
Was 'All right', or a grunt,
By pourin' water down his back
And—when he turned—his front.

"The billy biled, the tea was made,
They sat and ate their fill,
But Jack, upon his broad back laid,
Snored like a fog-horn still;
'We'll save some tea to scald him,' said
The peaceful Corney Bill.

"As they their beef and damper ate
And swilled their pints of tea
A bully notion all at wonst

Dawned on that rowdy three.
And Dublin Pat, in frantic mirth,
Said, 'Now we'll have a spree!'

"Well, arter that, I'm safe to swear,
The beggars didn't lag,
But packed their togs with haste and care,
And each one made his swag
With Johnnie's moleskins, every pair
Included in the bag.

"With nimble fingers from the pegs
They soon the strings unbent,
And off its frame as sure as eggs
They drew the blessed tent,
And rolled it up and stretched their legs,
And packed the lot—and went.

"And, scarcely p'raps a thing to love,
The 'Beauty' slumbered sound,
With nought but heaven's blue above
And Lambing Flat around,
Until in sight some diggers hove—
Some diggers out'ard bound.

"They sez as twelve o'clock was nigh—
We'll say for sure eleven—
When Johnnie ope'd his right-hand eye
And looked straight up to heaven:
I reckon he got more surprise
Than struck the fabled Seven.

"Clean off his bunk he made a bound,
And when he rubbed his eyes
I'm safe to swear poor Johnnie found
His dander 'gin to rise.
For there were diggers standin' round—
Their missuses likewise.

"Oh, Lor'! the joke—it warn't lost,
Though it did well-nigh tear
The sides of them as came acrost
The flat to hear Jack swear.
They sez as how old Grimshaw tossed
His grey wig in the air.

"Some minutes on the ground Jack lay,
And bore their screamin' jeers,
And every bloke that passed that way
Contributed his sneers;
Jack groaned aloud, that cursèd day
Seemed lengthened into years.

"Then in a fury up he sprung—
A pretty sight, you bet—
And laid about him with his tongue

*' "Hello ! Jem, here's a speck—crikey !" (George Lacy, watercolour)*

Advising us to 'get',
And praying we might all be hung—
I think I hear him yet.

"Then, on a sudden, down he bent,
And grabbed a chunk of rock,
And into Grimshaw's stomach sent
The fossil, with a shock,
And Grimshaw doubled up and went
To pieces with the knock.

"And in the sun that day Jack stood
Clad only in his shirt,
And fired with stones and bits of wood,
And with his tongue threw dirt;
He fought as long as e'er he could—
But very few were hurt.

"He stooped to tear a lump of schist
Out of the clinging soil,
By thunder you should heard him jist,
And seen the way he'd coil
Upon the ground, and hug his fist,
And scratch and dig and toil!

"'Twas very plain he'd stuck it fat,
The dufferin' Lunnon muff:
The scoff and butt of Lambing Flat
Who always got it rough,
Could strike his fortune where he sat;
The joker held the stuff.

"Well, that's the yarn, it ain't so poor:
Them golden days is o'er,
And Dublin Pat was drowned, and sure
It quenched his thirst for gore;
Old Corney Bill and Dave the Cure
I never heard on more.

"The Sleepin' Beauty's wealthy, too,
And wears a shiny hat,
But often comes to old Tom Pugh
To have a quiet chat;
I lent him pants to get him through
His fix on Lambing Flat."

*The Lambing Flat goldfield (which later became the town of Young) was famous in its time for the lawlessness of its inhabitants, not so much the diggers as the inevitable hangers-on who came for the pickings. Thievery and brutality were commonplace events, and one part of the camp rejoiced in the name of Blackguard Gully! The bushranger Darky Gardiner ran a butcher's shop there for a time, no doubt obtaining the raw materials for his business from among his cattle-duffing friends. The most notorious of the anti-Chinese riots in Australia took place there in 1861. Many Chinese were murdered, some were scalped, and I have read of diggers who wore the scalp with pigtail attached as a belt for years after the riot. After the Palmer rush in Queensland, most of the Chinese returned to China, but some lingered on, working mainly as cooks on station properties, though some worked as station hands and shearers. Some achieved local fame, as did Quong Tart in Sydney and the redoubtable publican Jimmy Ah Foo, of Longreach. Of Jimmy Ah Foo, it is related that on one occasion when the shearers' union decided to ask all publicans and boardinghouse keepers to sack their Chinese cooks and replace them with white men, Jimmy replied, "All li, boys. I go now sack-um blully Chinee cook. Sposen I no gettum white man cook I go longa kitsin, cookum dinner me blully self." It used to be said that you were nobody in Queensland unless you knew the Eulo Queen, Jacky Howe the gun shearer, and Jimmy Ah Foo. See* Roll the Summers Back *by Joseph Porter for some stories of this famous trio.*

# The Sheep Station

*Alexander Forbes*

(Air—"Young Man from the Country")

Now friends if you'll attention pay
And list to what I state
I'm certain you will pity feel
For my unhappy fate;
For here I am in Queensland's bush,
An awful sight to see,
And a Mandarin from China
To keep company with me.

My humpy from its looks was built
Soon after Noah's ark,
Roof, sides, and gable all composed
Of rotten sheets of bark.
On rainy days the heavy wet
Comes pouring down quite free
On the Mandarin from China,
But alas likewise on me.

Ye gods! to think that one whose sires
At Bannockburn have bled
Must now associate with a man
In China born and bred.
From the brave old "land of cakes" I hail,
While from the realms of tea
Comes the Mandarin from China
That keeps company with me.

In shape his lovely frontispiece
Resembles much the moon,
His mouth is like the Cove of Cork,
His nose is like a spoon.
A liver-coloured, whitey-brown,
Magenta skin has he,
This Mandarin from China
That keeps company with me.

His lingo is most horrible,
To listen gives much pain;
So I have a code of signals framed
His meaning to explain.
My English puzzles him no doubt,
God knows, his puzzles me,
Which makes this man from China
Most indifferent company.

The place of his nativity
I'm sure I cannot tell;
'Tis no great loss, for if I knew,
Its name I could not spell.
Some crackjaw words, you may depend,
Are in the pedigree
Of the Mandarin from China
That keeps company with me.

But still he has some first-rate points,
As who on earth has not;
Celestial is the way he works
The frying-pan and pot.
A splendid feed can be produced
While you'd be counting three
By the Mandarin from China
That keeps company with me.

To fetch up wood and water too
He never will refuse,
But, yet, if I could have my way,
Another mate I'd choose;
With whom, I feel quite confident,
I better could agree
Than with the Mandarin from China
That keeps company with me.

*From* Voices from the Bush, *Alexander Forbes*

*The Palmer River goldfield in North Queensland almost certainly had the biggest concentration of Chinese diggers ever to assemble at one time in Australia. No one ever worked out how many Chinese were on the field, for it was rumoured that for every one who entered legally through the port at Cooktown at least as many came overland from the deserted beaches of the Gulf where they were met by their compatriots and guided to the field overland. The Chinese seem to have been industrious, frugal, honest and to have kept very much to themselves. Those who remained in this country have made good citizens. I know of only one Chinese bushranger, for instance, and he was a failure at his profession. Apart from the widely held myth of European intellectual superiority over coloured races, and the fear that they would be deprived of employment by the immigrant who was prepared to work harder and for longer hours for less money, I can find little reason for the violence and trouble they encountered wherever they went. An old mate of mine, Bill Harris of Innisfail, once rode from the Mitchell River to Cooktown, leading a packhorse and living off the country, and he said he found many relics, pottery fragments, stone jars and brass opium tins in caves in some of the remote gorges of the Palmer. There could not have been many on Bendigo diggings when Thatcher wrote the following poem, though they arrived there in strength later. It would have been too good an opportunity for him to have missed listing the typical coolie hat in the song if it had been around at the time. Or perhaps popular opinion forbade mention of what newspapers often described as "the Mongol hordes" in a song meant to be popular with white diggers.*

*Ballarat Flat, from the Black Hill (engraving from* Victoria Illustrated, *S. T. Gill)*

# Coming Down the Flat

*Charles R. Thatcher*

If a body meet a body
Coming down the flat,
Should a body "Joe" a body
For having on a hat?
Some wear caps, some wide-awakes,
But I prefer a hat—
Yet everybody cries out"Joe",
Coming down the flat.

The squatter loves his cabbage-tree,
With streamers hanging down—
He wears it always in the bush,
And even when in town:
The cabbage-tree may be his choice,
But I prefer a hat—
Yet everybody cries out"Joe",
Coming down the flat.

The digger wears a wide-awake,
Wherever he may go—
At the windlass, when washing up,
And also down below.
The wide-awake may suit him well,
But I prefer a hat—
Yet everybody cries out "Joe",
Coming down the flat.

The peeler has a leather cap,
About two pounds in weight;
In pelting rain or broiling sun,
To wear it is his fate.
The leather cap won't do for me,
But I prefer a hat—
Yet everybody cries out "Joe",
Coming down the flat.

*"The Inimitable Thatcher" was an entertainer and prolific versifier who provided entertainment in hotels and places of entertainment on the Victorian diggings. He wrote many parodies and topical songs set to popular tunes of the time. The State Library of South Australia published a facsimile edition of many of Thatcher's songs in the 1960s, and the book may still be available from that source.*

*Thatcher, an unsuccessful digger who turned entertainer to make a living, was enormously popular and also an aggressive performer (on at least one occasion he leapt off the stage and beat up an interjector in the audience). He followed the diggers to the new rushes in the South Island of New Zealand, and eventually retired to England.*

# The Broken-Down Digger

*Anon.*

I've worked on the Nine-Mile, likewise on
  the River,
And out at the New-Chum, and Rocky Plains
  too;
At each of those places I did my endeavour,
But I've lately struck "duffers", with nothing in
  view;
And just now I'm longing to see the old places,
I'm longing to visit old Sydney again—
For I'm "full" of the Snowy's white hills and
  wild graces;
I'm a broken-down digger on Kiandra plain.

*Fragment of an "old song" in Charles MacAlister's* Old Pioneering
Days in the Sunny South

*A good, if sometimes fanciful, account of the Snowy Mountains diggings can be found in* Reminiscences of the Goldfields and Elsewhere in New South Wales *by Martin Brennan.*

*The invalid digger (from* Sketches of the Victoria Gold Diggings and Diggers As They Are [1852–53], *S. T. Gill)*

*Men, women and children on their way to the diggings (hand-coloured lithograph, on linen)*

# The Golden Gullies of the Palmer

*Anon.*

(Air—"Marching Through Georgia")

Then roll the swag and blanket up,
And let us haste away
To the Golden Palmer, boys,
Where everyone, they say,
Can get his ounce of gold, or
It may be more, a day,
In the Golden Gullies of the Palmer.

*Chorus*
Hurrah! We'll sound the jubilee.
Hurrah! Hurrah! And we will merry be,
When we reach the diggings, boys,
There the nuggets see,
In the Golden Gullies of the Palmer.

Kick at troubles when they come, boys,
The motto be for all;
And if you've missed the ladder
In climbing Fortune's wall,
Depend upon it, boys,
You'll recover from the fall,
In the Golden Gullies of the Palmer.

Then sound the chorus once again
And give it with a roar,
And let its echoes ring, boys,
Upon the sea and shore,
Until it reach the mountains,
Where gold is in galore,
In the Golden Gullies of the Palmer.

*Collected by Russel Ward from* Colonial Born, *G. Firth Scott. See also "The Old Palmer Song", Section II.*

# The Palmer Days

*Anon.*

The Palmer Days! To-night I camp beside a
  singing stream,
The fire casts a glowing light, and bright the red
  coals gleam,
And as the long night wanes apace I smoke away
  and dream.

The goldfields of the North! Upon them now the
  cattle graze,
The goldfields of the North! Ah, world-wide was
  their praise,
And who'll forget who ever knew the wondrous
  Palmer Days?

I see the ghosts of dead men pass who never
  knew the fears
Of wild and savage blacks who lay with nullas
  and with spears—
'Tis they who hold the foremost place, our
  Northern pioneers.

I see the diggers as they go, with dreams of
  wealth untold,
From every nation of the earth, from new lands
  and from old;
And the light that leads them, it is the wonder
  lure of gold.

I watch the pack teams pass, a score of horses in a
  line,
Their packs are filled with stores for men at many
  a mine,
They go to Maytown on the Palmer, where
  golden ingots shine.

The yellow hordes from China, in thousands they
  were there,
They follow where the white men lead, and
  where the white men dare,
And on the rich alluvial flats they steal the white
  man's share.

The police upon the Palmer road who knew the
  heat and damp,
I see their bright caps all agleam, I hear the
  horses tramp,
They fought the wild blacks side by side at far-
  famed Battle Camp.

The lights and life of Cooktown! All day and all
  night long

The gold dust flows o'er hotel bars where many
  miners throng,
And music halls are all aglow with laughter and
  with song.

I camp beside the Palmer road where poinciannas
  bloom and sway,
I see the spots where townships stood, and where
  all is bare today.
And gone is Maytown's glory, and Cooktown's
  fame has passed away.

# Far Cooktown

*Anon.*

Things are quiet in far Cooktown,
The days are dull and cold.
The festive goat has ceased to skip
Upon the mountains bold.

The Chinamen who run the show
Are tired, broke and weak.
The pub has got its shutters up.
The barmaid's in the creek.

No more the rich sweet scent of rum
Will roll across the plain;
For cash is gone and tick is done.
The red blind glares in vain.

A busy city by the sea
Has sunk and settled down.
A goat, two chinkies and a dog
Now own the bloody town.

# A Cry from the North

*Anon.*

'Neath a ragged banana a Northerner sat,
A-twisting the leaf of his cabbage-tree hat,
And trying to lighten his mind of a load
By reciting the lines of the following ode:

Oh, for a skipper and oh, for a ship,
Oh, for a cargo of niggers each trip,
Oh, for a shot at old Griffith and Brookes,
Oh, for a crack at those Liberal rooks.

Oh, that each man was as hard up as me,
Oh, that I'd money to go on the spree,
Oh, for the sugar to rig up a still,
Oh, that the storekeeper burnt his d——d bill.

Oh, that I'd water enough in the tanks,
Oh, that my credit was good at the banks—

And so he went oh-ing for what he had not,
Not contented with owing for all he had got.

*From* The Native Companion Songster

# The Wallaby Track

*E. J. Overbury*

You may talk of your mighty exploring—
Of Landsborough, McKinlay, and King;
But I feel I should only be boring,
On such frivolous subjects to sing.
For discovering mountains and rivers
There's one, for a gallon I'd back,
Who'll beat all your Stuarts to shivers;
It's the man on the Wallaby Track.

With a ragged old swag on his shoulder,
And a billy or pot in his hand,
'Twould astonish the new-chum beholder
To see how he'll traverse the land.
From Billabone, Murray, or Loddon,
To the far Tatiara and back,
The mountains and the plains are well trodden
By the man on the Wallaby Track.

*On the wallaby race (lithograph by J. A. Commins, reproduced from a contemporary postcard)*

When spring-time brings on the sheep-shearing,
'Tis then you will find them in droves,
For the West Country stations all steering,
Demanding a job from the "coves".
Should they fail in obtaining employment,
For grub they take care not to lack;
For cadging's a source of enjoyment
To the men on the Wallaby Track.

In the daytime they make themselves jolly,
And laze in the shade out of sight;
For they know 'twould be nothing but folly
To make any station till night.
But when the sun sets they'll be dodging
All up to the hut in a crack,
To secure a good supper and lodging
And not starve on the Wallaby Track.

There are many who don't care a button
As long as they're sure of a feed;
They believe in good damper and mutton,
But hard work is not in their creed.
There are others who stick during shearing,
Then shoulder their swags on their back;
For the rest of the year they'll be steering
On their well-beloved Wallaby Track.

But the most are both able and willing
To work when they can for their cash;
And then they will spend every shilling,
Delighting in making a dash.
For a day or two nothing can equal
Their joy in absorbing hard tack;
But I fear you will find in the sequel
They're again on the Wallaby Track.

There are many who'll stick to the stations,
But with sovereign contempt will refuse—
Though they get better wages and rations—
To work for the poor "cockatoos".
But still, when the harvest is ready,
There are hundreds to reap, mow, or stack;
For a month or two keeping quite steady,
Forgetting the Wallaby Track.

But, alas! you can prophesy plainly
That, directly they come to this town,
Our landlords, with "Mather" and "Ainley",
Will soon lamb the poor fellows down.
And, while the strong liquor is flowing,
They don't seem to care for the sack;
There's no end to their bouncing and blowing
When off on the Wallaby Track.

*From* Bush Poems, *E. J. Overbury*

*Part of the preceding poem seems to have become a widely known bush song, picking up a fine tune in the process. That version is included in Section II, page 193 of this book. The poem following was written during the Kanaka days in Queensland, when South Sea Islanders were recruited for work on properties in this State. For historical background on the local slave trade, see* Cannibal Cargoes *by Hector Holthouse, and also the contemporary* A Cruize in a Queensland Labour Vessel to the South Seas, *by W. E. Giles, reproduced in 1968 by the Australian National University Press.*

*The reaction of the "old hands" to the young Londoner seems to have been typical of the established Australian of this time to the newchum. See the note on "How the Sailor Rode the Brumby", in this section.*

*Diggers en route to deposit gold (from* Sketches of the Victoria Gold Diggings and Diggers As They Are [1852–53], *S. T. Gill)*

# The Sugar Plantation

*Anon.*

A gay young spark of a London clerk
Got tired of his station;
He heard of a billet, and he thought he could
   fill it
As boss of a sugar plantation.
Thought he it will be a continual spree,
No need to be worried with figures,
I'll dress all in white, and swell round at night,
And do nothing but wallop the niggers.

*Chorus*
Sing hey, for the life of a planter so gay,
The finest old game in the nation;
While rum makes us jolly and children suck lolly,
We'll back up the sugar plantation.

To the planters he came in pursuit of his aim,
But when they found what he wanted to do
They told him to go—to a warm place below—
For an impudent young jackeroo.
Oh, sorely he sighed, and bitterly cried,
When he found that no one would employ him;
The old hands, too, did seek to cure what they
   called "cheek",
Every means they could find to annoy him.

*Chorus*
Sing hey, for the life of a planter so gay,
The finest old game in the nation,
But a cockney is lost, as he'd find to his cost,
On a Bundaberg sugar plantation.

And oh, in the night the mosquitoes did bite,
Till often he muttered, "Tarnation!"
They peppered him well, and his features did
   swell,
Till he cursed every sugar plantation.
So, thinks he, I'll go home, and never more roam,
But stick to my desk and my figures;
And Queensland so hot may for me go to pot
With its old hands, mosquitoes and niggers.

*Chorus*
Sing hey, for the life of a planter so gay,
The finest old game in the nation,
But I'd rather live plain down in Petticoat Lane
Than be boss of a sugar plantation.

*From* The Native Companion Songster

# The Last of the Hand Cutters

*Bill Scott*

In the lounge at the White Horse one Saturday
   night
There were lavender bugs round the overhead
   light.
The rain belted down on the pavement outside
When an old drunk climbed up on a table and
   cried—

"Farewell to the days of the file and the knife
And the wandering canecutter's trouble-filled
   life.
Farewell to the Guns and the Saturday sprees
When the gang was eight men and the cook was
   Chinese.

"I've cut down at Childers where the cockys are
   mean,
They grizzle and moan if you don't top it clean.
I've sweated at Bingera through the hot days
For plantation bosses with tabletop drays.

"I've cut out at Marion, cursing my lot,
In Q. 44 that was tied in a knot;
But the worst place of all was at Condong,
   my boys,
For a fat cane inspector, all bullshit and noise.

"I've spent the slack seasons at ringing out West,
And I swear for big tallies the North is the best,
For from Ingham to Mossman as everyone knows
Are the best little towns where the sugarcane
   grows.

"Now the old days are gone with the good times
   we've seen
For the cutters are stuffed by this harvest
   machine
That thrashes along through the furrows and ruts
In a cloud of blown trash with hot gas in its guts.

"Now there's nothin much left for a cutter
   like me
But the pension and just the occasional spree!"
Then he fell from the table and flat on the floor
When a cocky there present let out this loud
   roar—

"Oh die, you old bastard and stop your
   complaining!"
So he snuffed it. Outside the rain just kept on
   raining.

Next morning at dawn when the sky was pale
   grey,
A harvester clanked in and took him away.

*This may be sung to the tune "Villikens and his
Dinah" if the following chorus is added after each
verse:*
   *Dinky-die, dinky-die,*
     *for I'm an old cutter and I can't tell a lie.*

# To the Gulf

*George Carrington*

(Air—"To the West, to the West")

To gulf, to the gulf, to Australia's fag-end,
Where all kinds of misery walk hand in hand,
Where a man is soon *done*, if he's willing to broil,
And the strongest soon finds himself under the
   soil;
Where the squatters are rapidly going to pot,
And the men are all dying like sheep of the rot.
When I'm tired of existence, my steps I will bend
To that "fair land of promise", Australia's
   fag-end.

To the gulf, to the gulf, to that blissful retreat,
Where roguery stalks *coolly* abroad in the heat;
Where a cheque is a cheque, if you live
   till it's got,
But the chance is a hundred to one, that
   you'll not;
For, unless you can live in a swamp like a frog,
You may reckon on dying the death of a dog;
Then if you are foolish, your steps you will bend
To that fair land of promise, Australia's fag-end.

To the gulf, to the gulf, to the land of the flies,
Where each insect tormentor for mastery vies
Which shall plague you the most, in the terrible
   heat;
The gulf is most truly a blissful retreat.
Carpentaria! high wages have no charms for me
In an atmosphere pregnant with death on the
   spree.
When I've no other refuge my steps I will bend
To that gulf full of horrors, Australia's fag-end.

*Collected by Russel Ward from* Colonial Adventures and
Experiences, *by a University Man (George Carrington, of Oxford).
The original song was well known:*

*Unlucky digger that never returned (from* Sketches of the
Victoria Gold Diggings and Diggers As They Are [1852–53],
*S. T. Gill)*

. . . the concerts, were thoroughly enjoyed, in-
cluding Henry Russell's rollicking sea songs,
"Cheer, Boys, Cheer," "A Life on the Ocean
Wave," etc. The favourite of all was:—

"To the West, to the West, to the land of the
   free,
Where the Mighty Missouri rolls down to the
   sea,
Where a man is a man, if he's willing to toil,
And the humblest may gather the fruits of the
   soil.
To the West, to the West, where the rivers that
   flow
Runs thousands of miles, spreading out as they
   go,
Where the young may exalt, and the aged may
   rest,
Away, far away, to the land of the West."

*From* History and Adventures of a Queensland Pioneer, *E. J.
Foreman*

*Scene of Gilbert's death (engraving from* Illustrated Melbourne Post, *24 June 1865)*

# The Daly River-Oh!

*Jim Burgoyne*

Now come all ye sports who want a bit of fun,
Roll up your swags and pack up a gun;
Get a bit of flour, sugar and tea,
And don't forget a gallon of Gordon's O.P.,
Crank up your Lizzie and come along with me
And I'll show you such sights as you never did
    see
Down on the Daly River-oh!

*Chorus*
There was Wallaby George and Charlie Dargie,
Old Skinny Davis and Jimmy Panquee,
Big-mouthed Charlie and old Paree,
The Tipperary Pong and Jim Wilkie;
And where'er you may roam
You will find yourself at home,
They are noted for their hospitality.

You are wakened in the morn and your heart's
    filled with glee
By a little dark maid with a pannikin of tea,
And she'll give you such a welcome, you won't
    wish to go
Away from the Daly River-oh!

I saw a buffalo and a fat Chinee
Run a dead heat to the foot of a tree;
The Chinaman flew, he didn't feel the ruts,
But the buffalo stopped with a bullet in the guts.
As the wild birds rose at the sound of the gun
The water dropped a foot in the silver billabong;
With geese, ducks and feathers, you couldn't see
    the sun
Down by the Daly River-oh!

While the buffalo kicked we poured in the lead,
We killed him ten times to make sure he was
    dead;
We drew out our knives and we all hopped in—
Three whites, two Chows, four bucks and a gin.

We tore off his hide and ripped him up the guts,
Took his little tit-bits, his fancy funny cuts.
Then we cranked up the Lizzie and we shouted
    "Right-oh!"
All aboard for the Daly River-oh!

Now I saw a nigger sitting in an old gum-tree,
The crows had picked his eyes out, so he couldn't
    see,
Never and never a word spoke he
For he was as dead as dead could be.
He was just about ripe and the smell was high,
Like a billabong of fish when the water goes dry,
When Dargie drew a gibber that hit him in the
    mush,
And the dead went "Phoosh" and we all went
    bush,
Down by the Daly River-oh!

*The late Bill Harney included this poem in one of his
first books,* North of 23°. *He sent a copy of the poem
to Douglas Stewart and Nancy Keesing for inclusion
in their fine book,* Australian Bush Ballads. *Bill is
buried under a gum tree he selected himself about a
week before he died, in the tiny graveyard on the
eastern slope of Buderim Mountain, overlooking
Maroochydore and Mooloolaba. I went to his funeral,
for I knew him, and have a great respect for his
writing and also had a fondness for the man himself.
His headstone is a simple one, showing an open book
with the words "Bill Harney, Author" as the
inscription.*

# Mick Dooley's Pants

*George Essex Evans*

They brought a boy from Tallaran to run Mick
    Dooley's tracks;
They yarded him the fastest blood among the
    station cracks;
With moles and shirt and sloucher hat and pipe
    with broken stem,
He slung into the saddle straight and waved his
    hand to them.

The Sub. was lately out from "'Ome", the
    troopers both were green,
The tracking of an outlaw was a game they had
    not seen;
This chippy little nigger and the antics that
    he played—
They were rolling off their saddles at the funny
    sight he made!

The tracker had a roving eye, he laughed a saucy
    laugh;
He grinned as they were grinning, and he gave
    them chaff for chaff;
The troopers both were solid men whose brains
    had run to beef,
But when the boy got moving all their mirth was
    turned to grief.

He was cautious 'mong the melon-holes, but
    where the plain was sound
He led 'em at a gallop with his eyes upon the
    ground;
And as odds are on a thoroughbred against a
    trooper's hacks
They were somewhat disconcerted at this mode
    of running tracks.

He took 'em down the Flinders where the spear-
    grass lined the brink,
Then crossed a stage of forty miles—without a
    drop to drink,
And down the beds of dried-up creeks they
    wandered all day long
Till life seemed, in a trooper's view, one endless
    billabong.

Then turned he sharply to the west—the blue
    McKinlay Range,
And gave them joys of spinifex, in case they
    wished a change;

337

And up and down the stony hills they tracked the
guilty Mick,
Except when they required a rest to be a little
sick.

They hauled their horses after them when hills
were tough and high,
And still the Sub. remarked, "Bai Jove!"—his
eyeglass in his eye;
And still the blackboy pointed to the tracks which
he had seen,
Until they fairly bottomed—they had struck a
blind ravine!

Then one sharp-eyed suffering trooper gave a
grunt of savage joy,
And called aloud unto the Sub. and pointed to
the boy:
"The name upon them trousers! sure as God
made little ants—
Look, sir, this imp of Satan wears a pair of
Dooley's pants!"

Like thought the tracker wheeled his mount and
vanished from their sight,
But as he thundered down the gorge he yelled
with all his might:
"Mick Dooley's crossed the Border now—no run
dat feller in—
Next time you want-um tracker, boss—don't get
Mick Dooley's gin!"

*Fred Ward, or Captain Thunderbolt, was the most
successful of all the New South Wales bushrangers, in
terms of time spent on the rampage. He repays
investigation by anyone interested in the bushranger
as hero. He was, for instance, one of the few men to
escape from Cockatoo Island gaol in Sydney Harbour, and he was free in the bush for some six years
before being killed by Trooper Walker. He had a great
many sympathizers in the New England area and had
the reputation of being a gentleman in the best sense of
the word. Judith Wright wrote a book for children
called* Range the Mountains High *based on a
reported incident in his career. His grave is in the
Uralla cemetery, and is well cared for. Annie Rixon
wrote* Captain Thunderbolt, *but it was privately
printed and I have seen only one copy. The author was
sympathetic to the bushranger, and seeks to prove that
he was not Fred Ward at all. I have tried to trace her,
but in vain. The book is still in my possession.*

# A Day's Ride

*Anon.*

Bold are the mounted robbers who on stolen
horses ride
And bold the mounted troopers who patrol the
Sydney side;
But few of them though flash they be, can ride,
and few can fight
As Walker did, for life and death, with Ward the
other night.

It seems the troopers heard that Ward,
well known as Thunderbolt,
An outlawed thief, was down near Blanche to
try a fresh-roped colt.
(Not far from Armidale, that spot for brilliants so
renowned—
Although the talked-of diamonds now are seldom
found.)

Said Alick Walker as he clapped his saddle
on his steed,
"If I catch sight of Ward today I'll try his
horse's speed;
Up hill or down, 'tis all the same, I know my nag
can stay"—
Then got his arms, and galloped off, all ready for
the fray.

Soon as he got near Thunderbolt, the first salute
he got
From that retreating party was a random
pistol-shot;
The robber fled, the trooper went in chase, his
spirits rose—
When Ward advised him to keep off, he
answered, "Bosh, here goes!"

As through the scrubby bush they sped, and
timber-tangled brake,
Both held their horses well in hand, nor made the
least mistake;
Easing his horse with judgment then, the light-
weight trooper raced—
Good jockey as the robber was, he found himself
outpaced.

Mile after mile, rough ground and smooth, up
hill and down the vale,
Steep rocky tracks they galloped o'er—Ward's
horse began to fail.

*Portrait of Frederick Ward, alias Thunderbolt (engraving from an early illustrated paper)*

Scant time he had for firing, for whenever he looked back
Onward his adversary pressed, fast nearing on his track.

On to a creek pursuer and pursued still headed straight:
One hastening to avenge the law, his foe to meet his fate.
Ward, almost hopeless of escape, devised a desperate scheme—
Dismounting from his horse he swam the wide and rapid stream.

Cried Walker, "May my mother's son for ever be accursed
If now I fail to take him, but I'll stop his gallop first."
His pistol flashed, the stockhorse fell; cut off from all retreat
At bay the reckless outlaw stood, defiant in defeat.

"I'll not surrender," was his cry; "before I do, I'll die!"
"All right," his brave opponent said, "now for it, you or I!"

A moment's pause—a parley now—the trooper made a push
To grapple at close quarters with the ranger of the bush.

A shot—a blow—a struggle wild—the outlaw with a shriek
Relaxed his hold, and sank beneath the waters of the creek.
'Twas thus the dreaded robber's evil spirit passed away,
Vanquished by brave young Walker, now the hero of the day.

Henceforth those loafing swagmen who around the stations coil,
Exchanging lies at night until they see the billies boil,
At lambing-down or shearing-time will tell with bated breath
Of Walker's fight with Thunderbolt, that ride for life and death.

*The capture of Thunderbolt near Uralla by Constable Walker (engraving from* Illustrated Sydney News, *8 June 1870)*

# The Fierce and Bloody Battle of the Weddin Mountains

*"Damphool Jnr"*

Nine valiant men of New South Wales all armèd
  to the teeth
Went forth to take one Gardiner, of bushrangers
  the chief;
And then Sir Frederick he did say, "Your reign
  will now be brief;
For all the fearful deeds you've done, your neck
  will come to grief!
Ho, yes," he said, "fierce Gardiner, your neck
  will come to grief."

Sir Frederick then and his nine men, set out one
  winter night
Towards the Weddin Mountains, as the moon
  was shining bright,
And how the jackasses did laugh upon the
  branches' height—
To see nine valiant cavaliers they thought a
  goodly sight!
And all to take one Gardiner they thought a
  goodly sight.

'Twas said in town, one Mrs Brown had got
  a house of call,
A little snug and quiet spot beneath a gum-tree
  tall;
A stable for his prancing grey behind the cottage
  wall,
And for himself a supper nice, the cosy bed
  and all—
"It pleasant is," quoth Gardiner, "the cosy bed
  and all."

Now of Sir Frederick's fighting men, two stood
  behind the pump,
And three bobbed down their valiant heads
  just hidden by a stump;
The others were placed in the rear to hit his
  horse's rump,
And then bold Pottinger did say: "His life's not
  worth a dump."
So thought the laughing jackasses, his life's not
  worth a dump.

And sure up rode bold Gardiner upon his
  prancing grey,
And then up jumped bold Pottinger, and said,
  "My friend, good day,

I've got nine valiant men at arms yourself to take
  away,
And to the gallows we will bear you, gallows-bird
  away."
"Ho, will you so?" says Gardiner, "I wish you
  then good day."

As Gardiner was trotting off, Sir Frederick took
  his gun,
And still he thought that Gardiner was poking of
  his fun,
From him and his nine valiant men, to think that
  he could run;
So taking aim at Gardiner he said, "My friend
  you're done,"
And all the laughing jackasses they thought that
  he was done.

And then instead of a report there only was a
  snick;
Said he, "Who loaded that there gun did do a
  scurvy trick."
But at the sight of Gardiner the valiant men
  turned sick,
While Gardiner he laughed aloud, and rode off
  like a brick,
And all the laughing jackasses they said he was a
  brick.

Sir Frederick then harangued his men, and said
  each scurvy knave
Should have the sack when he got back who
  could so bad behave;
So very careful were they all, their precious souls
  to save.
And then they took a little boy, they were so very
  brave,
Not one that day did run away! they were so very
  brave!

The military are ordered out, and troopers too,
  'tis said,
Commanded by one Hamilton, Sir Frederick
  instead;
Tremendous Black will show the track, who fills
  us all with dread;
And each for Gardiner's charmèd life will carry
  charmèd lead,
Cast at the solemn midnight hour when good
  folks are abed.

*Frank Gardiner was the natural born son of a Scottish migrant named Christie, and was christened Frank Christie. He was born near Goulburn. His mother was part Aboriginal, part Irish, and worked as a servant. He took to the bush early in his life, assumed the name of Gardiner, and was wanted for cattle and horse stealing while still in his teens. He must have had remarkable powers of leadership, for he was boss of a gang of duffers in the western district of Victoria before he was twenty. Arrested in 1850, he was sentenced to five years in gaol. He escaped after only five weeks. He later was caught and sent to Cockatoo Island gaol in Sydney. He served this sentence, making one unsuccessful bid to escape. In 1860 he set up the butchering business at Lambing Flat mentioned previously in these notes, which he closed in 1861. His was the first gang in Australia to rob a gold escort successfully. This took place at Eugowra Rocks, and later was the subject of a famous painting by Tom Roberts.*

*The story told in this ballad is essentially true. He was having an affair with a Mrs Kitty Brown of Wheogo. Sir Frederick Pottinger, in charge of police in the Lachlan district, tried to set an ambush to capture him during one of his visits to his paramour, taking with him a Sergeant and seven troopers. Pottinger actually tried to shoot Gardiner as he rode off, and his gun misfired. His report of the incident follows.*

"Being aware that Frank Gardiner, the bushranger, was enamoured of Mrs. Brown . . . and believing that he would take advantage of her husband's absence to tender his addresses, I proceeded on Saturday with eight men to the premises; I arrived at 12 p.m., and leaving four of the men in charge I went with Senior-Sergeant Sanderson and Trooper Holster to watch the place; I subsequently sent Sub-Inspector Norton and Trooper Holster to guard the front while Senior-Sergeant Sanderson and I hid ourselves in the bush. We discovered the house dark and silent as though everybody was asleep; after about half an hour we saw a light struck and in a few minutes a woman made her appearance and commenced to collect wood for the purpose of making a fire, but neither Sergeant Sanderson nor I could identify the woman, as we were concealed at a distance of 150 yards from where she was standing, in a thick pine-tree scrub; it might be 20 to 25 minutes after my seeing the woman that I observed a man mounted on a white horse approaching Brown's house at a quiet pace, upon which I called upon Sanderson to fall back, and we did so to our original position; suddenly the noise of the horse's hoofs sounded nearer and nearer, when I saw Gardiner cantering leisurely along; I waited until he came within five yards of me, and levelling my carbine at him across his horse's shoulder (the weapon, I swear, being about three yards from his body), I called upon him to stand; I cannot be mistaken, and on my oath I declare that the man was Frank Gardiner; deeming it not advisable to lose a chance I prepared to shoot him, but the cap of my piece missed fire; Gardiner's horse then began to rear and plunge, and before I had time to adjust my gun, he had bolted into the bush; as Gardiner was riding away on the back of the frightened animal, Sergeant Sanderson fired at him, as also did Holster; I called out to those who could hear me to 'shoot the wretch.' Gardiner, however, made his escape.

"We then proceeded to Mrs. Brown's house, and having seen her she frankly admitted that Gardiner had been at her place. I saw a bed made upon the sofa, and a four-post bedstead with a bed upon it in which two persons had been reposing; the boy Walsh was in it asleep and he declared that he had heard no noise and did not know what had happened; he had lodgings at his mother's and was not obliged to sleep where he was found; I immediately arrested him.

"On the table in the kitchen I saw the debris of a supper, a bottle of gin, a flask of powder and a box of revolver caps; some few days ago I received information that Gardiner had been seen, accompanied by a lad answering the appearance of Walsh, near to Mrs. Walsh's residence, and that while a man named Humphreys was stuck-up on the road a youth like Walsh held Gardiner's horse while he perpetrated the robbery. When I came across the bushranger's camp a short time since, I picked up a small monkey jacket, only large enough for a boy to wear; Walsh says he is seventeen years of age, but I don't think he is more than fifteen. I may add that the gun missing fire was purely an accident, as Sergeant Condell, when he loaded it, took every precaution to prevent the misadventure."

*Pottinger seems to have combined great ineptitude with shocking luck. On one occasion he went after Ben Hall and the outlaw stole his horse from him. One Queensland bushranger, known as the Wild Scotchman, travelled all the way south from the Burnett district to "fight a duel" with Sir Frederick, and* actually did exchange shots with him. After he attended a race meeting in 1865 where Ben Hall was present, he was called to headquarters in Sydney to explain his apparent inability to stop the bushranging that was so prevalent in the area under his control. While crossing the Blue Mountains on the way to Sydney, he wounded himself with his own pistol, and died. Some say that he suicided, but there is an apocryphal story that he was vaulting over a hedge at a stopping place of the coach to impress a lady passenger with his agility, fell over his sword and the impact of his fall set off his revolver. I cannot vouch for the story, but it sounds like the sort of thing that would have happened to Sir Frederick. His whole career seems to have been like that.

Gardiner escaped to Queensland and opened a store on the road to the Canoona goldfield northwest of Rockhampton. Kitty Brown joined him there, and he resumed his proper name of Frank Christie and became a respectable and trusted man in the district. An ill-advised letter from Mrs Brown to her sister led to his arrest and trial. He served ten years of his sentence, was pardoned and exiled, and went to San Francisco, where he was eventually shot in a dispute following a game of cards.

Ben Hall remains the bushranger who seems to have aroused the most sympathy among his fellow bushmen. Certainly there are more ballads and songs about him than about any other outlaw in the continent, including the Kellys. He and his gang once held up the little township of Canowindra for three days to have a spree. They paid for all the liquor and food consumed, and made the local policeman a guest of honour at the feast. Hall was eventually separated from the rest of his gang in 1865. Some say that they intended to leave for America and rejoin forces there. However, Hall was betrayed by one of his "bush telegraphs", a man called Mick Conolly, who had been a sort of banker for him. The party that went to capture him was led by a black tracker called Bill Dargin, who had been a schoolfellow of Hall's at one time. They came to the clump of trees where he was sleeping just at dawn, and tried to close in to capture him alive. Hall woke, and stood among the saplings. A Sergeant of police, named Condell, shouted, "In the name of the Queen, Ben Hall!" Hall reached for his revolvers, and the troopers opened fire. Badly hit, Hall called to Dargin, "Shoot me dead, Billy." He was still being hit by bullets after he lay dead on the ground. The police laid his body across a horse and took it back to Forbes, where it was paraded through the streets in triumph. He was buried at Forbes.

# Brave Ben Hall

*Anon.*

Come all Australian sons with me
For a hero has been slain
And cowardly butchered in his sleep
Upon the Lachlan Plain.

Pray do not stay your seemly grief
But let a teardrop fall
For many hearts shall always mourn
The fate of bold Ben Hall.

No brand of Cain e'er stamped his brow,
No widow's curse did fall;
When tales are read the squatters dread
The name of bold Ben Hall.

The records of this hero bold
Through Europe have been heard,
And formed a conversation
Between many an Earl and Lord.

Ever since the good old days
Of Dick Turpin and Duval,
Knights of the road were outlaws bold,
And so was bold Ben Hall.

He never robbed a needy man,
His records best will show,
Staunch and loyal to his mates,
And manly to the foe.

Until he left his trusty mates,
The cause I ne'er could hear,
The bloodhounds of the law heard this
And after him did steer.

They found his place of ambush,
And cautiously they crept,
And savagely they murdered him
While the victim slept.

Yes, savagely they murdered him,
The cowardly blue-coat imps,
Who were laid onto where he slept
By informing peelers' pimps.

No more he'll mount his gallant steed,
Nor range the mountains high,
The widow's friend in poverty—
Bold Ben Hall, good-bye.

*John Meredith collected this song from Mrs Sally Sloan in Sydney, in the 1950s. Judith Wright also knew of it from childhood, and it was from the final verse that she selected the title of* Range the Mountains High *for her book about Thunderbolt.*

*Ben Hall (engraving from* Illustrated Melbourne Post, *22 May 1865)*

# The Death of Ben Hall

*Anon.*

Ben Hall was out on the Lachlan side
With a thousand pounds on his head;
A score of troopers were scattered wide
And a hundred more were ready to ride
Wherever a rumour led.

They had followed his track from the Weddin
   heights
And north by the Weelong yards;
Through dazzling days and moonlit nights
They had sought him over their rifle-sights,
With their hands on their trigger-guards.

The outlaw stole like a hunted fox
Through the scrub and stunted heath,
And peered like a hawk from his eyrie rocks
Through the waving boughs of the sapling box
On the troopers riding beneath.

His clothes were rent by the clutching thorn
And his blistered feet were bare;
Ragged and torn, with his beard unshorn,
He hid in the woods like a beast forlorn,
With a padded path to his lair.

But every night when the white stars rose
He crossed by the Gunning Plain
To a stockman's hut where the Gunning flows,
And struck on the door three swift light blows,
And a hand unhooked the chain—

And the outlaw followed the lone path back
With food for another day;
And the kindly darkness covered his track
And the shadows swallowed him deep and black
Where the starlight melted away.

But his friend had read of the Big Reward,
And his soul was stirred with greed;
He fastened his door and window-board,
He saddled his horse and crossed the ford,
And spurred to the town at speed.

You may ride at a man's or a maid's behest
When honour or true love call
And steel your heart to the worst or best,
But the ride that is ta'en on a traitor's quest
Is the bitterest ride of all.

A hot wind blew from the Lachlan bank
And a curse on its shoulder came;
The pine-trees frowned at him, rank on rank,
The sun on a gathering storm-cloud sank
And flushed his cheek with shame.

He reined at the Court; and the tale began
That the rifles alone should end;
Sergeant and trooper laid their plan
To draw the net on a hunted man
At the treacherous word of a friend.

False was the hand that raised the chain
And false was the whispered word:
"The troopers have turned to the south again,
You may dare to camp on the Gunning Plain."
And the weary outlaw heard.

He walked from the hut but a quarter-mile
Where a clump of saplings stood
In a sea of grass like a lonely isle;
And the moon came up in a little while
Like silver steeped in blood.

Ben Hall lay down on the dew-wet ground
By the side of his tiny fire;
And a night-breeze woke, and he heard no sound
As the troopers drew their cordon round—
And the traitor earned his hire.

And nothing they saw in the dim grey light,
But the little glow in the trees,
And they crouched in the tall cold grass all night,
Each one ready to shoot at sight,
With his rifle cocked on his knees.

When the shadows broke and the dawn's white
   sword
Swung over the mountain wall,
And a little wind blew over the ford,
A sergeant sprang to his feet and roared:
"In the name of the Queen, Ben Hall!"

Haggard, the outlaw leapt from his bed
With his lean arms held on high.
"Fire!" And the word was scarcely said
When the mountains rang to a rain of lead—
And the dawn went drifting by.

They kept their word and they paid his pay
Where a clean man's hand would shrink;
And that was the traitor's master-day
As he stood by the bar on his homeward way
And called on the crowd to drink.

He banned no creed and he barred no class,
And he called to his friends by name;
But the worst would shake his head and pass
And none would drink from the bloodstained
    glass
And the goblet red with shame.

And I know when I hear the last grim call
And my mortal hour is spent,
When the light is hid and the curtains fall
I would rather sleep with the dead Ben Hall
Than go where that traitor went.

*The Victorian Police had boasted of their prowess during the reign of the bushrangers in New South Wales; and dared them to cross the border. Their words seemed to come true when "Mad Dan" Morgan crossed the Murray River at Peechelba, and was dead within forty-eight hours. What the troopers did not realize, perhaps, was that the 'rangers tended to stick to the wild bush country they knew so well, and where they could and did lose their pursuers. The troopers captured Harry Power with ease, once they were told where he was hiding. But their own private nightmare was in the making when the Kellys went into the bushranging business in earnest in the late 1870s. Perhaps they then realized the frustrations of trying to catch superb horsemen, experienced in the bush, and with the natural hide-outs of the ranges well known to them since childhood and a band of sympathizers across the country who could and did inform them of the movements of the police.*

*This is not the place to detail the rights and wrongs of the Kellys. There are many books on the subject, both for and against the gang. Superintendent Hare wrote one; friends of the family have kept* The Inner History of the Kelly Gang *in print to the present day. Max Brown wrote a fine book called* Native Son *just after World War II. There are also others. Let the interested reader look at the material and decide for himself. Kelly signed himself "a forced outlaw" in one of his open letters, and said at his trial, "If my lips teach the public that men are made mad by bad treatment, and if the police are taught that they may exasperate to madness men they persecute and illtreat, my life will not be entirely thrown away."*

*It has been claimed that part at least of the* following ballad was sung at the pub in Glenrowan on the fateful night when four desperate men waited for the train that brought them death. Probably most of the details are true in fact, if not in righteous sentiment. Note the treatment meted out to the Chinese cook in the fourth last stanza. It rings true.

## The Kelly Gang

*Anon.*

Oh, Paddy dear, and did you hear
The news that's going round,
On the head of bold Ned Kelly
They have placed two thousand pound.
And on Steve Hart, Joe Byrne and Dan
Two thousand more they'd give,
But if the price was doubled, boys,
The Kelly Gang would live.

'Tis hard to think such plucky hearts
In crime should be employed,
'Tis by police persecution
They have all been much annoyed.
Revenge is sweet, and in the bush
They can defy the law,
Such sticking up and plundering
You never saw before.

'Twas in November, Seventy-eight,
When the Kelly Gang came down,
Just after shooting Kennedy,
To famed Euroa town;
To rob the bank of all its gold
Was their idea that day,
Blood-horses they were mounted on
To make their getaway.

So Kelly marched into the bank,
A cheque all in his hand,
For to have it changed for money
Of Scott he did demand.
And when that he refused him,
He, looking at him straight,
Said, "See here, my name's Ned Kelly,
And this here man's my mate."

With pistols pointed at his nut,
Poor Scott did stand amazed,
His stick he would have liked to cut,
But was with funk half crazed;
The poor cashier, with real fear,
Stood trembling at the knees,
But at last they both seen 'twas no use
And handed out the keys.

*Examination and remand of Kelly in Melbourne gaol (engraving from* Australasian Sketcher, *14 August 1880)*

The safe was quickly gutted then,
The drawers turned out, as well,
The Kellys being quite polite,
Like any noble swell.
With flimsies, gold and silver coin,
The threepennies and all
Amounting to two thousand pounds,
They made a glorious haul.

"Now hand out all your firearms,"
The robber boldly said,
"And all your ammunition—
Or a bullet through your head.
Now get your wife and children—
Come man, now look alive;
All jump into this buggy
And we'll take you for a drive."

They took them to a station
About three miles away,
And kept them close imprisoned
Until the following day.
The owner of the station
And those in his employ
And a few unwary travellers
Their company did enjoy.

An Indian hawker fell in, too,
As everybody knows,
He came in handy to the gang
By fitting them with clothes.
Then with their worn-out clothing
They made a few bonfires,
And then destroyed the telegraph
By cutting down the wires.

Oh, Paddy dear, do shed a tear,
I can't but sympathize,
Those Kellys are the devils,
For they've made another rise;
This time across the billabong,
On Morgan's ancient beat,
They've robbed the banks of thousands,
And in safety did retreat.

The matter may be serious, Pat,
But still I can't but laugh,
To think the tales the bobbies told
Must all amount to chaff.
They said they had them all hemmed in,
They could not get away,
But they turned up in New South Wales,
And made the journey pay.

They rode into Jerilderie town
At twelve o'clock at night,
Aroused the troopers from their beds,
And gave them an awful fright.
They took them in their night-shirts,
Ashamed I am to tell,
They covered them with revolvers
And locked them in a cell.

They next acquainted the womenfolk
That they were going to stay
And take possession of the camp
Until the following day.
They fed their horses in the stalls
Without the slightest fear,
Then went to rest their weary limbs
Till daylight did appear.

Next morning being Sunday morn
Of course they must be good,
They dressed themselves in trooper's clothes,
And Ned, he chopped some wood.
No one there suspected them,
As troopers they did pass,
And Dan, the most religious one,
Took the sergeant's wife to mass.

They spent the day most pleasantly,
Had plenty of good cheer,
Fried beefsteak and onions,
Tomato-sauce and beer;
The ladies in attendance
Indulged in pleasant talk,
And just to ease the troopers' minds,
They took them for a walk.

On Monday morning early,
Still masters of the ground,
They took their horses to the forge
And had them shod all round;
Then back they came and mounted,
Their plans all laid so well,
In company with the troopers
They stuck up the Royal Hotel.

They bailed up all the occupants,
And placed them in a room,
Saying, "Do as we command you,
Or death will be your doom."
A Chinese cook, "No savvy" cried,
Not knowing what to fear,
But they brought him to his senses
With a lift under the ear.

*The capture of Ned Kelly (engraving from* Illustrated Australian News, *3 July 1880)*

All who now approached the house
Just shared a similar fate,
In hardly any time at all
The number was twenty-eight.
They shouted freely for all hands,
And paid for all they drank,
And two of them remained in charge,
And two went to the bank.

The farce was here repeated
As I've already told,
They bailed up all the banker's clerks
And robbed them of their gold,
The manager could not be found,
And Kelly, in great wrath,
Searched high and low, and luckily
He found him in his bath.

The robbing o'er they mounted then,
To make a quick retreat,
They swept away with all their loot
By Morgan's ancient beat;
And where they've gone I do not know,
If I did I wouldn't tell,
So now, until I hear from them,
I'll bid you all farewell.

*This poem about the Kellys shows how sentiment and brutal realism can be combined in the bush ballad. The versifiers were ubiquitous and of greatly varying standard of performance. What has never ceased to surprise me is that there were so many of them. The next poem, by Gibson, is probably his most popular one, and has fine touch of hurt reproof which would appeal to the bushman who expected his mate to stick to him under all circumstances, sharing good and bad fortune. But then, Sam Holt appears to have been something of a con man right through the writer's association with him.*

An Up-Country Coach

# A Ballad of Queensland

**"Over-landing" Jim apostrophiseth his quondam mate, who hath made his pile, and gone home**

Oh! don't you remember black Alice, Sam Holt,
　Black Alice so dusky and dark—
That Warrego "gin" with the straw through
　　her nose,
　And teeth like a Moreton Bay shark?
The villainous sheep-wash tobacco she smoked
　In the gunyah down there by the lake;
The grubs that she gathered, the lizards
　　she stewed,
　And the "damper" you taught her to bake?

Oh! don't you remember the moon's silver sheen
　On the Warrego sand ridges white?
And don't you remember the scorpions and
　　things
　We found in our blankets at night?
The wild trailing creepers, the bush buds, Sam
　Holt,
　That scattered their fragrance around;
And, don't you remember that chest-foundered
　　colt
　You sold me and swore he was sound?

They say you've ten thousand per annum, Sam
　Holt,
　In England, a park, and a drag,
And p'raps you've forgot you were six
　　months ago
　In Queensland a-humping your swag.
Who'd think, now, to see you a dinin' in state
　With lords, and the devil knows who,
You were "flashin' your dover" six short
　　months ago
　In a lambing camp on the Paroo?

Say, don't you remember that fiver, Sam Holt,
　You borrowed so frank and so free,
When the publicans landed your fifty-pound
　　cheque
　In Tambo, your very last spree?
Luck changes some natures, and yours, Sammy
　Holt,
　'Aint a grand one as ever I see,
And I guess I may whistle a good many tunes
　'Fore you'll think of that fiver, or me.

Oh! don't you remember the cattle you "duffed,"
　And yer luck at the Sandy Creek "rush,"
The "poker" you played, and the "bluffs" that
　　you bluffed,
　And yer habit of holdin' a "flush?"
Perhaps you've forgotten the pasting you got
　From the "Micks" down at Callaghan's store,
When Pat Flanagan found a fifth ace in his hand,
　And you'd raised him his pile upon four!

You weren't quite the cleanly potato, Sam Holt,
　And you hadn't the cleanest of fins;
But you lifted your pile at the Towers, Sam Holt,
　And that covers most of your sins.
When's my turn a-comin'? Well, never, perhaps,
　And its likely enough yer old mate
'll be "humping his drum" on the Warrego banks
　To the end of the chapter of Fate.

---

*"The Newchum's Farewell", or the parting curse, has been written about many places in Australia, but seldom with such feeling and enthusiasm; one feels the writer really meant it. It was probably popular because it gave the reciter and his audience a fine sense of their own toughness in being able to live under the frightful conditions described with such venom but possible lack of poetic talent.*

# Newchum's Farewell to Queensland

Queensland, thou art a land of pests,
From flies and fleas one never rests,
Even now mosquitoes 'round me revel,
In fact they are the very devil.

Sand-flies and hornets just as bad,
They nearly drive a fellow mad:
The scorpion and the centipede
With stinging ants of every breed.

Fever and ague with the shakes,
Triantelopes and poisonous snakes,
Goannas, lizards, cockatoos,
Bushrangers, logs and jackeroos.

Bandicoots and swarms of rats,
Bull-dog ants and native cats,
Stunted timber, thirsty plains,
Parched-up deserts, scanty rains.

There's rivers here, you sail ships on,
There's nigger women without shifts on,
There's humpies, huts and wooden houses,
There's men who don't wear trousers.

There's Barcoo rot and sandy blight,
There's dingoes howling half the night,
There's curlews' wails and croaking frogs,
There's savage blacks and native dogs.

There's scentless flowers and stinging trees.
There's poison grass and Darling peas,
Which drive the cattle raving mad,
Make sheep and horses just as bad.

And then it never rains in reason,
There's drought one year and floods next season,
Which wash the squatter's sheep away,
And then there is the devil to pay.

To stay in thee, O land of Mutton!
I would not give a single button,
But bid thee now a long farewell,
Thou scorching, sunburnt land of Hell.


*This poem is for me the example of the truly awful.
Not even "Bellerive", that Homer of the* Bulletin
*"Answers to Correspondents" column, ever did worse.
This writer shares Joe Tishler's complacency in the
possession of his poetic gift, however. The spelling is as
in the original book. Sideling Creek, incidentally, is a
tributary of the North Pine River, just north of
Brisbane.*

*The whole quote is from* History and Adventures
of a Queensland Pioneer *by E. J. Foreman.*

Then again in Ovid's Metamorphosises a young
chap when walking in the forest sees a beautiful
girl, clothed only in a flowing mantle of beautiful
hair. The girl spies him and sort of gives him the
glad eye, and runs away, knowing he would follow,
which he does, and just as he is putting his arms
around her waist she turns into a tree, and there you
are. Surrounded with all these wonderful books I
thought I could do a bit myself, so I wrote a few
verses about our creek and the old Sideling Creek
bridge. We used to take the "Queenslander," so,
being my first attempt, I sent the verses to that
paper, but, alas! the editor sent them back to me,
and wrote on the back of them, "The writer is no
poet, and the sooner he finds the mistake out the
better for himself and those about him." Of course,

that setback nipped my poetic effusions in the bud
for the time being, and made me very down-
hearted. Years after, however, I was on the
permanent staff of the same paper. The verses were
as follows:—

"I wandered by the creek bank, I stood upon the
   bridge,
I gazed upon the silent stream, then anon up the
   ridge.
The moon was shining bright and clear, no man
   or beast appeared,
But the screeching of the curlew was the only
   sound I heard.
I sauntered on across the flat, down to the river's
   brink,
Where the darkies oft are fishing and the cattle
   come to drink;
The darkies, they were safe in camp, I dare not
   them disturb,
Still the screeching of the curlew was the only
   sound I heard.

I wandered on amidst the trees, and giant trees
   they were!
The bloodwood, oak, and spotted gum, and the
   ironbark was there—
I gazed into their lofty tops, no leaves or
   branches stirred,
Still the screeching of the curlew was the only
   sound I heard.
The bush is very free, my boys, the bush is very
   wild,
But give to me that happy land where I dwelt
   when but a child,
Then three cheers for happy Queensland, with its
   mines of gold so pure,
Three cheers for good old England, for I once
   was happy there."

At the time I wrote these verses we had a man
staying with us for a while who had just arrived
from England. Now this man had a sister, who at
the time was writing with Miss Braddon, the
celebrated novelist. This chap tried all he could for
me to let him send the verses home to his sister, so
that she could publish them in the journal, "Bow
Bells," but I would not agree.

*On the tramp (engraving from* Australasian Sketcher, *24 January 1889)*

# Freedom
# on the Wallaby

*Henry Lawson*

Our fathers toiled for bitter bread
  While idlers thrived beside them;
But food to eat and clothes to wear
  Their native land denied them.
They left their native land in spite
  Of royalties' regalia,
And so they came, or if they stole
  Were sent out to Australia.

They struggled hard to make a home,
  Hard grubbing 'twas and clearing.
They weren't troubled much with toffs
  When they were pioneering;
And now that we have made the land
  A garden full of promise,
Old greed must crook his dirty hand
  And come to take it from us.

But Freedom's on the Wallaby,
  She'll knock the tyrants silly,
She's going to light another fire
  And boil another billy.
We'll make the tyrants feel the sting
  Of those that they would throttle;
They needn't say the fault is ours
  If blood should stain the wattle.

*The first of these two poems of Henry Lawson's sets
the problem as to which came first, this or the folksong
of the same title. It is saved from utter mediocrity by
the final couplet. The second poem describes what may
well have been one of the first communes in Australia.
Truly, there is nothing new under the sun.*

# The Bards Who Lived
# at Manly

The camp of high-class spielers,
  Who sneered in summer dress,
And doo-dah dilettantes,
  And scornful "venuses"—
House agents, and storekeepers,
  All eager they to "bleed"—
The bards who tackled Manly,
  Were plucky bards indeed!

With shops that feared to trust them,
  And pubs that looked askance;
And prigs who read their verses,
  But gave them not a glance;
When all were vain and selfish,
  And editors were hard—
The bard that stuck to Manly
  Was sure a mighty bard.

'Twas not the paltry village
  We honoured unaware,
Or welcome warm, or friendship,
  Or "tone" that took us there;
We longed to sing for mankind,
  Where heaven's breath was free
We only sought the grandeur
  Of sea-cliff, sands and sea.

And we were glad at Manly,
  All unaware of "swells,"
Of doctors and of nurses,
  And private hospitals;
With little fear of bailiffs,
  And great contempt for greed—
The bards who lived at Manly,
  They were a healthy breed.

What mattered floors were barren,
  And windows curtainless,
And our life seemed to others
  But blackguard recklessness?
We wore our clothes for comfort,
  We earned our bread alway,
And beer and good tobacco
  Came somehow every day.

Came kindred souls to Manly—
  Outsiders that we knew,
And with them scribes and artists,
  And low comedians too;
And sometimes bright girl writers—
  Called "Tommy," "Jack," or "Pat"—
(Though each one had a sweetheart
  The rest knew nought of that).

Oh! moonlit nights at Manly,
  When all the world was fair!
In shirts and turned-up trousers
  We larked like big boys there.
Oh! glorious autumn mornings—
  The gold and green and blue—
We "stripped" as well as any,
  And swam as strongly too.

The artist had a missus,
  Who rather loved the wretch,
And so for days together
  He'd stay at home and sketch.
And then—I fear 'twas only
  When things were getting tight—
The bards would shun each other,
  And hump themselves—and write.

When bailiffs came to Manly
  They'd find no "sticks" to take,
We'd welcome them as brothers—
  Their grimy hands we'd shake;
We'd send for beer in billies—
  And straightway send for more—
And bailiff nights in Manly
  Were merry nights of yore.

There are some things that landlords
  And law can't do at all:
They could not take the pictures
  We painted on the wall;
They could not take the table—
  The table was a door;
They could not take the bedsteads—
  The beds were on the floor.

The door of some old stable—
  We'd borrowed for a drink—
A page of rhymes and sketches,
  And stained with beer and ink:
A dead hand drew the portraits—
  And, say, should I be shamed,
To seek it out in Manly
  And get the old door framed?

They left the masterpieces
  The artist dreamed of long;
They could not take the gardens
  From Victor Daley's song;
They left his summer islands
  And fairy ships at sea,
They could not take my mountains
  And western plains from me.

One bailiff was our brother,
  No better and no worse—
And, oh! the yarns he told us
  To put in prose and verse,
And sorry we to lose him,
  And sorry he to go—
(Oh! skeletons of Pott's Point,
  How many things we know)!

The very prince of laughter,
  With brains and sympathy;
And with us on the last night
  He spent his bailiff's fee.
He banished Durkin's gruffness,
  He set my soul afloat,
And drew till day on Daley's
  Bright store of anecdote.

He said he'd stick to business—
  Though he could well be free—
If but to save poor devils
  From harder "bums" than he,
Now artist, bard and bailiff
  Have left this vale of sin—
I trust, if they reach Heaven,
  They'll take that bailiff in.

The bards that lived in Manly
  Have vanished one and one;
But do not think in Manly
  Bohemian days are done.
They bled me white in Manly
  When rich and tempest-tossed—
I'll leave some bills in Manly
  To pay for what I lost.

They'd grab and grind in Manly,
  Then slander, sneer, and flout.
The shocked of moral Manly!
  They starved my brothers out.
The miserable village,
  Set in a scene so fair,
Were honester and cleaner
  If some of us were there!

But one went with December—
  These last lines seem tonight
Like some song I remember,
  And not a song I write.
With vision strangely clearer
  My old chums seem to be,
In death and absence, nearer
  Than e'er they were to me.

Alone, and still not lonely—
  When tears will not be shed—
I wish that I could only
  Believe that they were dead.
With hardly curbed emotion,
  I can't but think, somehow,
In Manly by the ocean
  They're waiting for me now.

*The final two ballads speak of the bushman's idea of ethics and a possible afterlife which, no doubt, he had been assured was a certainty. They bear a remarkable resemblance in sentiment to some American country music and folksong; tunes such as "The Hellbound Train" and "The Ghost Riders in the Sky", for instance. The first ballad is sentimental to a fault, but it may have brought reassurance to simple men. The second, by the professional balladist, was equally popular; but has a more sardonic note. The final four lines are, almost word for word, a verse from Charles Flower's ballad "A Thousand Miles Away"; but who borrowed from whom is difficult to say. It doesn't matter, it's a good quartrain and bears repetition.*

# Limpy Bill

The Lord, He sat in judgment, close
   Inside St. Peter's gate.
When Limpy Bill from Coolibah
   Arrived to learn his fate.

A sunburned drover, old and grey,
   He pushed his shoulders square,
And said, "You'll want to know my life,
   And what I did down there."

"Church! Well, there weren't one very near,
   It didn't seem worth while
Just for to hear a parson preach,
   To ride near sixty mile.

I guess I've sworn a fairish bit,
   As stock-folk mostly do,
And drunk my whisky with the rest;
   I done some gambling too.

Oh yes, I did some fighting; some
   Great scraps; there was one—
But you're not interested though
   'Twas bad for Nigger John.

My good deeds! Kindness weren't my line,
   I dunno as I did
Anything extra special good
   'Cept when I saved that kid.

The bull meant business pretty bad,
   He couldn't run for fear,
But—I was old, and he was young,
   And no one else was near."

A smile broke on his wind-cracked face:
   "I thought I'd come here then,
But all I got was this 'ere leg,
   And 'Limpy Bill' from men.

I always hit in front and square,
   And clear above the belt,
I never pulled a horse I rode,
   Or stacked the cards I dealt.

I paid my debts—I did my work
   In sun, in dust, in rain;
I think that's all I'd try to do
   If I could live again.

My mother taught me all of this,
   I think she's somewhere here;
And she was with me often, for
   I used to feel her near.

And now I'm here to take my dose,
   I've always played the game,
I'll try whatever it may be
   To keep on just the same."

The Lord's face lit with gentleness:
   "I know your heart is clean;
I understand the thoughts you had
   Not what your words have been.

You shared your drop of water
   When thirty miles from more
With a weary, thirsty stranger whom
   You had not seen before.

You used your strength to help the weak
   As much as mortal can,
And facing all things with a smile,
   You proved yourself a man.

You proved yourself a man, and here
   You'll try a higher thing,
Come in and take your place among
   The workers of the King."

*From a* Bill Bowyang Reciter

# My Mate Bill

## (Jimmy the Hut-keeper, loquitur)

That's his saddle across the tie-beam an' them's
    his spurs up there
On the wall-plate over yonder, you kin see 's they
    ain't a pair.
The "daddy" of all the stockmen as ever came
    must'rin here—
Killed in the flamin' mallee, yardin' a scrub-bred
    steer!

They say as he's gone to Heaven, an' shook off
    his worldly cares,
But I can't sight Bill in a halo sot up on three
    blinded hairs;
In Heaven! what next, I wonder, for strike me
    pink an' blue
If I savvy what in thunder they'll find for Bill to
    do.

He'd never make one o' them angels with faces as
    white as chalk,
All wool to the toes like hoggets, an' wings like a
    eagle-'awk,
To sit on a throne an' trumpet an' 'arp like a
    bloomin' bard—
He'd no more ear for anthems than calves in a
    brandin' yard.

He could sit on a buckin' brumbie like a nob in
    an easy-cheer,
An' chop his name with a green-hide fall on the
    flank of a flyin' steer:
He could show the saints in glory the way that a
    fall should drop,
But sit on a throne?—not William—unless they
    could make it prop!

If the Heavn'ly hosts got boxed now, as mobs
    most always will,
Why who'd cut 'em out, an' yard 'em, or draft on
    the camp like Bill?
But to straddle a blazin' sunbeam, and muster a
    push that flew
Is graft that a man like William 'ud skearcely care
    to do.

He might'nt freeze to the seraphs, or chum with
    the cherubim,
But if ever them seraph johnnies get "pokin' it,"
    like, at him,

Well, if there's hide in heaven, an' silk for to
    make a lash,
He'll yard the lot in the jasper lake in a blinded
    lightnin' flash!

It's hard if there ain't no cattle, but p'raps they'll
    let him asleep,
An' wake him up at the judgment for to draft
    them goats an' sheep.
It's playin' it low on William, but p'raps he'll
    buckle-to
Just to show them high-toned seraphs what a
    mallee-man kin do.

If they saddles a big-boned angel—with a turn o'
    speed of course—
As can spiel like a four-year brumbie, an' prop
    like an old camp horse,
If they puts Bill up with a snaffle, an' a four or
    five inch spur,
An' eighteen foot o' green-hide for to chop the
    blinded fur,
He'll draft them blamed angoras in a way, its safe
    to swear,
As'll make them tony seraphs sit back on their
    thrones an' stare.

Stockwhip.

# Section V

# Oddments & Fragments

# Current Folk Tales

Too many writers seem content to write of folklore as if it were something that is dead or almost so. This supposition seems to me to be contradicted by instances constantly borne upon my notice. There are plenty of such beliefs still around, and new ones are constantly being added to the body extant. One of the more recent ones that is widespread is the one about trailing a piece of rubber from the boot of a car for the alleviation and relief of car sickness. People who would scorn to carry a potato against rheumatism or wear red flannel underclothes against flu nevertheless dutifully trail their piece of rubber. I don't doubt it works in certain cases. The mind is a wonderful physician. I cannot trace where the theory had its birth, but all over the eastern States of Australia are cars trailing little bits of rubber, to secure the occupants against bilious fits. It has even been claimed to me that wrapping the thorax in brown paper next to the skin makes assurance doubly sure. One can understand the manufacturers of car fittings sedulously fostering the use of insect deflectors, striped cushions in the rear windows, and dreadful little furry animals who nod at following drivers with ominous deliberation, but the mind hesitates to think that the manufacturers of little bits of rubber would do the same thing. It is all very mysterious.

Equally mysterious in origin are the folk tales of our time. These fall into two categories. There are the cycles of stories concerning a particular character or set of characters, and every now and then a single story worthy of much wider circulation which nevertheless retains its original identity and construction. Let us talk about the first type first.

When I first began to listen to such stories at school the cycle current was that of two Irish labourers called Pat and Mick. These redoubtable fellows were succeeded by a cycle of stories of bucolic humour concerning three Australians who were no doubt based upon three of the dramatis personae of the Steele Rudd "SELECTION" series, notably Dad, Dave and Mabel. Coming forward to modern times there have been cycles concerning Little Audrey, Confucius, Travelling Salesmen, Shaggy Dogs, and quite recently, elephants.

The fascinating thing about these stories is not so much their survival over a short period so much as the tremendous scope they have while at the height of their currency. It has never fallen to my lot to ever meet a man or woman who claimed to have started even one of these stories on its circulation. It has always been heard from someone else. In the mysterious way of the folk process they begin, flourish and die after a time, being in their turn replaced by another cycle. Some serious University person with time and inclination could well do a thesis on the rise and fall of such a cycle of stories. These entertainments are not necessarily verbal; around 1936 there was a fad for the clever gesture. Some of these remain in my mind to this day. For instance, if the interrogator pointed to his eye with his left hand while making snipping motions with the fingers of his right it indicated a China Clipper, while snapping the fingers of right and left hands alternately while varying their positions was a game of ping-pong. There were many such.

One particular theme that has its variants in all folk literature, written and verbal, is that of the tall story. This form of humour still flourishes in the backblocks of this country, and probably reached its height in the Paul Bunyan stories of the loggers in America, the Kentucky and New England stories about the Devil in the United States and the Crooked Mick and Speewah stories in Australia. Alan Marshall is the chief repository of the last named, and if you ever had the good fortune to meet him I hope you can get him to tell you a little about them. The other chief form of our own outback humour is that of the straight-faced understatement. A perfect illustration was given to me recently by the South Australian poet, Ian Mudie. Mudie tells of the bushman who was told of the Biblical occasion when it rained for 40 days and nights. "Yair," said the bushman. "We got half an inch out of that out home."

This brings me to the final example I have space to discuss. The specific story one meets over the years with minor variations but sticking remarkably closely to the original form. It is usually such a good story as to be credible, but barely so. I will quote two that have been extant to my knowledge for the past five years and which I meet occasionally still. The first is that of the Ready Mix Concrete Driver.

359

*Picnic party on Garden Island (engraving from* Australian Picture Pleasure Book, *W. G. Mason)*

Once upon a time there was a ready mix concrete truck driver who forgot to take his lunch to work with him. He had a delivery to make near his home at about 11 a.m. so determined to pick up his lunch at that time. He pulled up outside his house with a full load aboard at 11 exactly, and found a large opulent car parked there already. Cautious investigation revealed his wife in bed with a flash stranger. The driver withdrew cautiously and without being discovered. He lowered the window of the flash cove's car and deposited his cargo through it. He then drove away and the concrete dried before the unfortunate lover returned.

I have heard this story both in Cairns and in Adelaide and points between during the past five years. It is such poetic revenge, and barely credible. Therein lies its charm. But I have never been able to establish its veracity, though most versions agree that it occurred on the Gold Coast and the teller often claims to have been personally acquainted with the driver concerned.

The second and last story is about a fellow who saw an advertisement in a newspaper for a second-hand Mercedes-Benz (or Bentley, or Rolls) for ten pounds. He decided that it was a hoax but his curiosity led him to answer the ad. He is the only person to enquire. Sure enough he meets a mysterious widow in mourning at the address given, and she sells him the car at the advertised price. Later he discovers that the woman's husband has driven home late at night rather under the weather, and has gone to sleep in the car leaving the motor running. A gust of wind has slammed the garage door and the man has died from the effects of the exhaust gases. The widow wishes to be rid of the killer vehicle, but cannot legally give it away so she sells it for a nominal price, and the lucky fellow drives away in his new car for ten pounds.

So the stories and superstitions continue to flow from the inexhaustible reservoir. I can't wait to see what the next one will be.

*Bill Scott, in* Australian Tradition, *March 1969*

Dear Wendy,
Bill Scott's article on "Current Folk Tales" in No. 19 of *Australian Tradition* was highly interesting and suggests a few comments of my own.

The criticism that people all too often regard folklore as a dying thing is certainly true, as is the fact that this assumption is fallacious. Certain forms of folklore (the child ballads, the old fairy stories, etc.) come and go, but folklore as a whole never dies out where people congregate in groups for any length of time.

Much modern folklore, moreover, as well as older, rural material is found not only in Australia, but elsewhere in the English-speaking world (and beyond). For example, the last two stories Scott cites—about the cement mixer and the expensive car sold very cheaply, are widely told urban legends in the United States, and undoubtedly elsewhere. The name, place, and minor details of the narratives vary, but the stories are the same. The second anecdote seems to be a combination of two legends. The first finds a widow selling her husband's expensive car for $10, or a very cheap sum, because her husband willed the proceeds from the sale of the car to his secretary, young and beautiful, rather than to his wife. To spite the secretary, the wife sells the car cheaply. The second legend is the story of the Death Car. In this instance, a car is found in the woods or at a remote spot, with a badly decomposed body inside. The windows and doors have been shut tight and the body had deteriorated so badly that an unpleasant smell permeates the interior of this car, often a fairly expensive model. When the car is found, it is hauled off to the second-hand car lot, where it is fumigated and cleaned up, while the body is taken to the morgue. However, when the car is resold the

smell has so permeated the car that, in spite of all efforts to remove the odour, it lingers on, and the new owners are forced to sell the car once more. The car goes from owner to owner in a very short time, and is finally scrapped when no one will buy it, even for a fee of $5 or so, because the stench is too overpowering. This last story is especially widely told around the U.S. and is often reported in the newspapers as well. It is the kind of story which could be reinforced or stated anew by occasional happenstances of just this kind.

Urban legends—I use the term legend because most often there is an element of belief to these stories—can be divided into three broad categories: stories of the grotesque, the supernatural, and the anecdotal. Below are some capsule summaries of each:

### Grotesque:
A couple are out parking in Lovers' Lane on a summer night. The radio is on low and everything is very romantic. A news flash tells of a maniac with a hooked hand, who has escaped from the local mental institution. All citizens are warned of this dangerous individual. The couple decide it is late anyway, and that they ought to go home. When they arrive at the girl's house, they open the door of the car and there is a bloody hook hanging on the door.

A girl wears her long hair up in a bun at the back of her head, and for weeks and weeks never washes it or takes the bun down to comb out her hair. One day she collapses in a dead faint. She is observed to have blood running down the back of her neck. At the hospital, the doctors undo her hair and discover that cockroaches have eaten into the girl's brain.

### Supernatural:
The most famous example is the Vanishing Hitchhiker. A driver picks up a young woman at a lonely intersection, and drives her to the nearby town which she gives as her destination. When they arrive at the designated house, the driver looks around and sees the girl is gone. Puzzled, he wakes up the owners of the house and explains his predicament. The woman of the house explains patiently that the mysterious girl was her daughter, who was killed at the lonely intersection 13 years ago, and every year re-appears at the same spot and is driven home by yet another unsuspecting traveller. (There are many variations of this story; it has been found in Turkey, Japan, and in many other countries, as well as in the United States and

the English-speaking world. Orson Welles was in a movie which used this story as its theme.)

During World War II a submarine was sunk in the Pacific with all hands lost, but one guy, who was sick and on leave at the time his mates took off. Months later, the guy was standing watch on another ship which happened to pass over the exact spot where his navy comrades were entombed. The man had the watch to himself, was nodding at his post, when he heard a lot of noise and shuffling of feet on deck. When the next man came to relieve him, he could not be found, and the only trace or clue was the appearance of many footprints on the deck, and some seaweed.

**Anecdotal:**
These tend to be humorous. Included here would be the stories recounted by Scott of the cement mixer and the cheap car. But also one might cite the Nude Surprise Party.

A businessman was very attracted by his secretary, who seemed not to pay the slightest attention to him. Finally, one day she suggested shyly they go out to dinner. He jumped at the chance, and after dinner she suggested going to her apartment. He was again overjoyed. Once at her place, she told him she would be right back, that she was going to the next room to slip into something more comfortable. She was very seduc-

*An explorer's camp (T. Baines, from* Australia, *ed. Edwin Carton Booth)*

tive, and his hopes rose correspondingly. In fact, he was so eager to dispense with preliminaries that he decided to remove his clothing while she was out of the room. Finally, she called to him: "You may come in now, dear!" He charged furiously into the next room in his birthday suit as the whole office crew chorused: "Happy Birthday!"

This last story brings up the point that the same narrative may be told as a joke or a fictitious tale in some instances, and as a "true" story (a legend) in others. I have heard it told as both.

I'd be interested in hearing what other current folktale/legend material you people have "down under". Why not ask for contributions in *Australian Tradition?*

*Richard A. Reuss, in* Australian Tradition

Coaching by Night

Further to your section, "Current Folk Yarns," I would like to add a comment or two on the success or otherwise of such stories making the rounds. During 2 years in a Sydney University Department, I heard several such stories, some of thich seemed quite implausible to me, but all were related in deadly seriousness, and in many cases included details (e.g. name of a town) to add authenticity. Moreover, the listeners seemed to attend and comment equally seriously. Since I could not believe in the authenticity of some of the stories, I came to the conclusion that my colleagues did not either, but all acted the part in order not to spoil the story! Was I wrong? Were these yarns really believed as genuine?

The interesting question that then arises is why were the yarns which seemed most improbable to me (a Pommie) apparently accepted by my Aussie colleagues as true stories. I suggest that the answer lies in that intangible human characteristic known as a sense of humour. English friends of mine in Sydney thought that Australians had no sense of humour, but my experiences soon indicated that they had a different sense of humour. Something said or done which caused great laughter often left me thinking how childish, while I sometimes found myself giving offence where none was ever intended.

An English friend of mine from the north of England, but with many years spent in the south of England and latterly many years in Sydney, once suggested that the Aussie sense of humour was more akin to that of the north of England where, for example, someone slipping on a banana skin would arouse much amusement and cause much laughter, whereas the same event in the south might produce some embarrassment but not amusement. This suggests further that we should not simply refer to an Australian or an English sense of humour, but define our regions more closely.

Is it perhaps not too far fetched to consider "sense of humour" as a "collective folk" phenomena, worthy of study? It might be difficult to define, however. I would like to consider now two stories which I heard several times in Sydney.

In the first story a lady (sometimes known to a friend of the story teller) went into a department store (generally named). She went into the changing room to try on some clothes (alternatively, a ladies' toilet is specified) and put her handbag on the floor close to the door. While thus engaged, a hand shot under the door and snatched her bag. She reported the theft and returned home. She received a phone call from the store saying that they had the bag and could she come at once to identify and claim it (various reasons given for urgency, such as the shop closing). On arrival at the store, she discovered that they knew nothing of the bag or the phone call. On arrival back home, she found that her home had been broken into and the rooms ransacked.

The second concerns a driver of a ready-mix cement lorry who arrived home unexpectedly one mid-morning to find a car parked outside his home. On looking in the window of his house he saw a strange man with his wife (a bit more detail often given, depending on the company of the storyteller). He says nothing, but withdrawing quietly, he filled up the car with cement from his lorry and drove away. (In one version I heard, the raconteur adds, after a well-timed pause, that the car belonged to someone else!)

The first story is not humorous, and in fact certainly could happen. The details add authenticity. Many people have been persuaded to leave their homes for some reason or other, only to return and find they've been robbed. The fact that different names and details occur in various versions is no objection since this is the characteristic of stories, true or false, circulating by oral transmission.

The second story as I heard it never included any personal connections or place names, and it is unlikely that anyone knows anyone else who has found his car full of concrete. The story seems quite implausible to me. If the events actually happened they would give great amusement to the person with the "slipping on the banana skin" sense of humour, especially if present witnessing the events. In the absence of such participation, the recounting of the incidents must serve as a substitute. The success of the story then depends on its capacity for laughter, and its capacity to induce laughter depends on it being believed. My reaction, on the other hand, was to be amused by the story but not to believe it true. I suggest that this is because I would find it alien to laugh at such an event if it actually happened before my eyes, so that my amusement depended strongly on my believing that it was only a story.

I hope that I have included a few ideas to chew over.

*Greg Towner, in* Australian Tradition, *December 1970*

## More Current Folk Tales

We're decided to take up Richard Reuss's suggestion and run a section for current folk tales or legends. Contributions are invited.

This story, current in Melbourne, concerns a young middle-aged mother who found she was pregnant. Not only was she dismayed, but she was astounded, as she had been taking the Pill, and was certain that she hadn't made any mistakes. She told her teen-age daughter all about it, and the daughter, conscience stricken, admitted that she had been taking her mother's Pills and replacing them with saccharine tablets.

Reuss (see No. 20) says that stories can be reinforced by occasional happenstances of a similar kind. This one really got the contributor in. She tells that one night she went to spend the evening with a girl friend, and was told the story in great confidence. No names were mentioned, of course, but she was sure she knew who was concerned. The next day, greatly stirred by the unfortunate mother's predicament, she went off to work and told the story to the girls in the staff room, who discussed it in all its various aspects, and came up with the opinion that the daughter was morally responsible for the child, and that if she had any conscience at all she should adopt it.

The next morning one of the girls came in and said accusingly. "Well, you did make me look a proper Charlie. Fancy telling a story like that!" It seems that she in her turn had gone home and told her mother all about it, and mother had said, "But darling, that's been going around the bridge tables for weeks!"

*Wendy Lowenstein, in* Australian Tradition, *December 1969*

This one is not exactly contemporary, but was so about 15 years ago when I was a school kid.

A motor cycle, travelling at high speed, overtook a truck that was loaded with corrugated iron. As the rider swung out to pass, a sheet of iron blew off the load and neatly decapitated him. But the bike was already on course, and shot past the truck and on down the road. The truck driver took one look at the headless, blood-spouting corpse still astride the machine, and died instantly of a heart attack!

The other is one of the more apocryphal stories of the teaching service.

A teacher asked his class to write a composition on the topic, "Our Friend the Policeman." One effort was brief and to the point. "Cops," the child had written, "is barsteds."

The teacher, perturbed at such an attitude in one so young, made a phone call to the local police station. A few days later, a couple of constables arrived at the school on a "public relations" visit. They chatted with the children, let them play with sets of handcuffs, and finally gave them all a ride in the paddy-wagon to the local shop and bought them ice creams.

Shortly afterwards, the teacher again asked the class to write about "Our Friend the Policeman." He eagerly sought out the essay of the child whose first effort had so concerned him. This time, the child had written: "Cops is **cunning** barsteds."

*Brad Tate, in* Australian Tradition, *May 1970*

# You Can't Impress Australians

It is only a few years since one of our political correspondents was in Mt. Isa and was holding forth to a group of the better informed locals on how chummy he was with one John Gorton.

It was all "John told me this . . ." and "I told John that." This went on for some time with the locals politely nodding.

They then got a bit tired of it and one asked, "And who is John Gorton?"

The correspondent explained he was the Prime Minister. "Whatever happened to Menzies?" asked a local.

"He drowned," said another.

The correspondent gave it away and joined them in a conversation about one Ralph Johnson who was something of a local grass-fighter and much loved by all.

You don't have to travel to Mt. Isa to find out that Australia is the worst country in the world for name dropping. Unless the person you are trying to impress is the cousin of the person whose name you drop it is just as likely he has never heard of him.

It is part of the folk lore of the newspaper business that when President Kennedy was assassinated the man whose job it is to wait around at night for such things to happen rang the editor of a Melbourne newspaper and said with some emotion: "John Kennedy is dead."

The editor said: "Don't get too upset, Hawthorn will pull through without him."

The trouble is that you have to explain to everybody that a man named John Kennedy played with Hawthorn Football Club.

*From an unnamed newspaper cutting, quoted in* Australian Tradition, *October 1971*

# When Is a Yarn?

*Ron Edwards*

Wendy Lowenstein has rightly pointed out that the number of songs left to be collected must of necessity be small, and the number of informants dwindling, and she is suggesting that collectors turn to recording other aspects of our folklore, including yarns.

I fully agree with her, and have given the subject considerable thought, but to date I have been unable to formulate any sort of satisfactory definition as to just what a yarn is.

The tall story is another matter entirely, but my own experience has been that it is more often found in print than in the field. In all my years of collecting, and also living in country towns, I have only heard half a dozen tall stories, and I found these recitals rather embarrassing, as they seemed to be laboured re-workings of material from Bill Wannan's column in the "Australasian Post."

There are obviously some people who delight in this sort of thing as proved by the number of contributions sent in to the press, but where these contributors have obtained their material still remains a mystery.

Bill Wannan has undoubtedly suffered through more of these tall stories than anyone in Australia, and as a result has become quite an expert in their origins, frequently pointing out that some contributor's super-dinkum yarn is actually a re-working of an American item. There are indigenous tall stories, but perhaps not as many as we would like to believe.

Not long ago the ABC ran a competition on their third network to discover the best bush yarn of the year, and with hardly an exception the material sent in sounded as though it had been taken directly from Bill Wannan's column.

I have no doubt that some listeners would have found the material absolutely side-splitting, so much so that they would have felt compelled to write it down and send it off to the "Australasian Post" in the hope of Bill Wannan publishing it. Used in this way the tall story becomes the nearest thing to a perpetual motion machine.

The Speewah stories are a different problem. Alan Marshall has collected a number of these stories over the years mainly, I gather, in north-western Victoria, but other collectors do not seem to have gathered any in, with the exception of Bill

Wannan. I have always felt that the Speewah stories as originally collected by Alan Marshall were probably not widely known outside the areas in which he collected them.

However once he had published them the name caught on and soon many stories with a Speewah setting began being sent to Bill Wannan, giving the impression of a wide spread tradition. Bill Wannan, however, has pointed out that many of these stories were simply re-workings of Paul Bunyan stories, the American setting being changed to Australian.

Before proceeding I must point out that as well as being persecuted in this way Bill has also collected and published more real bush yarns than any other collector in this country, both in his "Post" column and in a number of collections in book form.

When I said earlier that I have not heard many tall stories I am talking about the laboured tall story, the "mosquitoes as big as bullocks" variety. These are not to be confused with the type of story very common in the bush that might be described as the embroidered truth. These yarns are always based on some true incident which the teller has consciously (or unconsciously) altered until it reaches the status of a yarn.

This alteration usually takes the form of stressing the action part of the story and diminishing any part that does not contribute to the action.

*Gold digging in Australia, 1852; "Bad results" (S. T. Gill, watercolour)*

For instance the late Alf Devey, of Yalkula, north of Cairns, had a brother-in-law who was once shot at by a passing motorist. This is how Alf explained the incident, or rather this is how the yarn was told to me by Jack Crossland, Alf's nephew, for the story had already begun circulating when I heard it.

"He was a lazy sort of joker, that George, and Uncle Alf used to send him out to dig out blady grass on a bit of a slope near the main road. Well George used to wear an old hat with the brim turned up into peaks on each side, and from the distance it made him look as if he had tall sticking up ears, like a kangaroo.

As well as this, when he got tired, which was pretty often, he would turn his hoe upside down and use the blade as a seat, so what with his own two legs out the front and the handle of the hoe sticking down the back he looked pretty well like a kangaroo sitting there when you got back a bit, especially with the two ears sticking up.

To make it look even more realistic when he went to roll a smoke he would hold the tobacco in his paws, like this, and the whole effect was so lifelike that before long all the tourists driving along the road used to be stopping and shooting at him."

Bushmen delight in yarns like these, and these are the ones that should be preserved, but the collecting of them is something of a problem. With songs it is possible to meet a stranger for the first time, explain what you are seeking, and record material all at one sitting, but this is not so with yarns.

With yarn spinning all the conditions have to be right before the informant can even begin, and this means that the story teller has to be fully at ease. Some masters of the craft, like the late Bill Harney, can tell a story straight off even if they have only met the listener minutes before but this is the exception.

Generally the collector has to spend considerable time with an informant before he will feel like yarning, and quite often this is impossible. One reason for this is that a yarn is seldom told by rote as a song or ballad is repeated, each rendition is a work of art in itself, enjoyed as much by the teller as by the listener.

Fiddling around with tape recorders is apt to put him off his stride immediately and turn what was probably going to be a lively yarn into a dull little story. But if the collector waits till he has the confidence of his informant and then asks if the informant will repeat yarns already told he is likely to find himself no better off. As the teller already knows that you know the end of each yarn he also knows that he is not going to get the enjoyment of your first reaction to the yarn, hence his recital is apt to be flat and usually shorter than on his first telling.

As well as gaining the confidence of the informant one must also be a good listener, and it also helps if one knows something of the area and the people in it, or can share some other knowledge in common. This means that collecting yarns while on field trips to distant areas can be very difficult, there is just not enough time to make sufficient contact.

An example of the growth of the embroidered truth may be seen in what happened to my friend Bill Fyfe. He set out from Cairns after one wet season to drive his car to Mount Mulligan, a deserted mining area. No one had used the road since the rain, so all the gullys were scoured out, and Bill had to stop every mile or even every half mile, and get to work with pick and shovel to fill in all the washaways.

Finally he crawled in to Mulligan exhausted after a day's hard work and had just started to boil his billy when a shiny new Holden roared up alongside him and the driver bounced out.

"They told me it was a rough road here, but it was no trouble at all, we made it in three hours!"

I was in a mining camp a few months ago and heard this story told once more, by a prospector, but already, within three years the story had grown to spread over three days, with Bill camping under his car every night in the pouring rain!

While I knew this story to be the embroidered truth, to the other listeners it was factual, and this poses another problem to collectors. While some yarns are so embroidered as to make them obviously folk yarns, what do we do about the many yarns which may in fact be simply recitals of true incidents?

A yarn going around Cairns at the present time concerns a fisherman who was caught by the fishing inspector with his ice box full of live female mud crabs, the catching of which is against the law. However, it was a very hot day out there in the Cairns inlet, the sea murky and tepid, and the fisherman's excuse was that because of this he had just caught the crabs and put them into the ice box to keep them cool. The actions of a true humanitarian.

The problem with this as a yarn is that it is actually fact and was reported in court evidence when the unfortunate nature-lover was fined. Even so it is being passed around just at the present by word of mouth, and many of the people telling it think it is actually a bit of embroidered truth, or even a straight out piece of fiction.

A collector meeting one of these people would be almost certain to record this as a yarn, that is if we take the definition of a yarn as being something that sounds like a yarn.

Which brings me to the question that I was going to ask at the start of this article, when is a yarn a yarn? Can any collector put forward a definition to serve as a guideline to collectors of Australian yarns. Must it be always untrue? Obviously not. Must it always be wildly exaggerated? Again no.

What then must it be?

*From* Australian Tradition, *December 1971*

*a Queensland Sugar Plantation.*

. . . I read with interest Ron Edwards' article about yarns in last issue, and disagree with most things he says. Ron says that other collectors have not gathered any Speewah stories. That is not so. I have gathered Speewah stories, and they were good ones, not "laboured re-workings" in any sense. What is more, I have collected them as far away as Western Australia, although in this case the informant said that his father told them to him, and that they had been learned in N.S.W. prior to the 1890 depression. The very fact of this depression led to the movement of many people from the east to W.A. as the Kalgoorlie rush broke out in 1893, and W.A. alone of Australian States, remained

prosperous because of the gold. If it was a fact that the informant, Tom Currey, learned it from his father, which I am sure is so, there is no chance of it having come from Alan Marshall, or Bill Wannan, which Ron suggests is the way Speewah stories have spread.

Also Ron says that he has heard only half a dozen tall stories which he found "rather embarrassing" being "laboured re-workings of materials from Bill Wannan's column in Australasian Post." I suggest that Ron has missed out on stories because he asks for songs. I have hours of wonderful tall stories from Ron's friend Sam Long, from whom Ron collected songs.

*Wendy Lowenstein, in* Australian Tradition, *June 1972*

## Yet More Current Folk Tales

*Since I wrote the original article back in 1969 I have had a number of unlikely stories brought to my notice, and I include these here to bring things up to date (1975).*

*My brother Alan tells me about a young man who owned a Volkswagen "beetle" car, who took his girl friend to a drive-in movie. During the performance four young men in an old Falcon next to them, who were drinking heavily, were using shocking language loudly while discussing the story line of the picture. The young man remonstrated with them, at their use of bad language in the presence of his lady friend, to be met with torrents of abuse. When the show was over, these louts all got out of their car and advanced on him. He hastily wound up the windows of his car, started the engine, and locked the doors. He was about to drive off, when three of the young men lifted the back of his car into the air, thereby robbing the wheels of traction, while the fourth tried to force the door open. The young man panicked, engaged low gear, and revved the motor. Eventually the weight of the car proved too much, it was dropped to the ground, and the spinning wheels carried it off with a tremendous jerk, leaving the larrikins behind. When the young man got home he found three bloody fingers jammed behind the rear bumper.*

*Another car story deals with a young couple who were taking their aged aunt across the Nullabor to Perth for a family reunion in midwinter. During one of the very long stretches across the bare desert, the aunt had a heart attack and died. The young man was in a quandary. His wife refused to travel with the body in the car with her, so he wrapped it in the canvas car cover, and strapped it to the luggage carrier on the roof of the vehicle. What with the cold weather and rigor mortis, aunty was soon literally a stiff. The horrified young people drove on to the limit of their endurance, eventually arriving exhausted at a motel outside Albany. They hastily booked a room and sank into deep sleep, leaving aunty strapped to the luggage rack to be taken to the hospital the following morning. During the night their car was stolen, aunty and all. The car has never been recovered.*

*Some sickening medical stories of the type quoted by Richard Reuss are around, but I find most of them too terrible to reprint in a book intended for family interest. One of the less noisome of these accidental disaster stories concerns a man who was about to sack one of his female employees with whom he had been having an affair but of whom he had grown tired. Workmen were fastening a steel plate designed for a neon sign outside the wall of the office building using an explosive rivet gun. Just as the tearful girl had pleaded that she not be discarded, and the man had scornfully refused, one of the exploded rivets entered through a weak spot in the mortar and pierced the back of the man's head, killing him instantly.*

*The only further comment I have to make on these stories is that they seem to epitomize that sense of poetic justice so apparent in the broadsides and street ballads of two hundred years ago.*

*There is the story of the husband who was always trying to score off his wife. This went on for years, until both were middle-aged people. Then on one weekend they went to the beach with friends for the day. This story is usually told about the Gold Coast in Queensland or Bondi Beach in Sydney. At any rate, husband was a keen surfer still, and he persuaded his wife to go swimming with him despite the big surf running this particular day. The inevitable happened, and the wife was caught by a dumper and rolled helplessly up the beach. In the process she opened her mouth to shout, and lost her false teeth, much to her dismay. Her husband went ostensibly to help her find the missing dentures, along with their friends who accompanied them on the excursion, and, winking hugely at them, he slipped his own false teeth out and then pretended to find them. He offered them to his wife, who rinsed them in the sea and then tried to fit them in. They would not fit, of course, and to the husband's horror she flung them far out into the breaking waves, saying, "It's no good, those aren't mine!"*

*There is another version of the above story that takes place on a fishing trip when a seasick angler loses his teeth over the side and another man offers his as a joke and loses them in the same way.*

*A fishing story that has been round the outback of Australia for many years concerns two men who go fishing for Murray cod and yellowbelly in a deep billabong. They are using the float system, to keep the bait off the bottom, and on this occasion one man is using crickets for bait and the other is using live small frogs. The fellow with the crickets catches fish after fish while his mate does not get a bite for hours. In desperation he shines his torch on to the dimly seen float, to discover that the frog has climbed out of the water and is sitting safely on top of the float. (In North Queensland, they are fishing for barramundi, and the little frog quoted is the small brown one called the "barramundi frog".)*

Twenty miles out of Cooktown (Qld.), a publican told a mate of mine of a bloke who had lounged about all day at the bar, drinking himself stupid. When the pub closed, the drunk staggered homewards in the moonlight, decided to take a short cut through the cemetery, and only succeeded in falling into a freshly-dug grave, where he promptly went to sleep.

Waking in the eerie half-light of the dawn, the startled boozer surveyed his surroundings and could not decide what had happened to him. Stretching up, he gripped the edge of the hole and hoisted himself till his eyes could see the tombstones stretching away in all directions.

"Now I know where I am," he muttered. "It's the bloody Resurrection, and I'm the first one up!"

*Bryan Clark, in* National Folk

*Ian Mudie, the South Australian poet, once told me a variant of the above. It went along the same until the the bloke woke in the newly dug grave. He moaned to himself, "I'm cold. I'm freezing!" and attracted the attention of another drunk who was also staggering homeward through the cemetery. The second drunk teetered on the edge of the grave, looking down for a minute, and then said gravely, "Course you are, you silly bugger. You've kicked all yer dirt off!"*

*My favourite story of graveyard humour concerns a navvy who died on the job, and was told me by Jack O'Neill who was ganger on the gang of navvies at Goondi sugar mill where I worked the slack season in 1952. Jack said that the dead man's mates acted as pall-bearers, but when they reached the grave ready to lower the remains of their mate, the coffin was the wrong way round. The Minister coughed, and said softly, "Reverse the corpse." They stared at him blankly. He said again, more loudly, "Reverse the corpse!" The ganger, quicker on the uptake than the rest, solved the problem simply, by saying, "End for end the bastard!" They knew what he meant straight away.*

*Jack has a lot of stories about navvies, especially those on the Kyogle branch line construction when the standard gauge line was extended to Brisbane to eliminate the transhipment of goods at Wallangarra when the standard gauge terminated there. Jack was an Ulsterman, and his accent was such that he had trouble with certain vowel sounds as pronounced by Australians. I remember him once on a bridge job telling us to "Putt a luttle bolt right through the muddle," which was a fair description of the stage the job had reached at that time.*

*Jack told stories about a navvy's wife whose tent was near the travelling bar that travelled with the camp from place to place. She had a daughter called Bridget, and he claims that when Bridget was milking the goat outside the tent one day her mother saw a loco crew coming. She called, "Bridget, come inside, I want you." When they had passed, she said, "You can go back to milkin' the goat now." A little later four navvies appeared on a pumper, and she called out frantically, "Bridget, Bridget, come inside and bring the goat with you!"*

*On another occasion, in the dead of night just after the bar had closed, footsteps were heard lurching along the track past their tent. Just outside the feet halted, and presently a vigorous splashing sound was heard. "Phwat's that?" asked Bridget. "Go back to sleep, it's only a horse or a navvy," said Mother.*

*He also told a yarn about an English nobleman and his wife travelling on a train that passed a gang of navvies working beside the line.*

*"What are those, dear?" asked the wife.*

*"Navvies, my dear," replied His Lordship.*

*"What do they eat?" asked the wife. When assured that they were human, she seemed lost in thought for a while. Later, she said, "And do they, er, sleep with, er, women?"*

*"Yes," said His Lordship. Again silence.*

*Then she said, finally, "Much too good for them."*

Scene on a Bush Road.

*Troops from southern States condemned to travel on troop trains in Queensland during World War II claimed that the theme song of the Department should be "I'll walk beside you"! There is an apocryphal story of a woman who approached the guard of a mixed goods train at Duchess in the northwest of Queensland. She was very pregnant, and demanded to know how much longer it would take to reach Mount Isa, because she didn't want to have the baby on the train. The guard told her severely that a woman in her condition should not have boarded a Queensland train.*

*"I wasn't in this condition when I boarded the train," she said.*

*"But of course, that was in the Northern Division," added the railwayman who told me the story.*

*This story, with variations, is told all over Australia; much the same as the popular name for a late train is often "The Midnight Horror", a name that bears thinking about!*

*Those interested in the folklore and customs of the*

*Bailed up (Tom Roberts, oil on canvas)*

Australian railwayman should acquire and read two books by that remarkable author Patsy Adam Smith, Folklore of the Australian Railways *and* Hear That Train Blow. *She was herself the daughter of a ganger, and lived most of her childhood beside the rails. She has travelled all over Australia by rail, talking to the men who roll the big ones through the night. My own experience of locomotives was confined to firing and driving the small sugar mill locos on the two-foot gauge tracks, bringing in the harvest, and working as a navvy in the slack season, as before mentioned.*

*One cannot leave the railways without mentioning the last big rail laying job undertaken in Queensland when the Mount Isa line was relaid with heavier track to carry the huge loads of lead and copper from Mount Isa to Townsville. Most of the construction gangs were Torres Strait Islanders; a warlike people in the past, as any student of the history of the Coral Sea will confirm, and they can be a warlike people still. Especially when they have had a few beers. My mate Bill Morrish tells of an occasion when his brother, who is a loco driver, was based in Cloncurry. He returned*

*to the pub where he was living, and climbed the steps to his room on the upper story of the building which came out on to the verandah that ran around the upper story. As he ascended, he heard two T.I. boys talking, and knowing there had been a blue earlier in the evening, he became cautious. But he is a very large man and a footballer of some note, so he continued to go up. As his head rose above the floor level he heard one say to the other, "Here's another one of those whitey blokes." He continued to rise through the floor, and as his height and weight became apparent, the other T.I. man said hastily, "Yeah, but this one's a GOOD whitey bloke!"*

*Incidentally, some twenty years ago there was a very different attitude in Cairns hotels between the treatment shown Aboriginals and T.I.s, as they were called locally. Ah, well, the Maori could fight like hell, too, and so won respect from the white man and equal status. One wonders what sort of treatment the Chinese digger and the unfortunate Aboriginal would have received in Australia had they too been effectively aggressive.*

*Prospecting for gold, or rewarded at last (hand-coloured lithograph from* Sketches of Australian Life and Scenery)

# A Comment on Australian Slang

*One of the chief difficulties facing novelists and other writers in Australia has been the prolific use of slang, which sets Australian off as being a different language from English, though basically allied to that tongue. The writer often has to decide between veracity of conversational prose and its consequent unintelligibility to people who do not speak the Australian language. It tends to limit the possible overseas market for his book. This slang is a development from the old thieves' cant, with many local catch-phrases and expressions added to the mixture, and some of the expressions have remained extant from the days of the*

*First Fleet. The word "pal", for instance, used so widely in America as well as Australia, is derived from the Romany (gipsy) word which means simply, "brother". Two comments are all we have room to include, and the study of idiomatic Australian language and its possible derivations is properly a study for lexicographers rather than folk investigators. One cannot help being fascinated, though, and it is a marvellous field for collection and speculation. Watkin Tench came with the First Fleet, and wrote two books on the colony, both published in London upon his return to England.*

A leading distinction, which marked the convicts on their outset in the colony, was an use of what is called the "flash", or "kiddy" language. In some of our early courts of justice, an interpreter was frequently necessary to translate the deposition of the witness, and the defence of the prisoner. This language has many dialects. The sly dexterity of the pickpocket; the brutal ferocity of the footpad; and the deadly purpose of the midnight ruffian, is each strictly appropriate in the terms which distinguish and characterize it. I have ever been of opinion, that an abolition of this unnatural jargon would open the path to reformation. And my observations on these people have constantly instructed me that indulgence in this infatuating cant, is more deeply associated with depravity, and continuance in vice, than is generally supposed. I recollect hardly one instance of a return to honest pursuits, and habits of industry, where this miserable perversion of our noblest and peculiar faculty was not previously conquered.

*From* The Settlement at Port Jackson, *Watkin Tench, Captain of Marines*

. . . Communication is indeed the problem. The following statement was heard in the public bar at Chardon's Corner Hotel in Brisbane, Christmas Eve, 1974: "You should've been here last night. Two wogs bunged on a blue. One of them got into holts with some young lair from Inala, but his china wouldn't back him, so he did his block and went the knuckle on his mate." End of quote. This communicated all right. The hearer said, "Go on!" The first speaker then said, "Yeah, we nearly pissed ourselves."

I submit that the above, and I vouch for its veracity, would convey the sort of fellows they were to another Australian who knew the language, but would be meaningless to someone who only spoke English. . .

*Bill Scott, in an article in* The Australian Author, *April 1975*

*From a distant land (David Davies, oil on canvas)*

*Stampede of pack horses, Northern Territory (T. Baines, from* Australia, *ed. Edwin Carton Booth)*

# Bush Rhymes and Sayings, Toasts and Curses

## As He Lay One Night

*F.H.*

As he lay one night neath a tall gum-tree, his
    reason came and went.
And he writhed in agonies by his fire, and he
    thought of his life illspent.
Then he calmly slept his last long sleep,
    starvation was his death,
He thought he lied neath the sunny smiles, of his
    mother sad bereft.
Next morning an old swagger, passing by the
    dell,
Saw the remains, stifled a sigh, and muttered
    another by hell.

*From the* Bulletin's *"Answers to Correspondents" column, 15 January
1898*

Shearer man like toast and butter,
Wolseley comb and Lister cutter.
Rouseabout like plenty joke,
Plenty rain and engine broke.

*This verse and the one immediately following are
widely known.*

A little bit of sugar and a little bit of tea,
A little bit of flour you can hardly see,
And without any meat between you and me,
It's a bugger of a life, by Jesus!

Ron Edwards collected the following "Rousie's
Hymn" from Don Johnson, shearer in the Winton
area in the thirties. It is, of course, sung to the tune
of the well-known hymn.

What a friend we have in Jesus,
Sending all the lovely rain,

*Sheep shearing in Australia (engraving from* Illustrated Sydney News, *15 October 1864)*

Fills the rousie's heart with pleasure
Fills the shearer's heart with pain

*From* Australian Tradition, *June 1972*

On the far Barcoo where they eat nardoo,
Jumbuck giblets and pigweed stew.
Fever and ague and scurvy plague you,
And the Barcoo Rot, but the worst of the lot
Is the Bellyando Spew[1].

*1. The Belyando River is a tributary of the Burdekin.*

*Rachel Henning in her* Letters *mentions that while on her way to Exmoor station from Port Alma, the party camped on a creek two days before they reached the Burdekin River. She says, ". . . Tom discovered some 'fat hen' in the creek, and when boiled it is not at all unlike spinach. I think it is a species of goosefoot; it is exactly like the English plant of that name." I remember being told as a boy that pigweed was edible, and have eaten it. The same weed (which grows in my garden in Brisbane) I have also heard called "fat hen". Possibly it is the same plant.*

*Rachel Henning also confirms that the standard ration given to shepherds on her brother Biddulph's station was "ten, ten, two and a quarter", as mentioned in the song "The Old Bark Hut". The figures referred to quantities of commodities, in this case, ten pounds of flour, ten of meat, two of sugar and a quarter of a pound of tea. These rations applied to station employees, not to travellers who were only entitled to, as Willoughby puts it in* Such Is Life, *"solicit the dem'd pannikin of flour". Of course, the experienced 'bo could usually raise more, as Lawson shows in one of his tales of Mitchell the Swagman.*

375

## Gow of Mount Gambee
*Anon.*

I've lived on beef and pigweed in the drought of
  sixty-three,
I've starved on yowah and munyeroo[1] adown the
  St-relec-kee,
But the hardest patch I ever struck was Gow of
  Mount Gam-bee.
He fed his blacks on 'roos and rats and
  "Wallapabraza pflours"[2].
His staggy meat was lively, and his sodden
  damper sour,
And weevils big as bull-ants played leap-frog in
  the flours.

*Collected by Russel Ward from* Bushmen All, *"Giles Seagram" (H. J. Driscoll)*

*1. In* Spinifex and Sand *David W. Carnegie gave this description: "A similar plant [to parakeelia], also found in Central Australia, is 'Munyeru'. In the centre of this a little bag of black seeds grows; these seeds are crushed and eaten by the natives. 'Munyeru', Breaden tells me, is quite a good vegetable for human consumption."*
*2. The Bathurst Burr was reputedly brought to Australia in the manes and tails of horses imported from Valparaiso, Chile around 1840. There must have been something euphonious about the name of the town which appealed to Australians. One of the bullocks in Tom Collins's* Such Is Life *was called "Vallaparaiser", and, as can be seen in the above verse, it was also used to describe the very poor quality flour supplied to some ration men with their "ten, ten, two and a quarter".*

*Rations were often of the cheapest and poorest quality. Another economy practised by station storekeepers was the supply of what the ration men called "post and rail" tea, mainly consisting of the stalks and roughest leaves. On one station when the shepherds were supplied with better quality tea because the cheaper variety had run out till the stores came, they complained about the quality, saying that "it didn't have the body"! The mispronunciation of the word must have been common enough; there is an English shanty with the chorus:*
  *Now it's come on, Jack; take in the slack,*
  *Get a turn around the capstan, heave aboard!*
  *In your part of ship you'll be handy, dandy,*
  *And we're off to Vallaparaiser round the Horn.*

Then there are those short pieces from two to six lines that are generally referred to as "bushmen's toasts", a convenient enough name, though not, of course, accurate. They act as conversation fill-ins, or comments on events or persons. While some of them are complete in themselves, others are undoubtedly fragments of longer verses, which have been cut adrift from the parent and exist as entities in their own right.

A particular sentiment or thought in verse form will appeal for some reason and be taken up by some particular group, be it boozers or shearers, until everyone in that group knows it. From there it may spread to similar groups, until the knowledge of certain of them act almost as passwords, and show that the speaker identifies himself with the group. For instance:
  A duck for a truck,
  And a drake for a rake,[1]
is an example of one, normally understood only by people in the sugarcane area along the north Queensland coast. This is an example of a specialised toast, but some of them are very general, and known to almost every adult male in Australia, for instance, "Things are crook in Tallarook", etc.

A number of these toasts are complete in themselves:
  We drank the old selection
  And the house upon the hill,
  We drank the ploughs and harrows
  And we're pretty thirsty still.
(Recorded from Tiger O'Shane, 26-1-65)

*1. "A duck for a truck, etc." This comments succinctly on the practice of bribing the crew of a sugar-cane hauling loco early in the season when trucks are short. A farmer who is anxious to get his cane hauled in to the mill will offer a duck or drake to the loco crew if they will give him extra empty trucks to load. Several empty trucks are known locally as a "rake" of trucks.*

*Ned Kelly, the bushranger (engraving from* Australasian Sketcher, *31 July 1880)*

Although many of the toasts seem to exist for no particular reason, yet they can often be used, because of a particular sentiment contained in them, to express an opinion of a certain event, and do it in such a way that it will only be understood by those "in the know". For instance:

> There was nothing to do, the shearer knew,
> But carry his swag outback.

When spoken in a bar, this is a comment on the publican, understood by all in the group, not because of anything hidden in those particular lines, but simply because the listeners mentally add the first two lines, which contain the message,

> The publican's words were short and few
> And the publican's looks were black.

Some toasts are recited seemingly to fill in lulls in the conversation, the purpose of others may be to change the conversation. Jack Crossland used this one quite often:

> Reach me down my fourteen foot malacca
> Where it hangs upon the wall,
> With three foot of greenhide thong
> And a foot of silken fall.

(Recorded at Innot Springs, 31-1-69)

Morris Jenkins had this to say when the party was quiet:

> Sing, you bloody bastards, sing,
> Make the bloody rafters ring!

(Recorded Cairns, 12-2-65)

Tiger O'Shane has a number of toasts:

> There he is, the dirty skunk,
> In the bar-room, stinkin' drunk.
> A fellow should be fined for knowing him,
> He was drinkin' here when I came in.
>
> Why don't you drink and make less noise?
> You make more noise than all the boys!
> Why don't you stand and drink in peace?
> God strike me dead, you'll bring the police.
>
> Here's to you, as good as you are,
> And here's to me, as bad as I am,
> And as good as you are
> And as bad as I am,
> I'm as good as you are,
> As bad as I am.

(All three above recorded at Holloways Beach, 21-1-65)

Some toasts refer to old trades, this one was from Mr Side, at Mount Kooyong:

> Bind 'em up tight,
> And pick 'em up clean,
> And keep out of the way
> Of the reaping machine.

(Recorded 20-4-65)

Jack Crossland learned the next one at Mount Surprise, in the Gulf country:

> Here's to good old whisky,
> Amber, pale and clear,
> Maybe not so sweet as a woman's lips
> But a damn sight more sincere.

Also this short one came from Jack:

> Necessity is the mother of invention
> And the father of halfcastes.

And last of all, short and to the point from Jock Dingwell:

> Sing, shout,
> Or get out.

(Recorded 2-2-65)

*From "Songs and Singers", Ron Edwards,* National Folk, *Number 33 (November 1969)*

Garden Island in a Fog

> Land of lags and kangaroos
> Of possums and the scarce emu,
> The farmer's pride but the prisoner's hell,
> Land of bums, fare thee well.

*This farewell curse was supposedly delivered from the top of the paddlebox of the steam vessel on which Frank the Poet (Frank Macnamara) was being sent back to Sydney from Van Diemen's Land. The emu was indeed scarce. It differed from the mainland species, and was extinct probably by the 1860s. The Tasmanian Aboriginals took a little longer to be eradicated, and the wary marsupial wolf, the Tasmanian Tiger mentioned in the song "Van Diemen's Land", took even longer to extinguish, the last known specimen dying in a zoo in the 1930s.*

*Queensland and the Territory seem to have drawn more than their fair share of curses and farewells. The following is an interesting one. Ron Edwards and Wendy Lowenstein collected it in 1969 from Charley Tarr, an elderly resident of Cooktown. He had found it written on a piece of paper he picked up casually in a Darwin street some years before. There is no indication of authorship. Re "stinging, stinking wogs" mentioned in the poem; these are undoubtedly the little beetles known in Innisfail as the "lavender" bug, or "stink" bug. When distressed, these squirt out a corrosive fluid or gas which stings severely, especially if it gets you in the eye. The smell is unmistakeable, like bitter almonds raised to the power of ten. It closely resembles the smell of lantana bugs, but is much more powerful. They are attracted to light, and are a great nuisance on a locomotive travelling tender foremost at night, when the headlight brings them in swarms at times, to the consequent distress and bad language of driver and offsider.*

## An Immigrant's Lament

We've flying ants with frilly pants,
And stinging, stinking wogs,
And clammy slugs and poison bugs,
And bloated croaking frogs.

We've crocodiles and miles and miles
Of snake infested scrub
We've fish that bite throughout the night,
Outside each flaming pub.

We've fever, bogs and dingo dogs,
And places fraught with vice,
And steaming days that wilt our ways,
And lousy little lice.

The mossies croon a songless tune
Around our tortured heads,
The sandflies bite throughout the night,
They're hatching in our beds.

Big ants and flies with avid eyes,
Eat every mortal thing,
Our Christmas cheer is third rate beer,
Oh death where is thy sting?

*The following curse was given to a member of the Victorian Folklore Society by Mr Lindsay Rose of Seymour, Victoria. He said, in 1962, in the accompanying letter that this "happened a few weeks ago". However, as "Lalla Rookh" was a commonly used name for Truganini, the last surviving full-blood member of the Tasmanian Aboriginal people, the chances are that it was written some time ago.*

May Satan, with a rusty crook,
Catch every goat in Tallarook;
May Mrs Mellon's latest spook
Haunt all old maids in Tallarook;
May China's oldest pig-tailed cook
Spoil chops and steaks in Tallarook;
May all the frogs in Doogalook
Sing every night in Tallarook;
May Reedy Creek create a brook
To swamp the flats in Tallarook;
May rabbits ever find a nook
To breed apace in Tallarook;
May Sin Ye Sun and Sam Ah Fook
Steal all the fowls in Tallarook;
May Ikey Moses make a book
To stiffen sport in Tallarook;
May sirens fair as Lalla Rook[h]
Tempt all old men in Tallarook;
May every paddock yield a stook
Of smutty wheat in Tallarook;
May good St Peter overlook
The good deeds done in Tallarook;
May each Don Juan who forsook
His sweetheart live in Tallarook;
May all who Matthew's pledges took
Get rolling drunk in Tallarook;
May every pigeon breed a rook
To spoil the crops in Tallarook;
May I get ague, gout and fluke
If I drink rum in Tallarook.

## Some Outback Definitions and Repartee

A Burketown mosquito net is a bottle of rum and a cowdung fire.

A Condamine roll is an emu between two dampers.

A Barcoo sandwich is a goanna between two sheets of bark, or a double rum between two beers.

A Wagga Rug is a sheet of paperbark between two opened out chaff bags. I have heard people still refer to a blanket as a "wagga", in Mount Isa in 1947.

Of tobacco, "She's strong, all right. Kill a brown dog at eight paces."

A stockman's lunch is a smoke and a spit.

A dingo's breakfast is a pee and a good look round.

Of a polysyllabic word used casually in conversation, "Where did you get that jawbreaker?" "I gave a bloke two ounces of tobacco for it!"

## Bush Cooks

Tug Moon was the cook at Rockedgiel, and apart from being a first-class cook he was a notable dancer, and his services as Master of Ceremonies were always in demand. I have seen several of the American square-dance callers, and Tug could have given any of them a lot of start.

*The men's dining room (engraving from* Australasian Sketcher, *22 April 1882)*

On the way to Coolah over Pandora Pass (where the beauty of the views again amazed me) he told a story against himself of an incident which had happened in that town a few years before. He was M.C.-ing a dance, and was drinking heavily. He tried to close the dance, but all there were enjoying themselves, and kept calling for more, and it looked like going on till morning. But in the first sets of the quadrilles, at "Ladies half-right, gents half-left," Tug shouted, "Harlots left, blankards right. He was knocked flat on his back by some offended husband or lover, and lay half-stunned for a moment, then sat up and yelled, "The moon's down, the dance is done."

When he finished his yarn he was quiet for a while, then remarked: "They should have shot me."

This story was vouched for by several people who were at the dance when it happened. And they bore him no ill-will. "Poor old Tug had a few in," was the explanation.

*From* Time Means Tucker, *Duke Tritton*

The babbling brook his shovel took
The damper to unfold.
"Another sod! So help me, God,
That beats the bloody world."

*Anon.*

*Shearers' cooks were not employed by the station but by the men themselves, being elected by the shearers after they had been signed on. Some of them were a law unto themselves, some of them were slightly mad, some of them could cook very well, some of them were "poisoners". Bill Harney had some wonderful stories about cooks he had known. Try to find a copy of that descriptive masterpiece of outback haute cuisine,* Bill Harney's Cookbook, *or find some lucky person who has a copy of the recording called "The Two Who Went Talkabout", which is simply an LP of Alan Marshall, that doyen of imaginative discursiveness about the bush, and Bill, talking to each other about things and other things as well. There is good cross talk on bush cooks on that record, including mention of one who was immortalized in verse as the Busted Oven. He earned his name by putting a crowbar through the stove at the end of the shearing so the squatter would have to buy a new stove for him by the time shearing came round again the next year. Other famous shearers' cooks included the Sitting Shot, "Gympie" Howard, Blue Bob from Borraloola and Jack without a shirt. There are many stories about bush cooks. Their traditional call was, "There's stew in the dixie, there's mutton on the dish, there's damper by the billy. You can have a feed or you can have the cook." Every bush cook was supposed to be ready to fight for his cooking.*

We were then introduced to another famous cook, "Jack without a shirt." No one seemed to know what his other name was. The story is that he was cooking at Boorooma many years previously, and, wanting to give the shearers a special treat, had knocked up a big duff, then discovered he didn't have a cloth big enough to hold it, so he used his shirt. At tea-time the shearers were praising the duff, and backing-up for second helpings, when one of them, going into the galley for a mug of tea, noticed the shirt bearing evidence of its use as a pudding-cloth. Being a bit fussy, he complained, and there was an argument, during which the shirt was torn to pieces. And it was the only shirt Jack owned. So till the cut-out he went about his babbling stripped to the waist, and the name stuck.

He didn't mind his nickname in the least; in fact, he seemed rather proud of it.

*From* Time Means Tucker, *Duke Tritton*

# Nicknames

Jack Wright was an interesting talker on the subject of nicknames:

"One of the cooks on the plains, the Liverpool Plains, was known as Fol-the-diddle-di-doh," he told Meredith. "He earned the name because he was always singing this song, 'Fol-the-diddle-di-doh'. When any of the travellers—any of the swagmen—came to the men's hut or the kitchen for a hand-out, his usual trick was to hand them the axe, and sing:

There's the axe and there's the wood,
Fol-the-diddle-di-doh,
When you think you've chopped enough,
Come and get a bit of duff.
Fol-the-diddle-di-doh.

"Another bloke had the name of Step-up. He used to walk with a limp—a step-and-a-limp and a step-and-a-limp; so he got the name of Step-up."

This fairly set him off. "Then", he said, "There was Bob the Frog. Bob was in Coolamon, and he was on the booze. He got in the horrors or something and took his clothes off and started to leap across the road like a frog. He was part aboriginal, and he looked a bit like a frog that way, so when he came out of the boob he got the name of Bob the Frog."

Wright laughingly told of the Baking-powder Cock. "The Baking-powder Cock addressed everybody as 'Cock', and the story is—whether it's right or not—he stole some money and the only place he could hide it was in the baking-powder tin; so that's how he earned the name of Baking-powder Cock."

*From* Folksongs of Australia, *John Meredith and Hugh Anderson*

## Nicknames around Coen and Cooktown, 1873 to 1896

Dick the Needle, Tom the Thread, Billy the Whip, Four Ton Jack, Billy the Pup, Dick the Dog, The Jumper, The Maggot, Lovely Les, Billy the Bludger, Pretty Boy, Twenty Foot, Wednesday Bob, Blue Bob the Bastard, Paddy the Fenian, Dick the Devil, The Great Australian Bite, The Nip, The Strangler, The Burner Off, Red Ned, Mick the Rager, The Sand Groper, Twentyfive to Six, Legs Eleven, The Bluetongue, The Human Bat, Tooth Brush.

*From Stan Boyd's "Notebook", quoted in* National Folk, *Number 39, along with many other nicknames*

*Nicknames I have met in my travels include Dungy, Bottler, Battler, Sinbad (from his habit of exaggeration), The Parrot, Walkie-talkie, Fish, Aspro, Big Red Mick and Little Red Mick, Onions, The Moaner, Knocker, Dusty (Miller, of course), Stuffer, Dingy (Bell), Bendy, Old Ek-ek (from the noise he made when he laughed), Zombie, Punchy, Slug, Emu-head, Hooky, Val Egg, and The Bony Herring.*

*From David Denholm I heard of the station master in Central Queensland who habitually wore a solar topee as issued by the Queensland Railways. He was short and very thin and the navvies always referred to him as "The Lead-headed Nail".*

# Children's Games and Rhymes

## Children's Games Around the World
*Alan Scott*

"Just have a go at this lot," says my mate, a second generation Australian, as he gazes at the collection of humanity at our place of employment, "the place is full of bloody wogs." The blokes referred to originated in Ireland, Quebec and many points in between. Their diverse origins gave me a way of passing the time, and for some years I have been asking what games they played as kids.

The question can evoke a variety of responses, all the way from blank amnesia to the ecstatic recall of a happy childhood. One man who described himself as an Armenian brought up in Jordan, regaled me for hours with recollections of games with tops. I was specifically asking about games not organised by adults. I was surprised to find, though perhaps I shouldn't have been, that we all played the same games regardless of differences in our national cultures.

We all flew kites, though my three Chinese informants had a more sophisticated version than the rest of us. They coated their kite strings with powdered glass and tried to saw through opponent's kite string. An Egyptian recalled running backwards off a flat roof in Alexandria trying to get his kite airborne!

When I was a boy we played a game called Kat, the Kat being a short piece of wood bevelled at both ends which we placed on the ground. We hit down on the tapered end with the stick we used as a bat, and when the Kat flipped up in the air, hit it as far as we could. I forget the actual method of scoring—I rather think we ran between wickets while the other side retrieved the Kat. A Cypriot and a Lebanese told me they played the same game.

Hopscotch was played by girls in most places, but a Lebanese said that boys and girls played it in his country, and a Pakistani recalled that it was a boys' game. But all over the world boys played with marbles and tops and girls skipped. The only informant who reported that marbles were not played by him or his immediate friends was a White Russian brought up in Harbin. However, he saw marbles played in Shanghai when he moved there. He thought this was due to British influence. But a Chinese boy from the island of Hainan told me that when he came to Australia at the age of 12, boys here played a game of marbles with exactly the same rules as the game played in Hainan.

Apart from those already mentioned, my informants came from these countries: Hong Kong, Greece, Yugoslavia, Mauritius, Mexico, Brazil, Malta, and many different parts Hong Kong, the British Isles. Though they were all adults, I am sure that the games are still current among children in those countries and indeed that kids play the same games all over the world.

Rene Garde recounts in "Tambaran" how he visited a village in New Guinea where the boys spun tops made from half coconut shells. When he returned some time later to take photos, not only had the tops been put away but the boys would only spin them in secret away from adults. Only then did he discover that the tops were spun to assist the sweet potato vines to twine around their poles. His second visit coincided with the period when the tubers were growing and tops were tabu.

Probably most children's games that rely on accessories like marbles, balls, skipping ropes, etc., had their origins in such sympathetic magic or related superstition. Most likely they were adult occupations used to influence spirits. Relinquished by adults under the influence of formal religion or as science explained the working of nature, the games were retained by children for their own sake.

One might theorise that compulsory education increased the opportunity for play while educating the fundamental reasons for the games out of existence. Certainly children keep alive a variety of games not sanctified by the sports field or gaming

table. In spite of the distractions of T.V., in spite of the attractions of cheap toys and play materials, and in spite of competition from organised sport, these games seem bound to continue.

Given the deeply entrenched tradition, the emotional satisfaction and the appealing properties of the objects used in these games it seems certain that not only will my children continue to play them, but also their children's children into the future.

*From* Australian Tradition, *December 1971*

RAILWAY POLITICS

*As pointed out in the preceding article, children seem to share a global tradition. There seems to be an unwritten code of conduct which is understood by the inhabitants of school playgrounds in most countries, especially those of the English speaking nations. Some of these show evidence of great antiquity, and possibly the best book to have been written so far on these origins is* The Lore and Language of Schoolchildren *by Iona and Peter Opie, published by Oxford University Press. How many readers in their childhood, wishing for a short cessation in a game while they made a point of order, shouted, "I'm bar!" The Opies show that this expression derives almost certainly from the Anglo-French word "parley", a truce between knights on the battlefield. Another example is the survival of shepherd's home-made numbers in counting-out rhymes, especially those that begin with "Eenie, Meenie, Minie, Mo".*

*The major study in Australia of such material was published by Heinemann Educational Publishers, and was called* Cinderella, Dressed in Yella. *It is being revised at present but will soon be available again incorporating much new material. You will find many old friends from your childhood in it. The collectors and collators of the material are Factor, Lowenstein and Turner. One of the curiosities of Australian publishing is that the original book, the contents of which had been collected from school children, was banned for a time in one Australian State because it might corrupt children! Fortunately this Gilbertian state of affairs did not last very long.*

*Much of the material quoted here is included in this book, and I am grateful that it was published. I had it in my mind to do something along these lines myself, even to the extent of writing an article at one time advising collectors who complained of the lack of new traditional material to begin in their own homes with their own children. This article was subsequently published in* Australian Tradition *under the title, "All Around You". My brother Alan had made a collection of such rhymes in Queensland and New South Wales, and the indefatigable Wendy Lowenstein of Melbourne had also made a collection, which has been published as an occasional paper by the Fish and Chip Press.*

*No collection of Australian traditional material would be complete without a selection of children's verses. I have included, among others, the ones that seem to me to show some signs of local composition or local alteration from existing overseas material.*

## Parodies

Half a pound of Mandy Rice,
Half a pound of Keeler.
Put 'em together and what have you got?
A couple of sexy sheilas.

Hark the herald angels sing
Beecham's pills are just the thing.
Peace on earth and mercy mild,
Two for adults and one for a child.

While shepherds washed their socks by night
All seated round a tub.
A bar of Sunlight soap came down
And they went rub-rub-rub.

Good King Wenceslas went out
In a Mini Minor.
Bumped into an atom bomb
And ended up in China.

(To the tune "Colonel Bogey")
Bullshit, was all the band could play.
Bullshit, they played it night and day.
Bullshit! it's always bullshit!
It's only bullshit the band can play.

(The tune is a corrupt version of the "Soldiers' Chorus" from *Faust*)
Oh Eliza, look at your Uncle Jim,
Paddling in the bathtub, learning how to swim.
First he does the backstroke, now he does a dive,
Now he's in the plug-hole, swimming against the tide.

*My father used to sing another set of words to this same tune, a soldier's song from World War I, with the initial words, "Corn beef, and bloody great lumps of fat". I never did get to hear all of it, so suspect it must have been considered too coarse for my ears.*

Screw Pine

## Counting Out Rhymes

Bake a pudding, bake a pie,
Take 'em up to Bondi;
Bondi wasn't in,
Take 'em up to black gin;
Black gin took 'em in—
Out goes she!

Melbourne City Council, one, two, three,
Melbourne City Council, you're not HE.

## Skipping Rhymes

Captain Cook was a very brave man,
He sailed the ocean in an old tin can.
The waves grew higher and higher
Until they went right over.

Old Miss Mason dropped her basin
Right in the middle of Woy Woy station.
How many pennies did it cost?
One, Two, Three, etc.

*From Woolloomooloo to Darlinghurst (engraving from* Picturesque Atlas of Australasia, *ed. Andrew Garran)*

Vote, vote, vote for Mr. Menzies,
In comes [Susan] at the door.
[Susan] was the one who gave us all the fun
So we don't like Mr. Menzies any more.
Shut the door.

## Ball Bouncing

Johnny and Jane and Jack and Lou,
Butler's Stairs through Wooloomooloo,
Wooloomooloo and through the Domain,
Round the block and home again.
Heigh ho, tipsy toe,
Give us a kiss and away we go.

## Playground Rhymes

*There are many versions and sorts of rhyme about
Captain Cook, who seems to have captured the
popular imagination. The three following are my
particular favourites.*

Captain Cook chased a chook
All around Australia;
When he got back he got a smack
For being a naughty sailor.

Captain Cook chased a chook
All around Australia;
He lost his pants in the middle of France
And found them in Tasmania.

(To be sung to the tune of "Clementine")
Come to our school, come to our school,
It's a place of misery,
There's a teacher in the doorway
Saying, "Welcome unto thee'.

Don't believe it, don't believe it,
It's a pack of dirty lies,
If it wasn't for the teachers
It would be a paradise.

Build a bonfire, build a bonfire,
Put the teachers on the top,
Put the prefects on the bottom
And burn the bloody lot.

Salvation Army, free from sin,
All went to Heaven in a cornbeef tin.
One had a kettle and another had a drum
And another had a pancake stuck to his bum.

(To be sung to the tune of "That's Peggy
O'Neill")
She barracks for Richmond, I bet you a zac,
Because her bloomers are yellow and black:
Face like a dragon bashed in by a wagon,
That's Peggy O'Neill.

I'm a navvy, you're a navvy
Working on the line,
Four and twenty bob a week
Besides our overtime.
Roast beef, boiled beef,
Pudden made with eggs,
Up come a copper
With a pair of sausage legs.

Holy Father, what'll I do?
I've come to confess my sins to you.
Holy Father, I killed a cat.
You'll have to suffer, my child, for that.
Holy Father, what'll it be?
Forty days without any tea.
Father dear, it's far too long.
You've done, my child, a very great wrong.
But Father dear, 'twas a Protestant cat.
Good, my girl, you did right to do that.

*From* Cinderella, Dressed in Yella, *Ian Turner*

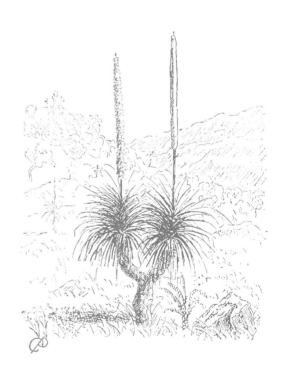

# Of Naval Tradition

I spoke of Alf's singing; and Jack the Shellback told me how the fellows at the station had persuaded him to give them a couple or three songs before he left.

"Wasn't he something wonderful?" I remarked.

"Well, no," deferentially but positively; "Nothing like what you'd hear in a foc'sle."

In fact, according to Jack's account, he used to be reputed a middling singer himself. And he straightway rendered a mawkishly sentimental song, and a couple of extremely unchaste ones, in a voice which made the tea-embrowned pannikins on the table rattle in sympathy.

*From* Such Is Life, *Joseph Furphy ("Tom Collins")*

"Oh, show me the way to go home,"
Said the girl on Bondi Beach.
"I had a little swimsuit 'bout an hour ago
And it floated out of reach.
Now all I have on now,
Is sand and sea and foam,
So give me a page of the Courier-Mail
And show me the way to got home."

*From Ron Edwards, who got it from Tony Davis of Fruitgrove, Queensland. The tune is self evident.*

*The following song has become reasonably well known from the show* Oh, What a Lovely War, *But the words used in that production differed from the ones my father used to sing meditatively as he watered the garden.*

I want to go home, I want to go home.
I don't want to go to the trenches no more
With the whizz-bangs and Jack Johnsons[1] flying galore.
Take me over the sea, where the Alleyman[2] can't get at me.
Oh, my! I don't want to die!
I want to go home!

*1. "Jack Johnsons" were shells that exploded with a dense cloud of black smoke. Jack Johnson was the famous negro boxer from the United States.*
*2. Possibly Allemagne.*

*There were many "private" songs peculiar to the Navy while I was engaged with that organization in the recent difficulties with Japan, Germany and Italy. One such was sprung on me as a complete surprise by an English matelot, a "scouser" from his accent, in the wet canteen at Small Craft Base at Colmslie in Brisbane around 1944. He said, "I know an Australian song." I expected the inevitable* Waltzing Matilda, *but to my surprise he sang the following in a tuneful voice, and although I heard it only once, I remember the words and music to this day.*

In an old Australian homestead, with the roses round the door,
A girl received a letter, just newly from the war.
With her mother's arms around her she gave way to sobs and sighs,
For when she read that letter, the tears came to her eyes.

*Chorus*
Why do I weep, why do I sigh,
My love's asleep, so far away.
He played his part that August day
And left my heart in Suda Bay.

She joined a band of nurses beneath the cross of red
And swore to do her duty to the soldier who lay dead.
Many soldiers came to woo her but were sadly turned away
As to them she told the story of the grave at Suda Bay.

*Chorus*

*I have never encountered it elsewhere since, though my mother now assures me that "Everybody knows that song."*

*Most of the "private" Naval songs were of a character not to be included in a book intended for family sale, and they are available from other sources. There was a private publication in Melbourne some years ago entitled* Lays and Snatches, *but I lost my copy in the recent inundation of the city of Brisbane. Brad Tate, a collector in New South Wales, has specialized in the collection of such ditties, and perhaps may some day be prevailed upon to publish the results of his labours.*

*I thought I had a good range of such songs until I met Stan Arthur, whereupon I bowed to the master. But there were songs that were popular in particular ships, e.g. the theme song of the H.M.A.S.* Kanimbla *while she was a merchant cruiser and before she was converted to a landing craft mother ship, or so I was assured by a former member of her crew who was watchmate with me on a mine-layer, the* Bungaree, *in 1943. The song was known on other vessels, but the* Kanimbla *regarded it as their own private property, he said. It went as follows.*

She's a tiddley ship, o'er the ocean she flits,
Sailing by night and by day.
And when she's in motion she's the pride of the
    ocean
And you can't see her backside for spray.
Side, side, tiddley ship's side,
The Jimmy[1] looks on it with pride.
But he'd have a blue fit if he saw all the spit
On the side of *Kanimbla*'s ship's side—
This is my story, this is my song,
We've been in commission too bloody long,
Roll on the *Rodney*, the *Nelson* and *Hood*
This one funnelled bastard is no flaming good,
Dinky-di, dinky-di,
I'm an old sailor and I can't tell a lie.

1. *The* Jimmy, *in Naval slang, is the First Lieutenant*

*Later, after the* Hood *was sunk during the battle with the* Bismarck, *the final stanza was altered by some messdeck bard as follows.*

    Roll on the Rodney, Repulse *and* Renown,
    *We can't say the* Hood *cause the bastard's
        gone down.*

*I never heard a shanty sung during the five years I spent at sea. I think they were working songs, and when the need for keeping time to the haul or the capstan was gone, the songs went also, as accompaniments for the jobs. There were still traditional calls and sayings, used by bosun's mates when piping orders outside the ears of Authority; and of course, there were traditional slang expressions that are probably still extant—the naval equivalent of thieves cant, perhaps—incomprehensible to the outsider but reassuring to the member of the "in" group. The Navy is very strong on tradition, as strong, in a way, as school children.*

*No doubt many of the familiar cries have now gone the way of all flesh and sound, one of them being the old familiar pipe, "Cooks to the galley", to advise the man responsible from each mess that the food was available from the cooks who actually did all the preparation. The pipe dates back to the days when each mess actually prepared the food for cooking and the cooks merely cooked it for them.*

*Another pipe of great antiquity was the old familiar traditional call for rousing men in the morning,, "Wakee, wakee, rise and shine, the sun'll burn your eyes out! Hands off ——, on socks, hit the deck me hearty tars! [Delivered in strongly ironic fashion, this last!] Show a leg, show a leg!" "Show a leg" goes back at least as far as the Napoleonic wars, when the conditions of life in the Navy were so bad that, on returning to England after foreign service, seamen were not allowed ashore in case they did not return. The Navy was not a popular service, and this led not only to the use of the press-gang for recruiting, but also to the impressment of men convicted of the milder forms of criminal charge. Naturally, no captain in his right mind was going to lose any of his already trained men if he could help it, so men were confined to the ship until it sailed again. It was the custom to allow wives and sweethearts aboard to live on the messdecks with their husbands, and the call "Show a leg" in the morning allowed the bosun and his mates to be sure that the body remaining comfortably asleep in the hammock was indeed a female and not a member of the crew who should have been on duty. I might hastily add that this custom was dead before I joined the Navy, but the call remained.*

*A song that was popular on Harbour Defence Motor Launch 1342 when I was serving aboard that vessel at Wewak and Madang in 1945 was brought aboard by a fellow called Don Croft, who had served in the R.N. for a while. It was a fine parody on the American traditional ballad "Frankie and Johnnie". The words went as follows.*

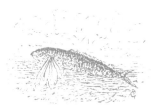

Listen, I'll tell you a story, it happened in Malta
   you know,
All about a great big beautiful blonde and a guy
   called Smoky Joe,
Who was her man, but who was doing her wrong.

Blondie was just four and twenty, Smoky was just
   thirty-two.
Smoky was running Blondie, and an O.D. winger
   too.
He was her man, doing her wrong.

Blondie went down to the Cairo, looking for a
   beautiful blue.
There in the corner sat her Smoky man with his
   O.D. winger too.
He was her man, but he was doing her wrong.

When Smoky saw his dear Blondie, "One sherry,
   waiter!" he cried.
"Sherry be damned!" said Blondie, "Take your
   hand from the O.D's side.
You are my man, but you're doing me wrong!"

The O.D. blushed quite crimson, the Cairo bar
   was packed,
A dirty drunken stoker yelled, "I bet that kid's
   been cracked!"
He was her man, but he was doing it wrong.

Blondie went down to the *Barham,* picked up a
   sixteen inch shell,
Trotted right back to the Cairo bar and blew the
   whole bloody place to hell.
She shot her man, and he was doing her wrong.

Now Blondie's gone down to Caroldina [sic],
   that's if she's still alive,
She's chamfering down that sixteen inch to the
   size of a five point five.
She shot her man, who was doing her wrong.

This story has no morals, this story has no end,
This story shows the trouble you get when an
   O.D.'s willing to bend.
And a man gets shot, for doing him wrong.

*Another song of Don Croft's was the happy-go-lucky
and extremely ironic comment on American servi-
cemen, written in England. To my knowledge this song
was not widely known in the Australian Navy, but it
is an excellent example of the English service song, and
could have been equally popular as the more famous
"Bless 'em All", which was bowdlerized into the hit
parade, or perhaps it was the other way round. It was*

*certainly popular among troops of all services. But
"Brother Sylvest" never achieved the same popularity, though it was widely known in the Royal
Navy. It was a drinking song, in that it followed the
shanty tradition of a single voice singing verse and
chorus but with anybody else who liked chiming in at
the end of some of the lines. The chorus was sung faster
than any other folksong I have ever heard, with the
possible exception of "The Hill of Ben Achee" from
Scotland, "The Rocky Road to Dublin" from
Ireland, and "The Bird's Courting Song" from the
East coast of America. The words went as follows, and
the parts in parentheses are those ejaculations made by
the entire company to assist the singer on his way.*

Have you heard about the big strong man (Strong
   man)
Who lived in a caravan? (Caravan)
Have you heard about the Johnson-Jeffries fight
   (Big fight)
When a big buck nigger beat a white?
You can bring all the heavyweights you've got,
   (Bring 'em all, etc.)
For I've got a guy can beat the lot,
He used to ring the bells in the belfry
But tonight he fights Jack Dempsey.

*Chorus*
He's my brother, (Who?) Sylvest,
He's got a row of forty medals on his chest, (Big
   chest)
He can lick any nigger in the west and need no
   rest
Bigga da mus., bigga da man,
Sonna da gun, don't push, just shove,
Plenty-a room for you an' me
He's got an arm, just like a leg (A woman's leg)
And a punch that'd sink a battle ship, (Big ship)
It takes all the army and the navy
To put the wind up, (Who?) Sylvest.

He thought he'd take a trip to Italy, (Big trip)
He thought he'd take a trip across the sea. (Big
   sea)
He dived in the harbour at New York, (Big dive)
An' he swam like a man made of cork. (Big swim)
He saw the *Lusitania* in distress, (What'd he do)?
He swallowed all the water in the sea,
He took the *Lusitania* on his great big chest
And he carried the bloody lot to Italy.

*Chorus*

*Children cradling for gold (contemporary engraving)*

There were other verses to this ditty, but I can't recall them now. I remember that he went to Japan, at least.

Recalled now in tranquillity, there are many Naval expressions with a ring of aptitude about them that have their own peculiar charm, for when I was afloat the Padre was always the "Sin-bosun", the cooks were called "Tucker-f———", and the plate of baked beans in tomato sauce, accompanied by a minuscule strip of bacon, was inevitably known as "Yippee-scran". In fact, on mornings when this was served, one did not need to go below to the messdeck to find out what the tucker was. The moment the cooks from each mess placed the "fannies" of provender on the table and the familiar smell wafted through the fug, the messdeck became a pandemonium of rebel yells, shouts of "Get along, little dogie," and "Bang! Bang!" as men shot each other from around the backs of rows of steel lockers. It was a harmless enough way of letting off steam, I suppose, and perhaps it is a traditional way with that particular form of nourishment, for I

found the same custom prevailed on the seamen's messdeck of the Commonwealth Lighthouse Vessel *Cape Leeuwin* when that particular breakfast arrived.

Men aboard small ships had their own customs peculiar to that vessel. In one Fairmile, we had what was called the Dead Horsie Club. Its membership rules were simple. Any member of the club could call out "Dead Horsies" at any time we were not actually engaged in official business, and all members present then had to immediately lie down upon their backs with arms and legs extended vertically, in the manner of a bloated dead horse or beast. Any one failing to do so had to buy drinks for all the rest of the club members. I once saw it happen at a wedding. Aboard another Fairmile, there was the Sydney Tram Club, which had no rules, except that members stood swaying in rows up and down the tiny messdeck between the two mess tables, holding on to imaginary straps and lurching from side to side as the tram went *around bends, while the coxswain solemnly sold imaginary tickets, rang the bell and swung along the running board in the best Sydney manner. There were other customs in other ships, all invented for the purpose of relieving boredom and raising laughter.*

*The matelot of today may eat in cafeteria fashion, but I am willing to swear that the songs and cries continue, for seamen still wear a two-inch black silk around their necks to lament the death of Nelson, and wear a collar with three stripes to celebrate his three major victories, the Nile, Copenhagen and Trafalgar. As I said before, the Navy is a traditional body, and holds to its traditions. No doubt the songs go on, and the equivalent of the Sydney Tram Club and the Dead Horsie Clubs. Or were these a wartime release for tension?*

# Traditional Dances in Australia

*Shirley Andrews of Melbourne is certainly the person who has, to my knowledge, done more to research and encourage the dancing of traditional dances in this country. Her fine booklet* Take Your Partners *contains not only music and directions for more than thirty dances, but also the results of much of her research into the history of dancing in this country. This section here quotes a little from her articles in* Australian Tradition, *and is intended as only an example of her work, and is in no sense a substitute for her booklet. This can be obtained readily from the Victorian Folk Music Club, Post Office Box 2025 S, Melbourne, Victoria 3001. This booklet will rapidly become a collector's item.*

*On the wallaby track (Frederick McCubbin, oil on canvas)*

## Folk Have Always Danced

It is rather unfortunate that folklore studies, at least in their popular image, have been somewhat distorted to fit the fiercely nationalistic thinking of the 19th and 20th centuries. It is rare enough for a language as spoken (and sung) to correspond strictly with national boundaries, music and dance styles never do. Styles of folk dancing are more likely to correspond with ethnic groups. An extreme example of this can be seen in the tremendous variety of folk dances of the Soviet Union and on a smaller scale in a country like Yugoslavia composed of many different groups of people.

What we think of now as folk dancing is only a tiny remnant of the dances done by most people in the past. We are concerned now mainly with the recreational dances done for pleasure on social occasions. In much earlier times dancing was an integral part of daily life, often with a serious purpose. It could include hunting dances, dances for the increasing of plants and animals, a vast variety of religious and ritual dances, courtship, marriage and fertility dances, processionals, dances connected with agricultural and other sorts of work, war dances and many others. Because of the

*A donkey race at Coogee Bay (engraving from* Centennial Magazine, *1888)*

intense enjoyment that man gets from dancing, dances just for recreation developed out of some of these and remained after the others disappeared with changed social conditions.

Although this recreational dance is only a small residue, its roots go back into our past. It is likely that dancing which is basically rhythmic movement is older than man himself. Probably some of his ornithological ancestors danced as well as the present day brolga and the lyre bird. Dancing is certainly as old as man himself and his desire to express himself—his body provided the most convenient instrument for this expression that he had at his disposal. Ancient cave paintings illustrate this for us. Dancing was a medium through which he tried to make contact with the mysteries of nature which surrounded him. Ritual hunting dances must have been one of the earliest forms. The Folklorico of Mexico recently gave us the opportunity to see a magnificent example, the deer dance of the Yaqui Indians of Northern Mexico.

Australia, of course, does have its own dance history that goes back for thousands of years. As well as its nationalistic attitude, Australian folklore has been guilty of a racialist attitude to its subject in that it has concerned itself mainly with the folklore of those "new" Australians who arrived only after 1788. There are some reasonably valid excuses for this. Firstly, most studies of Australian folklore have been made since the 1940s and have been done mainly by amateurs. By that time much of the Aboriginal culture had been completely destroyed and what remained was only to be found in remote areas of the continent. An even more important factor is that Aboriginal dance, music and song are in styles that are outside the normal experience of most people. They can only be properly studied by people who had already made a specialised study of primitive music and dance.

Unfortunately, although many detailed studies of Aboriginal life have been made by anthropologists and a few studies by musicologists, no really comprehensive study has ever been made of any Aboriginal dancing until recently so that a great deal of it has been lost forever. The noted American authority, Ted Shawn, made a brief visit here in 1947 and expressed amazement at the rich material still available for study even then. A fine effort has been made by another American dancer, Beth Dean, and her Australian husband, Victor Carell, in studying the dances still in existence in central and northern Australia. Her ballet, Corroboree,

based on some of these, was a feature of the cultural Olympics held in Mexico City at the time of the 1968 Olympic Games.

There is little doubt that among these Aboriginal dances are some which have been handed down with very little change for hundreds, possibly even thousands of years. Even after the tremendously disrupting influence of the white immigrants some continued unchanged. Descriptions and photographs of a Kangaroo totem ceremonial dance from 1898 (*The Native Tribes of Central Australia*, Spencer and Gillen, 1899 edition, page 225) tallied exactly with those taken by Victor Carell in 1953 in a ceremony of the same Kangaroo totem.

It seems that early man sought to appeal to the great unknown powers of nature through his dancing. One very ancient dance still performed by the Aranda people of Central Australia is an Increase Ceremony for the propagation of the tiny honey ants, once one of the only sources of sugar for these tribal people. It is rather a sobering thought to conjecture that this Increase Ceremony may have been performed in much the same way back in the days when our ancestors were still performing their tree-worshipping pagan dances in the thick forests of Ancient Britain.

The one thing certain is that the Australian Aborigines have a long rich history of folk dance in all its meanings with a tremendous variety of types of dances dating back into their dream time. At the extreme other end of the folk dance spectrum in Australia is the dance history of the newcomers since 1788, those migrants who came, some from peasant backgrounds, but more often from the new industrial society of Europe. By 1788 life in Europe had developed from its early tribal background through a feudal peasant society and was being shaken by the turmoils of the industrial revolution. Many of the ritualistic dances had vanished, but the social and recreational dances remained. The origins of these purely recreational dances are lost because they usually go back so far and are so inextricably mixed up with the other earlier forms of dance. So these links exist with the ancient past. For example, the English form of Sir Roger de Coverly or The Haymakers as now danced, can be traced back to a revival of this dance in the days of Charles II. However, it appears that it existed in an earlier form which can be traced back to an ancient dance called Rinncie Fadha, popular in pagan Ireland before the 5th century. And what was the form before that? Who knows?

Although dances and dancing styles were often confined to particular districts or to ethnic groups of people, there was also a lot of movement of dances and dance tunes throughout Europe, e.g. most European countries seemed to have a version of the Varsovienna, and The Soldiers' Joy turned up in many places. The many and varied peasant dances of Europe formed the basis of the ballroom dances developed by the new industrial society—the quadrilles, waltzes, galop, polka and the many other sets and couples dances of the 19th century.

These were also the dances of 19th century Australia along with some of the peasant dances brought out by the early migrants. Some of them have survived in a few places like Nariel, in Victoria, right up to the present day, and others have now been revived by those interested in this aspect of our folklore and culture. The Sydney Bush Music Club and the Victorian Folk Music Club have done much of the pioneer work in reviving these old dances. Unfortunately, partly because of this over-emphasis on the national approach to folklore there has been a tendency to deprecate them because they are not uniquely Australian. It is also an unjust criticism, as any study of the development of folk dance through the ages will soon make it plain that the social conditions necessary for the development of a characteristic style of dancing did not exist in Australia in the 19th century. By wanting to be unique, they miss the significance of these interesting links with our ancestors, particularly those that reach right back into our remote past. One of the fascinating aspects of folklore is that through it one studies some of the fundamental actions, emotions and characteristics of human beings. We find that habits that have been ingrained by centuries of repetition seem to linger on long after the logical reason for them has disappeared.

How many people, while superstitiously "touching wood", realise that this habit has come down to them from over 2,000 years ago from their tree-worshipping ancestors in ancient Europe. In their ritual dances, they circled round the tree and touched the wood to protect themselves from evil. Simple dances done just for fun now similarly have roots going back thousands of years. Many of the popular dance forms and steps have been repeated through the centuries. The oldest form was the closed circle in which every one circled round the object of worship and the circle must be closed for the magic to be successful. Later on, the ritual would become more complicated, and so the circling became more complex and the dancers begin to move in and out of the circle as well as round and round. Circassian Circle and the Stockyards are examples of this very ancient form.

Processional dances had their origin in very ancient tribal rites, the ceremonies of cleansing the community after the rigours of winter and the need to ensure the continued fertility of the community. It was common for the community to move in a procession through the whole settlement, sometimes in single file; but more often in couples. The famous Abbots Bromley Horn Dance in England is a survival of these ancient customs. It was common for people to move in separate files of men and women which would halt from time to time and the couples would join hands and dance together before continuing on with their procession. From these developed first the longways set dances, and finally the couple dances for social occasions.

Australian traditional dance had its origin in these same basic beginnings, although separated from them by a long process of development which took many hundreds, possibly even thousands of years. The natural urge to dance was always there wherever there were folk. In the early pioneering days of Australia when women were extremely scarce, solo dancing of hornpipes, jigs, etc., was quite common. Our eye witness accounts in this *Tradition* include one of an overlander's cook doing a hornpipe. One out-back dance—the Bullock-drivers' Schottische—was done by two men. Lack of women didn't stop the early shearers from holding a dance. They did all the traditional square dances and a few of the dances for couples in what they called buck sets.

This fundamental need to participate as a group to do things together, particularly to enjoy things together, is folk dancing's strength. A lot of very interesting ancestral ghosts are likely to join hands with us in the Stockyards, the Lancers, or any of our dances. They'll feel quite at home with 20th century Australians, who still share this fundamental enjoyment of dancing together in a group. So keep on dancing this way.

*Shirley Andrews, in* Australian Tradition, *December 1972*

## Reports from Eye Witnesses over 120 Years

1803: "On the evening of Saturday, the 7th instant, a Celebration of Nuptials took place on the Rocks, at which a numerous group of congratulants assembled to greet the enamoured Touchstone and his beloved Audrey. Compliments at an end, the circling planet of the board was briskly courted, and a fiddler with his merry crowd, received a universal welcome; the merry dance commenced, and the fair bride led down the Country Bumpkin, which was performed in character. The Cheshire Rounds and Irish Trot were also gone through with equal success, after which a contest for the Breeches ensued, but was determined in favour of Madam Beatrice, and the ladies in parting, withdrew in triumph.

On Monday evening, a good serenade of Culinary instruments waited on the new-married pair, which in harmony came little short of marrow bones and cleavers. The musicians demanded a fee, imposed by custom, and which being complied with, the young couple were left to their domestic quiet."

From the *Sydney Gazette,* No. 11, (15 May 1803)

The extremely florid prose (well larded with literary allusions to prove the erudition of the writer, as was customary in those days) is actually describing a wedding reception held in the district of Sydney we now call Woolloomooloo. The three dances mentioned had been well known in many areas of the British Isles for a long time. The old ceremony of the "Serenade of Culinary Instruments", otherwise known as a "tin-kettling", still survives today. Mrs. Con Klippel told us about one held very recently in the Nariel district.

### Sydney—1824:

"The ball and supper, given by Sir John Jamieson on the evening of Thursday the 1st, was of the most fascinating and splendid description. The ballroom was fancifully fitted up for the occasion. The company floated in from 8 to 9; the carriages were rolling rapidly down our streets between those hours.

Dancing, consisting of country dances, quadrilles and Spanish waltzes, presently commenced and was maintained with the utmost animation till midnight, when the guests were ushered into the supper-room. . . ."

From the *Sydney Gazette* (1 July 1824)

### Western Australia—1829:

"Even in its canvas tent period, Government House held receptions and dances that lasted all night. No one cared to cross the river in the dark because of quicksands and deep water, so quadrilles and gallopades went on until daybreak."

*Tales of Australian Pioneer Women,* F. H. Johnston Sydney, 1958, page 67

### Melbourne—1841:

"We were all nearly convulsed by a woman with a coronet on her brow dancing The Haymaker . . . . . I always observe that the Melbourne ladies look terribly stupid, never as if they were enjoying anything."

This somewhat acid comment is an entry dated October 22nd, 1841, from the fascinating hand-written diary of Christiana Cunninghame. It consists of five little notebooks of about 40 pages in the Mitchell Library and can be read only by earnest concentration with the aid of a large magnifying glass. The lady resided in Melbourne in 1841-2 and was not impressed with some of her contemporaries' efforts to maintain class distinctions at all costs.

### Goulburn, N.S.W.—1841:

"The Goulburn Annual Ball at the Argyle Hotel was opened with a double Scottish reel to the air of 'Clydesdale Lasses' by James Hunter, Esq., and lady, Thomas Brodie, Esq., Ross and Earl, Esq., with their ladies at 9 p.m."

From the *Sydney Gazette,* 7 September 1841

1838: "In the light of the camp fire an overlander saw his cook (who) . . . . . had mounted a box by way of stage, and was dancing a hornpipe in capital style to the music of a fife played by another of the party. At the conclusion he was warmly cheered by his companions, whose plaudits causing a rush among the sheep the bells of the flock tinkled in romantic concord!"

*From The Journal of a Journey from N.S.W. to Adelaide, performed in 1838,* Joseph Hawdon, page 13

### The 1840s:

"The dances of 'the long ago' were, in my opinion, far and away superior to those of the present day. I think, and have often said, that dancing went out when the polka came in, which I think is not 50 years ago.

The polka was the first of the new fashioned dances, as they were then called, which came out,

*The heights of Mount Macedon (engraving from* Illustrated Sydney News, *23 March 1878)*

and then by degrees following the more fan-dangled rubbish which is now called dancing. It is not dancing at all, consists of very few steps; indeed, I may say, none at all. There is nothing in it that any ordinary mortal could not learn in a couple of weeks at the most.''

James Kirby, of Minyip, wrote this in 1894 and published it in 1896 in *Old Times in the Bush of Australia; Trials and Experiences of Early Bush Life in Victoria during the Forties*, page 183. Describing a ball at which he had been present at Thompson's station in the 40s, he tells us that ''until supper time, nothing had been danced but fashionable dances'' and then describes how, during supper, the young Irish fiddler struck up a lively jig to amuse himself in the empty ballroom. Two of the staff, a waiter known as ''Micky'' and a girl ''Peggy'' danced this jig with great vim and vigour and then requested the ''Rocky Road to Dublin.'' They danced again to this and then ''first one lady and another joined in the dance and then the gentlemen joined in, each of whom could dance a jig or step dance quite as well as Micky . . . This put an end to any of the fashionable dances for that evening anyway; although dancing was kept up until daylight, there was nothing but reels, jigs, waltzes, country dances and the Highland Fling.''

## Melbourne—1850s:
''The room was filled with men and women of the working classes; in their every-day dresses; men in fustian coats, blue and red, and serge shirts, and the commonest cord or fustian trousers, trade-grimed or mud-bespattered: all with their hats on, and the majority with pipes or cigars in their mouths. The women, young and older, in common gowns, shawls, bonnets, and walking shoes. These people, in the most correct and orderly manner imaginable, were dancing quadrilles, polkas, waltzes, etc., generally with great precision and evident enjoyment, with perfect observance of dancing, sobriety and good manners.''

A description of the ''Shilling Balls'' seen during a visit to Victoria in the 50s from *Over the Straits: A Visit to Victoria,* Louisa Ann Meredith, London, 1861

## 1870s:
''The gaieties of Melbourne have reached a climax . . . they can no further go,'' wrote wealthy station owner, Neil Black, in this era of booming wool prices. He complained that he was quite worn down due to attending some 19 balls in two months. The Melbourne *Argus* of Saturday, 13 April 1872, advertises a ball in the Town Hall ''for the benefit of the sufferers by the late fire at the Theatre Royal'' with Stoneham's Quadrille Band that week and the Eight Hours Anniversary Select Ball at the Trades Hall for the following week, as well as four regular Quadrille Assemblies.

Mr. Mear's Select Quadrille Assembly was held at the Masonic Hall in Lonsdale Street every Saturday and Tuesday evening, with some competition from the Select Quadrille Assembly at the Trades Hall every Saturday and Monday evening. It doesn't sound like the staid Melbourne we know!

## 1880s:
''A Quadrille Party was being held in a small goldfields town in Victoria. The only place with enough floor room was the local store and hotel (a combined business). The floor had been cleared and liberally covered with candle shavings. Many of the young people present had walked several miles to get there as they had no transport.

The musician here was a dashing young Irishman, who played both the fiddle and the accordeon—and acted as M.C. and dancing instructor as well. He could also step dance and gave several fine exhibitions during the evening. His answer to all who were diffident about learning to dance was always the same: 'Shure, 'tis easy to dance if you'll awnly kape time with the music.'

Here they always begin with the First Set, as was usual. One of the things a spectator would have quickly noticed was the control exercised by the M.C. and the correct etiquette observed by the dancers—no slovenly turns or bows—no half executed figures—and certainly no lack of courtesy shown to the ladies by the beaus of the day, or the M.C. would know the reason why! There was also an almost fanatical adherence to dancing particular dances with the same partner, particularly the Polka Mazurka, the Varsovienna and the Circular Waltz.'' This account is as told by Mrs. Jane Bloodworth to her grand-daughter, Mrs. G. Bourke, some 50 years ago. Mrs. Bloodworth was born Jane Morgan in 1862 and lived in Back Creek, now Talbot, a small town in the Victorian ''diggings''.

''Balls of all kinds reminded one of the favourite entertainments of all classes from the squatters to the town larrikins. Those given by the publicans were open to all and held in their hotels if there was sufficient floor space. Men paid for their tickets, but women went in free. A German band, all brass and bristling moustaches, was essential equipment, seated on chairs placed on a high table at the extreme end of the room and under the leadership of a large powerful German with a pair of unexceptional whiskers and a spotless white vest."

The publicans dispensed brandy from behind the bar and the room whirled with the "white and light dresses of the ladies and the gaudy flaunting colours (red and blue shirts) sported by the men." At daybreak the dancers rode home, many of them to out-stations and farms miles distant. . . .

At all balls, whether under the auspices of the bachelors or the publicans, dancing was vigorous and lasted till daylight."

Margaret Kiddle in *Men of Yesterday,* quotes from a favourite writer for the *Argus* (31 January 1885), who wrote under the pseudonym of The Vagabond.

## 1890s:

The first half of a program from a dance held in the Cudgewa district in North-Eastern Victoria in the 1890s had the following list of dances: The First Set, the Schottische, the Caledonians, the Alberts, a Polkamerica, the Lancers, the Highland Schottische, the Waltz of Cartillions (sic), another Polkamerica, the Highland Fling, a Scotch Reel.

The delicate little printed program, still with its tasselled pencil attached, belonged to Mrs. Mary Tyrell, of Cudgewa. Mrs. Tyrell said that the other half of the night would have been made up of requests from the dancers and would have finished up at daylight with the First Set (i.e. the Quadrilles) and the Stockyards.

"A Shearer's Ball"—The decorations were green boughs tied to the posts in the woolshed, "the endless waltzes and lancers (kitchen lancers, not as stately as the old order but of a more frolicsome kind). One of the shearers would play a concertina, one a fiddle, sometimes singing would suddenly swell up from the dancers. It was only for the very strong—for no half-hearted waltzes or polkas went on here."

From *Among the Hills* by Hilda Abbott, describing her childhood in the 1890s. But this custom of finishing up the shearing with a dance in the woolshed had already been established for a long time by 1890. An account of life on the McConnell's station in Queensland in the 1860s in *Tales of Australian Pioneer Women,* by F. M. Johnson, says "Shearing was followed by the

Shearing Shed Dance, opened with a quadrille, followed by sets of lancers, polkas and country dances, with a caller to instruct us when to set partners and swing. Occasionally an Irishman obliged with a jig, and Mr. and Mrs. McConnell's piano duets were an indispensable part of the entertainment."

*Quoted in* Australian Tradition, *December 1972*

During these hard times the settlers used now and again to have a little enjoyment in the shape of corn husking, bees, dances in barns, etc. Sometimes two or three would go to town and go to the theatre, and stay in town all night. I remember about the first ball that was held on the North Pine. It was in Buchanan's barn. I was very young at the time, but I remember what pretty rosy-cheeked girls were there, with white dresses and long blue sashes floating behind them, and the men in their shirt sleeves. How they did enjoy themselves! The mothers would lay their sleeping infants on the floor at one end of the barn while they danced, and they could dance, I can tell you. There was no two-step or fox-trot in those days—just good square dances, waltzes, polkas, reels, schottisches, and other good old dances, and let me tell you everyone was happy. There was Billy Barber with his fiddle. Dear old Billy! He is alive yet. And McRobie was there. I have mentioned him before. Mac. made up these lines about that ball:

"What made the ball so fine, Aggie was there;
What made our glances shine, Maggie was there;
And the misses McGregors too sported their
    figures,
Which made us poor niggers to feel something
    there."

There was a splendid supper about 11 o'clock. After supper dancing was again indulged in until the sun was up. Then all left for home, some on horseback, while others rode home in drays and spring carts. Dear heart, how tired and happy everyone was. It makes me think of those lines:—

"Oh for the days of the Kerry dancing,
Oh for the clang of the piper's tune."

. . . The early settlers in the Rosewood scrub, of whatever nationality, were very sociable and friendly, and in spite of the monotony of the life there was often a dance held in a neighbour's barn, when both young and old would roll up from miles away. I often used to attend these dances, and being used to the bush, and able to play the concertina, I was made a very welcome guest. On one occasion I was staying with friend Hilworth at the time. The family got an invitation to a wedding about a mile distant. The invitation included myself. Ah me! what a time we had. The large barn was decorated for the occasion. There were seats all round the room. A barrel of beer and a cask of wine held conspicuous positions. How happy and jolly every-

body was! Old and young danced till daylight. I forgot to mention the roast fowls, joints of meat, besides puddings and cakes galore, and how the Hilworth family and I walked home in the morning, and in walking through the scrub how we all sang the "Mill Wheel." I sang in English, the others in German. You see, the "Mill Wheel" is a German song.

*Both extracts from* History and Adventures of a Queensland Pioneer, *E. J. Foreman*

## Australian Traditional Dances

*Compiled by Shirley Andrews*

### The Armatree Brown Jug Polka

**Formation:** 2 concentric circles, men on the inside with backs to the centre, partners facing. Either the old-fashioned ballroom hold or just hold partners' hands in a low position in front.

**Dance:** Commencing on man's left, heel and toe twice, jumping on other foot, then 4 slip steps sideways. Repeat to the other side. (8 bars-verse).

Release hold and clap partner's right hand 3 times (with rhythm clap-clap-clap to fit music. Clap partner's left hand 3 times. Clap both partner's hands 3 times. Clap hands on own knees 3 times. (4 bars chorus).

**Partners:** *Link right arms and skip 4 steps clockwise round one another, then link left arms and skip 4 steps back. (2nd 4 bars chorus).

*To make the dance progressive—partners skip only 2 steps round each other after linking right arms, then link left arms with the next partner and skip round 6 steps back to a position in the circle ready to start the dance again. Men move round the circle clockwise and women anti-clockwise.

**Notes:** The Armatree Brown Jug Polka was collected by folklorist, John Meredith at a Boxing Night Dance at Armatree, near Gulargambone, N.S.W., in 1955. It is identical with the Pat-a-Cake Polka in the English Folk Dance and Song Society's Community Dance Manual No. 1. It was also danced in America under the latter name.

## Dashing White Sergeant

**Formation:** Sets of six people in lines of three facing one another, the sets being arranged around the room like the spokes of a wheel. The lines should have one man in the centre with a lady on each side of him but can have one lady in the centre of two men.

The step used is the Skip-Change-Step or a hop-step together step.

**Circle left:** The dancers in each set take hands in a circle and move to the left with 8 slip steps, then 8 steps back to the right, finishing back in lines of 3. (A1)

**Set to right-hand partner:** The centre man sets with his right-hand lady, and turns her with right arms linked. (A2)

**Set to left-hand partner:** Centre man turns and repeats above step with his left-hand lady.

**Figure-of-eight:** (Also known as reel of three.) This starts with the man and his right-hand lady moving in a circular path round one another, passing left shoulders. While they are doing this, the left-hand lady moves to her left in preparation for passing right shoulders with the other lady. All three continue weaving in and out in a figure-of-eight path until they are back to their places at the end of the phase of music (B). (B1)

**Forward and back:** The lines of 3 facing one another move forward and back, hands joined. (B2)

**Pass through:** Drop hands and pass through (passing right shoulders with their opposites) forming up in a new set.

**Notes:** The Dashing White Sergeant is a country dance from the latter half of the last century. The tune is not Scottish, but was composed by Henry Bishop, well-known composer of "drawing-room music" such as Home, Sweet Home. However, it was sufficiently in the Scottish style to have won acceptance there and has been used for this dance. It includes some older traditional steps, such as the reel of three combined with newer forms such as the arming which were not characteristic of traditional Scottish dancing. It has now been adopted by Scottish dancers.

## Four Sisters' Barn Dance

**Formation:** Couples in a circle, facing anti-clockwise around the Line of Dance. Men on the inside holding partner's left hand.

**Dance:** All step on right foot, step left foot up behind right, then step hop on right foot, raising left foot in front, moving slightly diagonally but travelling forward. Repeat starting with the left foot. (Bars 1-2)

Repeat to the right and left. (Bars 3-4)

All move forward in the circle with 4 step hops commencing on the right foot. (Bars 5-6)

Ladies do 4 step hops turning under men's right arms, the men doing 4 step hops while turning ladies. (Bars 7-8)

**Notes:** This dance was taught to members of the Sydney Bush Music Club by a well-known dance music ensemble. This group, known as "The Four Sisters," played two button accordeons, concertina and fiddle. They remembered this dance as one that was popular in their youth.

A very similar dance was done at Nariel, where it was called "Uncle Ev's Barn Dance" after Mrs. Beat Klippel's Uncle Ev from whom it has been learnt.

## The Galopede

**Formation:** Longways set for 6 to 8 couples facing inwards, the 2 lines 8 paces apart. Top couple the one nearest the band. Ladies on the right.

**Everyone in and out:** All march 4 paces into the centre, bows slightly to partner, retreat 4 paces to places. (A1)

**Pass through:** Cross over passing right shoulders and turning towards right into opposite places.

**Everyone in and out:** Repeat 1st step. (A2)

**Pass through:** Cross over passing left shoulders and turn left back into original places.

**Everyone swing:** All swing partners with a cross-arm swing. (B1)

**Top couple swing down:** The top couple swings quickly down the centre of the set to the bottom and stays there. The other couples must drop quickly back to places out of the way of the top couple. (B2)

Repeat with a new top couple.

**Notes:** This is a revived dance. There was a whole series of dances known as Galopedes early last century. As often happens, most of these have disappeared and left only one or two of the most popular ones with the name.

Other suitable tunes are Bobby Shafto and Winster Galop.

## Highland Schottische

**Formation:** A couple's dance, old-fashioned ball-room hold

**Dance:** Man starts on left, lady on right foot—2 heel and toe steps while hopping on other foot, then 4 fast chassis (slip steps to the man's left). Repeat on other side. (8 bars)

Fast circular turns (as in Barn Dance but faster tempo). (8 bars)

**Music:** The Keel Row is an ideal tune for this.

**Notes:** This version as done at Nariel is the usual one. This is one of the 19th century couples dances based on earlier peasant dances.

The Highland Schottische first appeared in Great Britain about 1855. It combined part of the common schottische popular about that time with an old strathspey setting step also used in reels. It became an immediate favourite in Scotland, spreading into even remote areas very quickly.

# The Tempest

**Formation:** Progressive double longways. Lines of 2 couples facing 2 couples in sets down the length of the room, the lines of four being arranged across the room. On reaching either end, the fours "remain neutral" for one turn of the dance. They then turn round and couples exchange places so that those who have been "Outsides" become "Insides" and vice versa.

**Circle eight:** The two lines take hands and circle left, then circle right back to places. (A)

**Galop across:** Couples take ballroom hold and galop across (men passing back to back) to other side. They turn and galop back to places (ladies passing back to back). (B)

**Star round and swing:** The centre 4

people (insides) right hands across (ladies right hands on top) in a star and walk round clockwise, while the Outsides swing with their opposites. (C)

**Star back:** Insides left hands across and walk back in anti-clockwise direction while Outsides swing their opposites in the reverse direction as before.

**Advance and retire:** Take hands in lines of 4, and walk 4 steps forward and 4 back. (D)

**Pass through:** The lines with their backs

to the musicians raise their arms in an arch and the others pass under into new sets.

**Notes:** This is particularly interesting in that it is mentioned in some old dance instruction books as still being danced in city ballrooms at the end of the last century, and was the last one of that type of dance to survive in the cities, although others also survived in the bush. A version very similar to the one given here is printed in *Mrs. Charles Reid's Ballroom Guide*, 9th ed., published in 1895.

## Thady You Gander
## or The Irish Trot

**Formation:** Longways set for 4 couples, facing towards top of set.

**Lead down the set:** The first or top man leads partner down the centre; crosses behind her at the bottom of the set and they both come up on the outside (the man on the ladies' side, the lady on the men's side) to the top of the set. (A1)

**Top lady leads round:** The top lady leads the 3 men behind her round the outside of the set back to places. (A2)

**Top man leads round:** The top man leads the ladies behind him round the outside of the set back to places. (A3)

**Strip the willow:** Top couple arms right in the centre of the lines, then each links left arms with the next person of the opposite sex in the line, then right arms to partner in centre again, and so on down to the bottom of the set. Couple stays there. (B1 & B2)

Repeat with a new top couple each time.

**Notes:** This is a revived dance. It is a very old dance, well known in different areas of the British Isles 300 years ago. It is mentioned in the *Sydney Gazette* of 15 May 1803—see Reports from Eye-Witnesses.

I have not been able to find the meaning of the title which seems to have numerous variations of spelling. This one is that used by the English Folk Dance and Song Society and this is the version included in their Community Dance Manual No. 1. It seems unlikely that this dance would have survived up until the present day in Australia. The one collected by Warren Fahey (*Tradition*, No. 27, page 12) appears to be a revised version. The description given corresponds with that quoted in an Education Department's folk dance booklet which also describes it as a Scottish dance. Many country dances which were commonly known in large areas of the British Isles are still done in Scottish dance circles, although they may have no qualities that are typically Scottish. Thady You Gander was included in the 1st edition of the famous *English Dancing Master* published in 1650 by John Playford. This was a collection of 104 English country dances published for the guidance of town dwellers.

**Music:** The tune given is one known in Sydney Bush Music Club circles as the Flying Pieman, because they used it for a dance of that name, but it is actually an Irish Reel tune collected by John Meredith from Herb Gimbert, who had learnt it from his Australian-Irish grandmother. The first part should be played three times through, the second part twice. Another suitable tune is King of the Cannibal Isles, playing the first part three times and the longer second section only once, also There's Nae Luck about the House.

## Virginia Reel

**Formation:** Longways set for 6 or 7 couples, partners facing one another. Top couple nearest the musicians, lady on the right.

**Honour your partner:** Both lines walk forward, slight bow to partner, lines retire.

**Right hand swing:** A single turn around partner holding right hands.

**Left hand swing:** Single turn holding left hands.

**Two hand swing:** Single turn holding both hands.

**Do-si-do, right shoulder:** Partners pass back to back, men hold arms folded at shoulder level; ladies hold skirts.

**Do-si-do, left shoulder:** Same movement but passing left shoulders before moving past one another back to back.

**Top couple down the set:** The top couple take hands and galop down the set with sideways slip step, and back again.

**Strip the willow:** Top couple link right arms and skip round one another one and a half times. Then link left arms with person of opposite sex from second couple. Right arm to partner in centre again, and so on down the set, arm with partner at bottom and return to top of set, fitting this in so as to arrive back at the top at the end of that section of music.

**Cast off:** The two lines turn outwards, march down to the bottom of the set, the top couples make an arch, the second couple leads under it to the top of the set.

Repeat with the new top couple, and so on.

**Notes:** Virginia Reel is the American version of the old English dance, "Sir Roger de Coverly" or The Haymakers. It was very popular in Australia in the late nineteenth century. It suited the Australian bush tradition of liking vigorous dances as partners dance all the time in the first part of the dance; unlike the original, where only two couples are dancing at once.

**Music:** Any lively reel or jig can be used with a short section of march tune at the end. The Victorian Folk Music Club uses the following combination of tunes:

Kelvin Grove—twice through first section.

Muckin' O Geordie's Byre for the "Strip the willow" section, repeating each 8-bar sequence twice.

Bonnie, Bonnie Banks of Loch Lomond—Chorus only, for march.

## The Stockyards

**Formation:** Couples in a circle facing inwards—ladies on the right of partners. If circle too large, split into several smaller circles.

**Everyone in; Everyone out:** Everyone joins hands and walks 4 steps in towards the centre of the circle and 4 backwards again. Repeat above. (4 bars)

**Swing partners or**

**Swing corners:** Note: First time only swing with partner. At all other times each man swings with the lady on his left (i.e. his corner lady) who then becomes his new partner. (4 bars)

**Promenade:** Couples promenade round the circle anti-clock wise. (Hand-hold—with arms crossed in front) (4 bars)

**Swing partners:** Swing partners and finish back in circle again, ladies on the right of their partners. (4 bars)

**Music:** Another Fall of Rain. Eumerella Shore is also suitable.

**Notes:** This dance was collected at Nariel by the V.F.M.C. It was originally the last figure of the Quadrilles or First Set where it was, of course, done in sets of 4 couples. More recently it has been done in much larger circles. In another version of the Stockyards figure, the ladies only go into the centre first, and then the men only. This is very similar to the Big Circle Figure of the old English dance, Circassian Circle.

*Dancing between decks (engraving from* Illustrated London News, *6 July 1850)*

## Waltz Country Dance
## or The Spanish Waltz

**Formation:** Progressive Sicilian. Couple facing couple in sets of four arranged around the room.

**Dance:** Opposites take hands and balance forward and back in waltz time, everyone stepping forward on right foot, back on left foot. Men change places with opposite ladies, turning lady under their joined right hands. Men move clockwise round the set ladies anti-clockwise. (A1)

Repeat above.

The four people in the set join hands in a ring, and all balance forward and back in waltz time. Men release right hands and turn the lady on their left over to their right under their raised left hand. The lady dances a complete waltz turn and all finish with hands joined again in the circle. (B1 & B2)

This balance and change is repeated three more times, ending in a normal waltz hold with partners.

Couples circular waltz on to a new set—the couple facing anti-clockwise round the room will dance on the outside; the others on the inside of the room moving in the direction in which they were originally facing. (B3)

**Notes:** Spanish waltzes were mentioned quite often in accounts of dancing last century. This one was still being done at the end of the century. The earliest form of the Waltz Country Dance, also known as "The Guaracha" or Spanish Dance, was described in *The Ballroom* published in 1827. It had obviously been developed from the longways country dance by each alternate couple facing around to form fours and the waltz step introduced. The steps are identical with this version.

**Music:** Any 40-bar waltz or 32 bars plus 8-bar "waltz on." The 40-bar tune given here is Weary Waiting. Come over the Stream Charlie and Jenny Jones can both be used with an 8-bar "waltz on."

## The Haymakers' Jig

**Formation:** Longways sets for 5 to 6 couples. Partners face one another about 8 paces apart.

**Right hand swing:** Top lady and bottom man advance diagonally to the centre and swing once round with a right hand hold.

Top man and bottom lady repeat.

**Left hand swing:** Top lady and bottom man swing with left hand hold.

Top man and bottom lady repeat.

**Two hand swing:** Top lady and bottom man with two hand hold.

Top man and bottom lady repeat.

**Do-si-do:** Top lady and bottom man pass right shoulders and move round one another back to back. Men with arms folded in front; ladies hold skirts.

Top man and bottom lady repeat.

**Honour your partner:** Top lady and bottom man

408

*Sports on shipboard (engraving from* Australasian Sketcher, *26 August 1882)*

bow in centre. Lady takes three steps forward, places foot behind on 4th beat for small curtsey; man closes feet together and bows.

Top man and bottom lady repeat.

**Cast off:** Lines turn outward and march down to the bottom of the set. Top couple makes an arch others pass through.

Repeat with new top couple each time.

**Notes:** This version of the old English dance, Haymakers or Sir Roger de Coverly, was very popular in Australia last century. It survived after most of the other country dances and was often used to end a ball. Folklorist John Manifold remembers seeing it at country dances in his youth,

i.e. in the 1920s. This version is based on the revived version of the dance from the days of Charles II, but earlier versions date back to a dance popular in Ireland in the fifth century.

A more modern Irish version of the Haymakers is done in Australia by Irish dancers and has become popular in folk circles because of its more vigorous style, particularly in the swinging.

**Music:** V.F.M.C. has been using the tune The Quaker's Wife; the original Sir Roger de Coverly can be used; but a better one for giving guidance to the dancers is When Daylight Shines.

*From* Australian Tradition, *December 1972*

## Dance Notes
## and Booklist

*Compiled by Shirley Andrews*

Maybe the last copy of *Tradition* has inspired some other people to do some research into traditional Australian dancing. There is lots more information still to be gathered about dances done in the early days before living memory and also about styles of dancing, etc. Much of this useful information is waiting to be discovered in old newspapers, autobiographies and books of reminiscences.

Anyone who wants to make a more thorough study of traditional dancing might like to have a list of some of the basic reference books which I have found useful for this. One essential one, *The Social Dances of the 19th Century* by Philip J. S. Richardson, 1960, London; Routledge and Kegan Paul, covers this and earlier eras.

A broad knowledge of the development of folk dancing in Europe is also necessary so as to see Australian traditional dancing in its correct perspective. An excellent account is given in *European Folk Dance* by Joan Lawson, 1953, London; Sir Isaac Pitman. *The Dance: An Historical Survey of Dancing in Europe* by C. J. Sharp and A. P. Oppe, 1924, is also valuable. There are many books with fuller details of the folk dances of particular countries, too numerous to list here.

Other useful books on the historical aspects of dancing include *Some Historical Dances (12th to 19th Century)* by Melusine Wood, 1952; *A History of Dancing* by G. Vuillier, 1898. English Translation by Heinemann, London; *Dancing* by Mrs. Lily Grove, 1895, London; Longmans, Green & Co.; *Traditional Dancing in Scotland* by J. F. & T. M. Flett, 1964, London; Routledge and Kegan Paul; *Scotland Through Her Country Dances,* by George Emmerson, 1967, London; Johnson Publications Ltd., *Dancing* by C. J. S. Thompson, London; Collins; *The Dance: Its Place in Art and Life,* by Troy and Margaret West Kinney, 1914; *The Dance: An Historical Survey*, by C. J. Sharpe and A. P. Oppe, 1924.

For descriptions of folk dances from Great Britain, the Community Dance Manuals Nos. 1-7, published by the English Folk Dance and Song Society; also Cecil Sharp's Country Dance Books 1-6, and English Country Dance 1-9, and the Scottish Country Dance Society's Scottish Coun-try Dance Books 1-11. There are many useful books giving the instructions for the social dances of the nineteenth and early twentieth century under the names of Old Time Dancing. One authoritative one with very detailed descriptions is *Old Time and Sequence Dancing* by Michael Gwynne, 1950, London; Sir Isaac Pitman & Sons Ltd.

There are a few interesting old books of dance instructions published in Australia during the last thirty years of the nineteenth century in our main reference libraries. These include:

*Mrs. Chas. Read's Australian Ball Room Guide.* The 9th ed. is in the National Library at Canberra.

*Roberts' Manual of Fashionable Dancing*, 2nd ed. 1876, published by George Robertson, Melbourne, is in the State Library, Melbourne. The Messieurs and Miss Roberts ran a series of successful dancing academies at the time, one in Collins Street, one in St. Kilda and one in Sydney. *A Manual of Dancing and Etiquette* by Professor J. H. Christison, 1882, published by the *Mercury* Office, Maitland, is in the Mitchell Library, Sydney.

One depressing sidelight of this work has been the observation that the good collection of early books on this subject that was in the State Public Library in Melbourne is likely to be completely lost to us soon. When I first started consulting these, about 1962, most of those listed in the catalogue as being held upstairs could readily be produced by the library staff when requested. Recently I have found many of them to be missing. It seems that this library is so starved for finance and staff that there is no chance of the fine collection of books amassed in the early days being properly looked after.

There are some interesting books on social dancing in America where, apart from the American-style square dances, the dances done were very similar to those in Australia. *The Round Dance Book* by Lloyd L. Shaw, 1949, is one of the most comprehensive.

The best reference collection of books on folk dancing that I have found so far is that in the library of the Secondary Teachers' College at the Sydney University. They also have a magnificent index listing all the dances in all their books and where each may be located.

The information gathered about dances done in Australia in the early days is much more scattered and was obtained from many sources, far too numerous to list here. Margaret Kiddle's *Men of Yesterday*, 1961, Melbourne University Press, is one of the few serious historical studies I could find which has a number of accounts of dancing. Another is an M.A. thesis on *Social Life and Conditions in Early Melbourne prior to Separation*, by Rose McGowan, held in the Baillieu Library at Melbourne University. Most of the rest of my information came from brief accounts or comments on dancing in a variety of early books and newspapers. A selection of these was included in the last *Tradition*, but I am sure that there are many others that could be added to our collection.

N.B.: Alan Scott, in his *Collector's Songbook*, 1970, Bush Music Club, also mentions an article by Mr. Percy Gresser, called "The Songs They Sang and the Dances They Did", written about the Bathurst district. The article is in the Mitchell Library.

### Thady You Gander

The dance, Thady You Gander or The Irish Trot, was included in the last *Tradition* (Page 14) [see Page 404 in this book]. I said I had been unable to find the meaning of the first name. Jacko Kevins, well known as a fine player of dance music, particularly Irish music, has come to light with it. Jacko says that Thady is an Irish name so that the title is apparently somewhat an uncomplimentary remark addressed to some character of that name. Gander has its usual meaning as the husband of Mrs. Goose, traditionally represented as being rather silly.

This dance seemed to be known all over Great Britain, but as it was listed under its other title, Irish Trot, in the 1st edition of the *English Dancing Master*, published in 1650 by John Playford, it may have come originally from Ireland.

### The Tempest

The Tempest is one of those dances which combines some of the characteristics of the country dance with those of the social dances of the eighteenth century. An anonymous Ballroom Guide of the 1860s states that it was introduced into England from Paris about 1850 and "speedily became a favourite and for several seasons was much danced in London and the Provinces. It unites the cheerfulness of the quadrille with the sociability of the Country Dance."

It apparently became popular all over England and many parts of Scotland so that the English Song and Dance Society have a number of versions collected in different places. The version given in the last *Tradition* is almost the same as the one collected in Wiltshire. It is also reported by J. F. and T. M. Flett in *Traditional Dancing in Scotland* that it was done in various places there.

*From* Australian Tradition, *March 1973*

### A Further Note on The Tempest

The Tempest is one of those early Victorian ballroom dances which eventually turned up in the English and Scottish countryside where they were discovered around the turn of the century by folk dance collectors.

Under the ballroom name of "La Tempete", it is described in a number of ballroom dance guides from at least 1840. As "The Tempest," it is described today in the English Folk Dance and Song Society publication, Community Dance Manual, No. 3, and this description is almost identical to that given in the Dance Issue of *Australian Tradition*. (The difference being that the "Outsides" balance during the righthand star. The music is identical). As "Tom Pate" (a sort of anglicized spelling of the French title!), it is described in the Community Dance Manual, No. 6, although in a variation so sufficiently different that it could almost be regarded as another dance.

According to J. F. and T. M. Flett, in their *Traditional Dancing in Scotland* (1964), "La Tempete" was certainly still being taught in Scotland in the 1890s.

*G. D. Towner, in* Australian Tradition, *March 1973*

# Dunnymen and Garbologists

*There are many apocryphal stories about these heroes, the "wanderers of the day" and the "pilgrims of the night", but this is hardly the place to expatiate. Both jobs are among those that are threatened in our society by the onward technological tread of automation; and these workers are becoming fewer with the spread of sewerage and garbage disposal units. Among their customs was that of leaving a Christmas card printed with verse for their clients. The words range from classical allusions to the Pipes of Pan to odd stanzas that reflect what is often obviously the hard work of a number of hands. I find them a charming oddity, and have collected a number of them over the years.*

*Poetry is hard work, and I have no doubt that the men of various municipalities share the arduous annual toil of composition by swapping their efforts one with another. The whole traditional thing reflects the belief that seems to be common to us, that a ceremonial occasion requires a more formal approach than mere prose. The results are often entertaining and occasionally hilarious.*

MERRY XMAS 1968 AND A HAPPY NEW YEAR 1969

The days hurry by,
  We meet now and then,
And the first thing we know
  It's Christmas again . . .

The season for greetings,
  For special thoughts too —
The season for sending
  Best wishes to YOU !

*FROM YOUR*
**CLEANSING MAN**

*Christmas Greetings*

**1967 . . . . 1968**

Once more another year comes round,
  With all its hopes and fear,
I hope it may commence for you,
  With best of good luck near.

May you enjoy more than your share,
  Of health, wealth and content,
So that this year may prove to be
  The best you've ever spent.

☆

*from* **YOUR SANNO MAN**

**Christmas Greetings 1968**

**Happy New Year 1969**

A Merry Christmas to you all,
With plenty of Good Cheer,
And may you have prosperity
Throughout the coming year.

And though the Police keep order
There's no more useful man,
Than the Chap who calls at daybreak,
And juggles with the can.

We leave your pan quite clean and sound
And try not make a mess,
We leave our verses every year
And wish you all success.

**—YOUR SANITARY MAN**

## Christmas Greetings 1969

## Happy New Year 1970

We are the boys who take the pan
We slip round the back and make things right
Sometimes we know you get a fright
As we often look a sloppy sight.
With pan on shoulder, we look like logs
Fall over clothes lines, get bit by dogs
But just the same we have the last say
For what you leave we take away.
So now as Xmas time draws near
We wish you all the best of cheer
A Merry Xmas and a Happy New Year.

— YOUR SANITARY MAN

Christmas Greetings

1970—1971

My compliments I send you—
Upon this Christmas card,
I do my best to rhyme it too—
But somehow it's quite hard.

For mine's a job where hands play
part
And brawn is needed too;
But still my wishes are sincere,
With heart that's good and true.

And this kindly wish I send you—
To Greet you on this day,
May all the health and happiness—
With you in the future stay.

from THE ROVERS of THE DAY

MERRY XMAS
1969 1970
AND A HAPPY NEW YEAR

Around the town I wander
On every working day,
Picking up your garbage tins
And carting the rubbish away.
And when you see me coming
Don't turn your head and say
"Here comes the Garbage man
Let's go another way."
For an unpleasant job we do our best
To give you a service as you request,
And as I am no stranger here
May I wish you one and all
A Merry Xmas and a Happy New Year.

FROM YOUR
CLEANSING MAN

MERRY XMAS
1971 1972
AND A HAPPY NEW YEAR

Greeting you at Christmas time
With wishes most sincere
For all that makes you happy
At this season of the year;
And may the year that lies ahead
Be specially happy too,
And bring the finest and the best
Of life's good things to you.

FROM YOUR
GARBOLOGIST MAN

### Season's Greetings 1974-75

Some will sing their carols,
To sound their Xmas Cheer,
Some will toast in fruit cup
And others with their beer.

The bells will start a chiming,
For that's the church's way
Of telling all the people
That this is Xmas Day.

It may not pass as music
— A rattling garbage can —
but it sounds a jolly greeting,

*From the Pilgrims of the Day.*

### Season's Greetings 1975-76

*The King of Season's here again;*
*His magic weaves a spell*
*Of perfect joy and happiness,*
*Far more than words can tell;*
*So let us wish you all good cheer,*
*And may you have a day*
*That's rich with fun and laughter,*
*In the true old festive way.*

*From "THE PILGRIMS OF THE DAY"*

## With the . . .
## Season's Compliments

### "Pipes of Pan"

★★★★

The early Greeks have told you
About the "Pipes of Pan"
A guy from their Mythology
Who's partly beast and man.

Now this is all a myst'ry
It's flamin' Greek to me
For these can't be together
That's plain as plain can be.

You've either got the pipes laid
Or use a blooming pan
And this of course is serviced
By me — your Sanno Man.

So here's the Season's Greetings
From one you rarely see
And Happy New Year Also
From us — my mates and me.

## Your Friendly SANNO MAN

414

# Appendix

# Directory of Museums

These lists of museums and folk museums, transport museums and pioneer villages should not be looked upon as being final in any way. They were compiled from lists supplied by the tourist bureau authorities in each State, and are intended merely to serve as a reference to you for further investigation.

Tourist authorities in all States welcome enquiries from interested visitors, and in many cases supply brochures and descriptive pamphlets at nominal or no cost. Local officers can often advise of times of opening of these museums and if any charge is made, and enquiries should be directed to them in the first instance, especially if you are thinking of exploring interstate.

The author felt that people interested in folklore would also be interested in displays of equipment and clothing, furniture and implements, and other relics of the past age from which most of the material in this book originated. The technological conditions have made the old ways fade rapidly, so fast indeed that I often see items of historical interest in displays that were the commonplaces of life as recently as my own childhood.

I would like particularly to thank the people in tourist departments of all State governments for the willing assistance they have given in the compilation of this list.

# New South Wales

## Sydney and Environs

These are too numerous to list individually, but an excellent brochure covering most points of interest is available from the New South Wales Government Travel Centre, at 8 Martin Place, Sydney, or from branch offices in all other capital cities. The brochure, called "A Guide To Historic Sydney", is a booklet of 32 pages and is liberally illustrated in colour. It is most comprehensive. Separate smaller folders are available on specific areas—notably the Rocks district, where it is hoped to establish a Maritime Museum; and Parramatta. Displays of furniture and costume at the Museum of Applied Arts and Sciences at Ultimo, near Central Railway Station are very fine.

## Country Centres

| | |
|---|---|
| Albury | Albury Historical Museum, Wodonga Place |
| Armidale | Armidale Folk Museum, Faulkner & Rusden Streets |
| Bathurst | Bathurst Folk Museum, 1 George Street |
| | Museum, Applied Arts & Sciences (within the Technical College building), William Street |
| | Abercrombie House, 6km west of Bathurst on the Ophir Road |
| Berrima | Berrima Museum, Jellore Street |
| | Bakehouse Museum, Hume Highway |
| Berry | Berry Museum, Queen Street |
| Bingara | Historical Society Museum, Maitland Street |
| Boggabri | Historical Museum, 25 Brent Street |
| Canowindra | Historical Museum, Memorial Park, Gaskill Street |
| Carcoar | Stoke Stable Museum, Carcoar |
| Casino | Old Domestic Science School, Walker Street |
| Cobar | Technological Museum |
| Condobolin | Museum, Community Centre |
| Coonabarabran | Warrumbungle Historical Museum |
| Coonamble | Museum |
| Cowra | Historical Museum, Vaux Street (opp. Railway Station) |
| Dubbo | Historical Museum, Old Dubbo Gaol, Macquarie Street |
| Eugowra | Historical Museum, Norton Street |
| Faulconbridge | Home of Norman Lindsay (National Trust property) |
| Forbes | Folk Museum, Cross Street |
| | Lachlan Village, Newell Highway (old Forbes goldfield) |
| Glen Innes | History House, Fergusson Street & West Avenue |
| Gosford | Henry Kendall Cottage, Kendall Street, West Gosford |
| Grenfell | Historical Museum, Old School of Arts Building, Camp Street (Henry Lawson section, newspaper files to the 1870s) |
| Gulgong | Pioneers' Museum |
| Hartley Vale | Hartley Courthouse (National Trust property) |
| Hill End | National Parks Centre, High Street |
| Holbrook | Woolpack Inn Museum, Hume Highway |
| Inverell | Pioneer Village, Tingha Road |
| Kangaroo Valley | Hampden Bridge Pioneer Farm Museum |
| Kiama | Museum, Kiama Harbour |
| Lake Cargelligo | Historical Museum, Holt Street |
| Lake Tabourie | Museum, Princes Highway |
| Lismore | Richmond River Historical Society Museum, Molesworth Street |
| Lithgow | Esk Bank House, Bennett Street (especially period furniture) |
| Milthorpe | Golden Memories Museum, in Good Templars Hall, opp. Police Station, Orange-Blayney Road |
| Milton | Folk Museum, Croobyar Road & Wason Street |
| Molong | Historical Museum, Riddell & Gidley Streets |
| Mount Victoria | Historical Society Museum, Old Railway Station |
| Mudgee | Museum |
| Nowra | Shoalhaven Museum, Berry Street |
| Nundle | Historical Museum |
| Orange | Museum, Cultural Centre, Sale Street (mining relics) |
| Parkes | Henry Parkes Memorial Museum, 316 Clarinda Street (includes his personal library) |
| | Memorial Park, Pioneer Road (vintage farm machinery) |
| Port Macquarie | Historical Museum, Clarence Street |
| Tamworth | Calala Cottage Museum, Dennison Street |
| | Folk Museum, 13 East Street |
| Tenterfield | Centenary Cottage and Sir Harry Chauvel Gallery, Logan Street |
| | Sir Henry Parkes Museum, School of Arts, House Street |
| Tingha | Smith's Private Museum |
| Walcha | Pioneer Cottage Museum, Derby Street |

| | |
|---|---|
| Wauchope | Timbertown, re-creation of old timber settlement, with sawmill, bullock teams and steam tramway |
| Wellington | Museum |
| Wentworth | Old Wentworth Gaol |
| Wentworth Falls | Blue Mountains Historical Society, Hobbys Reach (documents, newspapers and photographs) |
| West Wyalong | Historical Museum |
| Wollongong | Illawarra Historical Museum, 11 Market Street |

# Queensland

## Brisbane and Environs

| | |
|---|---|
| Aspley | "High Barbaree", 109 Albany Creek Road (furnishings, coach house) |
| Bowen Hills | "Miegunyah", 31 Jordan Terrace (historic home) |
| Brisbane city | Observatory, Wickham Terrace Oxley Library, William Street (documents, historical works) |
| Cleveland | Redlands Museum, Show Grounds, Long Street, Cleveland (early agricultural implements, transport) "Ormiston", Wellington Street, near Cleveland (site of first commercial sugar production in Queensland) |
| Fortitude Valley | Queensland Museum (old household appliances, etc.) |
| Kuraby | Pioneer Valley Park, 537 Beenleigh Road (largest collection of horsedrawn vehicles in Australia, from all over the world) |
| Newstead | Newstead House, Headquarters of the Royal Historical Society of Queensland, Museum (oldest remaining home in the State) |
| Norman Park | "Early Street", 75 McIlwraith Avenue (old style pub, shop, slab hut, furniture, tools, etc.) |
| Wacol | Wolston House off Ipswich Road, built 1852 (National Trust property) |

## Country Centres

| | |
|---|---|
| Advancetown | Pioneer House, near Nerang on the Gold Coast (period furnishing) |
| Barcaldine | Folk Museum, Ash and Birch Streets (photographs, records, etc.) |
| Brisbane Valley | Bunya-Burnett House, 4 km from Brisbane Valley Highway, between Yarraman and Nanango, built 1848 |
| Buderim | Movie Museum, display of early movie cameras and film projectors in working order (short sequences from early films, with commentary) Pioneer Cottage, Ballanger Crescent |
| Bundaberg | "Blue Anchor", Branyan Road, near Bundaberg. Old cottage and slab hut, in herb gardens (furnishings, bush crafts) |
| Cairns | "House on the Hill, The," built 1896, restored, historical associations with military operations in World War II |

| | |
|---|---|
| Cooktown | James Cook Historical Museum |
| Cooyar | Pioneer Hut, built on the Cooyar-Crows Nest section of the New England Highway (split timber and shingle construction) |
| Dalby | Dalby Museum, 22 Drayton Street (farm equipment) |
| Drayton | Bull's Head Inn, Drayton Road<br>Early Settlers Museum, 8 Parker Street (furnishings)<br>St Matthews Church, Glennie Street (district records) |
| Gympie | Andrew Fisher Cottage, Brisbane Road<br>District Historical Museum, 194 Brisbane Road |
| Ilfracombe | Folk Museum, 28 km west of Longreach |
| Imbil | Museum Of Wonders, Island Road (mainly military museum) |
| Kirra | Gilltrap's Yesteryear World, Pacific Highway (an outstanding transport museum, general machinery, and historical items) |
| Laidley | Laidley Pioneer Village (cottage, bush school, blacksmith's shop and machinery shed, many vehicles) |
| Mount Morgan | Historical Museum, East Street (over 600 photographs) |
| Pittsworth | Folk Museum (agricultural equipment) |
| Port Douglas | Court House Hotel |
| Prosperine | Folk Museum, 57 Marathon Street (furnishings) |
| Toowoomba | Cobb and Co. Transport Museum, James and Water Streets<br>Goulds and Toowoomba Art Gallery, City Hall (paintings and antiques)<br>Lionel Lindsay Art Gallery, 27 Jellicoe Street (library, prints and manuscripts)<br>Tawa Pioneer Cottage, 9 Boulton Street |
| Warwick | Pringle Cottage, Dragon Street (pioneering relics) |

# Victoria

## Melbourne and Environs

| | |
|---|---|
| Elsternwick | "Ripponlea", Hotham Street |
| Fitzroy Gardens | Captain Cook's Cottage |
| Melbourne city | Governor La Trobe's Cottage, Birdwood Avenue<br>Old Melbourne Gaol, Russell Street (original cell block and museum) |
| Mitcham | Schwerkholt Cottage |
| North Williamstown | Railway Museum, Champion Road |
| Richmond | Post Office Museum, Swan Street |
| South Yarra | "Como", Como Avenue (National Trust property) |
| Sunbury | Emu Bottom Homestead |

## Country Centres

| | |
|---|---|
| Ararat | Langi Morgala Museum |
| Apollo Bay | Yadin Historical Farm, Grove Street extension |
| Ballarat | Historical Museum, Barkley Street<br>Montrose Cottage and Eureka Historical Museum, Eureka Street<br>Sovereign Hill Historical Park Tourist Tramways |
| Bairnsdale | Historical Museum |
| Beechworth | Burke Memorial Museum<br>Carriage Museum and Powder Magazine<br>Ned Kelly's Cell, below Town Hall |
| Bendigo | Central Deborah Gold Mine<br>Hammill Coach Building Works, Kangaroo Flat<br>Joss House<br>Sandhurst Town Folk Museum<br>Whipstick Eucalyptus Factory and Mallee Historical Farm<br>Museum and Log Lockup, Eaglehawk<br>Tramways Museum, Hargreaves Street |
| Benalla | Kelly Museum, Hume Highway |
| Casterton | Historical Museum, Railway Station<br>Pioneers' Museum<br>Warrock Homestead |
| Castlemaine | Historical Museum, Lyttleton Street |
| Chiltern | "Lake View" (National Trust property) |
| Corryong | The Man from Snowy River Museum |
| Creswick | Historical Museum, Town Hall |
| Dromana | McCrae Homestead (National Trust property) |

| | |
|---|---|
| Dunolly | Goldfield Museum, Broadway Main Street |
| Echuca | Historic port area |
| Eldorado | Museum |
| Geelong | Armytage House, 263 Pakington Street, Newtown |
| Harrow | Log Gaol, built in the 1860s |
| Heywood | Bower Bird's Nest Museum |
| Jeparit | Wimmera-Mallee Pioneers' Museum |
| Kaniva | Historical Museum |
| Kerang | Historical Museum, Riverside Drive |
| Korumburra | Coal Creek Historical Park |
| Kyneton | Historical Museum (Victorian era display) |
| Lake's Entrance | Antique Car and Folk Museum |
| Lara | Flinder's Gallery |
| Menzies Creek | Puffing Billy Steam Museum |
| Mildura | Aviation Museum, Mildura Airport Rio Vista Homestead |
| Moe | Gippsland Folk Museum, Princes Highway |
| Nagambie | Historical Museum, High Street |
| Port Fairy | "Riversdale", 98 Gipps Street |
| Portland | Caledonian Inn, Portland-Heywood Road "Cottage in the Gardens" Kurtze's Museum |
| Pyramid Hill | Historical Museum, McKay Street |
| Queenscliff | Historical Centre |
| Serviceton | Copeman's Homestead |
| Swan Hill | Folk Museum and Pioneer Settlement, Horseshoe Bend Tyntyndyer Homestead |
| Warracknabeal | Machinery Museum, Henty Highway Historical Centre, Scott Street Log Lockup Gaol, Deveraux Street |
| Warrnambool | History House, Gillies Street |
| Wedderburn | General Store Museum, High Street |
| Yarra Junction | Historical Society Museum, Old Railway Station |

*The Victorian Government Tourist Bureau will provide an informative booklet free to tourists and interested people on application*

# South Australia
## Adelaide and Environs

| | |
|---|---|
| Adelaide city | Ayers House, North Terrace (historical material) South Australian Museum, North Terrace State Historical Museum, Old Archives Building, North Terrace State Library, North Terrace (documents, publications) |
| Belair | Old Government House, National Park |
| Gawler | Folk Museum, Old Telegraph Building, Murray Street |
| Glanville | Port Adelaide Ketch Museum, 190 Semaphore Road |
| Grange | Captain Sturt's House |
| Glenelg | Historical Museum Art Display, The Esplanade |
| Mile End South | Railway Museum, Railway Terrace |
| Morphett Vale | Pioneer Village Museum |
| Peterhead | Austbuilt Maritime Museum, 95 Fletcher Road |
| Port Adelaide | Nautical Museum, 135 St Vincent Street |
| Semaphore Park | Fort Glanville, Military Road |
| Tea Tree Gully | Old Highercombe Hotel Museum, Perseverance Road |

## Country Centres

| | |
|---|---|
| Birdwood | Pioneer Art and Historical Motor Museum |
| Littlehampton | Baderloo Coach and Railway Museum, Balhannah Road |
| Lobethal | Museum, Main Road |
| Loxton | Pioneer Village |
| Lyndoch | Chateau Yaldara Antique Collection Old Telegraph Museum |
| McLaren Vale | Barn Gallery and Museum, South Road |
| Mallala | Historical Society Museum |
| Mannum | Paddle steamer "Marion" |
| Moonta | Moonta Mines Primary School (formerly) |
| Murray Bridge | Folk Museum, Johnstone Park |
| Saint Kilda | Electrical Transport Museum |
| Strathalbyn | National Trust Old Courthouse Museum, Rankine Street |
| Tanunda | Barossa Valley Historical Museum, 47 Murray Street |
| Victor Harbour | Cornhill Museum and Art Gallery, Cornhill Road Museum of Historical Art, Yankalilla Road Whaler's Haven Museum |
| Willunga | Old Police Station and Courthouse |

# Western Australia

## Perth and Environs

| | |
|---|---|
| Bassendean | Rail Transport Museum |
| Claremont | Old Depot, The |
| Fremantle | Round House, The |
| | State Museum, Fremantle |
| Guildford | Mechanics' Hall Museum |
| | "Woodbridge" (National Trust home) |
| Kalamunda | Kalamunda Museum, Historical Society |
| | Stirk's Cottage |
| Mahogany Creek | Old Mahogany Inn |
| Mundaring | O'Connor Museum, Mundaring |
| Nedlands | Stirling House, Historical Society |
| Perth city | West Australian Museum |
| Rockingham | "Rockingham", Historical Society |
| Rottnest | Rottnest Museum, Rottnest Island Board |
| Swanbourne | Tom Collins House, W.A. Fellowship of Writers |

## Country Centres

| | |
|---|---|
| Albany | Albany Residency Museum |
| | Old Farm, Strawberry Hill (National Trust property) |
| | Patrick Taylor Cottage, Historical Society |
| Beverley | Aeronautical Museum |
| Bridgetown | "Bridgedale" (National Trust home) |
| Broome | Police Station |
| Bruce Rock | Municipal Museum |
| Bunbury | King Cottage, Historical Society |
| Busselton | Butter Factory, Historical Society |
| | Prospect Villa, Historical Society |
| | Wonnerup House (National Trust home) |
| Carnarvon | Tourist Bureau Museum |
| Collie | Private Museum |
| Coolgardie | Bayley's Mine (private museum) |
| | Goldfields Exhibition |
| | Railway Station |
| Corrigin | Historical Society Folk Museum |
| Cunderdin | Municipal Museum |
| Dongara | Russ Cottage, Historical Society |
| Donnybrook | Anchor and Hope Inn |
| Dowerin | Municipal Museum |
| Geraldton | Maritime Museum |
| Greenough | Historical Society Pioneer Museum |
| Harvey | Knowles's Store, Historical Society |
| Kalgoorlie | Hainault Tourist Mine (private museum) |
| | Golden Mile Museum |
| | Trafalgar Fire Station |

| | |
|---|---|
| Kellerberrin | Historical Society Museum |
| Kojonup | Old Barracks, Historical Society |
| Leonora | Gwalia Historical Gallery (a President of the United States, Herbert Hoover, was once Mine Manager of the "Sons of Gwalia" mine) |
| Mingenew | Historical Society Museum |
| Moora | Berkshire Valley, Historical Society |
| Mount Barker | Police Station, Historical Society |
| Nanga Bay | Pioneer Cottage (private museum) |
| Nannup | Colonial House (private museum) |
| Narembeen | Historical Society Museum |
| | Machinery Museum |
| New Norcia | Garrido Hall (private museum) |
| Northampton | Chiverton House, Municipal Museum |
| Nungarin | "Mangowine" (National Trust home) |
| Pemberton | Pioneer Museum |
| Roebourne | Old Cossack Courthouse, Municipal Museum |
| Tambellup | Historical Society Museum |
| Toodyay | Old Gaol, Municipal Museum |
| Walkaway | Historical Society Station Museum |
| Welbungin | Farming museum |
| Wongan-Ballidu | Municipal Museum |
| Wyndham | Boab Tree, The |
| Yalgoo | Municipal Courthouse Museum |
| Yallingup | Mill Brook Sawmill (private museum) |
| York | Residency Museum |
| | Settler's House (private museum) |

# Tasmania

## Hobart and Environs

| | |
|---|---|
| Battery Point | Van Diemen's Land Folk Museum, 103 Hampden Road (especially for costume and fine arts) |
| Hobart city | State Library of Tasmania, 91 Murray Street (contains the W. L. Crowther Library, primarily Tasmanian material, especially maritime documents; also the Allport collection of ceramics, furniture, books and prints) Tasmanian Museum and Art Gallery, 5 Argyle Street |
| Newtown | "Runnymede", 61 Bay Road (National Trust home) |
| Taroona | Shot Tower, The |

## Country Centres

| | |
|---|---|
| Bruny Island | Bligh Museum, Adventure Bay (historic documents, Aboriginal artifacts and some material on Antarctic exploration) |
| Burnie | Pioneer Village Museum, High Street |
| Deloraine | Folk Museum, Emu Bay Road |
| Evandale | Clarendon House, Nile, near Evandale (furniture) Horseless Carriage, The, Village Centre Pleasant Banks (fine examples of early farm buildings) |
| George Town | Grove, The 25 Cimitiere Street, near Bell Bay |
| Grantham | Old Watch House, The (convict relics) |
| Hadspen Village | Red Feather Inn (an audio-visual presentation of coaching and nineteenth century living is presented at various times during the year) |
| Hampden | Entally House, Bass Highway (furniture and antiques) |
| Launceston | Queen Victoria Museum, Wellington Street Franklin House, Franklin Village, South Launceston |
| Longford | "Brickendon", built 1829 of handmade brick (furnishings) |
| New Norfolk | Old Colony Inn, Montague Street |
| Port Arthur | Museum and complex of buildings, on the Tasman Peninsula (the most important historical centre outside of Hobart) |
| Richmond | The old gaol is open to the public |
| Ross | Wool and Craft centre, housed in a building believed to be the original barracks for troops in the district |
| Swansea | Pioneer exhibition (historic artifacts and materials) |
| Westbury | White House (furnishings, stables and transport) |
| Zeehan | West Coast Pioneers Memorial Museum |

*A "Visitor's Guide To Tasmania" is available at nominal charge from the Tasmanian Government Tourist Bureau*

# Index